'From slavery to human trafficking, from orphan
Shaw ably shows how evangelicals have been at the heart of the action for more
than two hundred years. This thorough examination of Christian social
responsibility as it combined with gospel proclamation demonstrates how such
holistic or integral mission is not only supported by Scripture, but has been
blessed by God to the advancement of his kingdom.'
Ian Burness, former General Director, Echoes International

'Ian Shaw's beautifully written book explores the extensive social impact evangelicals in the eighteenth and nineteenth centuries created in their communities
and around the globe as both men and women tackled prison reform, education,
housing, employment, medical care and other social concerns. He emphasizes
the historical evangelical approach to minister to the whole person, defying
social norms that denigrated others. *Evangelicals and Social Action* is an
inspiring call to renew the historical evangelical emphases of conversion and
social activism.'
Lynn H. Cohick, Provost/Dean of Academic Affairs, Northern Seminary,
Illinois, USA

'This book is an excellent resource for anyone wondering whether evangelical Protestantism can contribute meaningfully to the common good. Using
well-crafted case studies, Ian Shaw provides a compelling account of the wide-
ranging social impact of holistic ministry by evangelicals around the world.'
Jeffrey P. Greenman, President, Regent College, Vancouver, Canada

'Dr Ian Shaw has put the challenge to "love your neighbour as yourself" firmly
back on the evangelical map. The welfare state and controversies over the
"social gospel" have held evangelicals back from their God-given task to be
good news as well as preach it. In this book, you will find tremendous challenge
and inspiration from the lives of everyone from John Wesley to John Stott –
almost a "who's who" of evangelical heroes whose compassion for the poor and
downtrodden blazes a trail for us to follow.'
Jeremy McQuoid, Chair, Keswick Convention

'This book brought me to tears, to a place of awesome wonder, and to gratitude
to God for the inspiration he has given to men and women of faith to work in
front, and behind the scenes, of society. It is not simply a sweeping historical
account of the kindness and grace of evangelicals, it is a substantial work, carefully researched. Ian Shaw illustrates the breadth of social action and political

involvement over this period, which changed society. He brings issues to life with character studies and has unearthed new material, even about well-known figures such as Hudson Taylor. The book is informative, inspirational and challenging. We see through the pages of the book the gospel walking hand-in-hand with social action. Many of the challenges of earlier centuries are still with us – modern-day slavery, human trafficking and racial inequality. All Christians should read this book and be proud of their Christian heritage. Then they should pray to God that he will raise up men and women of faith and courage such as Lord Shaftesbury and Josephine Butler, for our generation.'
Sheila Stephen, former Chair of the Christian charity Prospects, UK

'This superbly well-researched and engagingly written book brings so many unknown names of evangelical believers into the limelight, those who did the most amazing feats of social compassion and justice but have never received the fame and recognition of a Wilberforce, Shaftesbury or Elizabeth Fry. The sheer abundance of facts and statistics proves beyond question how evangelical commitment over two centuries saw no dichotomy, but natural and biblical integration, between evangelistic zeal to save sinners and conscientious activism battling against the social and economic evils that sin generates. Those of us who are glad to see such missional integration increasingly reinstated in global evangelicalism (not without resistance) welcome the historical lineage provided by this book. Yet, the underlying evils of inequality, poverty, slavery, racism, abuse of women and children, greed and corruption, are with us still. The battle goes on. And this book will encourage those evangelicals today whose calling is to engage in that battle in the power of the cross and living demonstration of the gospel, inspired by such a cloud of witnesses. May their tribe increase.'
Chris Wright, Global Ambassador and Ministry Director,
Langham Partnership

EVANGELICALS AND SOCIAL ACTION

EVANGELICALS AND SOCIAL ACTION

From John Wesley to John Stott

Ian J. Shaw

INTER-VARSITY PRESS
36 Causton Street, London SW1P 4ST, England
Email: ivp@ivpbooks.com
Website: www.ivpbooks.com

First published 2021

British Library Cataloguing-in-Publication Data
A catalogue record for this book is available from the British Library.

ISBN: 978–1–78359–658–4
eBook ISBN: 978–1–78359–659–1

Set in Minion Pro 10.75/13.75pt
Typeset in Great Britain by CRB Associates, Potterhanworth, Lincolnshire
Printed and bound in Great Britain by Ashford Colour Press

Produced on paper from sustainable sources

Inter-Varsity Press publishes Christian books that are true to the Bible and that communicate
the gospel, develop discipleship and strengthen the church for its mission in the world.

IVP originated within the Inter-Varsity Fellowship, now the Universities and Colleges
Christian Fellowship, a student movement connecting Christian Unions in universities and
colleges throughout Great Britain, and a member movement of the International Fellowship
of Evangelical Students. Website: www.uccf.org.uk. That historic association is maintained,
and all senior IVP staff and committee members subscribe to the UCCF Basis of Faith.

Contents

Part 1
THE BROADER PICTURE

Part 2
EVANGELISM AND SOCIAL ACTION: RESPONSES TO KEY ISSUES AND CHARACTER STUDIES

EVANGELICALS AND ISSUES OF ECONOMIC DEPRIVATION

Contents

Contents

Foreword: A text for our time

Exhilarated. Sobered. Hopeful.

Those were my emotions as I read this extraordinarily timely book. Indeed, as we seek to respond to a world that serially reels from disasters such as COVID-19 and their economic, environmental, emotional, mental, physical and spiritual impacts, Ian Shaw's compelling survey of evangelical gospel action over two centuries comes to us as an imagination-expanding well of wisdom. We do not, after all, just study history to avoid repeating its mistakes, we study it to learn from its successes.

I found myself exhilarated by the cornucopia of compelling examples of the fruitful union of gospel sharing and gospel action at a time when it might be easy to forego one or the other. Exhilarated by the extraordinary creativity of so many of the initiatives described. Exhilarated by the repeated testimony of how the word of God shaped people's hearts and minds and impelled them to love their neighbour, to be a neighbour to others, by both sharing and demonstrating the love of God in its holistic richness.

I was exhilarated too by the innovativeness of so many solutions – putting on services in which only work clothes could be worn so as to remove the sartorial barrier that 'Sunday best' church culture had erected; or recognizing, decades before almost any agency was even properly treating people with learning disabilities, that pets help.

Exhilarated too by the sheer unpredictable beauty of what an understanding of God's character might lead his people to do. The industrialist Titus Salt, for example, not only cut working hours in his factories, and improved working conditions, but built a new town to provide healthy living conditions. And then he provided a park, a music stand and even a cricket pavilion. 'Owzat' for holistic ministry? What a glorious reflection of the generous, joyous character of the God who sent his Son so that we might have abundant life, and died so that it might be so.

I found myself exhilarated too to see how many of the issues that evangelicals have wrestled with in the past forty years were pondered and often well answered one hundred or two hundred years ago.

Yes, there were mistakes. I was sobered by how easy it is to be blind to what is actually happening in our own towns. Sobered by how often biblical interpretation owed much more to the dominant culture than to good exegesis. Sobered too by how an emphasis on particular sections of the Bible had been used as a tool of social control – focusing the preaching to antebellum black slaves, for example, on passages about submission and obedience, and avoiding passages about liberation and freedom. Sobered too by how contemporary parallels abound.

But the book left me full of hope. Hopeful because it was clear that again and again God had, through his people, brought significant, deep, permanent societal change – in housing, in education, in the treatment of mental illness, in business practice and . . . Hopeful because of the sheer unpredictability and unlikeliness of some of the changes that occurred. When such things happen with God, what might we now hope and pray and work towards? When God works through individuals in such ways, what might he want to do through us in our time, in our contexts?

Ian is an inspired guide. Indeed, it is hard to imagine anyone more richly suited than he. He brings his experience of urban ministry in a deprived area, his compassion for the poor, and his understanding of the difficulty of social and spiritual change. He brings his experience of having known and worked directly with Christians from every country mentioned, and having visited every country mentioned. He brings his scholar's taste for historical accuracy and his teacher's ability to bring the context, the people and the issues to life. And he brings his deep grasp of the historical, theological and hermeneutical issues to highlight how the Bible has been used to fuel or inhibit action. And he weaves all those strands together to create a measured, inspiring but not triumphalist account of the extraordinary contribution that evangelicals have made to the communication of the gospel, the well-being of millions, and the transformation of many of the countries they found themselves in.

And Ian brings his heart to it. And so, while this book illuminates times past, I would be very surprised if it does not lead to contemporary action.

May it indeed be so.

Mark Greene
Mission Champion, LICC

Preface

The thinking behind this book grew out of a number of years spent in pastoral ministry in an urban priority area in Salford, England. Here, surrounded by the classic urban pathologies of poverty, unemployment, crime, addiction and family break-up, with domestic and other forms of abuse all too evident, a faithful group of evangelical believers had for more than a century sought to minister the gospel. Demonstrating God's love through evangelism and deep practical concern in a range of ways, they reached out to the local community, many of whom were in great need. The church had started life as a mission hall, and I remember in the late 1980s visiting an elderly man in the local community who did not attend the church, but who recalled with deep gratitude the soup kitchen run by 'the Mission', as it was locally known, during the Great Depression of the 1930s.

Those years in pastoral ministry led me to reflect on the ways Christian believers in the past have ministered in similar circumstances. That began a journey for me into researching urban ministry in the first half of the nineteenth century, when the modern industrial city was a new phenomenon. That research was an attempt at what one reviewer of the subsequent book called 'total history', exploring the social, economic, political, as well as theological, influences on urban ministry in Manchester and London.[1] The work challenged the misconception that Calvinist evangelicals were indifferent to the needs of those who lived in urban areas. This book extends that discussion to evangelicals more generally, and adopts a global focus, to assess the way they connected evangelistic efforts with social action. The evidence presented challenges the oft-made accusation against evangelicals that they are somehow so heavenly minded that they are of no earthly use.

Thanks are due to many for helping to make this book possible. Students I have taught in many different countries and institutions have journeyed with me into past times and contexts to study these issues. The questions they have asked, and the observations and experiences they have shared, helped to shape

---

[1] I. J. Shaw, *High Calvinists in Action: Calvinism and the City c.1810–60* (Oxford: Oxford University Press, 2002).

the following material. Many have been struck by the contemporary relevance of the issues raised and the approaches taken. Indeed, to walk into a vast informal settlement such as Kibera in Nairobi, or the slums of South Asia or the favelas of Latin America, is like walking back amid the sights, sounds and smells of an early industrial city in nineteenth-century Europe. I remember one student in a class in Kenya who stood up after a lecture I had given and said, 'You have given us all hope we can make a difference in our cities today.' Evangelical Christianity offers such 'hope' in pre-industrial, industrial, as well as post-industrial, contexts.

In the preparations for writing this book the late Donald Mitchell, librarian of Union School of Theology, Bridgend, Wales, was a great source of help in finding resources for the project during my three years working there as Provost. My gratitude is also due to Dr John Jeacocke, who has, as ever, provided invaluable support in proofreading, indexing, checking the text and formatting footnotes. Heartfelt thanks go to Mark Greene for contributing his inspiring Foreword for this book, and also to those who have kindly written commendations.

This book is dedicated to Dr Tony Sargent, former pastor of Worthing Tabernacle and Principal of International Christian College, Glasgow, who modelled in his ministry so much of what this book is about.

Introduction

Evangelicals have continued to debate into the twenty-first century the extent to which they should engage in social action. For some, the urgency of the task of evangelism means there is no time to devote to projects of social concern. To others, social action has become the essence of the gospel and a priority matter. There are also those who hold the view that faithfulness to Christ means taking equally seriously both evangelism and the teaching of the Sermon on the Mount, or the parable of the good Samaritan.

Activism has been identified as central to evangelicalism. Such activism includes not only evangelism, but also social action that expresses the ethics of the gospel.[1] This book explores how this was the predominant understanding among evangelicals in the eighteenth and nineteenth centuries. Then in the first half of the twentieth century evangelicals became significantly hesitant about social concern because it had become associated with what was termed the 'social gospel', which was closely associated with theological liberalism. However, since the 1960s, and especially after the Lausanne International Congress on World Evangelization in 1974, there has been a significant return to the pattern of previous centuries. At Lausanne, evangelicals from the West worshipped, fellowshipped and debated together with evangelicals from the Global South, who saw social action as a natural, and indeed essential, companion to evangelism. The resulting Lausanne Covenant reflected this re-evaluation: 'we express penitence both for our neglect and for having sometimes regarded evangelism and social concern as mutually exclusive'.[2] Billy Graham, who had helped to convene the Congress, declared, 'faith and good works are handmaids of the Gospel which cannot be divorced'. Stanley Mooneyham, President of World Vision, summed this up:

> There are two mandates in the New Testament. One is witness, the other is service. To ignore either of them is to seriously cripple the church . . . to

---

[1] D. Bebbington, *Evangelicalism in Modern Britain* (London: Unwin Hyman, 1989), 10–12.

[2] Lausanne Covenant, sect. 5, in J. D. Douglas (ed.), *Let the Earth Hear His Voice: International Congress on World Evangelization, Lausanne, Switzerland, Official Reference Volume, Papers and Responses* (Minneapolis, Minn.: World Wide Publications, 1975), 4–5.

engage in evangelism of soul without recognition that those souls also have bodies is foolish and unreal ... love which is demonstrated in tangible acts of Christian caring is irresistible.[3]

In 1984 John Stott suggested debate on the matter was over:

It is exceedingly strange that any followers of Jesus Christ should ever need to ask whether social involvement was their concern, and that controversy should have blown up over the relationship between evangelism and social responsibility. For it is evident that in his public ministry Jesus both went about 'preaching the good news of the kingdom' as well as 'healing every disease and sickness' (Matthew 4:23); in Peter's summary, 'he went around doing good and healing' (Acts 10:38). In consequence evangelism and social action have been intimately related to one another throughout the history of the church.[4]

Yet not all evangelicals have been convinced. One prominent leader declared in 2016:

The temptation is strong for believers to jump into the cultural fray as self-righteous social/political reformers and condescending moralizers ... those activities are not to be the Christian's chief priorities ... The church will really change society for the better only when individual believers make their chief concern their own spiritual maturity.[5]

He did, however, clarify this by defining 'spiritual maturity' as including the practical dimension, of 'living in a way that honors God's commands and glorifies His name'.[6]

Writings by Tim Chester at the turn of the twenty-first century explored the biblical and theological arguments surrounding this debate, and urged evangelicals to be both evangelists and activists.[7] This book is designed as a necessary historical companion to these studies, exploring the richness of the evangelical

---

[3] W. S. Mooneyham, 'Acts of the Holy Spirit '74', in Douglas, *Let the Earth Hear*, 445–449.

[4] J. R. W. Stott, *Issues Facing Christians Today* (Basingstoke: Marshall, Morgan & Scott, 1984), 3.

[5] J. MacArthur, 'Christian Duty in a Pagan Culture' <http://www.gty.org.uk/resources/articles/A122/christian-duty-in-a-pagan-culture>, accessed 27 December 2016.

[6] Ibid.

[7] T. Chester, *Awakening to a World of Need: The Recovery of Evangelical Social Concern* (Leicester: Inter-Varsity Press, 1993); T. Chester (ed.), *Justice, Mercy and Humility: Integral Mission and the Poor* (Carlisle: Paternoster Press, 2002); T. Chester, *Good News to the Poor: Sharing the Gospel Through Social Involvement* (Leicester: Inter-Varsity Press, 2004).

tradition that has united evangelism and social action, and making the thinking and action of the past available for discussions about current key social issues.

Evangelicals are the subject of this book. This is not to ignore the heritage of social action among other Christian traditions, including the Roman Catholic, Orthodox, Anglo-Catholic and mainline liberal churches. However, in the evangelical tradition social action has been far less recognized and reported on than the evidence suggests it should have been, which makes it an important field of study. The following chapters use the term 'evangelical' to refer to Protestants whose belief and practice centred on four main themes: the necessity of a personal conversion experience; the Bible as the authoritative source of Christian teaching and practice; salvation as possible only through faith in Christ's atoning work on the cross; and a pattern of living out these convictions, especially in evangelism and works of service to others.[8] Evangelicals formed a clearly identifiable and interconnected network of mutual recognition and spiritual kinship – linked by their shared personal experience and belief patterns, and factors such as what they read, personal correspondence, preachers they heard, conferences they attended, and by ties of friendship, family and fellowship. All these transcended international and denominational boundaries, allowing evangelicals to work and witness together, and keeping them from being confined to a narrow religious subculture.

For much of the period from the late eighteenth to the late nineteenth century such evangelical beliefs and practice became widespread in most Protestant denominations. They were common to most Methodists, Baptists, Congregationalists and a host of independent churches, as well as significant numbers of Presbyterians and Anglicans. The advance of theological liberalism in many mainline Protestant denominations in the early twentieth century reduced the prominence and influence of evangelicalism, and those who were evangelicals began to feel the need to self-identify as such and their numbers and influence became lower. However, evangelicalism remained a significant force in the USA, and grew again in confidence and prominence in the 1960s in Britain and parts of Europe. Much of the Christianity that expanded with such great rapidity in the Majority World (Africa, Asia and South America) from the 1950s onwards was significantly marked by evangelical belief and practices, including within the Pentecostal and charismatic traditions.[9]

The beginning and end points of this book are the ministries of two Johns – John Wesley, one of the key figures of eighteenth-century evangelicalism,

---

[8] Bebbington, *Evangelicalism*, 5–17. These four points have become known as the Bebbington 'quadrilateral', and have become a fairly standard definition of evangelicalism.
[9] I. J. Shaw, *Christianity: The Biography* (London: Inter-Varsity Press, 2016), 25–60, 266–268.

and John Stott, who helped formulate the Lausanne Covenant. The influence of their views will become evident in a number of the chapters. This study covers individuals from a range of national and denominational backgrounds to demonstrate how pervasive the connection between evangelism and social action has been.

As a prelude to the coverage of specific issues, two initial chapters in this book offer a bird's-eye overview of Christian perspectives on gospel proclamation and social concern from the early church to the Reformation, and then from the Reformation to the end of the twentieth century. In the following chapters a series of issues between the 1730s and the 1960s are discussed in detail. Each features a survey of responses to a social need, and then offers a short character study of the thought and practice of one significant evangelical. Throughout the book some attempt at global coverage is made, with examples drawn from contexts from North America and Great Britain to China, India, Australia and South Africa. The slight preponderance of material from Britain is not because of a lack of evangelistic and social activity elsewhere, but to do with the accessibility of sources for the issues covered. Were this study to focus on the period 1970–2020, examples from evangelicals in Africa, Asia and Latin America would predominate. Sadly, in earlier times their work often went unreported and unrecorded.

The areas of evangelical social action covered are loosely grouped into six – economic deprivation; education; people at risk; issues of race; health and well-being; and forensic and social pathologies. The case studies include seven women, reflecting their significant involvement, and deliberately range from well-known figures, such as William Wilberforce and Amy Carmichael, to less well-known evangelicals, such as Hsi Liao-chih, Clara Swain and Jeremiah Evarts. They also cover a representative range of theological perspectives found among professing evangelicals, from Arminian to high Calvinist.

For want of space, important areas in which evangelicals have been active are not covered. Much could have been said about their action in areas such as animal rights, the environment, care for sight- and hearing-impaired people, refugees, sailors and soldiers, efforts to protect the unborn child, the formation of trade unions, and so on. The areas featured are those in which the connection between social action and evangelism is most apparent. Although this treatment is historical, the contemporary nature of many of these issues is striking. The challenges of modern-day slavery, racial equality, the plight of street children and trafficked women continue to feature regularly in the media. The problems of addiction, and the care and rehabilitation of criminals, seem as intractable as ever.

In such a study there is a danger of 'pedestalling' those featured and setting them above criticism. While the book does focus mainly on their achievements, there are also places where their weaknesses or blind spots emerge. It is surprising and indeed, to many readers, encouraging to find that these people were evidently used in remarkable ways, despite having feet of clay. They would all have looked at their achievements and said, *soli Deo gloria* (glory to God alone).

As evangelicals the influence of the Bible was foundational, which from the Old Testament to the New is replete with injunctions to God's people to demonstrate compassion, justice and mercy to the poor, the dispossessed and the marginalized. They sought to demonstrate the 'heart' religion desired by God:

> If you do away with the yoke of oppression,
> > with the pointing finger and malicious talk,
> and if you spend yourselves on behalf of the hungry,
> > and satisfy the needs of the oppressed,
> then your light will rise in the darkness,
> > and your night will become like the noonday.
> (Isa. 58:9–10)

The teaching of Jesus in Matthew 25:31–46 was repeatedly alluded to as both an instruction and an inspiration, especially the words

> For I was hungry, and you gave me something to eat, I was thirsty and you gave me something to drink, I was a stranger and you invited me in. I needed clothes and you clothed me, I was ill and you looked after me, I was in prison and you came to visit me.

The following chapters serve as a practical exposition of the way these verses were applied by evangelical Christians.

Part 1

THE BROADER PICTURE

1a

Christian gospel proclamation and social action: from the early church to the Reformation

The socially marginalized formed a large proportion of the population of the Roman world into which Christianity was born. Because the literature of the time gave them scant attention,[1] the extent of destitution is significantly underestimated. To be poor, and that included many in work, was normally to be hungry.[2] Archaeological evidence from Corinth indicates high levels of infant mortality, widespread malnourishment and people working long hours under significant duress.[3] Up to 95 per cent of the population were highly vulnerable to any crisis in the food supply.[4] Some wealthy individuals in the Roman world were generous to those in need, although often for political purposes. When Roman writers praised good deeds, they were referring to actions done to receive a reward, something very different from the 'simple heartfelt compassion of the Christians'.[5]

Paul's letters mention a few wealthy and influential people, but most Christians were artisans, labourers or slaves (1 Cor. 7:21–22). In 1 Corinthians 1:26–28 he lists the 'weak', the 'lowly', 'the despised'. The majority of church members at Corinth 'appear to have been poor or very poor'.[6] 1 Corinthians 11 suggests some were living below the subsistence level.[7]

[1] L. L. Welborn, 'The Polis and the Poor', in J. R. Harrison and L. L. Welborn, *The First Urban Churches*, vol. 1: *Methodological Foundations* (Atlanta, Ga.: SBL Press, 2015), 189–191, 228.

[2] W. V. Harris, 'Poverty and Destitution in the Roman Empire', in *Rome's Imperial Economy* (Oxford: Oxford University Press, 2011), 33.

[3] L. L. Welborn, 'Inequality in Roman Corinth', in J. R. Harrison and L. L. Welborn, *The First Urban Churches*, vol. 2: *Roman Corinth* (Atlanta, Ga.: SBL Press, 2016), 57.

[4] Ibid. 65.

[5] G. Uhlhorn, *Christian Charity in the Ancient Church* (Edinburgh: T&T Clark, 1883), 18–23, 37, 43.

[6] S. J. Friesen, 'Poverty in Pauline Studies: Beyond the New Consensus', *Journal for the Study of the New Testament* 26 (2004), 348–353.

[7] Welborn, 'Inequality', 67.

Writing around AD 150, Aristeides set out the characteristic Christian social ethic:

> They labour to do good to their enemies . . . They despise not the widow, and grieve not the orphan. He that hath distributeth liberally to him that hath not . . . if there is a man among them that is poor and needy, and they have not an abundance of necessaries, they fast two or three days that they may supply the needy.

In contrast to wider society, Christian benevolence was not done for show or praise: 'the good deeds which they do, they do not proclaim in the ears of the multitude, and they take care that none shall perceive them'.[8] A similar point is made of Christians in the second-century *Epistle to Diognetus*: 'They love all men, and are persecuted by all . . . They are poor, and make many rich; they lack everything, and in everything they abound.'[9]

Justin, also writing in the second century, believed many were changed from opposition to faith through the care demonstrated by Christians to their neighbours.[10] He refers to a weekly collection taken for 'orphans and widows and all in want through sickness or any other cause', including 'those in prison, or strangers from abroad, in fact of all in need of assistance'.[11] Tertullian, writing from North Africa reports Christians donating to 'the deposit fund of kindness'. This was

> for the nourishment and burial of the poor, to support boys and girls who are orphans and destitute; and old people who are confined to the house; and those who have been shipwrecked . . . or banished to islands, or in prison, or are pensioners because of their confession.[12]

This powerful example, Tertullian noted, led non-Christians to declare 'how they love one another'.[13]

In the early centuries of the church contagious diseases had a devastating effect, especially the epidemics of AD 165 and 251. The first epidemic saw up to a third of the population of the empire wiped out, and at the height of the

---

[8] Aristeides, *Apology*, 15.1–12, 16.2, quoted in J. Stevenson, *A New Eusebius* (London: SPCK, 1987), 52–54.

[9] *Epistle to Diognetus*, 5.11–14, in Stevenson, *New Eusebius*, 55.

[10] Justin, *Apology*, 1, 16, in Stevenson, *New Eusebius*, 58–59.

[11] Justin, *Apology*, 1.17, in H. Bettenson (ed.), *The Early Christian Fathers* (Oxford: Oxford University Press, 1969), 62–63.

[12] Tertullian, *Apologeticus*, 39, in Bettenson, *Fathers*, 142.

[13] Ibid.

second some 5,000 people a day died in Rome alone, and perhaps two-thirds of the population of Alexandria.[14] Panic and social chaos ensued. Most who could, fled, abandoning the sick and dying: others threw infected family members out into the streets. Dionysius, however, reported the compassionate response of Christians: 'Unsparing of themselves . . . visiting the sick without a thought of the danger, assiduously ministering to them, tending them in Christ.' Many Christians caught the infection, 'and when they had cared for and restored health to others died themselves'.[15] Because the provision of food, water and basic nursing care can considerably reduce mortality in epidemics, many thousands of lives were saved by their courageous actions.[16]

In the fourth century the emperor Julian the Apostate, who turned in hatred on his one-time Christian faith, found his efforts to reintroduce paganism hindered by the 'moral character' of Christians. Their 'benevolence toward strangers' was something the pagans never matched. Christians had, in effect, created a 'miniature welfare state'.[17] Literally living out Matthew 25:35–40 proved highly attractive to those outside the faith.

The care of the poor and sick was seen in the holistic approach of Basil of Caesarea (c.330–79), who had the Basileias built, the first Christian hospital for the care of the poor, sick and dying.[18] Gregory of Nazianzus (c.329–90) asserted benevolence was a wise spiritual investment by believers, declaring Basil's hospital a

> storehouse of piety . . . in which the superfluities of their wealth, aye, and even their necessaries, are stored . . . no longer gladdening the eyes of the thief, and escaping both the emulation of envy, and the corruption of time.[19]

Gregory declared love for the poor a fundamental component of Christian discipleship.[20]

---

[14] R. Starke, *Rise of Christianity* (San Francisco, Calif.: HarperCollins, 1997), 76–77, citing W. H. McNeill, *Plagues and Peoples* (Garden City, N.Y.: Doubleday, 1976).

[15] Dionysius, *Festival Letters*, quoted by Eusebius, *Ecclesiastical History*, vol. 2, 7.22 (London: Heinemann, 1892), 185–187.

[16] Starke, *Christianity*, 89.

[17] P. Johnson, *A History of Christianity* (New York: Atheneum, 1976), 75.

[18] B. E. Daley, 'The Cappadocian Fathers and the Rhetoric of Philanthropy', *Journal of Early Christian Studies* 7.3 (1991), 431–461; G. B. Ferngren, *Medicine and Health Care in Early Christianity* (Baltimore, Md.: The Johns Hopkins University Press, 2009), 124–130.

[19] Gregory of Nazianzus, *Oration*, 43.63, in J. Stevenson, *Creeds, Councils and Controversies* (London: SPCK, 1966), 97–98.

[20] Gregory of Nazianzus, 'On Love for the Poor', *St. Gregory of Nazianzus: Select Orations*, tr. Martha Vinson (Washington, D.C.: The Catholic University of America Press, 2003), 39–71.

Augustine of Hippo believed that good works were 'faith expressing itself through love'.[21] He strongly denied that by giving alms people could 'purchase impunity to continue in the enormity of their crimes and the grossness of their wickedness'.[22] Good works did not make a person a Christian, but the 'purpose of the new birth is that we should become pleasing to God . . . we then begin to live piously and righteously'.[23] Augustine warned against giving attention to physical needs alone, rather than spiritual. It was foolish

> to think that we ought to be readier in running with the bread, wherewith we may fill the belly of a hungry man, than with the word of God, wherewith we may instruct the mind of the man who feeds on it.[24]

Gospel proclamation and social action belonged together.

In his highly influential *Pastoral Rule* (*c.*590) Gregory the Great explained that charity should be done 'humbly', out of 'understanding that the things which they dispense are not their own'. Because wealth already belonged to God, it also, in a sense, belonged to the poor. Quoting the *textus classicus* of social concern, Matthew 25:42–43, he warned of the spiritual danger faced by those who have 'indiscreetly kept' their own goods, by not responding to the needs around them.[25]

One statement appearing to question the connection between gospel proclamation and social concern, 'Preach the gospel at all times. If necessary use words,' is frequently attributed to Francis of Assisi (*c.*1181–1226). This is problematic for two reasons. The first is that Francis never said it. In chapter 17 of his *Regula non-Bullata* (1221) he did say, 'let all the brothers preach by their deeds', but the phrase was not included in the Rule of Francis itself. The second reason is that Francis was convinced that words were necessary. Indeed, the same chapter urges preachers to promote the 'utility and edification of the people, by announcing to them vices and virtues, punishment and glory', albeit with 'brevity of speech'.[26]

---

[21] Augustine, *Enchiridion on Faith, Hope, and Love*, tr. Albert Oulter (London: SCM Press, 1955), 18.67.

[22] Ibid. 19.70, 77.

[23] Ibid. 76.

[24] Augustine, 'On the Catechising of the Uninstructed', in P. Schaff (ed.), *Nicene and Post-Nicene Fathers of the Christian Church*, vol. 3: *St Augustin*, repr. (Grand Rapids, Mich.: Eerdmans, 1988), 15.298.

[25] Gregory the Great, *Pastoral Rule*, 20, Admonition 21, in P. Schaff (ed.), *Nicene and Post-Nicene Fathers, Leo the Great, Gregory the Great*, vol. 12, repr. (Grand Rapids, Mich.: Eerdmans, 1983), 45–46.

[26] See <http://www.Franciscan-archive.org>, *regula non-bullata*, 17.166; *regula bullata*, 9, on preachers. The Roman Catholic Church in 2008 reasserted the need for missionary activity to include more than humanitarian good works (*Christianity Today*, February 2008, 13, quoting a document from the Vatican Congregation for the Doctrine of the Faith).

Thomas Aquinas' vast *Summa Theologiae*, written between 1265 and 1274, notes how giving alms supplies one's 'neighbour's corporal needs', but also brings spiritual fruit by investing treasure in doing the commands of God, which 'bring thee more profit than gold'. However, this should not be the primary intention in the act of giving.[27] Unlike Francis, however, no clear connection is made by Aquinas between good works and Christian proclamation.

With such theological support the medieval monastic movement became a major provider of charitable aid, education and care for the sick. However, for all Aquinas' cautions, the popular misunderstanding that charity had direct personal spiritual value became widespread, drawing on the apocryphal text Ecclesiasticus 3:30, 'almsgiving atones for sin'. Benevolence became a means by which the rich could gain merit before God. As the fourteenth-century Italian Dominican monk Giordano da Pisa unfeelingly put it, 'God has ordered that there be rich and poor . . . Why are the poor given their station? So that the rich might earn eternal life through them.' By the late medieval period poverty was a growing social issue, with up to 75 per cent of Europe's urban population suffering some form of material need.[28]

In the sixteenth century the Reformers deliberately shifted the emphasis in salvation away from human activity – whether through actions of the church or the individual by good works – on to Christ's finished work. Luther's doctrine of justification by grace alone through faith left no salvific role for human works. Against the accusation that such theology undercut a powerful motivation to charity, Luther powerfully countered, 'Christians are to be taught that to give to the poor or lend to the needy is a better work than the purchase of pardons.'[29]

The 1522 Wittenberg Order created a common chest for collecting funds for the poor, offered cheap loans to workers and artisans and subsidized the education of the children of the poor. Practical service to one's neighbour, including care for the poor, was the outflow of a person's salvation, not an attempt to merit grace. Luther connected theology and praxis: accepting Reformed theology and worship involved a commitment to wholesale reform and renewal in social life. Social action was to be the work of the whole faith community, although Luther was frustrated that some were reluctant to contribute to social needs.[30]

---

[27] Thomas Aquinas, Second Part of the Second Part, *Summa Theologiae*, Question 32, Almsdeeds <www.newadvent.org/summa/3032.htm>.

[28] Giordano da Pisa, quoted in C. Lindberg, *The European Reformations* (Oxford: Blackwell, 1996), 113.

[29] Luther, Thesis 43 of the 95 theses, in H. Bettenson, *Documents of the Christian Church* (Oxford: Oxford University Press, 1963), 43.

[30] Lindberg, *Reformations*, 118–128.

This approach was repeated by the other Reformers. Martin Bucer wanted Christianity to permeate the whole of society, including social welfare. After he arrived in Strasbourg, he reorganized the system for poor relief so there were no beggars on the streets.[31] Ulrich Zwingli argued that it was the duty of the Christian to meet the needs of others and remove poverty. A system was established in Zurich by which a member of the clergy and a layperson distributed food and gifts from church funds to the poor in each district.[32]

During the Reformation Geneva's economic and social structure was placed under huge strain by a vast influx of refugees, almost doubling the population, many fleeing religious persecution in France. John Calvin's holistic theological and pastoral vision for Geneva involved 'every aspect of social life on earth' – family, education, economics and politics – believing it could be transformed into a Christian 'commonwealth'.[33] Calvin, quoting Isaiah 58:7, 'when you see the naked, to clothe him', believed that property and wealth were given by God to enable Christians to demonstrate social responsibility. Giving to the poor was giving to God. Christians should help the most vulnerable in society by buying the goods they produced.[34] Extreme wealth and extreme poverty were both evils. All economic and financial decisions should be examined in the light of Christ's law of compassion.[35]

Calvin entrusted the church's support of the poorest members of society to deacons, one part of his fourfold pattern of church officers, along with the pastors, elders and doctors (theological teachers), who offered parallel spiritual care. The deacons provided not just food and clothing to the poor, but helped them find housing, employment, education and training. Deacons oversaw the running of hospitals, found homes for orphaned children, the elderly and infirm, and provided clothing and bedding for asylum seekers.[36] This community-wide model of proclamation and social action shaped John Knox's work in Scotland.[37]

The Reformers saw social welfare as the outflow of the gospel, a response to God's gracious activity, which was to transform all of personal and community

---

[31] R. S. Wallace, *Calvin, Geneva and the Reformation* (Grand Rapids, Mich.: Baker, 1988), 21.

[32] W. C. Innes, *Social Concern in Calvin's Geneva* (Eugene, Ore.: Pickwick Press, 1983), 55–56.

[33] Wallace, *Geneva*, 27–28.

[34] J. Calvin, *Commentary on Deuteronomy*, Deut. 8:17, and *Sermon on Deuteronomy*, 24:1–16, quoted in Wallace, *Geneva*, 124.

[35] Calvin, *Sermon on Deuteronomy*, 15:7–10, quoted in Wallace, *Geneva*, 91.

[36] B. Patterson, *Poverty in the Theology of John Calvin*, Princeton Theological Monographs 68 (Eugene: Wipf & Stock, 2006), 139. See also J. E. Olson, *Calvin and Social Welfare: Deacons and the Bourse française* (Cranbury, N.J.: Susquehanna University Press, 1989); R. M. Kingdon, 'Social Welfare in Calvin's Geneva', *American Historical Review* 76.1 (February 1971), 50–69.

[37] Innes, *Geneva*, 298.

life.[38] As one historian observed of the Reformation, 'poor relief and the concern for philanthropy was . . . running through its story like a gold thread'.[39]

This comprehensive religious and social vision was continued by the Puritans, as seen in the town of Dorchester, England, where John White was appointed rector in 1605. He powerfully preached a strong Calvinistic message, held catechism classes and prayer meetings, and regularly visited his parishioners. White led a civic social-reform movement, in which the common funds of the town were used to care for the sick, educate children and buy food for the poor. A hospital was established that also gave accommodation for orphan children; a small weekly grant was offered to those in need, with food and clothes at Christmas. The council funded nursing for the sick and aged. At times of scarcity the council bought up grain supplies and sold them at subsidized prices; new almshouses were built for the elderly. Social change was accompanied by spiritual fruit. In 1620, out of a population of 1,200, it was estimated that more than 600 people were partaking of monthly communion, and the weekly congregation was significantly larger.[40]

In Dorchester, wider society was transformed: the illegitimacy rate fell from 7 per cent in 1597–1601 to just 1.2 per cent in the late 1630s. A wave of generosity was unlocked – making it the most philanthropically generous town in the west of Britain. White remained the minister of Dorchester for forty-three years, and his teachings were still widely followed ten years after his death.[41]

Puritan theologians remained convinced that the evidence of a person's changed relationship with God would be apparent in moral transformation and active social concern. As William Ames argued in 1627, love to God 'produces love toward men, they are in some sort partakers in the image of God, therefore we are said to love God in men and men in God'.[42] These sentiments were reflected in the Westminster Confession of Faith (1646), which stressed that good works were a duty incumbent on the believer, of which 'they are not hereupon to grow negligent'.[43]

Pietism, a seventeenth-century renewal movement within Lutheranism, also stressed that faith should be active. Preaching, visitation and pastoral care of the faithful were all given high priority.[44] Pietists developed a network of

---

[38] Lindberg, *Reformations*, 372.

[39] G. Rupp, *Patterns of Reformation* (London: Epworth Press, 1969), 102.

[40] D. Underdown, *Fire from Heaven* (London: Fontana, 1993), 106.

[41] Ibid. 107, 224.

[42] W. Ames, *Marrow of Theology*, 1.16.8, quoted in W. Dyrness, *Reformed Theology and Visual Culture* (Cambridge: Cambridge University Press, 2004), 166.

[43] *Westminster Confession of Faith*, 19.5.6; 16.3.

[44] On Pietist thinking see P. J. Spener, *Pia Desideria* (1675), tr. T. G. Tappert (New York: Fortress Press, 1964).

schools, orphanages and hospitals, including those started by August Francke at Halle in Germany, which proved highly influential.

The first 1,600 years of the church give consistent theological argument and practical demonstration that social action should accompany Christian witness. Although at times the role such works played in a person's salvation was misunderstood, the connection between faith and action, and between meeting a person's spiritual and temporal needs, was steadfastly maintained.

1b

Christian gospel proclamation and social action: from the eighteenth century to the twentieth[1]

There was a clear continuity between the theology and practice of the Reformers, Puritans and Pietists and that held by evangelicals from the eighteenth century onwards.[2] The emphasis on the necessity of works of love and mercy as the fruit of spiritual transformation continued, as did the practice of social action standing alongside evangelism.

Jonathan Edwards (1703–58), a foundational figure in eighteenth-century evangelicalism, emphasized the 'duty' of charity to the poor as 'absolute and indispensable'. It was as much a duty as to 'pray, or to attend to public worship'.[3] Although his family followed many others of his time in keeping a domestic slave, Edwards stressed the need for humane treatment of slaves and wrote opposing the slave trade.[4] He also condemned the unfettered operation of the free market whereby ruthless merchants bought grain cheaply and then sold dearly in times of shortage, which caused great suffering among the poor.[5]

This Edwardsean tradition was continued by Timothy Dwight (1752–1817), Edwards' grandson. As President of Yale, he preached a sermon to his students in 1815 entitled 'On Doing Good', based on Galatians 6:9–10. Dwight spoke of pursuing the 'duty' to labour in doing good with 'firm resolution and unremitted energy', and not becoming 'feeble and spiritless' in such causes as running day schools, Sunday schools, overseas mission and the relief of the poor. He offered

---

[1] Some of this discussion was initially included in I. J. Shaw, 'Theology and Transformation in Society: The Scottish Evangelical Theological Society Finlayson Lecture, April 2008', *Scottish Bulletin of Evangelical Theology* 26.2 (autumn 2008), 132–150.

[2] See M. A. G. Haykin and K. J. Stewart (eds.), *The Emergence of Evangelicalism* (Nottingham: Apollos, 2008) for a discussion of this, including a chapter by the author of this book.

[3] J. Edwards, 'Christian Charity: or, The Duty of Charity to the Poor, Explained and Enforced', *Works of Jonathan Edwards*, vol. 2 (1834), repr. (Edinburgh: Banner of Truth, 1979), 163–173.

[4] K. P. Minheenan, 'Jonathan Edwards on Slavery and the Slave Trade', *William and Mary Quarterly* (October 1997), 823–830.

[5] G. Marsden, *Jonathan Edwards, a Life* (New Haven, Conn.: Yale University Press, 2003), 304.

both anthropocentric and theocentric motivation for doing things 'not only to be beneficial to mankind', but with such a disposition as 'will render the performance morally excellent and lovely in the sight of God'.[6]

A series of personal religious transformations were worked out in terms of social transformation in the life of John Wesley (1703–91). His move from nominal Anglicanism to devoted High Church piety produced the ordered life of the Oxford 'Holy Club', with an active social concern that included charity to the poor and prison visiting, although this did not bring the assurance of salvation Wesley longed for. His evangelical conversion experience yielded that longed-for assurance, and brought renewed endeavours in social concern as an activist outflow of his experience of grace, as the following chapters will illustrate.

The need for faith, the fruitful reality of which was to be demonstrated in love and service to others, was emphasized by the heirs of the Evangelical Revival, be they Arminian, evangelical Calvinist or moderate Calvinist. Evangelical social compassion was the fruit of the gospel. The evangelical parochial work of Charles Simeon (1759–1836) in Cambridge included not only preaching and widespread pastoral visitation, but schemes to sell bread to the poor cheaply, the running of a Provident bank and supporting the poor.[7]

The Baptist Andrew Fuller (1754–1815), much influenced by Edwards' evangelical Calvinism, argued that the Divine Law, 'summed up by our Lord in love to God and our neighbour', was a binding duty on all men, believers and unbelievers.[8] His position was a restoration of that set out in the 1689 Baptist Confession of Faith, that 'obedience to the moral law remains for ever binding upon both justified persons and all others'.[9] Although for believers, 'as far as our works are good, they are produced by His Spirit', the Confession stressed the responsibility to show fruit: 'for they must be diligent in stirring into activity the grace of God that is in them'.[10]

A commitment to both spiritual and social transformation was also characteristic of a number of pioneers in the nineteenth-century Protestant missionary movement. William Carey (1761–1834) is rightly remembered for his inspirational cross-cultural work in India, especially in biblical translation, and evangelism. Yet he was a man of profound social concern, expressed in radical ways. In England he launched a campaign to boycott the use of sugar

---

6 T. Dwight, *Sermons*, vol. 1 (New Haven, Conn.: Hezekiah Have, Durrie & Peck, 1828), 535, 537, 552.

7 R. Carus, *Memoir of Rev. Charles Simeon* (London: Hatchard & Son, 1847), 80, 440.

8 A. G. Fuller (ed.), *The Complete Works of the Rev. Andrew Fuller* (London: H. G. Bohn, 1852), 976.

9 *The Baptist Confession of Faith of 1689* [rewritten in Modern English] (Haywards Heath: Grace, 1982), 13.5.

10 Ibid. 13.1; 16.5.3.

in order to undermine the use of slave labour on sugar plantations in the West Indies. In India he also campaigned for the rights of Indian women, especially against *suti*, the burning of a widow on her husband's funeral pyre, and for better care for lepers. He founded schools for children of all castes and promoted libraries.[11]

When John Venn (1759–1813) faced opposition to his ministry at Holy Trinity, Clapham, from 'solfidians' for stressing the importance of the fruits of personal faith, his father, Henry Venn, wrote to reassure him, 'Every Prophet and every Apostle insists as much upon the fruits of faith, as upon faith itself, and the glory of Christ's Person.'[12] His ministry at Clapham was attended by a group of noted evangelicals, the best-known of whom was William Wilberforce. As a subsequent chapter will show, evangelical conversion awakened both Wilberforce's concern for the evangelization of others and his social conscience, and led him to embrace the cause of anti-slavery. Around him gathered the 'Clapham Sect', who began to exercise a very significant moral and social influence through their conviction that they should live out their personal spiritual transformation by performing acts of social transformation. For politicians such as Wilberforce, who were politically and socially conservative, operating in a context overshadowed by the French Revolution, such tactics were extremely radical, and have been termed 'holy worldliness': a seeking, through alliance with the forces of the world, to achieve a greater Christian good.[13] To Hannah More (1745–1833), closely associated with the Clapham Sect, and subject of a character study in this book, such actions were essential: 'To neglect works of charity . . . is an infallible evidence that our professions of piety mean nothing.'[14]

The dominant figure in nineteenth-century Scottish Presbyterianism was Thomas Chalmers (1780–1847). He developed schemes that drew together evangelism and social concern. His vision was the establishment of a godly commonwealth within his parish, with the wealthy exercising responsibility for those less fortunate than themselves.[15] Chalmers' thinking was rooted in the Christendom model of the Reformation, and represented the classic Calvinistic

---

[11] See A. C. Smith, 'The Legacy of William Carey', *International Bulletin of Mission Research* 16.1 (1992), 2–8.

[12] H. Venn, letter to John Venn, 1 January 1796, in Rev. H. Venn (ed.), *The Life and a Selection from the Letters of the Late Rev. Henry Venn, M.A.* (London: John Hatchard, 1836), 530–531.

[13] H. Willmer, 'Holy Worldliness in Nineteenth-Century England', in D. Baker (ed.), *Sanctity and Secularity: The Church and the World* (Oxford: Blackwell, 1973), 200.

[14] H. More, *Moral Sketches of Prevailing Opinions and Manners Foreign and Domestic: With Reflections on Prayer* (London, 1819), 199.

[15] The forces influencing Chalmers, and his influence on others, are discussed in B. Hilton, 'Thomas Chalmers as a political Economist', in A. C. Cheyne, *The Practical and the Pious: Essays on Thomas Chalmers (1780–1847)* (Edinburgh: St Andrew Press, 1985).

holistic understanding of the Christian message, but was also significantly shaped by political economy and Malthusian–paternalist ideas. Although aspects of Chalmers' thinking have been much questioned, they sprang from the conviction that good deeds were incumbent upon believers: 'the proper remedy . . . for the wretchedness of the few, is the kindness of the many'.[16] It was combined with a strong evangelistic emphasis and a concern to promote education, a vital dimension in both social and spiritual transformation.[17]

Chalmers proved highly influential upon many others. One was Robert Murray McCheyne (1813–43), an earnest evangelistic preacher whose social conscience was awakened and who visited the poor of his needy Dundee parish extensively. Preaching on a *textus classicus* of socially active evangelicals, Matthew 25:34–45, he solemnly warned the well-to-do in his congregation:

> Your haughty dwelling rises in the midst of thousands who scarce have a fire to warm themselves at, and have but little clothing to keep out the biting frost, and yet you never darkened their door . . . Ah, my dear friend, I am concerned for the poor, but more for you. I know not what Christ will say to you in that great day . . . there are many hearing me who now know well they are not Christian because they do not love to give. To give largely and liberally, not grudgingly at all, requires a new heart; an old heart would rather part with its life blood than its money.[18]

This combination of evangelism and social concern, spiritual and social transformation, is epitomized by the English Congregationalist minister Andrew Reed (1787–1862), who will be the subject of another character study. Gospel proclamation combined with practical demonstration of the compassion of Christ to the most vulnerable was the natural outflow of his evangelical faith. In 1828 he advised a minister at an induction service:

> Whatever has a tendency to meliorate the sufferings of humanity, to disperse the darkness of the mind, to subdue the vices of society, to restore man to a divine obedience, and to attach his hopes and thoughts to an unseen eternity, you will see as in perfect harmony with the spirit and letter of your commission.[19]

---

[16] T. Chalmers, preface to 1851 edn of *Christian and Civic Economy*, vol. 1 (Edinburgh: Constable, 1851), x.

[17] On Chalmers and urban mission see I. J. Shaw, 'Thomas Chalmers, David Nasmith and the Origins of the City Mission Movement', *Evangelical Quarterly* 76.1 (January–March 2004), 31–46.

[18] Quoted in T. Keller, *Ministries of Mercy: The Call of the Jericho Road*, 2nd edn (Phillipsburg, N.J.: Presbyterian & Reformed, 1997), 40.

[19] A. Reed, *The Man of God: A Charge Delivered at the Ordination of the Rev. Ebenezer Miller, M.A.*

The memorial tablet to Reed in the London Orphan Asylum, which he founded, exemplifies this holistic emphasis. It depicts him reaching down to care for a group of small children: in one hand is a Bible, in another he offers a plate of bread. Bread for life, the means of social transformation, and the Bread of Life, the means of spiritual transformation, were to be provided together.[20]

The way 'evangelistic work was intimately associated with social concern'[21] in the middle and later nineteenth century was ably demonstrated in the life and ministry of Lord Shaftesbury (1801–85), whose engagement with a number of issues covered in this book will be seen. He felt deep compassion for those who suffered, and feared for society if its poorest and most vulnerable members were not helped. Alongside this was a strong sense of duty, again shaped by Matthew 25. As he noted in his diary in 1857, the goats mentioned there were condemned 'not for the sins they have *committed*, but for duties they have *omitted*'. To know of the good that needed to be done, and not to do it, was sin.[22]

In a speech to the Social Science Congress in Liverpool in 1858, Shaftesbury explained how he was regularly told that spiritual remedies for the problems of society were sufficient, and that he laboured too much for the body, which was only perishable. Against this, he argued how difficult a purely spiritual approach was when faced by disease, deprivation, starvation, unsanitary living conditions and scenes where crime and immorality flourished. He reminded his hearers that 'the same God who made the soul made the body'. The body was created for 'fitness for His service', and the Christian's 'great object' was to do everything possible to remove obstructions to this great purpose: 'our bodies, the temples of the Holy Ghost, ought not to be corrupted by preventable disease, degraded by avoidable filth, and disabled for His service by unnecessary suffering'.[23]

Among Baptists in Britain the evangelical Calvinist C. H. Spurgeon (1834–92) continued to stress the importance of Christians engaging in both evangelism and social concern. His Metropolitan Tabernacle ran a range of different social-relief agencies, as well as innumerable evangelistic endeavours. Spurgeon urged Christians to 'meditate on methods of working, plan designs of good, act out deeds of mercy, persevere in labour, and continue in service

---

(London, 1829), 23.

[20] I. J. Shaw, *The Greatest Is Charity: The Life of Andrew Reed, Preacher and Philanthropist* (Darlington: Evangelical Press, 2005), 382.

[21] D. Bebbington, *The Dominance of Evangelicalism: The Age of Spurgeon and Moody* (Leicester: Inter-Varsity Press, 2005), 93.

[22] Lord Shaftesbury, diary, 1 October 1857, quoted in G. F. A. Best, *Shaftesbury* (London: B. T. Batsford, 1964), 54–55; emphases original.

[23] Lord Shaftesbury, speech to the Social Science Congress, 1858, quoted in B. Blackburn, *Noble Lord: The Seventh Earl of Shaftesbury* (London: Home & Van Thal, 1949), 170–171.

before God'. The agency God had appointed for doing good was the Christian's showing forth the fruits of salvation: 'if the poor be fed, it must be by these hands'.[24]

Even those widely considered to have a purely evangelistic focus, such as D. L. Moody (1837–99), were also committed to encouraging social-concern projects. Action to promote better housing for the poor was encouraged by his gospel preaching in Glasgow after he encouraged the evangelical leaders in the city to engage in social reform.[25]

From Arminian evangelicals to moderate Calvinists and evangelical Calvinists the connection between evangelism and social action was widely stressed. English high Calvinists also demonstrated themselves as active in the field of social concern. Although they rejected the view that the Law was the believer's rule of conduct, they did not dispute that good works were to be present in the life of the true Christian. As the more cautious John Gill expressed it, 'sanctification is absolutely necessary to salvation'.[26] A lack of evidence of good works was a sign of absence of grace.

Robert Hawker (1753–1827), the high Calvinist vicar of Charles Church in Plymouth, was even accused of antinomianism, yet demonstrated great generosity and compassion. His pastoral work included visiting the town's garrison at great risk to himself at a time of typhus fever. He established a female penitentiary, an orphanage and a society for the relief of the poor. As his friend and biographer commented, although Hawker 'denied progressive sanctification', his life gave ample evidence of it.[27] The high Calvinist Baptist William Gadsby (1773–1844) developed a special ministry to the poor handloom weavers of Manchester. He spoke out strongly against the Corn Laws, which kept the price of bread artificially high and thereby hurt the poor. In his obituary in the *Manchester Times* he was remembered as 'animated by an enlarged philanthropy. Benevolent, hospitable, and kind to all who needed admonition, advice, or assistance, he was constantly engaged in acts of mercy and in dealing out bread to the hungry.'[28]

There has been justified criticism of some nineteenth-century evangelicals for their adherence to prevalent social and economic philosophies, such as

[24] C. H. Spurgeon, 'Where to Find Fruit', Sermon Preached on 28 February 1864 at the Metropolitan Tabernacle, Newington, in *Spurgeon's Expository Encylopaedia*, vol. 8, repr. (Grand Rapids, Mich.: Baker, 1984), 85–87.

[25] I. G. C. Hutchison, *A Political History of Scotland, 1832–1924* (Edinburgh: John Donald, 1986), 136–138.

[26] J. Gill, *A Body of Divinity* (London, 1770), repr. (Grand Rapids, Mich.: Baker, 1971), 559.

[27] J. Williams, *Memoirs of the Life and Writings of the Rev. Robert Hawker, D.D.* (London: E. Palmer, 1831), 262.

[28] *Manchester Times*, 3 February 1844.

political economy. There has also sometimes been too much focus on individuals and symptoms, without tackling root causes of social injustice – although campaigns such as those against slavery and the Corn Laws did attempt to deal with structural issues. Yet, despite limited political opportunities for many, as will be seen, a number of evangelicals stood for election to local councils and sought to deal with structural issues by working to improve sanitation, drinking water, housing and education.[29] Many churches were also comprised largely of poor members, and a great deal of social action was by the working classes, for the working classes.[30]

In the later nineteenth century the tide began to turn against this integration of evangelism and social responsibility, introducing a significant discontinuity with what had gone before. It was a response to a series of pressures at the time. The movement was gradual, but by 1914 unmistakeable. As pressures grew on evangelicalism from factors such as biblical criticism and Darwinism, a more defensive, and inward looking, form of piety gained ground, especially represented by the holiness movement. This did not mean a wholesale rejection of social action, and the following chapters include examples of holiness proponents with a deep and practical social concern – such as Amy Carmichael and William Booth. The shifting of emphasis was encouraged by the popularity of premillennialism, which brought urgency to the task of evangelism before the imminently expected return of Christ, and less place for social action in a world that was passing anyway. Again, it should be noted that premillennialism and social concern were not mutually antagonistic: Lord Shaftesbury was capable of combining the two, as was D. L. Moody. The tendency, however, was towards a gloomy view of what could be achieved: Christ's return alone would bring a kingdom fit for people to live in.

Politics became a less common field for evangelical engagement, and there was less comfortableness with the 'holy worldliness' approach of Wilberforce and others. In North America postmillennialism increasingly became the domain of those who focused their intentions on the creation of the golden age of the kingdom of God on this earth. The 'social gospel', which had little emphasis on personal conversion, became closely linked to theological liberalism.[31] Alongside these factors should be noted the increased prosperity and suburbanization of much of evangelicalism. Many ministers and

---

[29] See e.g. C. Brown, '"To Be Aglow with Civic Ardours": The "Godly Commonwealth" in Glasgow 1843–1914', *Records of the Scottish Church History Society* 26 (1996), 169–195.

[30] R. Smith, 'Charity, Self-Interest and Welfare', in M. Daunton (ed.), *Self-Interest and Welfare in the English Past* (Cambridge: Cambridge University Press, 1998), 58.

[31] Bebbington, *Evangelicalism*, 194, 211–217.

congregations no longer experienced the daily converse with chronic poverty and need that had been a powerful motivation to urgent activity. Local authorities, and then national governments, increased their role in the resolution of social issues, such as education and health care, which reduced the space in which evangelicals could operate.

As the twentieth century progressed, the 'social gospel' came to be seen as the antithesis of evangelicalism, breaking the previous close connection between urgent evangelism and active social concern, although figures such as F. B. Meyer (1847–1929) maintained the balance of evangelicalism and social concern into the 1920s.[32] The pattern was repeated in the USA, although the trend was more gradual than is often depicted. Fundamentalism is usually seen as the antithesis of the social gospel, yet one of the papers in the series *The Fundamentals*, 'The Church and Socialism', included the appeal

A true gospel of grace is inseparable from a gospel of good works. Christian doctrines and Christian duties cannot be divorced … These social teachings of the Gospel need a new emphasis today by those who accept the whole Gospel, and should not be left to be interpreted and applied by those alone who deny essential Christianity.[33]

Later fundamentalists did not see things in the same way, and argued that social concern was a distraction from the 'main thing', which was urgent evangelism. The process has been termed 'The Great Reversal'.[34]

The tide gradually began to turn in the 1960s, and this became pronounced in the 1970s.[35] This reversal of the great reversal was expressed in the Lausanne Covenant, produced at the end of the 1974 International Congress on World Evangelization. Here an understanding of mission was articulated that embraced both evangelism and social concern. Evangelism is described in the covenant as 'the proclamation of the historical, biblical Christ as Saviour and Lord, with a view to persuading people to come to him personally, and so be reconciled to God', and then, 'The results of evangelism include obedience to Christ, incorporation into his church and responsible service in the world.'[36]

---

[32] I. Sellers, *Nineteenth-Century Nonconformity* (London: E. Arnold, 1977), 47.

[33] C. R. Erdman, 'The Church and Socialism', in *The Fundamentals*, 1904–15, vol. 12, 1911, 116.

[34] D. O. Moberg, *The Great Reversal: Evangelism Versus Social Concern* (London: Scripture Union, 1973).

[35] B. Stanley, *The Global Diffusion of Evangelicalism* (Leicester: Inter-Varsity Press, 2013), 151–153.

[36] Lausanne Covenant <https://lausanne.org/content/covenant/lausanne-covenant>, accessed 18 January 2020.

Such views passed into definitive statements of evangelicalism in the West, such as that from the National Evangelical Anglican Congress in 1977, which declared:

> We believe that the example of Christ, his teaching (especially as focused in his 'Great Commission') and the nature of the gospel together constitute a compelling summons to his people to give themselves in both witness and service. Both evangelism and social action are therefore universal obligations laid upon us by the authority of Christ. Both are also expressions of Christian compassion, and Christian social action makes the gospel visible.[37]

The following chapters explore how this deep-rooted pattern of connecting evangelism and social action among evangelicals from John Wesley to John Stott was evident in a number of key issues and across a range of international contexts.

---

[37] *The Nottingham Statement: The Official Statement of the Second Evangelical Anglican Congress Held in April* 1977 (London: Church Pastoral Aid Society, 1977), sect. A3, Christian Mission.

Part 2

EVANGELISM AND SOCIAL ACTION: RESPONSES TO KEY ISSUES AND CHARACTER STUDIES

2

Care for the poor

Until the development of a welfare state in Western countries in the early twentieth century state authorities at best provided a very basic safety net for those facing destitution. Most support for the poor came through the work of charities or individuals, and in this evangelicals played a considerable role. Kathleen Heasman estimated that three-quarters of charitable organizations in London in the nineteenth century were 'evangelical' in character and control.[1] Similarly, David Bebbington asserts that although philanthropy was a common feature of all religious bodies, evangelicals led the way.[2]

Evangelicals sought to bring fresh perspectives on the experience of poverty itself. John Newton comforted an impoverished friend with the thought that 'sanctified poverty is an honourable estate', providing opportunity to experience God's 'grace, and the faithfulness of his promises in the sight of men'. He noted that riches were often bestowed on those who 'have no portion but in the present life'.[3] From the eighteenth to the twentieth century evangelicals consistently found that their message of salvation by grace found a resonance among the poor. They taught that acceptance with God was not dependent on a life of good works or benevolent charity, which was easier for the rich to achieve.[4]

Yet there were questionable attitudes. The London Congregationalist preacher Joseph Parker declared from the comfort of his City Temple pulpit in

---

[1] K. Heasman, *Evangelicals in Action* (London: Geoffrey Bles, 1963), 14.

[2] D. Bebbington, *The Dominance of Evangelicalism: The Age of Spurgeon and Moody* (Leicester: Inter-Varsity Press, 2005), 120.

[3] J. Newton, 'Letter XXII, On the Advantages of a State of Poverty', *Works of Rev. John Newton*, vol. 1 (London: George Virtue, 1839), repr. (Edinburgh: Banner of Truth, 1985), 290–298.

[4] J. Walsh, 'The Origins of Evangelicalism', in M. A. Noll, D. W. Bebbington and G. A. Rawlyk (eds.), *Evangelicalism: Comparative Studies of Popular Protestantism in North America, the British Isles, and Beyond 1700–1900* (Oxford: Oxford University Press, 1994), 33.

1885, 'the world would be poorer but for its poor', suggesting that poverty enabled Christians to demonstrate the grace of giving.[5] Such unfeeling teaching reduced incentives to restructuring society to eradicate economic inequalities.[6] Others circumscribed the bounds of charitable giving to the 'Lord's poor', or to the 'deserving poor', although this was not the predominant view. Some discern the absence of a coherent social theory among evangelicals in their response to poverty, as Bradley observed: 'The basis of the Evangelicals' response to poverty and suffering was emotional rather than ideological.'[7] However, this chapter shows there was more significant thinking on the issue than evangelicals have been credited with, together with extensive practical action.

Jonathan Edwards, the great preacher and theologian of the Great Awakening in North America, emphasized the 'duty' of charity to the poor as 'absolute and indispensable'. This was modelled on the example of Christ. It was also evidence of the new spiritual life that followed conversion. Edwards argued that charity was as much a duty as it was to 'pray, or to attend to public worship'; indeed, there was no command in the Bible more urgent 'than the command of giving to the poor'. Although discouraging indiscriminate giving in the case of 'idleness or prodigality', he cautioned against too much 'scrupulosity as to the object on whom we bestow our charity . . . it is better to give to several that are not objects of charity, than to send away one that is'. Poverty occasioned by an imprudent act was not 'an unpardonable crime', and even if a person continued in 'vicious ways', help should not be denied to their dependants. Even the existence of a legal provision did not free 'from the obligation to relieve . . . by our charity'.[8]

The personal generosity of John Wesley, which will be explored in the character study below, was also demonstrated by George Whitefield (1714–70). Hearing in 1741 of a widow in distress whose landlord had taken her furniture because she could not pay her rent, Whitefield gave her all the money he had with him – 5 guineas. When his friend rebuked him for being too generous, Whitefield replied, 'When God brings a case of distress before us, it is that we can relieve it.' As they travelled on, a highwayman stopped them and demanded their money. Because of his earlier generosity, Whitefield had none to give, but the friend who had rebuked him now had to hand over his money. Whitefield

---

[5] J. Parker, in *Congregational Year Book*, 1885, 63, quoted in K. S. Inglis, *Churches and the Working Class in Victorian England* (London: Routledge & Kegan Paul, 1963), 250.

[6] F. K. Brown, *Fathers of the Victorians* (Cambridge: Cambridge University Press, 1961), 119.

[7] I. Bradley, *The Call to Seriousness: The Evangelical Impact on the Victorians* (London: Jonathan Cape, 1976), 120.

[8] J. Edwards, 'Christian Charity: or, the Duty of Charity to the Poor, Explained and Enforced', *Works of Jonathan Edwards*, vol. 2 (1834), repr. (Edinburgh: Banner of Truth, 1979), 163–173.

commented it was better that his money was with the poor widow than with the highwayman. A little later the highwayman returned and demanded Whitefield's coat, which he gave on the condition that he received the robber's torn and threadbare coat in exchange. They had not gone much further when yet again they heard the highwayman's horse returning and now fearing for their lives, they raced to the nearest house for shelter. Safe inside, Whitefield took off the tattered old coat, and found wrapped in one pocket a parcel containing more than £100 – the reason the highwayman was so keen to catch up with them again![9]

Charity became central to Methodist practice. Francis Asbury, the pioneer of Methodism in North America, followed Wesley's example of simple living and personal generosity. In 1813 he was carefully restricting his expenditure to $12 per month, leaving him $56 of the $200 per year given to him by the Methodist Conference, which he could use to help those in need. When visiting Ohio, he heard of a widow whose only cow was about to be sold for debt. He gave her what money he had, and begged the rest from bystanders, until what she owed was cleared.[10]

Charles Simeon's evangelical Anglican parochial work in Cambridge included visitation schemes to administer relief to the poor.[11] By 1799 John Venn had followed his example in dividing his Clapham parish into districts in which lay visitors arranged charitable support.[12] Venn was convinced that benevolence and compassion were the inevitable outflow wherever the gospel was faithfully preached and truly believed:

> The sinner will be awakened, faith will be strengthened and hope enlivened. The fruits of love to God, and of cheerful obedience to his law, will be produced, and a spirit of benevolence and charity to man will be diffused.[13]

The activities of many local churches in relieving poverty became very significant. By the 1820s the Kensington Congregational Church, London, alongside its schools and evangelistic agencies, provided a Benevolent Society for visiting and offering support to the poor and sick; a Blanket Society giving

[9] L. Tyerman, *Life of Whitefield*, vol. 1 (London: Hodder & Stoughton, 1876), 525–526.

[10] F. Asbury, *Journal of Rev. Francis Asbury*, vol. 3, entry for 30 July 1813 (New York: Eaton & Maine, n.d.), 416.

[11] R. Carus, *Memoir of Rev. Charles Simeon* (London, Hatchard & Son, 1847), 80, 440.

[12] M. Hennell, *John Venn and the Clapham Sect* (London: Lutterworth Press, 1958), 142–145.

[13] J. Venn, 'The Importance and Difficulties of the Christian Ministry', in *Sermons by the Rev. John Venn, M.A.*, vol. 1 (London: Ellerton & Henderson, n.d.), 4.

free blankets to the poor in winter; an Infants' Friendly Society, providing food and clothing for mothers and newborn babies; as well as regular collections in the church services for the poor.[14] Other churches had similar agencies, offering coal for heating, soup kitchens for the impoverished and maternity parcels for pregnant mothers.[15]

The most comprehensive and ambitious approach among evangelicals to tackling poverty in the parish came from Thomas Chalmers in Scotland. When he arrived in central Glasgow in 1815, he was shocked at the extent of both financial and spiritual poverty, and saw a connection between the two. He found that only around one in every hundred of his parishioners attended his church.[16] His 'godly commonwealth' scheme involved extensive parish visitation by elders and deacons to provide spiritual and moral instruction, and identify cases of genuine need. His holistic vision saw the parish church bearing responsibility for both the spiritual and material welfare of the people in the parish. He withdrew his parish from Glasgow Council's complicated system of poor relief and took up regular collections in the church. The deacons used these funds to support people in need, after careful enquiry as to whether the case was 'genuine'. Chalmers believed that devolving this responsibility from ministers to the deacons reduced the 'sordid and mercenary expectations' of the large numbers of people begging for money from clergymen, which allowed the clergy to concentrate on cases of spiritual need and thus enhance the promotion of the gospel.

For drawing a distinction between the 'deserving' and the 'undeserving' poor, Chalmers has received some justifiable criticism. He feared creating a class of people entirely dependent on charity. Such 'pauperism' was to Chalmers a 'deadly antagonist to the morality of our nation', breeding indolence and a lack of self-respect. Instead, people should be encouraged 'to repose on their own capabilities'. Savings banks were started to help working people save for hard times.[17]

Accepting responsibility for providing poor relief for all those in the parish was part of a bold, ambitious and comprehensive Christian scheme for social regeneration, but placed a huge financial responsibility on the parish church. As a brilliant preacher, Chalmers attracted both a large wealthy congregation able to donate generously and lay volunteers who had time to sustain the work.

---

[14] Bebbington, *Evangelicalism*, 122.

[15] Ibid.

[16] S. J. Brown, *Thomas Chalmers and the Godly Commonwealth* (Oxford: Oxford University Press, 1982), 94.

[17] T. Chalmers, *Christian and Civic Economy*, vol. 1 (Edinburgh: Constable, 1851), 300, 430.

He preached to them on their social responsibilities, and their duty of charity to the poor. In this he was effective – the church-door collection for the poor averaged £400 per annum. Chalmers was convinced that 'the proper remedy . . . for the wretchedness of the few, is the kindness of the many'.[18]

The scheme showed a preference for offering personal charity to the poor, rather than through impersonal state officialdom. Chalmers also maintained an evangelistic priority:

> We do not hesitate to affirm that it is better for the poor to be worse fed and worse clothed, than that they be left ignorant of those scriptures that are able to make them wise unto salvation through the faith that is in Christ Jesus.[19]

He therefore combined discriminating poor relief with pastoral, evangelistic and widespread educational effort (running day schools and Sunday schools), to promote moral, spiritual and social transformation.[20] This challenges the assertion that evangelicals lacked any integrated social vision. Indeed, in the words of one of his biographers, Chalmers' scheme represented 'the pursuit of social justice, particularly through the spiritual, moral, and material elevation of the oppressed labouring poor of industrializing cities'. The spiritual transformation of individuals happened alongside genuine social reform.[21] Rooted in the Christendom model of the Reformation, his scheme reflected the classic Calvinistic holistic understanding of the Christian message.

Although Chalmers enjoyed some success with his scheme in Glasgow, it had flaws. The model failed to account for the cyclical nature of industrial economies, by which many workers in cities such as Glasgow were suddenly thrown into unemployment and poverty as a result of trade conditions beyond their control.[22] Chalmers was also influenced by Thomas Malthus, who argued that indiscriminate charity would give people no incentive to limit their family size. As a result, not all the domestic visitors from the church were as sympathetic to the needs of the poor as they could have been. Most other churches willingly embraced Chalmers' scheme of extensive visitation in their neighbourhoods,

---

[18] Ibid. x.

[19] T. Chalmers, *The Influence of Bible Societies on the Temporal Necessities of the Poor* (Edinburgh: Oliphant, Waugh & Innes, 1814), 6.

[20] On Chalmers and urban mission see I. J. Shaw, 'Thomas Chalmers, David Nasmith and the Origins of the City Mission Movement', *Evangelical Quarterly* 76.1 (January 2004), 31–46.

[21] Brown, *Thomas Chalmers*, 148. For analysis of the scheme see 90–151.

[22] See R. A. Cage and E. O. A. Checkland, 'Thomas Chalmers and Urban Poverty: The St John's Parish Experiment in Glasgow, 1819–37', *Philosophical Journal* 13 (1976), 37–56.

but not his social-relief proposals. Indeed, they were abandoned within a few years of his departure from the parish in 1823. Chalmers' project presupposed the existence of an Established Church, but many evangelicals were in other denominations, without legally defined territorial parishes.

The fear of 'pauperism', with people becoming institutionally dependent on charity, which undermined the incentives to find work, shaped government reform of the Poor Law safety-net system in England in the 1830s. It was rendered harsher and demeaning to those who resorted to it, in an attempt to discourage claims.

While Chalmers stressed the responsibility of the church to care for those in wider society, others stood appalled at the failure of churches even to look after their own. The English Congregationalist Edward Miall (1809–81) lamented seeing church members forced into dependency on poor relief:

> it seems to have been in great measure forgotten, that men have bodies to be cared for as well as souls to be saved, and that they who evince no concern for the former are not likely to be confidingly listened to in relation to the latter.[23]

In the 1830s the evangelical factory reformer Michael Sadler declared, 'We are now called upon strictly to observe the command of the Divine Author of our religion to relieve those who have none to help them.'[24] The motivation was compassion and love towards those in need, but also a desire to be found faithful before God at the final judgment, when 'the King', might declare, 'I was hungry and you gave me nothing to eat, I was thirsty and you gave me nothing to drink' (Matt. 25:41–43).[25]

Because of their emphasis on the sovereignty of God, high Calvinists have been assumed to have little place for social action. However, this was far from the case.[26] Many came from impoverished backgrounds, and were convinced they were called to minister especially to the poor and oppressed. William Huntington suffered acute poverty as a child, and recalled how early in his marriage his own children cried for lack of food. A number of his congregation

---

[23] E. Miall, *The British Churches in Relation to the British People* (London: British Anti-State Church Association, 1849), 436–437.

[24] Quoted in R. J. Morris, *Class, Sect and Party: The Making of the British Middle Class, Leeds 1820–1850* (Manchester: Manchester University Press, 1991), 216.

[25] See F. K. Prochaska, *Women and Philanthropy in Nineteenth Century England* (Oxford: Oxford University Press, 1980), 121–122.

[26] See I. J. Shaw, *High Calvinists in Action: Calvinism and the City c.1810–60* (Oxford: Oxford University Press, 2002).

were very poor, and part of his message was the uncertainty of worldly riches and the preciousness of faith.[27] The poor were exhorted to go on 'trusting in the providence of God'.[28] Despite espousing High Tory politics late in his life, he was unsparing in his denunciations of those who oppressed the poor. In 1796 he condemned unscrupulous merchants charging 18–20 shillings per bushel for 'hog corn', and warned, 'Will not God visit for these things, and shall not his soul be avenged on such oppressors as these.'[29] Huntington was a man of great generosity. When down to his last 2 pence, he recalled giving away a halfpenny to a beggar. Late in life he supported a number of pensioners out of his own pocket. Such a lifestyle, Huntington believed, was pleasing to God, and was honoured: 'Dwell in the land and do good, and verily thou shalt be fed.'[30] His generosity extended beyond the household of faith, and his chapel raised £201. 15s. 6d. for the widows and orphans of those killed in the Battle of the Nile.[31]

Similarly, William Gadsby was reared in poverty, and as minister of a Strict Baptist Church in one of the poorest areas of Manchester he built up a congregation of around a thousand. He became well known for speaking out against forms of political and social oppression, campaigning vigorously against the Corn Laws, which kept the price of grain, and hence bread, artificially high, in order to protect the income of farmers. They were, to Gadsby, a tax on the urban poor. He was also a man of enormous generosity, giving away around one third of his salary to the socially deprived living around him. Such generosity, he believed, was a gift of God: 'O my dear friends, what a mercy it is to have a heart to give to the really needy.'[32] James Wells, the Strict Baptist minister of the Surrey Tabernacle, London, had spent a period in the workhouse as a young child. His church eventually attracted congregations of 2,000 people, many from the poorer parts of Southwark. Regular collections for the 'Poor's Fund' were taken, and he established a Sick Fund and a Benefit Society, to which members contributed each week, and could claim benefits if they were unable to work due to lack of work or accident, or if a family member died.[33] Wells urged a compassionate response to beggars:

---

[27] W. Huntington, *The Bank of Faith, or God, the Guardian of the Poor* (London: 1786), repr. (London: C. J. Thynne, 1913), 38, 7–8.

[28] Ibid. 15.

[29] T. Wright, *The Life of William Huntington S.S.* (London: Farncombe & Son, 1909), 104.

[30] Huntington, *Bank*, 169, 58–61.

[31] E. Hooper (ed.), *Facts, Letters and Documents (Chiefly Unpublished) Concerning William Huntington, His Family and Friends: Forming an Addenda to the 'Celebrated Coalheaver'*, 2nd edn (London: W. H. & L. Collingwood, 1872), 42.

[32] W. Gadsby, letter to a friend, 17 April 1842, in *Gospel Standard Magazine*, vol. 14, March 1848, 72.

[33] Shaw, *Calvinists*, 268–270.

I always sympathise with such . . . if they are a little bit roguish, they are dreadfully poor, and poverty is a very trying thing; so don't be too hard on them; you don't know what poverty might tempt you to do.[34]

In his comprehensive strategy for relieving personal and spiritual deprivation, evocatively titled *In Darkest England and the Way Out*, William Booth (1829–1912) of the Salvation Army rejected claims that support for the poor would deflect from evangelism. Instead, the relief of 'temporal misery' would make it 'easy where it is now difficult, and possible where it is now all but impossible, for men and women to find their way to the Cross'. He maintained that poverty was a barrier to people hearing the gospel, and left some with the stark choice 'starve or sin'.[35]

In his comprehensive survey of late nineteenth-century London Charles Booth reported on the immense efforts of local churches to support the poor. One evangelical mission hall in 1890, whose attendees were themselves by no means affluent, was raising funds to provide 'shoes for naked feet, coals for empty grates, food for empty stomachs, furniture for empty rooms, money for empty pockets'.[36] The soup-kitchen work of the independent missions was also highly significant, located as they often were in areas of significant poverty to prevent starvation. Free meals for poor children were also provided.[37] Much evangelical charity, often unseen and unrecorded, was from the poor to the poor.

As well as these efforts by churches and charities, the philanthropic endeavour of evangelical individuals was also considerable. Henry Thornton (1760–1815) was a successful merchant banker and Member of Parliament (MP). Before he married he gave away 85 per cent of his income, up to £7,500 per year. After he was married and was raising a family, he was still giving away more than a third of his income, up to £3,000 per year, a vast sum when £50 per year was the income of many.[38] The Congregationalist industrialist and merchant Samuel Morley commented, 'I have not had much difficulty making money, but I have often been at a loss how to spend it.' He carefully researched the needs

---

[34] J. Wells, 'A Rod for the Lazy and a Crumb for the Hungry', Sermon in *Surrey Tabernacle Pulpit*, vol. 2, no. 61 (London, G. J. Stevenson, 1860), 32.

[35] W. Booth, *In Darkest England and the Way Out* (London: Salvation Army, 1890), 3. For a fuller discussion of Booth's work see chapter 15 below.

[36] C. Booth, *The Life and Labour of the People of London*, 3rd series, *Religious Influences*, vol. 7 (London, Macmillan, 1902), 320.

[37] Ibid. 285.

[38] R. Coupland, *Wilberforce, A Narrative* (Oxford: Clarendon Press, 1923), 251; M. Hennell, *John Venn and the Clapham Sect* (London: Lutterworth Press, 1958), 188.

of the individuals, churches and charitable bodies he gave to. His biographer commented, 'he could not see suffering without seeking to relieve it'.[39]

The North American Evangelist D. L. Moody, renowned for the emphasis in his ministry on urgent and immediate gospel proclamation, was also a man of great generosity. In 1860, early in his ministry, he was already distributing food and clothing to the poor, combining this with working for the salvation of the recipients. He reported of his work in 1867:

> Earnest working Christianity is apt to be comprehensive, and to care for both soul and body. No harm ordinarily comes from doing good in both simultaneously . . . It was the same Jesus who preached the gospel all day to the multitudes, that then fed them miraculously.[40]

The evangelical politician Lord Shaftesbury worked tirelessly to ease the suffering of the poor and dispossessed, which he believed could be a barrier to their seeking God. He declared that he was 'committed to looking on all men as the children of God, and relieving them of temporal obstacles to the fulfilment of their spiritual destinies'.[41] He believed that legislation to deal with the failures of the system combined with philanthropic giving was the best way to help individuals, but it should be done without robbing them of their own initiative and responsibility. They should be helped until they were able to help themselves: 'laws may remove obstacles and sympathisers give aid, but it is by personal conduct, by sobriety, by order, by honesty, by perseverance that a man, under God, becomes the architect of his own fortunes'.[42]

The effectiveness of this concern to relieve poverty has been questioned by some. The acute observer Charles Booth, in his survey of London, felt that 'the charitable relief given by missions of every description is rarely wise'. He highlighted much overlap of provision, and feared that the unsubtle offering of 'material assistance on one hand and the gospel in the other' reflected mixed motives and brought mixed results. It encouraged 'an atmosphere of meanness and hypocrisy, and brings discredit on both charity and religion'.[43] The North American Presbyterian John Nevius (1829–93) in his mission work in China similarly noted how the 'opprobrious epithet, "Rice Christians"' had been applied to those who had found their way into churches simply to benefit from

---

[39] E. Hodder, *Life of Samuel Morley* (London: Hodder & Stoughton, 1887), 196, 288, 499–501.

[40] *Advance*, 1, 7 November 1867, 4, quoted in J. F. Findlay Jr, *Dwight L. Moody: American Evangelist 1837–1899* (Chicago, Ill.: University of Chicago Press, 1969), 104–105.

[41] G. B. A. M. Finlayson, *The Seventh Earl of Shaftesbury 1801–1885* (London: Eyre Methuen, 1981), 50.

[42] Lord Shaftesbury, letter to the *London Times*, 6 December 1872, in Finlayson, *Shaftesbury*, 602.

[43] Booth, *London*, 278, 294.

food and material provisions. He recognized that '[t]hey have been connected with the Church, and probably will be, in all lands and in every age,' but the missionary method he outlined included advocating an end to the practice.[44] However, when charitable giving was accompanied by genuine compassion towards those in deep poverty, there could be a genuine response. Charles Booth quoted a report from a Baptist Mission in London in 1890:

> our soup kitchen has been opened all the winter, and besides sales of soup and puddings, thousands of quarts have been given away . . . This place has also proved the meeting place of needy sinners and a full Saviour.[45]

Indeed, the Baptist social investigator R. Mudie Smith, in his survey of religious life in London in 1904, applauded the work of churches and their faithful and often successful gospel preaching. But he went on:

> The gospel that does not concern itself with body, mind, and environment, as well as his soul, is a contradiction in terms . . . we need not expect the masses to take seriously either it or us . . . The Spirit of the Lord is not upon us unless our tidings to the poor are 'good tidings'.[46]

By the early twentieth century in Britain there was a growing recognition that the state had both the resources and moral duty to be involved on a wider scale. F. B. Meyer, who developed large inner-city churches in Leicester and London in the early twentieth century, began to call for the state to play a part in correcting systems that 'make the few rich and the many poor', and should also 'level up women's wages'.[47] State intervention reduced the space in which churches and charities could operate in the West.

However, deepening awareness among evangelicals of global need and their responsibility lay behind a series of initiatives in the second half of the twentieth century. In 1950 World Vision was founded by Bob Pierce and Frank Phillips, in Portland, Oregon, initially to meet emergency crisis needs, but by the 1970s it was teaching agricultural skills and installing water pumps, enabling people to improve their food-growing skills so they were less likely to fall into poverty.[48]

---

[44] J. Nevius, *Methods of Missionary Work* (New York: Foreign Mission Library, 1895), 15–16.

[45] Booth, *London*, 278.

[46] R. Mudie Smith, *The Religious Life of London* (London: Hodder & Stoughton, 1904), 13.

[47] F. B. Meyer in *British Weekly*, 26 April 1906; *Free Church Year Book* (London: National Council of the Evangelical Free Churches, 1909), 29.

[48] R. Balmer, 'World Vision International', in *The Encyclopedia of Evangelicalism* (Berkeley, Calif.: Westminster John Knox Press, 2002), 765–766.

The Evangelical Alliance Relief Fund (Tearfund), committed to relief and development work overseas, was launched in the UK in 1968. It sought to relieve poverty, and also to tackle its causes, and consequent suffering and disadvantage.[49]

In the Lausanne Covenant John Stott included a call for evangelicals to live in radically different ways: 'All of us are shocked by the poverty of millions and disturbed by the injustices which cause it.' It called on evangelicals to develop a 'simple lifestyle' in order to contribute more generously to both relief and evangelism.[50] This challenge reflected Stott's own practice and his awareness of the experience of millions of Christians in the Majority World.[51] The parallels between Stott's holistic vision and that of John Wesley and the early Methodists are notable, as will be seen in the following character study.

Character study: John Wesley (1703–91) – England

John Wesley oversaw the rapid development of the Methodist movement, which quickly became international, while undertaking a vast volume of literary production, including theological treatises, sermons and hymns. He is best known as a preacher, reckoned to have travelled some 250,000 miles by horseback in his itinerant ministry. His evangelical preaching was combined with an active social concern, which included the promotion of education, opposition to slavery and calls for prison reform. J. Wesley Bready in *England Before and After Wesley* (1938) outlines the wave of social reform that followed the Evangelical Revival, although his assertion that 'Wesley was the master-figure'[52] is something of an overstatement. The issue of poverty probably attracted John Wesley's attention more than any other. There is evidence of a bias to the poor in his ministry: he held their faith in higher regard than that of the rich, because it was 'pure, genuine grace, unmixed with paint, folly and affection'. The 1748 Methodist Conference even debated whether rich adherents should have a longer probationary period before membership than the poor.[53]

His personal background made Wesley acutely sensitive to those in financial need. He was one of nineteen children, born to an improvident father who, despite being an Anglican clergyman, was in 1705 jailed for unpaid debts.

---

[49] For further discussion of World Vision and Tearfund see chapter 3.

[50] Lausanne Covenant, 1975, sect. 9, 36–37 <https://lausanne.org/content/covenant/lausanne-covenant>, accessed 18 January 2020.

[51] See T. Dudley-Smith, *John Stott: A Global Ministry – A Biography: The Later Years* (Downers Grove, Ill.: InterVarsity Press, 2001), 216. Because of the phrase, Ruth Graham, wife of the famous evangelist, refused to sign the covenant, arguing 'simple' was hard to define, and preferring the word 'simpler'.

[52] J. Wesley Bready, *England Before and After Wesley* (London: Hodder & Stoughton, 1938), 12.

[53] J. Telford (ed.), *Letters of John Wesley*, vol. 3 (London: Epworth Press, 1931), 229.

Wesley knew what it was to go without, and learned from his mother, Susanna, the importance of economical and prudent living.[54] As a student he was conscience stricken when he was unable to help a poor girl because he had recently spent his money on decorating his rooms, lamenting that it was at the cost of the 'blood of the poor'. In 1731, when a Fellow of Lincoln College, Oxford University, he resolved to live on the £28 per year income he then received, and to give the rest away.[55] After three years his income had jumped to £90 and he gave away £62. As he became a successful author he gave away profits of up to £1,000 a year. One writer estimates he gave away £30,000, a vast sum even in those days.[56]

Any ostentation or unnecessary spending was eschewed. When the government Commissioners of Excise wrote in 1776 to all those believed to be owners of silver plate, demanding the payment of the tax duty owed on it, Wesley replied, 'Sir – I have two silver spoons at London and two at Bristol. This is all the plate I have at present, and I shall not buy any more while so many round me want bread.'[57]

At his death, the only money he had left was a few coins in his pocket and on his dresser – the rest had been given away.

The complaint that evangelicals proposed no radical social theory is countered by the idea proposed by Wesley of a return to the shared community of goods as practised in Acts 2:44 and 4:32. The Moravians, who were for a while influential on Wesley's evangelical spirituality, had operated within a communal economy. However, when Wesley discussed this model with the Methodist Societies in 1744, he received a lukewarm response. He came to believe that such an ideal was possible only among Christians living at the highest level of love and fellowship.[58]

Wesley asserted that failing to heed the needs of others was robbing God, as well as the poor, the widow and the orphan. Such neglect left a person accountable before God for all 'the want, affliction and distress which might have been removed, but had not done so'.[59] In May 1741 those belonging to the Methodist

[54] H. D. Rack, *Reasonable Enthusiast: John Wesley and the Rise of Methodism* (London: Epworth Press, 1989), 49–50.

[55] Wesley, 'Sermon LXXXVIII, On Dress', in *Works of John Wesley*, vol. 7 (London: Wesleyan Conference Office, 1872; repr. Grand Rapids, Mich.: Zondervan, n.d.), 21; 'Sermon LXXXIX, The More Excellent Way', in ibid. 36.

[56] T. Coke and H. Moore, *The Life of the Rev. John Wesley* (London: G. Paramore, 1792), 434.

[57] Quoted in R. Watson, *The Life of Rev. John Wesley, A.M.* (New York: Mason & Lane, 1839), 229.

[58] John Walsh, 'John Wesley and the Community of Goods', in K. Robbins (ed.), *Studies in Church History*, Subsidia 7 (Oxford: Blackwell, 1990), 25–50.

[59] See W. J. Warner, *The Wesleyan Movement in the Industrial Revolution* (London: Longmans, 1930), 210.

Society in London were urged to bring clothing and a penny a week to help clothe and support its poor members. Wesley was still raising money for poor Methodists when he was aged 80, but his social concern was not restricted to the household of faith. In 1740 he was also raising funds for the poor who were unable to get assistance from the Poor Law.[60]

Charity was a key Christian duty to Wesley, although the man who sold all his clothes to support the poor was described as 'mad'.[61] Actions were to be matched by a heart of love and compassion. Wesley wrote, 'Put yourself in the place of any poor man, and deal with him as you would God should deal with you.'[62] In 1744 the Methodist Conference instructed, 'Give none that ask for relief either an ill word or an ill look.'[63] Nor was charitable relief to be given in a cold and impersonal way: 'How much better it is . . . to *carry* relief to the poor than *send* it! And that both for our own sakes and theirs.' Such visits allowed opportunity to offer spiritual as well as temporal support, and blessed both receiver and giver: 'it is far more apt to soften our hearts and makes us naturally care for each other'.[64]

However, Wesley did not advocate the poor remain passive in their poverty – self-improvement was also enjoined. He was uncomfortable with excessive wealth being passed on to children. The challenge was that, as some Methodist converts adopted self-denying practices, they inevitably grew in affluence and became upwardly socially mobile. Methodism became a diverse and complex movement, ranging from poor labourers to businessmen and aristocrats. Wesley was anxious to break down the distinction between the 'deserving' and the 'undeserving' poor. The mark of the true Christian was 'universal benevolence', embracing 'neighbours and strangers, friends and enemies, the froward, the evil, and unthankful'.[65] In the 1780s Wesley called on Methodists to start 'Strangers' Friend Societies' to assist financially people in new industrial areas unable to claim relief from the Poor Law because they had relocated from their place of origin, often to find work. The first was started in Bristol in 1787.[66]

Wesley's approach is epitomized in his sermon 'The Use of Money', first preached in 1744, based on Luke 16:9. The problem was not money, but its use: 'It may be used ill . . . but it may likewise be used well.' He encapsulated his teaching in a classic three points: 'Gain all you can'; 'Save all you can'; 'Give all

[60] Rack, *Wesley*, 361.
[61] G. Whitefield, *Journals* (London: Banner of Truth, 1960), 267.
[62] J. Wesley, *Journal of John Wesley*, ed. N. Curnock, vol. 4 (London: Epworth Press, 1938), 301.
[63] Methodist Society Minutes (1744), quoted in Rack, *Wesley*, 363.
[64] Wesley, *Journal*, vol. 4, 358, 422; emphases original.
[65] *Works of Wesley*, vol. 10, 68–69.
[66] Rack, *Wesley*, 448.

you can.' It was the 'bounden duty' of Christians to earn money through honest trades, as long as others were not exploited. Saving ensured money gained was not wasted on 'the pleasure of sense'. Once family and dependents had been provided with food, clothing and 'that which preserves the body in health and strength', the remainder was to be given away, especially to the poor. Christians were to question themselves over whether they were acting as a 'steward of my Lord's goods?' Giving was not to be seen just as offering God a portion of their income, for 'all that is God's'.[67]

He believed that showing love to all, including the poor, was part of offering the gospel of salvation to all. There are, however, complexities in Wesley's thinking, in part because of the traditions he drew on. An element of asceticism came from the Anglican High Church tradition he practised with the Oxford Holy Club, who made almsgiving an aspect of the discipled lifestyle. After his evangelical conversion in 1738, he was drawn to Moravian communitarian ideals. Unlike most other leaders of the Evangelical Revival, who saw sanctification as progressive and not complete until death, Wesley also believed Christians could attain what he called 'Christian perfection' in this life. Nonetheless, Wesley's conversion to evangelicalism by no means diminished his social concern. Social action was to him an important, demonstrable evidence of conversion. Devotion to Christ was to be characterized by service to the poor, for that had been the example of Jesus himself.

---

[67] J. Wesley, *Sermons on Several Occasions by the Rev. John Wesley, A.M.* (London: Wesleyan-Methodist Book-Room, n.d.), 704, 705, 706–707, 710, 713, 716.

3

Disaster relief

Natural disasters, especially famines, were a significant feature of the experience of God's people in the Bible, from the book of Genesis through to the New Testament (e.g. Acts 11:28). By the eighteenth century the ravages of disease and food shortage had not ceased to be a part of the experience of large numbers of people, despite industrial development in Western economies. The cyclical pattern of economic activity saw surges of growth, interspersed by periods of trade recession. This was something of which evangelicals were all too aware, and sought in different ways to bring relief to those in greatest need.

One such severe economic downturn occurred in 1772, creating much unemployment and poverty. Wesley set out his thoughts on the problems in a letter to the editor of *Lloyd's Evening Post* in December 1772. This was published as a tract the following month, entitled *Thoughts on the Present Scarcity of Provisions*. Wesley movingly recounted the scenes of suffering he had witnessed, including seeing poor people picking 'stinking sprats' from a dunghill to eat them, and gathering up bones left by dogs in the streets in order to make 'broth of them, to prolong a wretched life'. He blamed the country's economic ills on luxury, waste and unnecessary taxes. Wesley also believed that the price of bread corn was inflated because of the demands of the distilling industry, with many distillers avoiding paying duty. Instead, the duties required to raise state expenditure were being paid by those least able to afford them. This was nothing less than 'selling the flesh and blood of their countrymen'. Wesley bitterly condemned extravagant waste on horses and carriages, and other desires for opulent display, when thousands were perishing 'for want of food'. Wesley's solution to the problem of starvation faced by thousands was not just to give money, but also to create employment opportunities: 'Find them work, and you will find them meat. They will earn and eat their own bread.' He did not shirk from strong political comment, and called for a rebalancing of the economy away from luxury consumption, to the production of staples. He also urged paying off the national debt, removing government sinecures and reducing the size of farms so farmers could focus on food production.[1]

One natural disaster that haunted Britain and Ireland in the nineteenth century was the Potato Famine of the 1840s. The population of Ireland and parts of north-west Britain had increased significantly and the cultivation of potatoes had become widespread. This brought a ready supply of a cheap and easily grown foodstuff, but left large parts of the population dependent on a single food source. When, in the autumn of 1845, the potato crop failed badly in Ireland and the Highlands and Islands of Scotland, hundreds of thousands were left on the verge of starvation. The crop failed even more drastically in the following year. The tragedy deepened in 1847 when epidemic diseases, especially typhus, swept through the starving populations in the already famine-stricken areas.

More than a million people died in the famine in Ireland, and more than a million emigrated. As the new Whig government in London drew back from the previous policy of public works and soup kitchens, crowds of thousands dressed in rags descended on the workhouses in Ireland pleading for help. Workhouse staff were unable to cope and many starving people died outside the walls of the institutions that had been built as the place of last resort when things became absolutely desperate for the population.[2]

Churches were stirred into action to bring famine relief. The Free Church of Scotland, which had only separated from the Church of Scotland in 1843, and faced huge financial demands for the building of new churches and manses, led the way among Scottish churches. Galvanized by the challenge of Thomas Chalmers from November 1846 onwards, more than £15,000 was collected by this new evangelical denomination to help relieve the suffering in Scotland and Ireland. Chalmers' role was both influential and significant. Some refused to contribute to the relief efforts, arguing that the natural disaster was an outworking of the law of population outlined by Thomas Malthus. This proposed that when population exceeded the capacity of agriculture to supply its needs, there would be a 'check' such as a famine, which would reduce numbers to a sustainable level. Supporters of Malthusian thinking argued it was not only improper but also impossible to intervene in these natural laws to prevent the drop in population. Nature was to be left to take its course, no matter how many hundreds of thousands died. Others in the government propounded a laissez-faire economic doctrine that it was not the role of the state to intervene in the

---

[1] J. Wesley, *Thoughts on the Present Scarcity of Provisions* (1773), in *Works of John Wesley*, vol. 11 (London: Wesleyan Conference Office, 1872; repr. Grand Rapids, Mich.: Zondervan, n.d.), 54, 55, 57.

[2] C. Ó Murchadha, *The Great Famine* (London: Continuum, 2011), 179–180.

economy, and even began to close relief efforts such as public-works projects and soup kitchens.

Early in his career Chalmers had shown some support for the overall thinking of Malthus, although never to the extent that it overrode his Christian compassion. However, in the face of the deepening tragedy he was appalled by those who were indifferent or hostile to the relief efforts. In the 1840s his views were more developed, and somewhat altered, as he outlined in a letter of March 1847, published in the *Witness*, a newspaper edited by the evangelical Hugh Miller. In this he strongly rebutted the arguments of those (including some evangelicals) who claimed that people facing starvation had brought the disaster on themselves by having too many children and not endeavouring to improve their own situation. Chalmers urged that 'the agonies and cries of those dying creatures' should 'reach our ears to the awakening of an effectual compassion'. He solemnly warned that if they did not, 'they shall reach the ears of Him who sitteth above, to the effect of a fearful retribution upon ourselves'.[3] He argued that this situation was to be viewed as a 'Special Providence' in which God called for a compassionate response. Along with private philanthropic efforts, he urged the government to step in, creating a partnership to deal with the desperate situation, because the scale of the problem was beyond the capacity of private philanthropy to resolve. He later called for at least £30 million in government aid – the threat of starvation to a significant portion of Britain's population was so serious. He also urged an end to using grain to distil beer and spirits: it was unconscionable that Scots should luxuriate in whisky and the English in beer when so many of their fellow citizens were dying for want of grain. Chalmers' prayer was that 'with the guidance and guardianship of the Holy Providence above, a harvest of good will result from this temporary evil'.[4]

The Irish famine awakened concern among evangelical Protestants not only for relief work but also, alongside this, for mission in Ireland, with the efforts of the so-called 'second Reformation' gathering pace in the late 1840s. The Society for Irish Church Missions opened schools for children that offered not just education but also food and clothing. Scripture readers were employed. The Revd Alexander Dallas, founder of the Irish Church Missions, using the medium of the Irish language, set up a series of 'feeding schools' and mission stations across Connemara, which saw several thousand converts. They were to face considerable opposition from a determined subsequent counter-mission

---

[3] *Witness*, 5 June 1847, quoted in S. J. Brown, *Thomas Chalmers and the Godly Commonwealth in Scotland* (Oxford: Oxford University Press, 1982), 368.

[4] T. Chalmers, 'The Political Economy of a Famine', *North British Review* 7 (1847), 282–289.

led by the Irish Catholic Church. Converts were criticized as 'soupers', converting only for the sake of the material support they received.[5] However, those who provided the relief worked hard to avoid drawing any connection between the aid they offered and a need to accept their message.

The Revd Frederick Trench, perpetual curate of Cloghjordan, described the desperate efforts of his fellow Church of Ireland clergy, working sometimes in partnership with Roman Catholic priests, to bring relief to the poor and dying in the famine, and to start 'eating houses' to give the famine-stricken population a meal each day. His account, contained in published letters, described visiting areas such as Schull, where he found streets eerily silent, devoid of the sound of children at play. Instead, tragically, they lay dying where they had once played. He was horrified to find dozens of bodies left unburied in the fields or in the houses, where they were gnawed by dogs or rats. Wherever the clergy went, they were surrounded by crowds of people clasping their dying children in their arms, pleading for help.[6] Trench believed that the tragedy had opened up opportunities for gospel ministry among the poor Catholic population that had not been available before the famine. However, despite the chronic need, he deprecated 'in the strongest manner holding out of any carnal inducements to the reception of the spiritual good'. He declared that he loathed 'from my innermost soul, the iniquity of holding out an inducement to the miserable to do that to which their poverty, and not their will, might consent'. It was not morally right to induce or put pressure on desperate people to change their religion. But, quoting the promise of Christ 'Let your light so shine before men that they may see your good works and glorify your Father which is in heaven,' he did believe that charity might open the door to promotion of the spiritual welfare of the population.[7]

Later in the century, in 1862 and 1863, the American Civil War caused immense disruption to already difficult trade conditions in Britain, and cut the supply of cotton to the mills in Lancashire from the southern slave-owning Confederate states. The so-called 'Cotton Famine' saw up to half the cotton-factory operatives thrown out of work, and those in work on greatly reduced wages. Visitors found houses stripped almost bare as the unemployed sold everything they had for food, and were forced to sleep on straw on the floor. In some areas up to half the population applied for poor relief and large numbers migrated. Despite their suffering, the cotton workers were largely resolute in

---

[5] Ó Murchadha, *Great Famine*, 185–186.
[6] F. F. Trench, 'Letters Concerning the Famine', Appendix to W. S. Trench, *Realities of Irish Life* (London: Longmans, Green, 1869), 394–402.
[7] Ibid. 410–411.

their support of the cause of the northern states against the slave-owning southern states. Their plight aroused great compassion among churches. Adding their efforts to other public-relief projects, the Lancashire Baptist Relief Fund distributed £7,000.[8] Other churches from further afield were similarly involved. In December 1862 James Wells of the Surrey Tabernacle in London preached sermons in support of those affected by the shortages, and in the following month travelled to Lancashire to distribute personally the significant sum of £189 raised.[9]

Disaster relief also became a significant part of the ministry of evangelical missionaries in the late nineteenth century, especially in China, which became the focus of considerable mission efforts. Timothy Richard (1845–1919), a Welshman who had experienced a personal awakening to faith during the 1859 revival, was in 1869 accepted by the Baptist Missionary Society. He served in the Shantung and Shanxi provinces.[10] Richard pushed mission into new avenues when a devastating famine was experienced in northern China in 1876–9, which cost some 9.5 million lives. He used the famine to call people to repentance and to turn to God, but also disseminated news of the devastation in wealthy areas of China, and overseas. Richard and the North American Presbyterian John Nevius took a lead in distributing relief in the winter of 1876–7, but tens of thousands were dying. Timothy Richard, and David Hill of the English Wesleyan mission (see the character study below), thereafter became the key figures in distributing relief funds. Such compassionate activity won the gratitude of many Chinese towards the mission: for some the first contact they had with Christians was through their role in disaster relief. It was a decisive moment in the developing missionary consciousness, making emergency relief a continuing concern of overseas mission. Famine relief was undertaken not simply to pave the way for evangelism, but as compassionate service that followed the pattern of Christ, who fed the five thousand. Mission was about being and doing, as well as preaching.[11]

James Hudson Taylor and the China Inland Mission (CIM) have generally been associated with giving a very strong priority to evangelism above social concern. However, as chapter 16 in this book shows, they placed a strong focus

---

[8] J. Lea, 'The Growth of the Baptist Denomination in Mid-Victorian Lancashire and Cheshire', *Transactions of the Historic Society of Lancashire and Cheshire* 124 (1972), 142–143.

[9] I. J. Shaw, *High Calvinists in Action: Calvinism and the City c.1810–60* (Oxford: Oxford University Press, 2002), 270.

[10] See also A. Walls, 'The Multiple Conversions of Timothy Richard: A Paradigm of Missionary Experience', in *Cross Cultural Process in Christian History* (Maryknoll, N.Y.: Orbis Books, 2002), 236–258.

[11] On Richard see B. Stanley, *History of the Baptist Missionary Society* (Edinburgh: T&T Clark, 1992), 175–190.

on care for opium addicts. Alongside that, CIM workers played important roles in famine relief in the devastating famine of 1876–9. It was an event of biblical proportions, involving floods, locust plagues and drought, and affected seventeen provinces. After the drought came floods that stripped away the topsoil, and then drought returned, particularly devastating Shanxi province.

Hudson Taylor, alerted to the terrible conditions, wrote an article in *China's Millions* on 'Concern for the Poor', based on Psalm 41:1–3, and commented:

> Do not let us spiritualise the text so as to lose its obvious meaning (of not merely sympathy but action). How much of the precious time and strength of our Lord was spent in conferring temporal blessings on the poor, the afflicted and the needy?[12]

This challenge, and the reports he published from CIM missionaries, led to £8,000 in donations being sent to the CIM. In all, mission societies and the Shanghai Famine Relief Committee received more than £50,000, vast sums of money. But this paled into insignificance in the face of the £150,000 per week being derived from the sale of opium in China. The September 1877 edition of *China's Millions* devoted fourteen pages to the famine, two to the opium scandal and only two pages to the normal work of the mission.[13] In March 1878, using funds for the ordinary work of the mission, Hudson Taylor instructed missionaries in the famine-affected areas, where there were many refugees, to take on the support of 200 destitute children, prioritizing the orphans. This work was headed up by his wife, Jennie, who travelled to China to undertake the project, leaving behind two infant children under the age of 3 in order to do so. The CIM missionaries worked with Hill and Richard, despite there being some significant theological disagreement with the latter over the broader theological views he was taking. They distributed relief in the worst-affected parts of Shanxi.[14]

Women also played a significant role in disaster relief. The indomitable Charlotte ('Lottie') Diggs Moon (1840–1912), standing just 4 feet and 3 inches tall, left her work as a teacher in Georgia to begin work as a Southern Baptist Missionary in China in 1873. She saw significant evangelistic success at P'ing-tu, where many converts won through her ministry were gathered into churches,

---

[12] Quoted in A. J. Broomhall, *Hudson Taylor and China's Open Century*, bk 6: *Assault on the Nine* (London: Hodder & Stoughton, 1988), 167.

[13] Ibid. 171.

[14] A. Austin, *China's Millions: The China Inland Mission and the Qing Society, 1832–1905* (Grand Rapids, Mich.: Eerdmans, 2007), 102.

and she helped to train indigenous pastors for the work. Within twenty years the Chinese pastor at P'ing-tu had baptized more than 1,000 converts. Lottie Moon was a person of profound compassion. Conflicts in the region had a significant impact on her work, particularly the Sino-Japanese War (1894), the Boxer Rebellion (1900) and then the Chinese Nationalist uprising, as a result of which the Qing Dynasty was overthrown in 1911. As well as the huge dislocation occasioned by war, these events cast frequent shadows of famine and plague over her work. When famine struck in her region, she could not bear to keep food for herself when starving children came to her door, and gave generously to them. The malnutrition occasioned by her generosity is considered in some accounts of her life as a contributory factor in the rapid decline in her physical and mental health before her death in 1912.[15] Yet the impact of her work endured. In 1888, to raise funds among Southern Baptist women for missionary work in China, she initiated a Christmas offering. After 1918 it became the Lottie Moon Christmas offering: in 1992 it raised $80 million.[16]

Such relief efforts in China continued into the twentieth century, as is seen in the work of Alex Macpherson, a missionary with the CIM. In 1922 a disastrous flood occurred in Chenghsien. With no help available from the Chinese government, the Chinese–Foreign Famine Relief Committee was formed, with Macpherson together with the local chief magistrate as co-chairmen, which showed how evangelicals were willing to work in partnership with the authorities. They oversaw work to buy and distribute foodstuffs and clothing for the needy.[17] Part of the motivation for Macpherson's social concern was belief in Christ's second coming. Not only were Christians to be found actively engaged in works of service at Christ's return, but the sense of imminence of that event also spurred evangelistic concern. From this, Macpherson believed, came a strong motivation for believers to manifest 'a spirit of true charity'. He was convinced that 'those who truly are watching for the return of their Lord will be most unceasing in their work of loving sympathy and relief'.[18]

After the Second World War, evangelical responses to humanitarian crises became more organized and large-scale, their awareness heightened by the condition of the seven million displaced persons in Europe alone after 1945. This renewed interest in social concern among evangelicals came after the

---

[15] The traditional account of her unsuccessful struggle with her missionary society for more funds to relieve the poor, and its effect on her health, is challenged in a more recent study; see R. D. Sullivan, *A Southern Baptist Missionary to China in History and Legend* (Baton Rouge, La.: Louisiana State University Press, 2011).

[16] See C. B. Allen, *The New Lottie Moon Story* (Nashville, Tenn.: Broadman Press, 1980).

[17] A. K. Macpherson, 'Famine Conditions in Chekiang', *China's Millions*, April, 1923, 56.

[18] Ibid. 57.

decades in which social action had increasingly been viewed as synonymous with the liberal social gospel. This fresh interest was combined with a conviction that this should be closely associated with gospel outreach. Evangelicals were concerned that other major relief and developmental organizations, such as Oxfam (founded in 1942 by Quakers and other social activists in Oxford) and Christian Aid (founded in 1945 by mainline Protestant denominations), lacked this dual focus. These evangelicals took the view that social concern alone, without an evangelistic dimension, was an insufficient expression of the Christian message, and a form of the social gospel. Evangelical convictions that Word and deed were inseparable led them to seek avenues for giving to organizations and projects which made sure that gospel witness was an intrinsic part of compassionate service in the world.

In 1947 Bob Pierce (1914–78), a North American Youth for Christ Evangelist, undertook a highly successful evangelistic campaign in China, and was deeply affected by the poverty he saw there. He was introduced by a local worker to an abandoned girl called White Jade. Pierce began sending funds to China each month for her upkeep and education. His desire to do more led him to found World Vision in 1950, to help children orphaned by the Korean War. Soon funds were being received to care for children in need in other Asian countries, then in Latin America, Africa, Eastern Europe and the Middle East. Pierce's motto was, 'Let my heart be broken with the things that break the heart of God.'[19] By the second decade of the twenty-first century, World Vision was one of the largest relief agencies in the world, working in nearly 100 countries.

The readiness with which evangelicals supported its humanitarian efforts, initially among victims of war, pointed to their growing desire to express their social conscience practically. World Vision's mission statement asserted its dual focus on both social concern and Christian witness, describing its ministry as

an international partnership of Christians whose mission is to follow our Lord and Saviour Jesus Christ in working with the poor and oppressed to promote human transformation, seek justice and bear witness to the good news of the Kingdom of God.[20]

---

[19] On Pierce's life see J. R. Hamilton, 'An Historical Study of Bob Pierce and World Vision's Development of the Evangelical Social Action Film', PhD dissertation, University of Southern California, 1980.

[20] See <https://www.worldvision.org.uk/who-we-are/our-history>, accessed 20 January 2020; T. Stafford, 'The Colossus of Care' and 'Imperfect Instrument', *Christianity Today*, March 2005, 51–56.

Pierce was also adept at using visual media, notably film, in raising awareness of humanitarian crises.[21] Pierce left World Vision in 1967, and in 1970 founded Samaritan's Purse, another evangelical Christian relief organization designed to meet emergency needs in crisis contexts, working with evangelical mission agencies and local churches.

In response to World Refugee Year (1959/1960) *Crusade*, the monthly magazine sponsored by the Evangelical Alliance in the UK, gave over a whole issue to the plight of refugees worldwide. Without any appeal for funds, donations poured in from individuals and churches, who requested that they be sent to those in need by the hands of evangelical Christians.[22] As a result, an Evangelical Alliance Refugee Fund (EAR Fund) was established. Because the Evangelical Alliance was not itself a relief agency, the funds donated were distributed to other charities considered suitable. In 1967 the Evangelical Alliance employed the Anglican curate George Hoffman (1933–92) to develop this work, and in the following year he became one of the founders of The Evangelical Alliance Relief Fund (Tearfund), which he led for many years.[23] This organization, formally registered as a charity in 1973, played a key role in broadening the scope of evangelical social concern. Hoffman had been much influenced by the teaching of John Stott that both evangelism and social action were obligations laid on Christians, and expressions of Christian compassion.

Tearfund emphasized that the gospel was 'good news to the poor', and its relief work included an emphasis on both physical and spiritual needs. Its ministry was largely conducted through partnership with local churches in the areas to which relief was sent. One prominent supporter was the singer Cliff Richard, who between 1969 and 1984 raised £300,000 for the charity through a series of benefit concerts, and served as Tearfund's Vice-President and President. In the 1970s Tearfund was not just administering emergency aid, but also investing heavily in longer-term development projects. John Stott was also an early supporter of Tearfund, and served as its President. In 1975 he wrote *Walk in His Shoes: The Compassion of Jesus*,[24] which Tearfund described as 'a life changing moment of understanding' for many staff.[25] Tearfund spread globally, with Tearfund Canada (formerly World Relief Canada) founded in 1970, Tear Australia in 1971, Tear (based in the Netherlands) in

---

[21] For the use of visual media see Hamilton, 'Bob Pierce'.

[22] *Church Times*, 2 March 2018.

[23] T. Chester, *Awakening to a World of Need: The Recovery of Evangelical Social Concern* (Leicester: Inter-Varsity Press, 1993), 13–14, 41.

[24] J. Stott, *Walk in His Shoes: The Compassion of Jesus* (Leicester, Inter-Varsity Press, 1975).

[25] Letter from Stephen Rand, Tearfund to John Stott, quoted in T. Dudley-Smith, *John Stott: A Global Ministry – A Biography: The Later Years* (Downers Grove, Ill.: InterVarsity Press, 2001), 274.

1973, Tearfund (New Zealand) in 1975, Tearfund Belgium, in 1979, and Tearfund (Switzerland), 1984. The organization's income rapidly grew from £34,000 in 1968, to reach more than £15 million by the time of Hoffman's death in a road accident in 1992.

Through organizations such as World Vision, Samaritan's Purse and Tearfund, late twentieth-century evangelical Christians were not only awakened to a world of need but were also provided with a vehicle by which they could offer compassionate practical support, and in which the gospel message would also be a part of the ministry offered to those in need.

Character study: David Hill (1840–96) – China

A leading figure in the provision of relief during the 1876–8 famine in China, in which millions died, was the Methodist missionary David Hill. Born in York, England, after completing theological studies he was in 1864 appointed by the Wesleyan Methodist Conference to the Central China Mission, which had been formed just two years earlier.[26] He was strongly influenced by the example of John Wesley, and gave away as much as possible of his income, keeping expenditure on himself to 'the absolute minimum of need'.[27] His missional practice combined evangelism with social action: 'Let evangelistic work be accompanied by benevolent activity to the physical wants of men so long as I have it in my power to do so . . . even to the disposal of all personal property.'[28]

Hill proved a highly effective missionary evangelist, and was instrumental in the conversion of the Confucian scholar Hsi Liao-chih.[29] The 'Rice Christian' problem was a particular concern in China. Nonetheless, Hill believed un-equivocally in the call to 'love and do good even to our enemies', and took as his model the parable of the good Samaritan. He saw the missionary task as setting forth the 'Christ-life' alongside the words of the Christian message.[30] He chose deliberately to live near scenes of poverty and to 'mix with those burdened with it, and, as far as we can, relieve it'.[31] Following the Son of Man meant 'to be identified with the poor, and to place himself as far as possible on a level with them'. To accomplish this he chose never to marry.[32]

---

[26] W. T. A. Barber, *David Hill: Missionary and Saint* (London: Charles H. Kelly, 1898), 1–48.

[27] G. G. Findlay, *History of the Wesleyan Methodist Missionary Society*, vol. 5 (London: J. A. Sharp, 1924), 468; Barber, *David Hill*, 158.

[28] Findlay, *History*, vol. 5, 468.

[29] On Hsi see chapter 16 in this book.

[30] Barber, *David Hill*, 158–160.

[31] Letter to his brother, J. R. Hill, 19 June 1877, quoted in Barber, *David Hill*, 158.

[32] A. Foster, letter, quoted in Barber, *David Hill*, 193, 222.

After the terrible drought started in China in 1876, Hill moved to Shanxi when he heard it was the worst-affected province. Hill recalled people 'were mown down by millions'. The problem was exacerbated by the number of farmers who had switched from growing grain to growing opium. By November 1877 people were eating weeds and bark from trees, as three to four million Chinese were reduced to starvation. Although there was some grain in other provinces, the response of the Chinese government was slow and inadequate, and the heavy snow of the winter of 1877 further hindered their response.[33]

The scenes in Shanxi were horrific. Everywhere was 'the stench of dead bodies lying in houses by the side of the living, who had not the strength or means to bury them ... Wailing and lamentation and woe wafted on every breeze.' The roads were 'strewed with men and women who had sunk down unable to move further'. Wherever he walked he was beset by people looking like skeletons clutching at him and begging for relief.[34]

The Chinese government focused on either sending a lump sum of funding to an area, some of which was often appropriated by officials, or shipping bulk quantities of food, substantial amounts of which was taken by intermediaries. At the height of the famine, despite its large resources, the Chinese government was still offering starving people only two pints of rice a month despite there being supplies in other parts of the country.[35]

Evangelical missionaries from different denominations worked closely together. Hill was among those who travelled to Shanghai to receive some of the funds sent there by the missionary societies. In Shanxi Hill worked with Joshua Turner of the CIM, who had arrived in China in 1876. They sought to work alongside the local authorities if possible. When arriving in a new location, the missionaries spoke to the district magistrate, requesting a list of families in most need, so they could visit them first, although not all co-operated. Hill and Turner went systematically from village to village, and then house to house, visiting between ten and twenty houses a day. In Shukow they relieved 16,000 destitute people. Their relief was given in small copper coins that did not need to be exchanged. They were shocked to find banks and money changers profiteering in the crisis by charging up to 8 per cent for changing silver coins into copper. By giving money, Hill felt he was offering some dignity to famine-stricken people, allowing them to choose what food they could buy, and where.[36]

---

[33] Barber, *David Hill*, 184, 187–189.
[34] Ibid. 196–198.
[35] Ibid. 190, 197, 245.
[36] Ibid. 190, 193–195, 197.

In 1878 the death rate in Ping Yang reached 73 per cent. Five women were executed for kidnapping children from the streets, and then killing and eating them. Wolves also came in from the surrounding countryside, predating on the dead and even the living. The urgency of the crisis left Hill with an acute dilemma. Should he stop and preach the gospel to everyone he helped, knowing that would slow his progress in reaching others who might die before he got to them with aid? Hill decided that the immediate priority was saving as many lives as possible, and then he could go back and preach to them later. In the direst of emergency there was 'no time then to preach any gospel but that of deeds'.[37]

He was horrified when one of his most trusted agents embezzled funds, deceiving him in the most desperate of times. In all his charitable efforts Hill stressed the need for careful discrimination. Of some he found idling in a lodging house he noted, 'Give them money – they gamble it away, as they do the clothes you may give them.' Once starvation had been averted, it was his preference to pay people to undertake small-scale work projects, such as repairing a road or giving widows some cotton to sew and sell, rather than just give away funds. All was done with compassion, 'with a smile' and a 'few sweetmeats'.[38]

The spiritual fruit of Hill's and Turner's work became clear as the famine receded. Many turned from the idols that had failed them when they had frequented the shrines of the rain god, Lung Wang, and Lao Tien (Ancient Heaven), crying unavailingly for the drought to end. Hill and Turner started services in their home, gathering together those who had shown most interest in their message. The 'preaching' of their charitable relief efforts had proved attractive. When Hill and Turner revisited villages affected by the famine the following year, at first the poor feared they had come back to reclaim their money. When assured this was not the case, they 'prostrated themselves to the earth before them' with gratitude. Others, however, had quickly fallen into a culture of dependency and some missionaries were beset by angry Chinese people expecting free meals and rice even when the crisis of the famine was over.[39]

The outcome of Hill's work was lasting. His biographer believed the 'fine chain of prosperous and self-supporting Christian Churches in the north is due under God's Providence to the practical love shown during the awful famine'.[40]

---

[37] Ibid. 199–202.
[38] Ibid. 204–207, 210.
[39] Ibid. 200, 206, 217, 246.
[40] Ibid. 183.

Throughout the remainder of his ministry Hill continued to connect evangelism and social action in his ministry. In 1882 he founded a school in Hankow offering education and employment skills for blind children. A foundling hospital, to rescue abandoned baby girls, was also established. In 1887 a medical mission, hospital and some almshouses were also opened in Hankow. Despite his recurrent fear that he might create 'Rice Christians', he rejoiced that many became Christians and showed genuine spiritual fruit.[41]

For all Hill's investment of time in social action, his biographer observes, 'itinerant evangelism from first to last was Hill's chief joy'.[42] Hill inspired others to mission. After his furlough in England in 1881, it was said that 'almost all the Methodists to Central China for the next ten years were due directly or indirectly to his personal advocacy'.[43] As one of his friends declared, 'I never met one . . . who, looking to his work and character as a whole, has awakened in me a desire to have for myself such a life, such a character, and such an influence as he possessed.'[44]

Hill died in 1896, after catching typhus in Wuchang, still doing the work for which he is best known – distributing relief funds during a famine. The text on his tombstone reads 'The Son of Man came not to be ministered unto, but to minister.'[45]

---

[41] Ibid. 268–282.
[42] Ibid. 271–272; T. Richard, *Forty-Five Years in China: Reminiscences by Timothy Richard* (London: T. Fisher Unwin, 1916), 145–146.
[43] Findlay, *History*, vol. 5, 474.
[44] Barber, *David Hill*, 336.
[45] Findlay, *History*, 483–484; Barber, *David Hill*, 337.

4

Care for the unemployed and employees

Evangelical Christian attitudes to work and unemployment were shaped by the biblical presentation of work as mandated by God (Gen. 2:15), something from which satisfaction and fulfilment were to be derived (Eccl. 2:24; 3:22), and the responsibility for providing for self and family (2 Thess. 3:10). How these principles shaped the attitudes and actions of evangelicals towards unemployment and employee care is the focus of this chapter, and the character study looks at the work of Lord Shaftesbury in tackling some of the issues where children and adults were suffering as a result of harsh and exploitative working practices.

Economic growth accelerated in Britain during the eighteenth century and in Europe and North America in the early nineteenth century. The Industrial Revolution brought an employment revolution, as the workforce began to shift from agriculture to industry. In 1780 just 25 per cent of Britain's population was engaged in manufacturing, mining and building. By 1851 this was 42 per cent. Economies of scale resulted in progressively larger-scale industrial units, which by the mid nineteenth century saw huge mills producing goods, especially of cotton and wool. Although industrialization brought more stable employment and better wages, working conditions for many deteriorated.[1] Working for twelve hours or more in a hot cotton factory, the air filled with choking dust, was not only unpleasant; it was harmful to health. One witness to a British parliamentary inquiry in 1834 declared, 'no man would like to work in a power loom shed . . . there is such a clattering and noise it would almost make someone mad'.[2] Significant numbers of children were employed in mills and mines, and some suffered horrific accidents at work, or succumbed to diseases brought on by poor working conditions. Although employment was generally more stable, there were still sudden dips in the trade cycle when suddenly thousands could be rendered jobless. Because they now had only one specialized skill, they

---

[1] I. J. Shaw, *Churches, Revolutions and Empires: 1789–1914* (Fearn: Christian Focus, 2012), 68–70.
[2] 'Evidence to Select Committee on Handloom Weavers, 1834', *Parliamentary Papers*, vol. 10 (London: Great Britain, Parliament, House of Commons, 1834 [556]), 432.

could not move to other employment easily. Unemployment was one of a series of new and rapidly changing issues confronting evangelicals in the new industrial world, together with the interconnected issue of working conditions. The next chapter will consider the related issue of housing problems.

The eighteenth-century Evangelical Revival coincided with the social dislocation at the start of the Industrial Revolution. George Whitefield and John Wesley demonstrated a particular affinity for manual workers. These included the miners of Kingswood, near Bristol, or those employed in the potteries in the English Midlands, who responded to their evangelical message in great numbers. For some, this was at great cost. A number of employers dismissed workers who embraced Methodism, and landlords evicted others from their homes because of what they deemed 'extreme views'. Wesley's economic philosophy was encapsulated in his 'Use of Money' sermon (see chapter 2), which placed emphasis on hard work – 'Gain all you can'; personal responsibility for what was earned – 'Save all you can'; and the accountability to care for others – 'Give all you can.' The motivation behind this was to be the ethical principle of love to one another. Methodists became renowned for their mutual aid and sense of community.[3]

Wesley declared it 'wickedly, devilishly false' to assert that people were poor simply because they were idle.[4] Instead, he argued, most people were in want 'through scarcity of business'.[5] He was particularly concerned about those rendered unemployed through factors beyond their control, calling for compassion and understanding to be shown to them. He believed most people were desperate for work. In his *Thoughts on the Present Scarcity of Provisions* (1772) he questioned, 'Why have all these nothing to eat?', and answered simply, 'They have no meat because they have no work.'[6] Nor did he simply blame employers for the lack of work – they too were affected by the adverse economic conditions, which left people with little surplus income to purchase their products, and so could no longer employ people: 'They cannot, as they have no vent [sic] for their goods, food now bearing so high a price that the generality of people are hardly able to buy anything else.' Instead of condemning the unemployed, the proper response was to 'Find them work, and you will find them meat. They will then earn and eat their own bread.'[7]

---

[3] Max Weber was incorrect to suggest that Wesley's teaching promoted the view that the more possessions acquired, the more this was a sign of God's grace. Max Weber, *The Protestant Ethic and the Spirit of Capitalism* (New York: Charles Scribner & Sons, 1958), 142–143.

[4] Wesley, 'Journal', in *Works of John Wesley*, vol. 2 (London: Wesleyan Conference Office, 1872; repr. Grand Rapids, Mich.: Zondervan, n.d.), February 1753, 269–270.

[5] Ibid., vol. 3, 482, November 1772.

[6] Ibid., vol. 5, 349–350 (letter to the editor, *Lloyd's Evening Post*, 8 December 1772).

[7] Letters to the editor, *Lloyd's Evening Post*, in J. Telford (ed.), *Letters of John Wesley*, vol. 5 (London: Epworth Press, 1931), 353–354.

Although he was no economist, and his views often reflected a pre-industrial world view,[8] Wesley called for governmental action to create suitable economic conditions in which there was a market for goods to be bought and sold. This included limiting rises in food prices, 'for then people will have money to buy other things'.[9] Wesley also used his best endeavours to start a number of projects to give employment to those without work, such as one established in 1740 for the processing of cotton.[10]

Methodists were taught that all employment relationships should be modelled on the example and principles of Christ. This was the guiding principle in the nineteenth century of Joseph Wilson, a Primitive Methodist factory owner in Bradford. He argued for mutual respect and support between employer and worker:

> I tried to understand the worker's point of view . . . and lean to his side. I must try to serve them and do what I can for them so that my whole business life . . . would bear investigation on the basis of the highest standards.[11]

The Bradford industrialist Titus Salt (see also chapter 5) sought to work out his evangelical principles in his business life. He recognized that his business and workforce were at times in the hands of economic forces beyond his control, especially in the recession of the 1840s. He contributed generously to a fund for the unemployed, when hungry and angry men, women and children filled the streets.[12] In 1848, although his mills were losing the huge sum of £20,000 per month, he still gave employment to a further 100 unemployed woolcombers. During times of trade depression Salt preferred to reduce wages rather than lay workers off, which meant the hardship was shared. In 1876 this prompted a brief strike by some workers. Salt compromised, and did not impose the full reduction, and all the strikers were subsequently re-employed.[13]

Salt was concerned in 1846 that legislation which was proposed by advocates of the 'Ten Hours movement' to reduce working time to ten hours per day would create unemployment in the face of overseas competitors working

---

8 On Wesley's economic thought see T. W. Madron, 'Some Economic Aspects of John Wesley's Thought Revisited', *Methodist History* (1965), 33–45.

9 Telford, *Letters of John Wesley*, vol. 5, 353–354.

10 Wesley, 'Journal', vol. 1, December 1740, 292.

11 J. Wilson, *Joseph Wilson, His Life and Work* (Bradford: Lund Humphries, 1923), 29.

12 J. Reynolds, *The Great Paternalist: Titus Salt and the Growth of Nineteenth-Century Bradford* (Hounslow: Maurice Temple Smith, 1983), 164–165.

13 I. C. Bradley, 'Titus Salt: Enlightened Entrepreneur', *History Today* 35.5 (May 1987), 31; Reynolds, *Paternalist*, 317–319.

fourteen hours a day. Nonetheless, he limited the working hours in his factory to ten hours a day well before legislation required him to do that. Salt also supported the campaign for establishing Saturday as a half-day holiday, to allow people time for recreation and shopping so they could attend churches on Sunday.[14] Salt's wider pastoral concern for his workers included the tradition of an annual works outing to the Yorkshire Dales, started in 1849. The *Bradford Observer* hailed this as a demonstration of 'Practical Christianity'.[15] He was also environmentally conscious, and fitted special burners to his mill chimneys to reduce the emissions of sulphur.[16]

The Congregationalist Francis Crossley's carpet-making mills in Halifax, employing up to 5,000 workers, were, in the middle of the nineteenth century, the largest in the world.[17] He was hesitant about opposing The Hours Movement, being fearful it would create unemployment. During the trade depression of 1847–8 he generously contributed to assistance for the unemployed,[18] preferring such a spontaneous and heartfelt response of fellow feeling to the institutionalized, hierarchical, parish relief system dominated by Anglican clergy. Such actions he saw as part of his religious duty to create harmonious relationships between all classes of society. In contrast to many other manufacturers, the Crossleys did not lay off employees who became involved in Chartism, the radical movement of the 1830s to 1840s to extend democracy. Francis Crossley even voted for the Chartist candidate in the 1847 Halifax Borough election.[19] In 1852 he argued that his views sprang from his daily contact with working people:

> I have met them daily and conversed with them, talked with them, done business with them, had arrangements to make with them. I have also had to do with the middle class, and I stand here to tell you that I have found as much fair dealing, as much honesty, as much integrity, amongst the working classes of my country, as I have found in higher grades in which I have mixed.[20]

These Christian principles of social partnership with his workers led Crossley in 1864 to change his business into a limited liability company, and offer shares

---

[14] Reynolds, *Paternalist*, 130–131, 320; R. Balgarnie, *Sir Titus Salt: His Life and Its Lessons* (London: Hodder & Stoughton, 1877), 65.

[15] *Bradford Observer*, 20 September 1849.

[16] Bradley, 'Titus Salt', 32.

[17] On Crossley see F. Crossley, *Sir Francis Crossley, Bart, M.P.* (London: John Stabb, 1872).

[18] T. Iwama, 'The Middle Class in Halifax, 1780–1850', PhD thesis, University of Leeds, 2003, 178, 180.

[19] Ibid. 168, 204, 252.

[20] *Halifax Guardian*, 10 July 1852, in Iwama, 'Middle Class', 205.

to his employees at favourable conditions. This opportunity for them to share in the profits of the company was widely accepted. He went on to build almshouses (paying a weekly pension to residents), an orphanage and an endowed school.[21]

The welfare of the workers in the paper mill run by the evangelical Cowan family, near Edinburgh, Scotland, was considered of high importance. The company provided for the education of the children of its 600 employees from 1823 onwards, and in 1849 built a school for them. By 1868, 120 children were enrolled, together with 80 young people already working in the mills, who attended evening classes. Well before the Factory Acts of 1847 and 1850, the Cowans stipulated that no child under 13 was to work in the mill, and that no young person should be employed before he or she could read and write. All employees were to join a medical club, which, in return for a small payment, provided financial assistance in the event of ill health.[22]

Personal contact was considered essential in the application of Christian principles. John Wood, a Bradford worsted spinner, was an evangelical Anglican who supported factory legislation, and sought to apply his faith to the work environment. One employee, John Clark, called the working conditions in his mill 'a blessing'. Whenever Wood entered the factory, Clark reported 'all seemed glad to see him, as if it were felt and fully recognized that his was the grateful task to watch over them and promote their general good and that only one common interest existed between them'. However, this personal contact was lost after Wood retired to Hampshire, and left the running of the mill in the hands of a business partner. A very different environment ensued, for the new master was 'an unjust and tyrannical man, his actions mean and he treats the work people with all the austerity and harshness of a despotic ruler; he excites the envy and increases the malice of the poor against him'.[23]

This raises the question of whether the Industrial Revolution improved life for working people. This was discussed by Thomas Chalmers in his *Political Economy*,[24] and the subsequent 'The Supreme Importance of the Right Moral to a Right Economical State of the Community'.[25] Chalmers accepted that there

---

[21] G. C. Boase, 'Crossley, Francis', in *Dictionary of National Biography, 1885–1900*, vol. 13 (London: Smith, Elder, 1885–1900).

[22] A. D. Macleod, *A Kirk Disrupted: Charles Cowan MP and the Free Church of Scotland* (Fearn: Mentor, 2013), 204–205.

[23] John Clark, *History and Annals of Bradford* (Bradford, 1840), 183–191.

[24] T. Chalmers, *On Political Economy in Connexion with the Moral State and Moral Prospects of Society*, 2nd edn (Glasgow: William Collins, 1832).

[25] T. Chalmers, 'The Supreme Importance of a Right Moral to a Right Economical State of the Community: With Observations on a Recent Criticism in the Edinburgh Review', in T. Chalmers, *Collected Works of Thomas Chalmers*, vol. 20 (Glasgow: William Collins, 1835–42), 145–225.

had been a general improvement in material living standards since 1780, but this was at the expense of increased hours of work and declining working conditions. Modern industry, he argued, robbed the worker of comfort and dignity, condemned children to work up to fourteen hours a day and reduced the labouring man 'into an animal, or rather, into a mere piece of living enginery'. He had much sympathy with the factory reformers, but feared their efforts would only increase unemployment among adults, as well as children, as factory owners responded by reducing their workforce.[26]

The social need to prevent unemployment was an important consideration for evangelicals. Scottish Free Church minister James Begg argued that the aim of society should be to provide paid employment for as large a number of people as possible. This was the God-given order of things to enable the poor to have food and clothes, and increase health and well-being: 'The earth is, by the kindness of the adorable Jehovah, a vast and inexhaustible magazine of human food. But that food must be extracted by persevering toil. For every mouth sent into this world there are two hands.'[27]

The principle of the avoidance of future unemployment among the boys educated at the Mount Hermon School of Boys, which opened in 1881 in Northfield, Massachusetts, was central to D. L. Moody's thinking. The boys ran a boot-black brigade and a barber shop, and set up stands to sell newspapers, all giving work experience. Self-motivation was key – boys were not to 'eat the bread of idleness'.[28]

The scheme of 'Social Salvation' set out in 1890 by William Booth explored the need of a 'comprehensive method of reaching and saving the perishing masses'. It was necessary to meet basic human needs, such as food and shelter, before people were able or willing to listen to the gospel.[29] One of the issues that needed to be addressed directly was that of unemployment.[30] In London in 1888 the official estimate of unemployment was put at 20,000, but Booth thought it much higher. He saw it as a problem, 'appalling enough to make us despair'. The Salvation Army's scheme for helping the unemployed started with the City Colony, which provided rescue shelters and relief from immediate starvation. Work was provided, in return for shelter, because Booth wanted to avoid

[26] Ibid. 184–192, quoted in S. J. Brown, *Thomas Chalmers and the Godly Commonwealth in Scotland* (Oxford: Oxford University Press, 1982), 202–203.

[27] James Begg, letter to the *Witness*, in T. Smith, *Memoirs of James Begg, DD*, vol. 2 (Edinburgh: James Gemmell, 1888), 136. See also Begg's pamphlet *Pauperism and the Poor-Laws* (Edinburgh, J. Johnstone, 1849).

[28] J. F. Findlay Jr, *Dwight L. Moody: American Evangelist 1837–99* (Chicago, Ill.: University of Chicago Press, 1969), 310–312.

[29] W. Booth, *In Darkest England and the Way Out* (London: Salvation Army, 1890), ii, iii–iv.

[30] See also chapter 15 below for Booth's approach to tackling alcohol abuse.

creating dependence on charity through 'being treated to anything which they do not earn'. The next stage were the small factories that provided training and employment as carpenters, cobblers, painters and mat makers. The Salvation Army's factory in Whitechapel was in 1890 employing ninety people, with eight hours' work for food and shelter and a weekly allowance of 5 shillings. These were to be 'harbours of refuge' where 'the storm-tossed workman may run and re-fit', before returning to the regular labour market.[31]

The Salvation Army also sought to find employment for those rescued, and a Labour Exchange was established. Between June and September 1890 Booth recorded 2,670 people were registered, and 369 of them had found work through its services. A brigade was also established to collect household waste and unwanted items, many of which could be recycled. The final stage of the scheme was the Farm Colony, where people learned agricultural skills, and in 1897 there were 260 men living and working on a farm at Hadleigh in Essex. From here they could seek settled employment opportunities on other farms, or be helped to migrate overseas to South Africa or Canada.[32] At the heart of the scheme was enabling people to return to gainful employment.

In each of the projects the gospel was shared openly, for Booth said, 'it is the very light and joy of our existence'. However, there was no difference between the help offered to those who made a Christian profession and those who did not. Yet Booth believed that without a spiritual change to accompany the social support offered, there was every likelihood people would return to the dire situation they had come from.[33] Booth sought £1 million to fund the plan fully, but in the first year only £128,000 was raised, and thereafter the inflow of funds dwindled. This meant that only some parts of the plan were implemented. There were those within the Salvation Army, such as Frank Smith, for a time a commissioner, who wanted to focus exclusively on the social scheme. When this was resisted, and the twofold evangelism and social-concern emphasis was upheld by Booth and the other leaders, Smith resigned.[34]

One of the great evangelical entrepreneurs was F. B. Meyer (1847–1929), who conducted highly successful ministries in Leicester and London. He was a fine preacher, wrote devotional Bible commentaries and was a regular speaker at the Keswick Convention.[35] Alongside his earnest evangelistic ministry he was

---

[31] *Darkest England*, 35, 105, 107, 108–109.

[32] Ibid. 111–112, 115, 125–128, 143–147.

[33] K. S. Inglis, *Churches and the Working Class in Victorian England* (London: Routledge & Kegan Paul, 1963), 208.

[34] Ibid. 202–210.

[35] I. M. Randall, *Evangelical Experiences: A Study in the Spirituality of English Evangelicalism 1918–1939* (Carlisle: Paternoster, 1999), 14–15.

a man of practical social action. His ministry at Melbourne Hall in Leicester attracted a congregation of some 1,400 people and was a hive of activity, with eighty-three meetings of one form or another being held each week.[36]

Meyer started a series of agencies linked to his church.[37] A key place was given to providing gainful employment for those assisted. He began a wood-chopping business for unemployed men, and a firewood merchant's business to sell their work.[38] At the home for discharged prisoners he established, residents lived 'under Christian influences' and paid their way by wood-chopping.[39] Meyer bought some ladders, pails and wash leathers and commenced a window-cleaning brigade for unemployed people, giving his name to the business to establish its credibility. He then bought very long ladders to enable the men to clean windows in the local factories. Such projects gave work to the unemployed, and often led to more permanent jobs. Sometimes, after a period of stability in work, a worker might return to alcohol abuse, but Meyer ensured the door to restoration was kept open.[40] His focus was on dealing with the individual as a whole person. Meyer was always grateful that this congregation 'were not scandalized at the eminently practical side of their pastor's character'.[41]

When Meyer moved to London, a similar range of ministries was established, blending gospel outreach and social action. This was particularly seen in his ministry at Christ Church, Westminster, from 1892 to 1909. Here congregations numbered up to 2,300 people. He was particularly concerned with the social deprivation in Southwark and Lambeth, which made 'virtue difficult and vice easy'.[42] He became a borough councillor and used his efforts to close 'disreputable houses' and rescue hundreds of prostitutes. For them he established a society for 'Befriending the Unmarried Mother and Child', a savings bank and a labour bureau. Through these efforts, one of his biographers explains, Meyer 'strove mightily not only to preach the Gospel of salvation, but to labour for the betterment of physical conditions, and the elimination of elements which were inimical to righteous living and Christian citizenship'.[43]

The spectre of unemployment haunted the working classes in the late nineteenth and early twentieth centuries. The introduction of national insurance payments brought a measure of support, but even in the 1920s tens of thousands

---

[36] W. Y. Fullerton, *F. B. Meyer: A Biography* (London: Marshall, Morgan & Scott, 1929), 52–54.

[37] Ibid. 60.

[38] Ibid.

[39] Ibid. 62.

[40] A. C. Mann, *F. B. Meyer: Preacher, Teacher, Man of God* (London: George Allen & Unwin, 1929), 90–91; Fullerton, *Meyer*, 63.

[41] Mann, *Meyer*, 91.

[42] Ibid. 54; Fullerton, *Meyer*, 78.

[43] Fullerton, *Meyer*, 155; Mann, *Meyer*, 85.

of unemployed people ended up in workhouses. Government assistance, in the form of the 'dole', was hated by those who applied for it because of the demeaning and intrusive questioning about personal circumstances and need. Others felt it bred indolence. One London City missioner, who worked among coster-mongers, street traders, casual labourers and street sweepers, believed that the 'something for nothing' policy of the 'dole' served to breed 'a dislike for work, and brings temptation in its train. It has increased street gambling, and attendance at billiard saloons, cinemas, and public houses'.[44] Yet even those who received the benefit could barely make ends meet. Another London City missioner helped to support a retired soldier and his family who were in a pitiful state after their small business failed. The missioner found them accommodation, bought them furniture and helped the man to find work. Both father and mother came to faith in Christ through the help they had received. The missioner wrote in his report, 'spiritual good often follows so-called social effort'.[45]

The need to integrate faith with business practice was illustrated in the twentieth century by John Laing (1879–1978), a faithful member of the Brethren. He built up his father's building company in Carlisle into one of Britain's largest, in an industry renowned for its cut-throat mode of operation. Laing was loyal to good workers, many of whom stayed with the company throughout their lifetime, but had no time for slackers or shoddy workmanship. He drove himself hard, but as early as 1905 had worked out that excessive working hours did not increase productivity, and so ensured that the hours of his workers were significantly below the industry average. Laing's company introduced payment for time lost by bad weather well before others did. No man was to be laid off in the weeks leading up to Christmas. Bonus schemes were introduced, holiday pay and a savings scheme. Even in slack times workers who had been with the company for more than twelve months were kept in employment. To assist with their rehabilitation Laing was also prepared to offer work to men who had served prison sentences. Laing's workers knew their employer would be there to support them. When he heard of a former worker who had fallen seriously ill and become destitute, Laing immediately sent a telegram to the Carlisle office 'Relieve immediate distress and report.' At the heart of his business philosophy were his resolutions made in 1909 in the middle of a very difficult set of circumstances that nearly ruined his company: 'First, the centre of my life was to be God – God as seen in Jesus Christ; secondly I was going to enjoy life, and help

<hr>

[44] I. Howat and J. Nicholls, *Streets Paved with Gold: The Story of the London City Mission* (Fearn: Christian Focus, 2003), 161.
[45] Ibid. 159.

others enjoy it.' Providing stable work for his employees was part of that. Laing described how he invited God to be a participating partner in his business. With this came a resolution that if his income reached £3,000 he would live on just £500, give away £1,000, and save the rest to invest or provide a reserve for the company in difficult times. He was content to live in a middle-income bracket, even when his earnings were far larger than this.[46]

In his 1964 work *The Christian in Industrial Society* the industrialist Fred Catherwood (1925–2014), son-in-law of the renowned preacher Martyn Lloyd-Jones, outlined the ethical responsibilities of Christian employers. Based on discussions held by a group of Christian industrialists, the key principles enunciated included the need for a 'minimum wage which will give a reasonable basic standard of living . . . No-one should be able to take people into his employment unless he is able to pay them'. If redundancies were economically necessary, 'the Christian will want to be foremost in minimizing the effect'.[47] Catherwood presented the high moral standards for Christians in the business and workplace as an aspect of faith-sharing, although 'the Christian has no right to impose his standards on the private lives of his employees'. Christian employers also had a pastoral responsibility for their workers, so 'that those who get in a mess' could approach these employers more easily. Being known as a Christian in business needed to be backed by consistent behaviour, for, based on how the employer lived, 'a great many people will have the opportunity of judging the effects of the Christian faith'. Without the need to 'import chaplains or evangelists to bear a Christian witness', he argued, 'there are a thousand and one ways in which he can show Christianity in action'. Witness by deeds in the workplace would open the door to words: 'People are more likely to listen if the sort of life we lead makes them think that there is something worth listening to.'[48]

In his chapter on unemployment in *Issues Facing Christians Today*, published in 1984, a time of industrial unrest and growing unemployment, John Stott urged the church to be for the unemployed the 'voice of the voiceless', for they 'have no union to represent them, or plead their cause'. He believed most people longed to work, and the 'work-shy' were a tiny minority. Stott called churches to 'repent of ever looking down on the unemployed, and of ever imagining that the words "workless" and "worthless" might be synonymous'. He encouraged churches to start their own local initiatives to create small-scale employment

[46] R. Coad, *Laing: The Biography of Sir John W. Laing C.B.E.* (London: Hodder & Stoughton, 1979), 40, 46–52, 68, 92–94.

[47] H. F. R. Catherwood, *The Christian in Industrial Society* (London: Tyndale Press, 1964), 95, 96.

[48] Ibid. x, 98, 99, 100.

or run training initiatives, and promoted the biblical understanding of work as 'self-fulfilment through the service of God and neighbour'.[49]

Undoubtedly, there were inconsistencies and mixed motivations among these evangelical responses to employee care and unemployment. Not all activity was disinterested. For all the sense of pastoral responsibilities on employers, there was a realization that a well-cared-for workforce would be productive and profitable. However, behind it was a belief in a God-given dignity in work, and that unemployment represented the inability of individuals to fulfil what they were created to do. Charity was essential in times of crisis, but the best way for families to avoid falling into poverty was for them to have fulfilling and properly remunerated work.

Character study: Lord Shaftesbury (1801–85) – England

Anthony Ashley Cooper, who became the Seventh Earl of Shaftesbury in 1851, endured an unhappy childhood in which the only loving care he experienced came from Maria Milles, a family servant who was an evangelical believer. Through her influence he made a profession of faith as a child, and throughout his life continued the pattern of daily prayer and Bible reading he learned from her. His experiences provoked in him a deep concern over anything that caused suffering or unhappiness. At the age of 25 he was elected to the British Parliament, where he worked for the next fifty-nine years, first as an MP, and then as a Lord in the House of Lords.[50] His evangelical beliefs gave him a strong sense of personal responsibility for the welfare of others, convinced that humans were made in the image of God and that their immortal destinies were being influenced by their living conditions. He argued that potential 'temples of the Holy Ghost, ought not to be corrupted by preventable disease, degraded by avoidable filth, and disabled for His service by unnecessary suffering'. The duty of society was to give each person 'full, fair and free opportunity to exercise his moral, intellectual, physical and spiritual energies'.[51] Shaftesbury argued that both individual philanthropy and state intervention should be designed as a safety net to raise individuals to the point at which they could help themselves.

---

[49] J. Stott, *Issues Facing Christians Today* (Basingstoke: Marshall, Morgan & Scott, 1984), 166–171.

[50] On Shaftesbury see E. Hodder, *The Life and Work of the Seventh Earl of Shaftesbury* (London: Cassell, 1887); G. B. A. M. Finlayson, *The Seventh Earl of Shaftesbury 1801–1885* (London: Eyre Methuen, 1981); G. Battiscombe, *Shaftesbury: A Biography of the Seventh Earl* (London: Constable, 1974).

[51] Shaftesbury, 'Address to Social Science Congress Liverpool, 1858', on sanitary legislation, in *Speeches of the Earl of Shaftesbury, K.G., Upon Subjects Having Relation to the Claims and Interests of the Labouring Class* (London: Chapman & Hall, 1868).

To go beyond this was to rob the individual of initiative and responsibility, which rendered socialist approaches unattractive to him.

In 1830 a group of evangelicals from the north of England, led by the MP Michael Sadler and, from Bradford, Parson G. S. Bull,[52] began a campaign against the long working hours of both children and women in the mills. Their misery was captured in a letter to the *Leeds Mercury* in 1830:

> thousands of little children . . . from seven to 14 years, are daily compelled to labour from six o'clock in the morning to seven in the evening . . . the very streets . . . are every morning wet with the tears of innocent victims at the accursed shrine of avarice.[53]

Evidence showed that children working in factories were prone to bodily deformities – some were badly injured by the machinery they worked alongside or under. The campaign to reduce working hours for children was fiercely resisted by mill owners, who rejected such government intervention in the free market. Shaftesbury[54] assumed leadership of the campaign after 1833, convinced it was his 'duty to God and the poor'. He believed that reducing working hours would allow children time for education, including Christian instruction. As in the struggle against slavery, the campaign required dogged persistence. He joined forces with the press and working-class men to mobilize public opinion in the cause. Concessions were gradually won over a number of years, but it was not until 1847 that a bill was passed in Parliament limiting the hours of work for women and children to ten hours.[55]

Alongside the moral impetus given to the campaign by Christian politicians such as Shaftesbury, other factors were at work. There was increasing recognition of the economic inefficiency of overworking and exploiting labour. Factory owners also recognized that a more educated workforce was more efficient, and began making available opportunities for schooling.

Shaftesbury brought reform in other areas of employment. In 1840 he saw a bill through Parliament to stop the employment of boys in climbing and sweeping chimneys.[56] He also worked to secure the 1842 Coal Mines Regulation

---

[52] See J. C. Gill, *The Ten-Hours Parson: Christian Social Action in the 1830s* (London: SPCK, 1959); R. B. Seeley, *Memoirs of the Life and Writings of Michael Thomas Sadler* (London, 1842).

[53] R. Oastler, letter to the *Leeds Mercury*, Saturday 16 October 1830.

[54] Until the death of his father in 1851 he was known as Lord Ashley, and able to stand for election to the House of Commons. After the death of the Sixth Earl, he became Lord Shaftesbury and could no longer sit in the Commons.

[55] Gill, *Ten-Hours Parson*, 82.

[56] Finlayson, *Shaftesbury*, 228–232, 249–251.

Act after revelations of the dreadful conditions under which women and children worked, often naked, and exposed to serious physical and sexual abuse. The Act outlawed the employment of women and children under the age of 10 in mines.

Another cause that impacted the employment experience of millions of nineteenth-century working people was the attempt to enforce stricter observance of the Sabbath. Shaftesbury, driven by a genuine concern to give workers a rest day, and having the hope that by being freed of the demands of work most people would have opportunity to attend religious services, sought through both persuasion and legislation to reduce the work people were required to do on a Sunday. In 1849 Shaftesbury saw a measure through Parliament to stop postal collections and deliveries on Sundays. More controversial was the endeavour in 1854 to close public houses on Sundays, a move rescinded after rioting.[57] A product of this campaign was measures to make Saturday a half-working day, so that people could shop or play recreational sport on Saturday afternoon, leaving Sunday free for religious observance.

Shaftesbury's Christian humanitarian concern was vast, ranging from promoting the care and protection of those suffering from mental illness to supporting the welfare of animals and opposing animal experimentation. He took particular interest in societies that combined addressing social problems with advancing the gospel, such as the London City Mission and the Ragged School Union, which feature in later chapters of this book. Shaftesbury was regularly asked to preside at the annual meetings in London of a host of religious and philanthropic societies in which he was active, and was a man of great personal generosity.[58] It was his policy to make a personal investigation of an issue before embarking on a cause, whether that meant visiting the depths of a coal mine, or going to the worst slums in London. For his concern for those in need he became known as the Poor Man's Earl. Shaftesbury was so convinced that God had called him to 'labour among the poor' that in 1855 he declined an invitation from Lord Palmerston to join the government as Chancellor of the Duchy of Lancaster.[59]

According to one writer, Wilberforce and Shaftesbury 'removed more sin and misery than any other British social reformers inside or outside Parliament'.[60] In the words of Charles Smyth, Shaftesbury helped to heal 'the worst

---

[57] On the campaigns for Sabbath observance see J. Wigley, *The Rise and Fall of the Victorian Sunday* (Manchester: Manchester University Press, 1980).

[58] J. Stephen, *Essays in Ecclesiastical Biography*, vol. 2 (1849) (London: Longmans, Green, 1907), 248.

[59] J. L. and B. Hammond, *Lord Shaftesbury* (London: Constable, 1925), 171.

[60] M. Hennell, *Sons of the Prophets, Evangelical Leaders of the Victorian Church* (London: SPCK, 1979), 50.

sores of the industrial revolution'.[61] His interventions on social issues challenged the prevailing non-interventionist philosophy of the state and strengthened the understanding of the moral right and duty of Parliament to interfere paternally in economic and social issues for the welfare of citizens.

Shaftesbury's work demonstrates the profound evangelical social conscience, and its causes. He was impelled by a sense of responsibility to use his position, his wealth and his time for the glory of God. He expected to be called to account by God for how he had spent every moment of his life, and was concerned to be found in God-honouring activity should Christ imminently return. He often felt he had fallen short of his own high standards, and was plagued with dark feelings of inadequacy and despair, despite his enormous record of achievement.

The great Baptist preacher C. H. Spurgeon, a close personal friend, said of Shaftesbury after his death:

> we have, in my judgment, lost the best man of the age . . . He was a man most true in his personal piety . . . a man most firm in his faith in the gospel of our Lord Jesus Christ; a man intensely active in the cause of God and truth . . . he was faithful to God in all his house, fulfilling both the first and second commands of the law in fervent love to God, and hearty love to man . . . Both man and beast may unite in mourning him: he was the friend of every living thing. He lived for the oppressed; he lived for London; he lived for the nation; he lived still more for God.[62]

---

[61] C. Smyth, 'The Evangelical Movement in Perspective', *Cambridge Historical Journal* 7.3 (1951), 160.

[62] C. H. Spurgeon, 'Departed Saints Yet Living', *Metropolitan Tabernacle Pulpit Sermons*, vol. 31 (London: Passmore & Alabaster, 1885), 541–542.

5

Action to improve housing conditions

The fact that in his life on earth Jesus said 'the Son of Man has nowhere to lay his head' (Matt. 8:20; Luke 9:58) gave the plight of homeless people a particular resonance to evangelical Christians. Although such Christians longed for the heavenly home the Lord was preparing for them, they invested significant time and effort in supporting those without homes in this world. And the need was enormous. The explosion of population growth in Europe and North America in the nineteenth century has been called the 'contagion of numbers'. Between 1800 and 1900 the population of Europe almost doubled, from 146 million to 295 million, and it became increasingly urban. In Britain by 1851 town dwellers outnumbered those in rural areas, and by 1891 the same applied in Germany. Although North America had no cities of more than 100,000 people in 1800, by 1890 the population of twenty-eight cities exceeded that. London's population rose from nearly 2.4 million inhabitants in 1850 to 7.2 million in 1910.[1] Between 1880 and 1899 some 8.5 million migrants arrived in the USA, and 10 million between 1905 and 1914. They tended to converge on urban areas: in 1890 around 40 per cent of Chicago's population had been born outside the country, its population rocketing from 109,000 in 1860 to 2.7 million in 1920.[2]

Such rapid, unplanned urban growth inevitably led to poor urban living and sanitary conditions, with frequent outbreaks of disease. Bad diet, polluted drinking water, poor ventilation and limited understanding of hygiene were a fatal combination. The supply of houses did not increase quickly enough, so existing houses were divided up, and gardens built over, creating damp, airless conditions. In Liverpool in 1840, 86,000 people lived in 2,400 overcrowded courtyards, sometimes with population densities of 1,000 per acre. One observer in Manchester described courtyards with one privy (a bucket toilet) for 50 people, which was often 'in a short time completely choked with excrementitious

---

[1] I. J. Shaw, *Churches, Revolutions and Empires: 1789–1914* (Fearn: Christian Focus, 2012), 442–444.
[2] M. Bradbury and H. Temperley, *American Studies* (London: Longman, 1998), 132; R. A. Mohl, *Urban America in the Industrial Age, 1860–1920* (Arlington Heights: Harlan Davidson, 1985), 13–17.

matter. No alternative is left to the inhabitants but adding this to the already defiled street'.[3] Many families were condemned to living in rooms with dimensions 8 feet by 10 feet, with broken windows stuffed with sacks, the property riddled with vermin, and lice infesting bedding and clothing. The rate of disease and death was enormous. The highest death rate was experienced among children under the age of 10, which reached 20.8 out of 1,000 in 1838,[4] and among children the highest risk was in the first year of life. In 1899 some 163 out of every 1,000 children born in Britain died before their first birthday; in Liverpool it was 218.9 per 1,000 in the 1870s.[5]

The hold on life of most remained short and tenuous: in the years 1838–54 life expectancy was around 40 for men, and 42 for women. Environment was a highly significant influence on lifespan, which for a child born in Manchester, England, in 1840 was half that of a child born in Surrey. Scarlet fever and typhus remained major killers, and cholera epidemics struck periodically in each decade from the 1830s to the 1860s, with the outbreak of 1832 killing 31,376 people. Tuberculosis, fuelled by cramped housing conditions and bad hygiene, remained the greatest killer, reaping a death toll of around 59,000 lives in 1838.[6]

The dominant free-trade philosophy brought the expectation that social problems, such as housing, were matters that would resolve themselves in time, but it was clear that this 'inevitable' process was not happening. The 1840s saw local authorities in Britain introducing building regulations for new houses, followed by housing acts in the 1850s and 1860s. Among those making calls for such interventions were evangelical Christians, who were concerned that bad environmental conditions were contributing to moral and religious decline. Evangelicals highlighted problems, promoted legislation to improve conditions and worked both individually and through their churches to bring practical change.

Whenever the evangelical paternalist Lord Shaftesbury took on a social concern project, his practice was to survey needs personally, meet those suffering and assess suitable responses to alleviate problems. His biographer Edwin Hodder stressed the spiritual perspective he brought to these visits: 'He saw in the miserable creatures before him not thieves and vagabonds and reprobates,

---

[3] P. Gaskell, *Artisans and Machinery* (London: J. W. Parker, 1836), repr. (London: Cass, 1968), 78.

[4] M. Flinn (ed.), *Scottish Population History from the Seventeenth Century to the 1930s* (Cambridge: Cambridge University Press, 1977), 19–20, 377–379; 'Report to the Select Committee on the Health of Towns', in H. J. Dyos and M. Wolff, *The Victorian City: Images and Realities*, vol. 1 (London: Routledge & Kegan Paul, 1973), 389.

[5] F. Crouzet, *A History of the European Economy, 1000–2000* (London: University Press of Virginia, 2001), 19–30.

[6] F. Crouzet, *The Victorian Economy* (London: Methuen, 1982), 19–30.

but men with immortal souls that might be saved, and with human lives that might be redeemed from their corruption.'[7] It was said that he hardly ever passed a street child without speaking to him or her, offering a smile and gentle words of encouragement. Because of his deep interest in supporting their needs he never reported receiving any sort of insult from the poor, the prostitutes, the beggars, the thieves or the drunkards he met.

Shaftesbury believed that offering meaningful help to the physical and spiritual condition of the poorest, especially children, was futile if they had nowhere to live, or if they lived in conditions of absolute degradation. In early 1846 he visited the slum areas of London, such as the Rookery of St Giles, renowned for its filthy and squalid living conditions, with rickety and massively overcrowded housing, where thousands packed together like rooks massed on a tree. Sunlight rarely, if ever, penetrated. Walls were covered in filth and slime. Courtyards were deep in sewage or refuse, with putrid pools in which foul-smelling bubbles of gas periodically rose to the surface. The smell, particularly in the heat of the summer, was overwhelming, sometimes causing even the stout-hearted to faint. Crime and immorality flourished, as did drunkenness and blasphemous language. Disease spread rapidly, especially typhus and sometimes cholera. The inhabitants of this nether world begged Shaftesbury to send officials to remove the filth that was more than ankle deep, or to get them a supply of clean water to drink. Sometimes there was only one bed for the whole family, including adults and children; in other places a pile of rags in the corner sufficed as a sleeping place for the lice-ridden inhabitants.[8] When Shaftesbury visited the wynds, the slum areas of Glasgow, he observed:

> I did not believe . . . that so large an amount of filth, crime, misery and disease existed in one spot in a civilised country . . . Health would not be possible in such a climate . . . is moral propriety and moral cleanliness, so to speak, more probable? Quite the reverse![9]

Shaftesbury was also appalled at the huge profits slum landlords were making from the misery of their poor tenants, who had nowhere else to live. Often one family had only a corner of a room, with other families in the other corners and one in the middle – with no opportunity for privacy or decency. He appealed for efforts to redress the 'lamentable' state of housing, and with the intention

---

[7] E. Hodder, *The Life and Work of the Seventh Earl of Shaftesbury*, vol. 2 (London: Cassell, 1887), 157.
[8] Ibid. 160–165.
[9] Lord Shaftesbury, 1839, quoted in S. Laidlaw, *Glasgow's Common Lodging Houses and the People Living in Them* (Glasgow: Glasgow Corporation, 1956), 20–21.

of securing 'great moral, social and political blessings for those who are the noblest material God ever gave a nation – the working classes of this country'.[10]

Shaftesbury was convinced of the link between poor environmental conditions and crime and immorality, and this encouraged him in 1842 to help to found what became the 'Society for Improving the Condition of the Labouring Classes'. This encouraged the building of Model Dwelling Houses for working people, which provided decent standards of accommodation, charged affordable rents, but also achieved a reasonable return to investors – as opposed to the vast profits made by slum landlords and rack-renters. Through the provision of such accommodation, Shaftesbury argued, 'the moral were almost equal to the physical benefits'.[11] He applauded the efforts of schools, but questioned the value of a policy in which one takes and teaches a young girl

for six hours a day the rules of decency and very virtue, and then send her back to such abodes of filth and profligacy as to make her unlearn by the practice of one hour the lessons of a year, to witness and oftentimes share, though at first against her will, the abominations that have been recorded.[12]

He questioned the assumption that those in early life who are 'treated as swine' would afterwards be able to 'walk with the dignity of Christians'.[13]

He was also deeply concerned for the housing conditions of newly arrived migrants, often in search of work. They were often forced into the lowest level of housing provision – the common lodging houses, which were usually dirty, overcrowded and disease-ridden. Here crime flourished, and often prostitution. In 1850 he introduced parliamentary legislation to allow local councils to build Model Lodging Houses and to regulate those that existed. Shaftesbury also highlighted the short-sightedness of slum-clearance schemes if no alternative housing was provided to replace those that had been demolished, which served to increase overcrowding. He was also involved in the passing of acts allowing for the compulsory purchase and demolition of the worst housing. He believed that humans, made in the image of God, should not live in conditions unfit for animals. Freeing people from the harsh struggles for existence would give them opportunity to consider matters spiritual. Shaftesbury remained convinced that

---

[10] Quoted in Hodder, *Shaftesbury*, vol. 2, 155.

[11] Lord Shaftesbury, article in the *Nineteenth Century*, vol. 14, 934, quoted in Hodder, *Shaftesbury*, vol. 2, 155.

[12] Lord Shaftesbury speech, quoted in B. Blackburn, *Noble Lord: The Seventh Earl of Shaftesbury* (London: Home & Van Thal, 1949), 169.

[13] Ibid.

the efforts of individuals or philanthropic societies that paid a modest return to investors were the best solution, rather than vast government schemes that resulted in a culture of dependency. To encourage the building of replacement housing, Shaftesbury supported further housing bills in 1867 and 1875, and the 1885 Housing of the Working Classes Act.[14] These increased the power of local councils to take down unhealthy properties and to raise loans for the building of replacements. They paved the way for a further act of 1890 that permitted the wide-scale building of council houses. Provision of decent, clean, sanitary housing was to Shaftesbury an expression of Christianity. He believed that until the homes of the poor were 'Christianised . . . all hope of moral or social improvement was utterly vain'.[15] In all his activities to promote better housing Shaftesbury declared his aim was to glorify God by promoting 'the advancement of His ever-blessed name, and the temporal and eternal welfare of all mankind'.[16]

The Scottish Free Church minister James Begg followed Shaftesbury in connecting a poor environment with widespread immorality. In 1849 he argued that there could be no expectation of morality without decent housing – and asserted that dwellings comprising just a single room 'are utterly incompatible with delicacy or even decency'.[17]

Glasgow's 'Civic Gospel', developed in the third quarter of the nineteenth century, had a distinctly evangelical flavour. A number of evangelicals elected on to the Glasgow Council had the strong support of many evangelical ministers. The 'Civic Gospel' combined the work of voluntary agencies for the spiritual and moral improvement of the populace, with local legislative solutions to urban problems. As well as the introduction of strict alcohol licences to reduce the incidence of drunkenness, there was a focus on improvements in sewage disposal, and policies to demolish slums. When middle-class rate-payers rebelled at the mounting cost of constructing the vast Loch Katrine reservoir that was being built to ensure clean water for Glasgow, the Free Church of Scotland minister the Revd Robert Buchanan preached a special sermon connecting unsanitary living conditions to the spread of immorality and ungodliness: 'filth is a great enemy and hindrance to godliness. To live in it, is almost inevitably to lose that self-respect which lies at the bottom of all moral and social progress.'[18] By the end of the century the civic-gospel ethos

---

[14] Hodder, *Shaftesbury*, vol. 3, 491–493; J. L. and B. Hammond, *Lord Shaftesbury* (London: Constable, 1925), 172.

[15] Quoted in Hodder, *Shaftesbury*, vol. 2, 349.

[16] Lord Shaftesbury, diary, 25 December 1851, quoted in Hodder, *Shaftesbury*, vol. 2, 359.

[17] T. Smith, *Memoirs of James Begg, DD*, vol. 2 (Edinburgh: James Gemmell, 1888), 138.

[18] C. Brown, '"To Be Aglow with Civic Ardours": The "Godly Commonwealth" in Glasgow 1843–1914',

was being superseded by the rise of municipal socialism with the building of council houses and flats, but a role for the churches in dealing with the issue of poor housing was still recognized. As one housing commission reported in 1891:

> it is essentially the function of the Christian church to organize such agencies and to bring to bear such influences as shall move the poor to live decent and clean lives in the decent and clean houses provided for them.[19]

The 'Civic Gospel' in Birmingham was even more sweeping, involving reorganization of the functions and finance of local government, and the running of major utilities for the benefit of the community. Those involved were from mixed denominational and theological backgrounds. Headed by Joseph Chamberlain, of Unitarian background, in 1873 the Liberals swept to power in the city. His backers included a range of influential Nonconformist ministers, including the evangelical Congregationalist R. W. Dale. Christians were urged to engage in society as councillors, as Guardians of the Poor and on school boards and hospital committees. Holding such office was deemed to be a form of Christian ministry. Local gas and water companies were purchased by the council, to be run for the benefit of the community, and profits used to fund civic improvements. Slums were demolished, art galleries, libraries and parks were provided, and the centre of Birmingham was redeveloped.[20]

In 1888 another Glasgow Presbyterian minister, Donald Macleod (1831–1916), observed the connection between environment and religious practice. He highlighted the striking parallel between the number of people living in homes comprising just one room, so overcrowded they were unfit for habitation, who numbered around 126,000 (more than 25 per cent of the population), and the 120,000 in the city who did not attend church. The figures included whole families and sometimes lodgers as well, living in only one room. The death rate in such dwellings was twice that of other properties. Overcrowding drove people on to the streets, where crime flourished, or to the public house, where drunkenness ensued. Macleod argued that:

Records of the Scottish Church History Society 26 (1996), 177–178.

[19] *Report of the Commission on the Housing of the Poor in Relation to their Social Condition*, Glasgow, 1891, quoted in R. J. Morris and R. Rodger (eds.), *The Victorian City: A Reader in British Urban History 1820–1914* (London: Longman, 1993), 73.

[20] See A. Briggs, *A History of Birmingham 1865–1938* (London: Oxford University Press, 1952); D. Judd, *Radical Joe: A Life of Joseph Chamberlain* (Cardiff: Cardiff University Press, 1993).

The pressure of the struggle for existence, and the hard battle for the necessities of life – which bring many of our decent working people to the one-roomed house, and compel them to live under the burden of anxieties that often alienate their interest from spiritual things – most undoubtedly influence the habit of church-going.

Macleod called for careful reflection on the 'close connection between the physical and the moral or spiritual life', and urged the churches to 'embrace within the field of our operations everything which tends to the physical and social as well as spiritual welfare of the people'. It was not sufficient simply to 'assault them with armies of district visitors, and shower upon them tracts and good advices, while we are leaving them to swelter in dens, and under conditions where Christian life is so difficult, if not impossible, to realise'. There were also things the church could do to make itself more welcoming to the poorest, who did not have respectable clothes to wear to meetings or money to rent pews. It could build more churches so the poor did not have large distances to travel. The church was to use its influence to bring a change in government thought that might prompt action.[21]

In 1883 the English Congregationalist Andrew Mearns (1837–1925) produced a small pamphlet about social and religious conditions in London entitled *The Bitter Cry of Outcast London*, which is considered a pivotal document in calls for housing reform. Describing the slums with language from the anti-slavery campaigns, he wrote of thousands

crowded together amidst horrors which call to mind ... the middle passage of a slave ship ... courts reeking with malodorous gases arising from accumulations of sewerage and refuse scattered in all directions ... dark and filthy passages swarm with vermin.

He also connected environmental conditions with harmful moral and religious results, describing the existence of 'a vast mass of moral corruption, of heart-breaking misery, and absolute godlessness'. Mearns, who drew extensively on reports from agents of the London City Mission, concluded 'That people condemned to exist under such conditions take to drink and fall into sin is surely a matter for little surprise.'[22] Poverty, bad housing and bad sanitation created a context in which crime, disease and suffering flourished. Mearns concluded that

---

[21] D. Macleod, *Non-churchgoing and the Housing of the Poor: Speech Delivered in the [Church of Scotland] General Assembly, 30 May 1888* (Edinburgh: W. Blackwood & Sons, 1888), 8–18.

[22] A. Mearns, *The Bitter Cry of Outcast London* (London: James Clarke, 1883), 4, 7, 11.

the problem was so great that state intervention was needed to improve the terrible conditions in which people were condemned to suffer and die, before 'the Christian missionary can have much chance with them'. Such thinking paralleled that already observed in the work of David Hill or William Booth, who had argued that when people are starving, their hunger needed to be allayed before they were in a fit state to listen to the claims of the gospel. To Mearns, squalid housing was a similar urgent need to be addressed to clear away barriers to people receiving the gospel. He described a scheme being developed by the Congregational Union that combined 'wise and practical' relief of material needs with visitation of houses for the purpose of offering compassionate care and the gospel. The area of London chosen for the scheme was filled with 'reeking courts, crowded public houses, low lodging houses, and numerous brothels . . . Poverty, rags, and dirt, are everywhere'. Mearns called upon Christians to share the heart of Christ, who 'had compassion on the multitude', and who looked 'with Divine pity in His eyes, over this outcast London'.[23]

Norman Macleod (1812–72), brother of Donald Macleod, was one of the nineteenth-century evangelical ministers who willingly chose a ministry in an area of urban deprivation. His ministry at the Barony Church, in one of the poorer parts of the East End of Glasgow, offered a range of social provisions to meet need. These included dinner rooms offering cheap, wholesome food for working men, and evening services for people who were allowed in only if they were wearing working clothes. This was an attempt to overcome the expectation that people had to wear their 'Sunday best' clothes to attend church, which was considered a barrier to the attendance of poor people. Macleod, believing that spiritual and social transformation went together, argued that if the temporal was separated from the spiritual, we 'leave the world to Satan, and give him the advantage over us'. Why leave it to 'infidels' to offer 'better houses or better clothing'. He questioned, 'does Christ only have to do with Sundays?'.[24]

Alongside these efforts by evangelical leaders to promote action to improve housing conditions by church bodies, local councils and even the government were also significant individual efforts to remedy the situation. One notable example was that of David Dale (1739–1806), a member of the Scotch Independent Church, who in 1786 built an entire community at New Lanark on the upper reaches of the river Clyde for his factory workforce of 2,000 people. It included a school, church and local shops. New Lanark was a clean and healthy location for work, and Dale himself lived in the heart of the community

---

[23] Ibid. 24, 31, 32.

[24] D. Macleod, *Memoir of Norman Macleod*, vol. 2 (London: D. Daldy, Isbister, 1876), 7–8.

for a number of years. New Lanark was later taken over by his son-in-law Robert Owen, who rejected Dale's evangelical Christian convictions and operated the village on co-operative and socialist, but strongly paternalist, lines.[25] Owen is often given credit for a project that was initially the work of an evangelical Christian. After selling New Lanark, Owen became a socialist lecturer and toured far afield promoting his views and deriding Christian teachings.

The character study of Titus Salt that follows shows how another evangelical Christian industrialist invested his fortune in improving the living conditions of his workforce by building a complete village. Another Yorkshire evangelical factory owner, who sought to improve the living environment for his workforce, was the carpet manufacturer Francis Crossley of Halifax. Crossley, an evangelical Congregationalist, built areas of good-quality housing for his workforce. He also promoted building societies, enabling working people to take out mortgages with which to buy their own homes. Crossley saw it as his duty to care for the poor and was generous in supporting relief efforts at times of unemployment. It was his view that if the Lord blessed him in his work, 'the poor shall taste of it'.[26] He also promoted the creation of a 'people's park' in Halifax, believing that giving people opportunity to appreciate landscape would help reduce their spiritual alienation from God.[27]

While most evangelicals, such as Shaftesbury and Mearns, sought a balanced response that combined both urban and spiritual renewal, others, feeling overwhelmed by the enormity of social problems in their contexts, shifted the balance strongly on to social action. One such was Walter Rauschenbusch (1861–1918), who ministered in New York and underwent a theological shift from evangelicalism to become the 'Father of the Social Gospel in America'. Born in Rochester, New York, of German immigrant parents, Rauschenbusch was raised in a pious conservative Baptist family. During his theological studies questions were already being raised about the orthodoxy of his views of the Old Testament. His period from 1886 to 1897 in pastoral ministry on the edge of the notorious 'Hell's Kitchen' slum in New York left him traumatized. He encountered in full force the classic symptoms of urban deprivation – poverty, poor housing, malnutrition, disease, ignorance and crime. He was left drained and disillusioned by urban pastoral work and a succession of funerals for

---

[25] On Dale see A. Liddell, *Memoir of David Dale* (Glasgow, 1855); D. J. McLaren, *David Dale of New Lanark*, 2nd edn (Milngavie: Heatherbank Press, 1999).

[26] T. Iwama, 'The Middle Class in Halifax, 1780–1850', PhD thesis, University of Leeds, 2003, 180, 252, 282.

[27] S. J. Daniels, 'Moral Order and the Industrial Environment in the Woollen Textile District of West Yorkshire, 1780–1880', PhD thesis, University of London, 1980, 206.

children.[28] Although his initial emphasis was upon evangelism, Rauschenbusch argued that individual conversion and individualistic philanthropy were ineffective responses to poverty, ill health and economic insecurity, which were rooted in the capitalist system.[29] In his frustration he sought for a new expression of Christianity in the writings of liberal theologians such as Horace Bushnell, Albrecht Ritschl and Adolf Harnack. Although friends warned him he was substituting social work for religious work, his emphasis in preaching switched to Christ the man, a unique religious personality who initiated the kingdom of God. The result was set out in *Christianizing the Social Order* (1912) and *A Theology for the Social Gospel* (1917). Although his view that a gospel message 'confined to the soul and its personal interests was an imperfect and only partially effective salvation' had already been asserted by evangelicals such as Shaftesbury, Norman Macleod and Mearns, Rauschenbusch went further and rejected traditional evangelical teachings.[30] The unifying principle of Rauschenbusch's theology became the 'kingdom of God'. He now saw the message of Christianity as about seeing 'a divine social order established on earth'.[31] The kingdom of God, he believed, was to be found not just in the church, but in the family, in the industrial organization of society and in the state: it 'realizes itself through them all'.[32]

Most nineteenth-century evangelicals working in the worst of urban conditions did not see the need to shift away from the balance between evangelism and social concern, or to embrace a social gospel that focused largely on this world, rather than both the present and future orders, in order to address issues of housing and insanitary environmental conditions. But Rauschenbusch's views did foreshadow the 'Great Reversal', which hampered evangelical engagement in social action between the First World War and the 1950s.

Character study: Titus Salt (1803–76) – England

By the time he was 50 Titus Salt had made his fortune as a mill owner in Bradford, especially through pioneering the utilization of alpaca wool, used extensively in the crinolines worn by Victorian ladies. Knighted in 1869, he was one of Yorkshire's great textile barons. He served with distinction as Bradford's

---

[28] C. H. Hopkins, *The Rise of the Social Gospel in American Protestantism, 1865–1915* (New Haven: Yale University Press, 1940), repr. (New York: AMS, 1982), 216.

[29] W. Rauschenbusch, 'The Stake of the Church in the Social Movement', *American Journal of Sociology* 3 (July 1897), 29–30.

[30] W. Rauschenbusch, *A Theology for the Social Gospel* (New York: Macmillan, 1917), 49, 95, 99, 178.

[31] W. Rauschenbusch, *Christianizing the Social Order* (New York: Macmillan, 1912), 67, 69, 96–102.

[32] Rauschenbusch, *Social Gospel*, 144–145.

Lord Mayor from 1848 to 1849, and as an MP from 1859 to 1861. Having achieved all he could wish for in life, his plan was to sell his businesses and buy a rural estate on which to retire.[33] The plan was never carried out, and he instead embarked on a remarkable project for the religious, social, physical and intellectual improvement of those who worked for him.

The Salt family were Congregationalists, and Titus attended the famous Horton Lane Chapel, Bradford. Although closely involved in the life and work of the church, he became Sunday School Superintendent but lacked assurance of faith and refused invitations to pray publicly. Then in the early 1850s he heard a sermon illustration about a caterpillar in search of leaves climbing what it thought was a tree. Reaching the top, it found instead the 'tree' was a flagpole, with a fine view, but no leaves to satisfy its hunger. The preacher applied this: 'Thus it is with men! . . . wealth says, "Come up to me!" . . . and honour says, "Come up to me!" Yet such things left only a void, for God is not there.' The preacher went on, 'Is not Christ the Living Vine? Oh! when the soul begins to feed on Him it begins to live.' Salt was deeply affected. He prayed 'to be directed aright, and to put my whole trust in Christ, which is the only sure foundation'. He found Christ to be the source of his 'public and . . . private peace'. He also began to feel a deep sense of responsibility over the great wealth given to him, which ought to be consecrated to the glory of God, and for the good of his fellow men. Salt's motto became 'Deeds, not just words'.[34]

The project that rose to prominence in his mind was that of providing a healthy living and working environment for his thousands of workers. Between 1831 and 1851 the population of Bradford had accelerated from 43,527 to 103,778, the fastest growth in the country, but huge overcrowding followed. As Mayor of Bradford Salt increased investment in drainage and improved sanitation, and opened a soup kitchen for the unemployed. He was convinced that issues such as alcohol abuse and widespread immorality could be tackled only by dealing with poor housing, sanitation and working conditions.[35]

Salt took the huge, and extremely costly, decision to relocate his factory and workforce from the centre of Bradford, to a greenfield site four miles away beside the river Aire. Here he built the vast Victoria Mill, opened in 1853 and one of the first fully integrated woollen factories in the world – with washing, dying, spinning, weaving and finishing all on one site. Working conditions for

---

[33] I. C. Bradley, 'Titus Salt: Enlightened Entrepreneur', *History Today* 35.5 (May 1987), 30–31. On Salt's life and career see also J. Reynolds, *The Great Paternalist: Titus Salt and the Growth of Nineteenth-Century Bradford* (Hounslow: Maurice Temple Smith, 1983).

[34] R. Balgarnie, *Sir Titus Salt: His Life and Its Lessons* (London: Hodder & Stoughton, 1877), 118–124.

[35] Bradley, 'Titus Salt', 32.

the workforce of some 3,500 people were improved by large windows to let in plenty of light, and by placing the shafts for the machinery under the floor to reduce noise. Alongside the mill he built a village called Saltaire, complete with all civic amenities, designed as 'a pattern to the country', housing 4,500 people in 22 streets containing 850 houses. There were a further 45 almshouses for the elderly. Each house had a living room, kitchen, scullery, three bedrooms, water and gas supply, and a small back garden. Salt built a fully equipped wash house, with the latest in equipment including wringers, spin driers and heated drying rooms. Along the main street were shops, a post office and savings bank. Rents were kept at a moderate level to allow all workers to live close to the mill.[36]

Opposite the factory a dining hall was opened, providing a dinner of meat and vegetables for 2 pence, or a bowl of soup for a penny. It was even possible for workers to bring their own dinner there and have it cooked for them. Salt built a hospital for the workers and established a fire brigade. He constantly sought to improve facilities. In 1871 a 14-acre park was added, including a music pavilion and cricket ground. All was designed to promote the health and well-being of the workers. Smoking, gambling, swearing and the consumption of alcohol were not permitted in the park; indeed, public drunkenness and violence were almost absent from Saltaire.[37]

Significant emphasis was placed on education. Schools opened in 1868 had spaces for 750 children and extensive playgrounds. The Inspector of Schools declared them 'the handsomest in my district'. There was one notable absence from the village – a public house. As a Bradford magistrate Salt was distressed by the adverse social consequences of alcohol abuse. Of crime he often said, 'Drink and lust are at the bottom of it all.' Salt believed instead in 'innocent and intelligent recreation', and this was provided in the institute he built, offering the advantages of a public house without its evils. The institute was the cultural centre of the village, looking like a university college, including library, reading rooms, classrooms for adult education, and a lecture hall capable of seating 800 people, where orchestral concerts and art exhibitions were held. There was a scientific laboratory, a large billiard room and a gymnasium.[38]

To Salt, *Quid non, Deo juvante* (With God nothing is impossible). He lived his religion, believing it was his responsibility to spend his large wealth wisely during his lifetime. He expended more on the village and its facilities than on the vast mill. Age and infirmity left him only more determined than ever to work for God, before 'the night cometh when no man can work'. He endowed

---

[36] Ibid. 33.
[37] Ibid. 34; A. Holroyd, *Saltaire and Its Founder* (Bradford, 1873), 68.
[38] Reynolds, *Paternalist*, 278–279.

scholarships at local schools and gave large sums to local mental hospitals, the Bradford Infirmary and the fever hospital. Salt's preference was for his benevolent actions to be known only to God and the recipient.[39]

Salt welcomed to his home missionaries such as Robert Moffatt and David Livingstone, and famous preachers such as Thomas Binney from London and Thomas Guthrie from Edinburgh. On business visits to London he heard C. H. Spurgeon preach. Salt's was a deep, but childlike, faith, with a profound reverence for the Bible and preference for preachers who 'told simply with great plainness of speech and directness of personal appeal the old, old story of the Cross, of man's need and God's love'. He was treasurer of the Bradford Town Mission for a number of years, which worked particularly in the slum areas. Salt took on the support of ten Bible women who visited the poorest homes and families. Each month he purchased large quantities of books and tracts for the missioners to distribute.[40]

In the centre of the village, directly opposite the vast mill complex, a large Congregational church was opened in 1859. It contained a family pew but Salt preferred to sit with the rest of the congregation. Salt preferred Congregationalist church order, which vested the choice and support of the minister and the running of the church in the members, but considered it 'a joy and a privilege to co-operate with Christians of all evangelical denominations, in furtherance of Christian work'. Other denominations were provided freely with sites to build chapels in Saltaire village, including Methodists and Baptists. Having been a Sunday school teacher, the construction of Sunday schools in Saltaire, which opened in 1876, gave him particular delight. These had capacity for 800 children, including more than twenty classrooms, a lecture room, library and a large hall.[41]

As his life drew to a close, Salt longed that his faith might be stronger, but nonetheless declared, 'all my trust is in Him. He is the only foundation on which I rest. Nothing else!' One minister friend said:

> If ever mortal man had merited heaven by 'good works' it was Sir Titus Salt. But, no! he never referred to anything he had done, or made it a ground of boasting . . . in the prospect of eternity, he appeared as a man stripped of all self-righteousness, and clothed with the righteousness of Christ as his only raiment.[42]

---

[39] Balgarnie, *Titus Salt*, 148, 189.
[40] Ibid. 148, 152, 158, 189, 160, 163; Reynolds, *Paternalist*, 172.
[41] Balgarnie, *Titus Salt*, 125, 172.
[42] Ibid. 178, 179.

On the day of his funeral in 1877 the busy streets and mills of Bradford fell silent. The representatives of some thirty charities and religious societies in which Salt had been involved followed his coffin. Crowds of 40,000 filled the streets of Saltaire. The funeral sermon concluded with the words 'Well done, good and faithful servant, enter thou into the joy of thy Lord.' Outside the church door stood Saltaire, living proof of 'wise philanthropy and simple faith'.[43]

---

[43] Ibid. 184–186, 188–189.

6

Day schooling

During the Reformation and Puritan periods significant emphasis was placed on education, from primary to university level. John Knox's vision for the social and spiritual regeneration of Scotland was based on the twin and closely connected forces of the kirk and school. Education enabled people to read the Bible and other Christian teaching, and went hand in hand with publishing Bibles, Christian literature and tracts. Evidence of the fulfilment of the hopes of Knox and other Reformers is seen in how all the converts of the Cambuslang revival in Central Scotland in 1742, who were interviewed about their conversion, were able to read, including men and women.[1]

The school and orphanage established in 1698 by August Hermann Francke (1663–1727) at Halle, the centre of Pietism in Germany, was to prove a key influence. Francke connected educational programmes with the care of the poor. The daily pattern followed by the children at the orphanage's school included prayer times (some led by the children themselves), study and work, with passages of Scripture read during meal times. The school aimed to promote both Christian understanding and godliness. Between 1695 and 1806 up to a quarter of orphanage schools in Germany were founded on the Halle model. There was also a training seminary for teachers, who assisted with the education of the children, the most gifted of whom went on to university. Francke's appeal to donors stressed the blessing afforded to givers as well as receivers of such work:

> I set forth these notions for the benefit of those who have been blessed by God with temporal wealth and who fear God as the giver of wealth, and

---

[1] T. C. Smout, 'Born Again at Cambuslang', *Past and Present* 97 (1982), 122.

who seek to use it so they may do good and be rich in good works and store up treasure in heaven.[2]

The composer Georg Friedrich Händel (1685–1759), the most famous of Halle's orphan children, served on the board of the London Foundling Hospital from 1750 until his death. After Francke's death in 1727, the orphanage and school declined somewhat, but John Wesley visited Halle within a few weeks of his evangelical conversion in 1738, and used it as a model for his Kingswood School in Bristol.[3]

Halle's influence also reached North America. When Whitefield visited the Ebenezer Orphanage in Georgia, founded by two Halle teachers, he was so impressed he immediately resolved to found his own. This was the Bethesda Orphanage in Savannah, Georgia, started in 1740,[4] which included a school. Its goal was that the children 'learn to labour, read and write, and at the same time be brought up in the nurture and admonition of the Lord'.[5] During his sermons George Whitefield also collected for charity schools, including the Blue Coat schools, raising in 1737 at least £1,000 for them.[6] Wesley and Whitefield worked together in founding the school at Kingswood where the local colliers were renowned for 'cursing and blasphemy . . . full of wars and fightings', before the gospel left many 'singing praise unto God their Saviour'. Children were taught to 'read, write and cast accounts', and to know 'the things which make for their peace'.[7]

The extension of education proved a key contributory factor in the eighteenth-century Evangelical Revival in Wales. The early evangelical Anglican Griffith Jones (1683–1761) pioneered the 'circulating school' movement in the 1730s as a way of promoting reading the Bible, which was used as the main teaching tool. Teams of teachers visited areas, many of them remote, and for a concentrated period of around three months taught children and adults the basics of reading, before moving on to a new location. The scheme, using the medium of the Welsh language for teaching, eventually saw more than 158,000 people attending schools in over 1,600 locations. The high point came two years after Jones' death, when there were 279 schools operating, with 11,770 scholars. Large

---

[2] A. Francke, *A Sincere and Thorough Report Concerning the Inward State and Importance of the Work of the Lord in Halle* (London, 1704), 60.

[3] J. Wesley, *Journal of John Wesley*, vol. 2 (London, Wesleyan Office, 1872; repr. Grand Rapids, Mich.: Zondervan, n.d.), 26 July 1738, 112–113.

[4] On Francke and Halle see D. H. Shantz, *An Introduction to German Pietism: Protestant Renewal and the Dawn of Modern Europe* (Baltimore, Md.: Johns Hopkins University Press, 2013), esp. ch. 5.

[5] L. Tyerman, *Life of George Whitefield*, vol. 1 (London: Hodder & Stoughton, 1890), 348.

[6] G. Whitefield, *Journal*, ed. W. Wale (London, 1905), 80–81.

[7] Wesley, *Journal*, vol. 2, 27 November 1739, 251–252.

numbers of those educated were converted in the revival, which spread across Wales from 1735 onwards.[8] A similar educational project, with significant spiritual fruit, took place in the Highlands of Scotland.[9] In both, the use of the local vernacular – Welsh and Gaelic – was central to the success.

However, there was some hesitancy by the Evangelical Revival leaders over making the education of children central to their work. This was in part because of their focus on reaching adults with the gospel. The Countess of Huntingdon, who started two charity schools, was frustrated at the lack of progress children made without parental support, and commented, 'a school will never answer the end of bringing forth any of the Gospel fruits of holiness till the parents are first made Christians. The parents must lay up for the children.'[10] Although there were Methodist-funded charity schools in places such as London, Bristol, Bradford, Halifax and Ironbridge, the major educational movement among evangelicals was to take place in the nineteenth rather than the eighteenth century.

It might have been a slowing in the rate of recruitment from adults of the artisan class that had been a strong source of new members up until 1820, which led to the shift of resources on to work with children. This was coupled with rapid population growth, with an increasing preponderance of young people. By the end of the nineteenth century many churches and chapels saw children as their primary mission field.[11] The result was heavy investment in not only day schools, the focus of this chapter, but also in Sunday schools, ragged schools and children's rescue organizations, which will be explored in subsequent chapters.

There was no state provision for education in England and Wales until 1870, and 1872 in Scotland. Before then education was provided by a mixture of private schools, 'public' fee-paying schools for the wealthy, charity schools, church schools and the poor-quality 'dame' schools.[12] Education was believed by Christian leaders to be a core part of the ministry of the church. Yet there was an awareness of its limits. Because of the fallen state of humanity, it could bring only a certain amount of personal reform. Real change would come only

---

[8] See F. A. Cavenagh, *The Life of Griffith Jones of Llanddowror* (Cardiff: University of Wales Press, 1930); M. G. Jones, *The Charity School Movement* (Cambridge: Cambridge University Press, 1938), 407.

[9] See D. E. Meek, 'Scottish Highlanders, North American Indians, and the SSPCK: Some Cultural Perspectives', *Records of the Scottish Church History Society* 23.3 (1989), 378–396.

[10] Letter to John Wesley, in A. C. H. Seymour, *The Life and Times of Selina, Countess of Huntingdon*, vol. 1 (London: W. E. Painter, 1840), 51.

[11] A. D. Gilbert, *Religion and Society in Industrial England, 1740–1914* (London: Longman, 1976), 159–160.

[12] M. Sturt, *The Education of the People, A History of Primary Education in England and Wales in the Nineteenth Century* (London: Routledge & Kegan Paul, 1967), 6.

from regeneration. Yet John Venn of Clapham observed in 1804 that although it could not in itself make a person 'a real Christian', education could free a person from prejudices, and bring deliverance from 'the dominion of dispositions highly favourable to temptation and sin'.[13]

The educational work started in 1798 by the Quaker Joseph Lancaster (1778–1838) rapidly grew in popularity, and became in 1813 the British and Foreign School Society. It attracted support from across the denominations, including that of William Wilberforce, although it became increasingly associated with Nonconformist churches. In 1851 it was educating 123,000 children. Lancaster's 'monitorial system' involved the more capable older pupils teaching groups of younger children. This allowed cheap and large-scale provision of education, but had obvious educational weaknesses and was criticized for turning schools into educational factories. However, because costs were lower than those of conventional methods, this brought some form of education within the financial reach of many more families than would otherwise have been possible. Although not always directly under the instruction of a qualified teacher, the system allowed children to work in smaller groups differentiated according to age and ability, and there was a system of rewards and prizes.[14] Lancaster got around denominational rivalries by adopting a Bible-only-based approach to religious education, making use of a catechism in which the answers were entirely in the form of Scripture texts: 'Neither the master nor the monitor should ever give an opinion, but let the scriptures be their own interpreter.'[15]

The Anglican National Society for the Education of the Poor in the Principles of the Christian Church, founded in 1811 by Andrew Bell (1753–1832), similarly used the monitorial system. It was by 1851 providing schooling for 465,000 children, with other Anglican schools educating a further 336,000. Bell's system was a direct Anglican rival to Lancaster's, and made use of the Anglican liturgy and catechism in religious education. Evangelicals played a role in the National Society until the middle of the century, when High Church voices came to prominence. The horizons of the National Society's educational provisions were limited. In 1805 Andrew Bell expressed his fear that, through 'indiscriminate education', those facing the 'drudgery of daily labour' would be rendered 'discontented and unhappy in their lot'. He believed that it was 'sufficient to

---

[13] John Venn, 'Charity Schools', *Christian Observer*, September 1804, 542, quoted in M. Hennell, *John Venn and the Clapham Sect* (London: Lutterworth Press, 1958), 37.

[14] C. F. Kaestle, *Joseph Lancaster and the Monitorial School Movement: A Documentary History* (New York: Teachers' College Press, 1973), 1–18.

[15] *British and Foreign School Society Manual* (London: British and Foreign School Society, 1831), 28.

teach the generality, on an economical plan, to read their Bible and understand the doctrines of our Holy Religion'.[16]

There was considerable competition between the schemes of Bell and Lancaster. Although this was sometimes hostile, it served to increase the number of schools across Britain. Both schemes began to receive government grants for school building in England and Wales in 1833. Other denominations also provided day schools. By 1851 there were 47,000 children in Congregationalist schools and 37,000 in Wesleyan schools, but the appropriateness of accepting state funding troubled Nonconformists, who feared state interference in religious teaching. This gave a considerable advantage to Anglicans in terms of resourcing – in 1861 Anglican schools were educating 76 per cent of all day-school children in England.[17] In 1847 the Wesleyans decided to accept governmental financial assistance.

Denominational rivalries, and debates about what form religious education should take, held back the introduction of state education.[18] The Lancasterian system was widely adopted across Europe, and especially North America, where it was popular because of its non-denominational 'scriptural' religious education, well suited to a North American context, where there was no established church.

The evangelical Lord Shaftesbury remained convinced of the significance of investment in education, which had 'control over and possession of the youthful mind of the country, and the temporal and eternal destiny of millions'.[19] Alongside this, there was a conviction that education must have a Christian basis. As the evangelical Anglican Hugh Stowell declared in Manchester, 'I believe that it were better almost for man that [education] were crushed, than it were given unless it were Christianised.'[20] Nonetheless, many remained uneducated. In 1864, 57 per cent of children in Manchester were still receiving no education at all.[21] Some factory owners, including the Congregationalist Titus Salt, at his vast textile mills in Saltaire, near Bradford, and the famous mustard manufacturer J. J. Colman, in Norwich, provided schools for the children and young people they employed.[22]

---

[16] A. Bell, *An Experiment in Education*, 1805, quoted in Sturt, *History of Primary Education*, 28.

[17] G. Kitson Clark, *Churchmen and the Condition of England, 1832–85* (London: Methuen, 1973), 125.

[18] See F. Smith, *A History of English Elementary Education 1760–1902* (London: University of London, 1931).

[19] Lord Shaftesbury, in Hansard, Parliamentary Debates, 3rd series, 48, 270, quoted in G. B. A. M. Finlayson, *The Seventh Earl of Shaftesbury 1801–1885* (London: Eyre Methuen, 1981), 118.

[20] Quoted in S. E. Maltby, *Manchester and the Movement for National Elementary Education, 1800–1870* (New York: Longmans, 1918), 67.

[21] A. Kidd, *Manchester* (Keele: Keele University Press, 1933), 53–55.

[22] H. C. Colman, *Jeremiah James Colman* (London: privately printed at the Chiswick Press, 1905), 126.

Education was at the heart of Thomas Chalmers' urban ministry in Glasgow. He believed that through education society could be 'civilized', raising society's intellectual and moral tone, preparing the way for the reception of the Christian message. This educational mission model, which grew out of the Scottish Reformation understanding of church and school as the redemptive units for society, was to prove central to mission at home and abroad in the nineteenth century. Chalmers was aware of the significant role schools had played in the evangelization of the Scottish Highlands, where, alongside preaching and Bible distribution, education had been a means of cultural and religious transformation. By 1823 there were two day schools in Chalmers' parish, with 800 pupils. David Stow, one of Chalmers' helpers in this work, went on to become a pioneer in infant-school education and the professional training of teachers.[23] Others involved in urban mission repeated the pattern, including the Anglican William Pennefather in St Jude's Parish, Mildmay, in the East End of London. Here he started a primary school for the poorest children, and a soup kitchen for the poor and sick.[24]

The effort and resource ploughed by churches and chapels into education was enormous. However, by the 1860s it was clear that the voluntary efforts of churches, chapels, charities and the other providers of day schools were not matching the rapid rise in population, and were failing in their ambition to be the source of religious, moral and educational guidance for the nation. With large numbers of children receiving little or no education, government intervention followed, with the 1870 Education Act in England and Wales and the 1872 Act in Scotland. These legislated for new schools to be funded using local taxes (rates), and to be run by locally elected school boards, to which many Christian leaders sought election.[25] Religious education was offered in these schools on a non-denominational basis, as Lancaster had advocated. The 1870 Act spurred denominations into further efforts to build schools, and the two systems continued side by side. The number of voluntary schools peaked at 14,479 in 1890, but from then on they were outcompeted by the board schools with their greater financial resources and facilities.[26]

Questions remain about what was achieved by this large investment of resources in education by churches and Christian organizations. Certainly, a level of 'civilizing' was achieved, spreading a diffuse awareness of Christian

---

[23] See J. Roxborough, *Thomas Chalmers: Enthusiast for Mission* (Carlisle: Paternoster Press, 1999), 71–72, 116–117.

[24] Ed. R. Braithwaite, *Life and Letters of Rev. William Pennefather* (London: J. F. Shaw, 1878), 391–392.

[25] O. Chadwick, *The Victorian Church*, vol. 2 (London: A&C Black, 1970), 300.

[26] Ibid. 305.

teaching and morality, but the impact in directly bringing children to a personal faith commitment is harder to assess. It was the opinion of the London social observer Charles Booth that the Christian hope of planting seed through education, which would later be brought to life by the outreach work of churches, was on the whole unfulfilled. Workers were 'often disheartened, and sorely tried by failure, the world continually claims the children, and God's kingdom seems to come no nearer'.[27] However, if the intention instead was simply a widespread introduction of a basic Christian understanding and ethos, this was achieved. According to David Bebbington, it 'helps [to] explain the continued esteem for Christianity in the non-church going population'.[28] Nonetheless, it proved a shock to chaplains in the First World War to find how little understanding of Christianity the soldiers had, despite most having attended Sunday school at some point, and many having attended church schools. The rapid growth in the provision of state education was one aspect of the secularization process in which religious bodies in Europe lost their central place in life and society.

The importance given to education among Protestant evangelicals in Europe was repeated in their mission endeavours overseas. The Danish–Halle mission, which reached Tranquebar in India in 1706, was led by the inspirational Bartholomew Ziegenbalg (1682–1719), a former Halle student. His work included a focus upon education, Bible translation and understanding local culture, with the goal of the establishment of an indigenous Indian church.[29]

The Baptist missionary William Carey (1761–1834), who worked in India from 1793 onwards, undertook mission work that included a partnership between gospel proclamation and education. Carey had been a teacher early in life, and was a gifted preacher and translator. He worked closely with Joshua Marshman, a skilled linguist and educator. By 1818 some 10,000 pupils were being educated in ninety-two schools.[30] Serampore College was established initially for the training of future Indian Christian leaders, but the curriculum included studying Hindu culture and Indian languages, and eventually Hindu and Muslim students were admitted. Carey and his colleagues were clear that the evangelization of India would come only through the work of indigenous

---

27 C. Booth, *Life and Labour of the People of London*, 3rd series, *Religious Influences, vii, Summary* (London: Macmillan, 1902), 12–13.

28 D. Bebbington, *The Dominance of Evangelicalism: The Age of Spurgeon and Moody* (Leicester: Inter-Varsity Press, 2005), 124.

29 D. D. Hudson, *Protestant Origins in India: Tamil Evangelical Christians, 1706–1835* (Grand Rapids, Mich.: Eerdmans, 2000), 1–29.

30 B. Stanley, *History of the Baptist Missionary Society 1792–1992* (London: T&T Clark, 1992), 51, 53.

converts who had the Christian Scriptures in their own languages, and who were educated so they could read, study and preach in those languages.[31]

In West Africa education was also central to the Sierra Leone project. Established in 1787 by friends of William Wilberforce in the Clapham Sect, it was a part of Africa where freed slaves could settle. The former slaves were to be introduced to Christianity, and the primary means by which this was done were preaching and education. In 1827 the 'Fourah Bay Institution' was established by the Church Missionary Society (CMS), including in its remit the education of liberated Africans, who were equipped to be future indigenous leaders. From Sierra Leone these gifted preachers, teachers and evangelists fanned out across West Africa, often undertaking mission among the peoples they had originally been taken from when they were enslaved, before their subsequent rescue. One of the first students trained at Fourah Bay was Samuel Ajayi Crowther (c.1806–91), a rescued slave who converted to Christianity. He proved a very capable linguist and preacher, and in 1864 was ordained the first African bishop in the Anglican church.[32]

The influence of Thomas Chalmers' educational approach to mission is seen in the work of Alexander Duff (1806–78), who studied under Chalmers at St Andrew's University. Duff was sent out as the first Church of Scotland missionary to India.[33] Duff believed that in order to help Hindu audiences to understand biblical revelation and the Christian world view, there was a need to develop a spirit of Western rational enquiry and intellectual renewal in India. Just as the apostles had preached in Greco-Roman societies prepared by 'civilization' for the gospel, such a seedbed needed to be created in India. Education would prompt such 'enlightened' minds inevitably to ask the religious questions that would lead people away from false or superstitious religious notions to embrace Christian truths.[34]

In 1830 Duff opened a school in Calcutta, with the help of the Hindu reformer Ram Mohan Roy, offering the children of higher castes a high-quality Western Christian education in English. He hoped that the religious, moral and social influence of any converts would percolate down through the other castes in Indian society.[35] Educationally, the project was a success, with enrolment

---

[31] Ibid. 48–51.

[32] A. Walls, *The Missionary Movement in Christian History* (Edinburgh: T&T Clark, 1996), 86–87, 102–109.

[33] S. Piggin and J. Roxborogh, *Thomas Chalmers and the St Andrews Seven* (Edinburgh: Banner of Truth, 1985).

[34] I. D. Maxwell, 'Civilisation or Christianity? The Scottish Debate on Mission Methods, 1750–1835', in B. Stanley (ed.), *Christian Missions and the Enlightenment* (Grand Rapids, Mich.: Eerdmans, 2001), 136–140.

[35] Duff set out his approach in *A Vindication of the Church of Scotland's India Missions* (Edinburgh: J. Johnstone, 1837).

averaging 800 over ten years, but the Calcutta School produced only around 50 converts, and they were often ostracized by their own families, who directed great outrage against the school. Most pupils were more interested in self-advancement through education than in the Christian principles behind their education. Nonetheless, the converts came from prominent families, and a number went on to serve as ministers or Christian lay leaders.[36] Similar institutes were established in Bombay (1832), Madras (1837) and Nagpur (1844).

The educational model of mission was prominent in the first half of the nineteenth century. The Lovedale Institution in South Africa, started by the Glasgow Missionary Society in 1841, provided a comprehensive educational model of elementary education, training for school masters, catechists and mission agents, and artisan and agricultural skills.[37]

However, thereafter views began to change in the light of the limited numbers of converts. Rufus Anderson (1796–1880), of the American Board of Commissioners for Foreign Mission, began to argue that civilization would follow as the result of scattering the gospel seed, rather than being preparatory for the gospel. Education was valuable only in so far as it furthered the work of evangelism.[38] Some schools were closed in the 1850s as statistical evidence for the limited returns from the large expenditure mounted and confidence in the strategy flagged. The emphasis shifted to direct evangelism and itinerant preaching.[39] Francis Wayland (1796–1865), the Baptist President of Brown University, declared in 1853, 'the son of God has left us no directions for civilising the heathen, and then Christianising them. We are not commanded to teach schools in order to undermine paganism, and then, on its ruins, to build up Christianity.'[40] Seventy years of mission work in India, with large investments in education, had produced a body of just 30,000 Christians, just one hundredth of one per cent of the population of the country.

British and North American evangelicals attracted to the immediacy of the revivalist approach of Charles Finney began to prioritize evangelistic activism, using indigenous workers preaching in the vernacular. Those marginalized by caste or tribal background, illness, poverty or social problems responded in greater numbers to the message of the missionaries than those who had received

---

[36] Maxwell, 'Civilisation?', 136–140.

[37] See R. H. W. Shepherd, *Lovedale in South Africa: The Story of a Century 1841–1941* (Lovedale: Lovedale Press, 1941).

[38] R. Anderson sermon 'Theory of Missions to the Heathen', 1845, 73–74, quoted in W. R. Hutchison, *Errand to the World: American Protestant Thought and Foreign Missions* (Chicago, Ill.: University of Chicago Press, 1987), 82.

[39] Ibid. 78–82.

[40] F. Wayland, *The Apostolic Ministry* (Rochester, N.Y.: Sage & Brother, 1853), 19, quoted in Hutchison, *Errand*, 84.

high-level education. Some mission leaders now feared that Christianity would be overwhelmed by poor and uneducated Christians.[41] One result of this shift in focus was the failure to produce well-qualified and well-trained local leaders.

The decline in emphasis on social action, such as in the area of education, has been attributed to the influence of premillennialism, which informed the approach of influential evangelists such as D. L. Moody, who argued that the key task of the preacher was to save as many as possible from eternal condemnation before Christ returned. He famously said, 'God has given me a lifeboat, and said "Moody save all you can."' However, he was still a man of social action, including running large schools in Northfield, Massachusetts. With a high level of racial integration, by 1886 some 500 boys and girls who were orphans or from impoverished backgrounds were being educated.[42]

Moody's urgent evangelistic emphasis influenced leaders of 'faith missions', such as James Hudson Taylor, founder of the China Inland Mission (CIM) in 1865, to focus on preaching and itinerant evangelism. Compared to the 15,271 schools British mission agencies reported they were running in 1889, the CIM reported they were running none.[43] In 1900 Hudson Taylor was still presenting two alternative ways of mission – working for the gradual enlightenment of the people, or preaching for instant conversion without any embellishments.[44] Despite this, education had become a significant part of the CIM's work by the start of the twentieth century. Schools were run to consolidate the work of local churches, as a follow-on activity after initial evangelistic work. The historian of the CIM's work reported, 'Propagating the gospel of reconciliation with God through the death of Christ could not but result in social reform.' By 1915 the CIM was running 237 day schools with 5,412 pupils, and 135 boarding schools with 4,295 pupils.[45]

In the late nineteenth century, schools, hospitals and social projects again began to become a key part of mission strategy.[46] An important figure in this change was the Baptist Timothy Richard, who argued that education was vital to seeing mass conversions to Christianity in China. He hoped that through Western education (including higher education) Chinese culture, especially its

---

[41] A. Porter, *Religion Versus Empire? British Protestant Missionaries and Overseas Expansion, 1700–1914* (Manchester: Manchester University Press, 2004), 165.

[42] J. F. Findlay, *Dwight L. Moody: American Evangelist, 1837–1899* (Chicago, Ill.: University of Chicago Press, 1969), 306–321.

[43] Jeffrey Cox, *The British Missionary Enterprise Since 1700* (London: Routledge, 2008), 202.

[44] Christopher E. M. Wigram, *The Bible and Mission in Faith Perspective: J. Hudson Taylor and the Early China Inland Mission* (Zoetermeer: Uitgevers Boekencentrum, 2007), 133.

[45] J. H. Broomhall, *Hudson Taylor and China's Open Century*, bk 7: *It Is Not Death to Die* (London: Hodder & Stoughton, 1989), 525, 531.

[46] Hutchison, *Errand*, 83–89, 99.

rising intellectual class, would be permeated with Christian ideals.[47] Although Richard was accused of developing a Confucianized form of Christianity, missionary educational efforts in China multiplied. By 1906 there were as many as 58,000 Protestant schools in China, with 400 higher-education institutions. Shandong Christian University was founded in 1905 by Baptist and Presbyterian missionaries.[48] Other explicitly Christian universities were founded in other parts of China, Hong Kong and Beirut, areas where Christianity was not the dominant religion. Similarly, in India the number of children being educated in missionary-run schools grew from 64,043 in 1851 to 299,051 in 1890.[49]

The education provided by evangelicals offered the socially marginalized a means of self-improvement, as well as the ability to read the Bible. As state-funded education reduced opportunities for educational involvement in the West, efforts by evangelical missionaries overseas multiplied. However, they remained clear that education was not to be an end in itself, but to be balanced with an evangelistic intent. As the influential missionary thinker John Mott wrote:

> The value of medical, educational, literary, and all other forms of missionary activity, is measured by the extent to which they prepare the way for the Gospel message, promote its acceptance, manifest its spirit and benefits, multiply points of contact with human souls . . . In some parts of the world, more people have been led to accept Christ through educational effort than through any other agency.[50]

Character study:
Hannah More (1745–1833) – England

Hannah More regularly divided opinions. Samuel Johnson considered her 'the most skilled versificatrix in the English language', whereas the writer and politician Augustine Birrell called her 'one of the most detestable writers that ever held a pen'.[51] In her time her books, later largely forgotten, sold more copies

---

[47] Stanley, *History*, 175–190; and A. Walls, 'The Multiple Conversions of Timothy Richard: A Paradigm of Missionary Experience', in A. Walls, *Cross-Cultural Process in Christian History* (Edinburgh: T&T Clark, 2002), 236–258.

[48] I. J. Shaw, *Churches, Revolutions and Empires: 1789–1914* (Fearn: Christian Focus, 2012), 419–420.

[49] G. Smith, *The Conversion of India from Pantaenus to the Present Time AD 193–1893* (London: John Murray, 1893), 200, 205, 206.

[50] J. Mott, *The Evangelization of the World in This Generation* (New York: Student Volunteer Movement, 1905), 11–16.

[51] A. Stott, *Hannah More: The First Victorian* (Oxford: Oxford University Press, 2004), vii–viii.

than Jane Austen. Her midlife conversion to 'vital religion', or evangelicalism, brought a complete change of direction in life.

She was the fourth of five daughters born to Jacob More, an impoverished Gloucestershire schoolmaster. The More girls were educated with the expectation they would gain an independent living.[52] Although courted by several suitors, to one of whom she was engaged for six years, as he repeatedly postponed the wedding day, More never married. Around 1773 she visited London and was introduced by friends to Samuel Johnson, the actor David Garrick and the painter Sir Joshua Reynolds. They encouraged Hannah's early literary efforts and she became a member of the Bluestockings, an influential group of literary women. A series of her plays were successfully staged in London and her poems and novels became immensely popular. But as her religious convictions deepened, she felt growing unease about her associations with fashionable society, and especially attending parties on Sundays.[53]

Leading evangelicals in London, including Thomas Scott, befriended More.[54] Her conversion to evangelicalism took place contemporaneously with that of Wilberforce in 1785–6. After they met in 1787, they became friends and John Newton became spiritual advisor to them both.[55] More became the only woman, other than those involved through marriage or kinship, to be considered a member of the Clapham Sect, and she produced poems and writings opposing slavery. Wilberforce and Henry Thornton became financial supporters of her schools and tract writing.[56]

Former friends were shocked at the change in her religious views, and in 1785 she retired from London society, buying a house in Somerset. Here she wrote her *Cheap Repository Tracts*, promoting the values of respect for order in society, humility, hard work, sober living and reverence for God. Costing just a penny, several millions were sold. After a visit by Wilberforce to her village in 1789, he challenged her, 'Something must be done for Cheddar.'[57] This galvanized Hannah and her sister Martha (known as Patty) into action. That year they started the Mendip Scheme, a comprehensive programme of education, religious instruction and social welfare. There were no other charity schools in the area, so Hannah leased a house for a schoolmistress, and converted an

---

[52] W. Roberts, *The Life of Hannah More: With Selections from Her Correspondence* (Boston: Roberts Brothers, 1872), 11–23. Roberts' biography is now widely criticized for its inaccuracies and for omitting the vitality and humour central to her nature.

[53] Stott, *More*, 80–84.

[54] Ibid. 85–86; J. and M. Collingwood, *Hannah More* (Oxford: Lion, 1990), 59.

[55] Stott, *More*, 90.

[56] Hennell, *Venn*, 170; Stott, *More*, 92–101.

[57] Collingwood, *More*, 73.

outbuilding into a school. Parents were visited and exhorted to send their children to school.

Similar schools were started in Shipham and Nailsea, with classes on weekdays providing education and training in employment and domestic skills. A Sunday school was also commenced, together with reading classes for teenagers and young adults who had missed out on education. A comprehensive system of social care was developed alongside the schools, including what became the Cheddar Friendly Benefit Society. For a subscription of a halfpenny a week women could receive 3 shillings a week when ill, and 7 shillings and 6 pence a week during childbirth. There were also funeral benefits – all vital resources in the days before state-welfare provision.[58] In all this Hannah was hugely engaged, travelling on horseback through all weathers to teach impoverished children to read, while still corresponding with leading politicians and royalty.[59]

In 1790 the school in Shipham was also flourishing, with 140 children attending. It was reported in 1796 that every house in the parish was sending children to the school. When fever spread through Shipham in the depths of the winter of 1792, Hannah paid for a wagonload of coal to be distributed to the poorest. Her comprehensive social action extended to buying up the production of the local 'calamine' mine during times of trade depression, so the workers could be paid.[60]

By 1800 Hannah and Patty had started twelve schools spread across ten parishes, with overall attendance of around 1,700 children.[61] However, some leading local famers believed that education might render their workers discontented, and discouraged them from sending their children to the schools. Some of her opposers eventually became supporters, but the opposition never entirely disappeared. Despite their woeful neglect of the area, there was also opposition from clergy. When she arrived in the area, no Anglican clergyman had lived in Cheddar for forty years, and there was only one Bible in the parish. Hannah and Patty were shocked to find 'as much knowledge of Christ as in the interior of Africa'.[62]

The schools work brought growing spiritual fruit. Groups of adults began meeting in the schools on Wednesday evenings to study the Scriptures. Before too long, 20–30 young people were doing the same. Hannah encouraged this,

[58] Ibid. 74–75.
[59] Stott, *More*, x.
[60] Collingwood, *More*, 83–84.
[61] Ibid. 92.
[62] Ibid. 80.

and sometimes would read a sermon to them. When John Venn visited the schools at Cheddar in 1793, he found 150 children 'praising God in loud hallelujahs who but four years ago knew nothing of God but to swear by his holy name'. He found them 'well instructed' in the Bible, some having memorized up to eighty chapters of it. He declared it 'the Lord's doing'. He noticed some who

> seemed to feel very deeply the power of the truth, and others who have . . . brought their fellow prentices, their masters and mistresses, or their parents, to pray to God night and morning. Indeed I never saw anything which affected me, or which promises more to glorify God.[63]

Although a loyal Anglican, for her work Hannah More was accused of Methodism. This came to a head in Blagdon, where opposition was led by a local High Church curate, Thomas Bere. It was a parish where education had been deeply neglected, and crime and disorder prevailed. Hannah More's school flourished, criminality declined and order returned to the parish. But Bere turned against the school and its schoolmaster, Henry Young, who was holding weekday evening meetings. Bere argued these were Methodist meetings. After a long and bitter conflict, Blagdon school was eventually closed, although the others remained open.[64] More's friends rallied to her support, including Venn, who declared her a 'much-injured lady, who has devoted talents and learning . . . to the improvement of the lowest; and whose benevolent labours, like those of her great Master, have been rewarded with calumny and reproach'.[65]

Some criticized her for taking a leadership role as a woman, and others for the supposedly politically subversive policy of teaching poor children to read and so improving their condition, arguing this would destabilize society. More responded, 'My object is not to make fanatics, but to train up the lower classes in industry and piety.'[66] Although criticized at the time for being too radical, ironically in the twentieth century her views were rejected as being patronizing and attempting social control of the lower orders by the higher classes. Certainly, More's primary hope was for personal spiritual revolution rather than a major eradication of inequalities in society. However, she remained convinced that education not only enabled people to read the Bible, but also gave them better

---

[63] John Venn, letter to E. Edwards, 1793, quoted in Hennell, *Venn*, 183.

[64] On the conflict see A. Stott, 'Hannah More and the Blagdon Controversy, 1799–1802', *Journal of Ecclesiastical History* 51.2 (April 2000), 319; Collingwood, *More*, 98.

[65] John Venn, *Christian Observer*, 1801, 543.

[66] Quoted in B. N. Schilling, *Conservative England and the Case Against Voltaire* (New York: Columbia University Press, 1950), 79.

opportunities for employment and benefitted society. She cared deeply for the poor, both in soul and body, and invested prodigious amounts of time and money in helping them. Her tract *Thoughts on the Importance of the Manners of the Great* (1788) strongly criticized the gentry for failing to do likewise.[67] Education was a key part of her comprehensive social and religious concern for the poor, and she declared, 'Action is the life of virtue, and the world is the theatre of action.'[68]

Facing growing age and infirmity she retired from the schools, spending her last years advising other philanthropists who approached her, and who regularly paid tribute to her inspirational influence.

---

[67] M. G. Jones, *Hannah More* (Cambridge: Cambridge University Press, 1952), 104–107.

[68] H. More, *An Estimate of the Religion of the Fashionable World* (London, 1808), 146, quoted in Bebbington, *Evangelicalism*, 12.

7

Sunday schools

The use of Sunday for religious instruction outside church services had a long and rich tradition. From the Reformation onwards, especially in the Puritan period, Sunday afternoon was often used for catechizing children and families. Although Sunday schools existed before the 1780s, the pioneer of the Sunday school movement in Britain is widely considered to be Robert Raikes (1735–1811). He promoted their work through his newspaper *The Gloucester Journal*. These reports spread rapidly, and thereafter the idea of educating the children of the poor became closely associated with Sunday schools.

Early Sunday schools shared a number of characteristics. They were free, being financed by donations, aimed at the spiritual well-being of the very poor, and instruction was based on the Bible and the catechism. In the late eighteenth century little education was available for the children of the poor. Many were in employment during the week but were left unsupervised on Sundays, with rowdy and disruptive behaviour sometimes resulting.[1] Raikes' own school, started in Gloucester in 1780, combined education and compassionate care with a desire to control unruly elements in society socially. He bought clothes and shoes for some of the poorest children, and sought to instil personal habits of discipline and cleanliness – Bible passages and hymns could be recited only by those who attended with clean hands and face. He was surprised at the alacrity with which the children participated, and even found some beginning to attend early morning prayers in the cathedral at 7 am.[2]

The elderly John Wesley was enthusiastic about what he saw, declaring the Sunday school 'one of the noblest institutions which has been seen in Europe for some centuries'. In 1784 he reported, 'I find these schools springing up wherever I go.'[3] Accounts circulated of the great change in the atmosphere on

---

[1] M. G. Jones, *The Charity School Movement* (London: Frank Cass, 1964), 143.

[2] Ibid. 146–147.

[3] Letter from Wesley, quoted in *Wesleyan Methodist Magazine*, 1845, 118; J. Wesley, *Journal of John Wesley*, vol. 20, entry for 18 July 1784, in *Works of John Wesley*, vol. 4 (London: Wesleyan Conference Office, 1872), repr. (Grand Rapids, Mich.: Zondervan, no date), 284.

Sundays in large towns as a result of Sunday school work, with 'noise, profaneness and vice' among children replaced by quietness and order.[4]

In the 1780s to 1790s Sunday schools were largely non-denominational and often independent of local churches. They included the Stockport Sunday School, founded in 1784, which, with 5,244 scholars, was reported in 1833 to be the largest in the world. After 1800 Sunday schools were increasingly attached to churches and chapels, and the focus became more strongly religious. This was not always without controversy. In 1824 the Bennett Street Sunday School in Manchester, which had more than 1,800 scholars, and had been for many years connected to St Clement's Church, severed its connection after the minister, William Nunn, sought to appoint teachers who shared his Calvinistic doctrinal views. The Sunday school eventually attached itself to what it felt was a more theologically congenial church, and St Clement's began its own Sunday school, which prospered.[5]

Sunday schools proved to be a significant educational success. Between 1780 and 1830, when the population of England increased by 100 per cent, the numbers of those able to read increased by 500 per cent. In 1830 it was reported that for more than half the children in Manchester, the only education they were receiving came through the Sunday school.[6] After 1810 Sunday schools had an increased religious rather than educational focus: 'Sunday' being emphasized above 'school'.[7] This led to a controversy as to whether writing was an activity that served to further the gospel, and whether it should be taught on a Sunday. The 1823 Wesleyan Methodist conference passed a motion that '[t]he Sunday School is a strictly and entirely religious institution, and that it must not teach writing.' Other Nonconformists such as Baptists and Congregationalists were less exercised about the matter.[8] Some Sunday schools circumnavigated the problem by teaching writing, and other subjects such as arithmetic, on weekday evenings.

Until the middle of the nineteenth century teachers were often from the working classes, and in some schools received a small payment. There is debate as to whether Sunday schools were institutions run by middle-class people who imposed their values on the lower orders of society, or whether they were led

---

[4] Jones, *Charity School*, 148.

[5] I. J. Shaw, *High Calvinists in Action: Calvinism and the City c.1810–60* (Oxford: Oxford University Press, 2002), 86–91.

[6] E. R. Royle, 'Evangelicals and Education', in J. Wolfe (ed.), *Evangelical Faith and Public Zeal* (London: SPCK, 1995), 121.

[7] R. B. Cliff, *The Rise and Development of the Sunday School Movement* (Redhill: National Christian Education Council, 1986), 73, 78, 87.

[8] Ibid. 81–83.

and run by the working class for their own betterment.[9] An example of the latter was the Sunday school started in 1824 by William Gadsby, the minister of St George's Road Baptist Chapel, in Manchester, who had risen from the poorest of backgrounds. Gadsby became a steadfast supporter of Sunday schools, and produced a hymn book specifically for their use. Children, who came from the inappropriately named Angel Meadow, a notorious slum, were taught not only how to read, but also how to write and spell. A society was started in 1836 to help provide destitute children associated with the school with clothing and footwear. One such was Thomas Vickers, who arrived at the school barefoot. Through personal care, religious teaching and general education he was converted to Christ, became a successful businessman and treasurer of the Sunday school.[10] Gadsby saw the potential of Sunday schools for promoting religious and moral change and social advancement:

> Can any person with the fear of God in his heart, believe that the labouring poor ought to be bond slaves either to the highest class or the middle class of society, and all means be kept from them of enabling them, if they are steady, industrious, and prudent, of raising themselves in society.[11]

Sunday schools often met before the Sunday morning service, with some children then being accompanied to the morning service, before reconvening in the afternoon. The Bible was the primary textbook for teaching reading. Children learned Scripture verses (some children were prodigious learners, memorizing whole books of the Bible), as well as the catechism in some schools, and hymns that were sung. Facilities became increasingly specialized during the nineteenth century, with the construction of separate Sunday school buildings, many of which were busy with different classes on other days of the week.

The growth in the number of children being taught in Sunday schools in England was extraordinary, rising from 206,100 in 1801 to 3.5 million in 1871. In 1888 some 75 per cent of all children were attending a Sunday school. Total attendance peaked at 6 million in 1903.[12] Numbers were especially high in

---

[9] See T. W. Laqueur, *Religion and Respectability: Sunday Schools and Working Class Culture, 1780–1850* (New Haven, Conn.: Yale University Press, 1976), which is challenged by M. Dick, 'The Myth of the Working Class Sunday School', *History of Education* 9 (1980), 27–41.

[10] Shaw, *High Calvinists*, 130–134.

[11] W. Gadsby, 'The Utility of Sunday Schools', in *Works of William Gadsby* (London: John Gadsby, 1851), 305.

[12] Cliff, *Sunday School Movement*, 102, 125, 164; O. Chadwick, *The Victorian Church*, vol. 1 (London: A&C Black, 1970), 256.

urban industrial areas: a survey of young people aged over 15 working in Lancashire cotton mills in 1852 found that 90 per cent had at some point attended a Sunday school.[13] Confidence in the potential of Sunday schools seemed unbounded, as a speaker at the 1846 Wesleyan Conference eulogized, 'if we do but cultivate this interesting field of Christian toil . . . we shall be an increasing people, while the sun and the moon endure'.[14]

The Sunday School Society, founded in 1785, enabled Anglicans and Nonconformists to co-operate in promoting such schools. Its first president was Henry Thornton, of the Clapham Sect. This interdenominational co-operation faded in the 1790s as the French Revolution spread fear of Jacobin principles, of which Nonconformists were (unjustifiably) suspected by Anglicans.[15] The absence of such fears about Sunday schools in North America enabled Americans to follow a strongly non-denominational path. In England and Wales, however, Sunday schools became increasingly denominational. By 1851 the Anglican Church was the largest provider, with 10,427 schools, accounting for 42 per cent of all enrolments. The Methodists accounted for 29 per cent, the Independents 13 per cent and the Baptists 7 per cent.[16]

Sunday schools were given a central role in missional strategies, especially in urban areas. Thomas Chalmers gave the Sunday school a prominent place in his urban ministry in Glasgow from 1815 to 1824. Using his principle of 'locality' as the way to facilitate connections between church and people, he broke his parish down into small districts. He argued that there should be one Sunday school for every 300 people. Sunday school teaching provided significant ministry opportunities for the mobilized laity, who were essential to Chalmers' scheme, including many keen young men starting out in business or the professions. They visited and befriended local people in their allotted districts, and encouraged parents to send their children to the Sunday school. Children were to be taught to read, using the Scriptures, and to be instructed in 'judgement and conscience' based on the lessons of Scripture.[17]

David Nasmith, the founder of the London City Mission (LCM), was much influenced by Chalmers and gave Sunday schools a prominent place. It was claimed that between 1869 and 1884 the LCM's agents had brought 115,412 people to worship services and helped 173,000 children to attend Sunday school.

---

13 Laqueur, *Religion*, 89.

14 Wesleyan Conference Minutes, 1846, 359–361, quoted in A. D. Gilbert, *Religion and Society in Industrial England, 1740–1914* (London: Longman, 1976).

15 Jones, *Charity School*, 152.

16 Cliff, *Sunday School*, 102.

17 T. Chalmers, *Christian and Economic Polity of a Nation* (Edinburgh: T. Constable, 1851), 72–79, 98.

Even as late as 1955, LCM workers were educating 10,498 Sunday school children.[18]

Hannah More similarly gave Sunday schools an important place in her mission strategy in villages and small towns. The Sunday school she started in the Mendip Hills saw attendance increase from 100 to 200 between 1791 and 1795, and the weekday evening reading class numbered 200 in the winter. However, supervising the unruly behaviour of the children could be a challenge – the Sunday school at Axbridge attracted 'poor, little, dirty, wretched-looking creatures' who were half-starved.[19]

One major question is over the effectiveness of Sunday schools. John Bright, the Radical MP of Quaker background, declared hyperbolically, 'I don't believe all the statesmen in existence ... have tended so much to the greatness and true happiness, the security and glory of this country, as have the efforts of Sunday School teachers.'[20] Yet, to the historian Owen Chadwick, most Sunday schools before 1870 were inefficient, with poor educational standards, untrained teachers and limited resources and expectations.[21] For all their limitations, for much of the century Sunday schools were the only educational opportunity available to most of the children of the working classes.[22]

By the middle of the nineteenth century the expressed aim of evangelicals in running Sunday schools was to help to bring children to personal faith in Christ.[23] These evangelicals certainly succeeded in introducing the Bible, *Pilgrim's Progress* and other literature given as Sunday school prizes, into homes, and children were given the ability to read them. Conversions did happen.[24] However, after the age of 11, especially among boys, attendance tended to drop, and the numbers from non-churchgoing families who moved from Sunday school directly into church or chapel attendance were not high. Within eight years of the optimistic declaration at the Wesleyan Conference of the potentiality of Sunday schools, a Wesleyan spokesman sombrely reported, 'vast multitudes of children are incessantly passing through our Sunday Schools, and then becoming ... utterly alienated from our religious fellowship'.[25]

---

[18] I. Howat and J. Nicholls, *Streets Paved with Gold: The Story of the London City Mission* (Fearn: Christian Focus, 2003), 190.

[19] J. and M. Collingwood, *Hannah More* (Oxford: Lion, 1990), 82, 89.

[20] J. Bright, *Church Congress Reports*, 1888, 363; 1894, 393, quoted in Chadwick, *Victorian Church*, vol. 2, 257.

[21] Ibid. 258.

[22] E. Baines, *The Social, Educational, and Religious State of the Manufacturing Districts* (London: Simpkin, Marshall, 1843), 23.

[23] Laqueur, *Religion*, 160.

[24] Ibid. 169.

[25] *Wesleyan Sunday Schools as They Are and as they Ought to Be*, 1854, quoted in Laqueur, *Religion*, 80.

In Nottingham, of 12,000 Sunday school pupils in 1822 only 87 progressed immediately into church membership. Over James Roby's forty-seven years as an Independent minister in Manchester, attendance at the church's Sunday school averaged 1,000 children a year, but only 260 eventually joined the church. Based on his studies, Laqueur concluded that only between 1.5 per cent and 4 per cent of children enrolled in a particular Sunday school would later belong to the church or chapel with which it was associated.[26] As agents of moral and social control, success could also be limited. One chaplain in Leeds prison reported that of 282 prisoners, 230 had attended Sunday school.[27]

This was a disappointment to those who had switched their ministry focus from seeking adult conversions in the late eighteenth century on to children in the nineteenth. Much of the available time of church and chapel volunteers, together with significant resources, was absorbed into working with children. Fewer people were available for domestic visitation, and R. W. Dale lamented the decline by the 1880s of lay preachers' societies in Congregational churches.[28] One corollary of the focus of centring evangelistic resources on children was the unwitting portrayal of religion as being for children rather than for adults, and especially for men. Although the Sunday school remained the one religious institution 'which the nineteenth-century public had any intention of using',[29] it did so on the public's terms rather than those of the churches that ran the Sunday schools, especially to gain a cheap education. The widening availability of free day-school education during the 1880s corresponded with the beginning of a decline in Sunday school attendance.[30]

The success of Sunday schools needs to be measured in less quantifiable ways. Sunday schools inculcated habits of punctuality, cleanliness and order; literacy rates rose; a general awareness of Christian teaching and morality was spread. They created a pool of young people who had some basic instruction in the Christian faith, and who might later in life return to attendance or be attracted by one of the outreach activities surrounding most churches. Sunday schools formed an important social focus. The annual Sunday school service filled the church, and Sunday school outings were high points of the calendar for children and their parents. In 1856, 23,000 Sunday school scholars attended the Halifax 'Big Sing', accompanied by a band of 560 individuals, including 83 trombones.

[26] Laqueur, *Religion*, 80.
[27] Chadwick, *Victorian Church*, vol. 2, 257.
[28] R. W. Dale, *History of English Congregationalism* (London: Hodder & Stoughton, 1907), 600.
[29] W. R. Ward, *Religion and Society in England, 1790–1850* (London: B. T. Batsford, 1972), 135.
[30] Laqueur, *Religion*, 148–157.

Sunday schools also offered welfare provisions, many running associated sickness and burial benefit societies.[31]

Not all the work of Sunday schools was aimed at children. Those of the north of England in particular included significant numbers of adult classes. In 1888 it was stated that more than 25 per cent of attendees in the Wesleyan Lancashire and West Riding Sunday schools were aged over 15. Chadwick noted that many working men 'would not go inside a church. Offer them a Bible Class, and their attitude was often different.'[32] The churches most successful in seeing children continuing into church attendance or other church activities were those running classes for teenagers and adults.[33]

This ability to bridge the ages and maintain an interdenominational focus helped Sunday schools to remain a central component of religious life in North America. In 1790, with no free school education available in Philadelphia, several denominational leaders formed the non-denominational First-Day or Sunday School Society of Philadelphia. All reading lessons were from the Bible, and even primers and spelling books used words and sentences from the Bible. Their purpose was combining education with aspirations for 'the virtue, liberty and happiness of the people'. Although non-denominational, Sunday school pupils were strongly encouraged to attend local places of worship, and met before and between service times.[34]

Within twenty years most major cities had a similar body. A significant development was the large adult classes established. The first major union of North American Sunday schools in 1817 was initially called the Sunday and Adult School Union, before it became in 1823 the Sunday School Union (SSU). It had by then 723 schools and some 50,000 pupils. The SSU emphasized the non-denominational approach, with agreement on 'the essential truths of the Bible as held by all Christians, and in a neutral attitude on those doctrines upon which they differed'. These 'essential truths' were evangelical, including

the supremacy of the inspired Scriptures as the rule of faith and duty; the lost state of man by nature and his exposure to endless punishment in the future world; his recovery only by the free, sovereign and sustaining grace of God, through the atonement and merits of a divine Redeemer . . . ;

[31] I. J. Shaw, *Churches, Revolutions and Empires* (Fearn: Christian Focus, 2012), 217.

[32] Chadwick, *Victorian Church*, vol. 2, 259, 262.

[33] I. Sellers, *Nineteenth-Century Nonconformity* (London: Edward Arnold, 1977), 37.

[34] E. W. Rice, *The Sunday-School Movement 1780–1917 and the American Sunday-School Union 1817–1917* (Philadelphia, Pa.: American Sunday-School Union, 1917), 45–47.

the necessity of faith, repentance and holy living with an open confession of the Saviour before men.[35]

The leaders of the SSU came from the main denominations, described as 'Big hearted, consecrated men of affairs', who, 'seeing the multitudes who neglected the Church and religion' were 'united in the great mission of teaching the truths of the Bible to those who were otherwise unreached by the gospel'. Their hope was that new birth and spiritual growth would 're-create and renew the human source of all reforms', which 'creates the strongest motive for every reform and for the betterment of every community and of every life therein'.[36]

The Sunday school movement in North America saw itself as primarily missional, focused increasingly on areas where churches were having little impact – new settlements further West and deprived urban areas. In 1856 evangelical leaders in Chicago declared, 'We consider the Sabbath school as the only hope for city heathenism. The church has no other means by which she can enlighten its darkness, or penetrate its interior.'[37] Considerable evangelistic success was reported by the SSU in the early 1880s, with between 10,000 and 20,000 conversions of children a year, especially in rural communities, where there was little gospel witness. Their non-denominational basis meant that children attending were not confined to those families from the specific denomination running the school. Often Sunday schools were the first religious institutions founded in newly settled areas, and sowed seeds of Christian witness, with churches being established over time in the wake of these Sunday schools. Winter evangelistic campaigns were common, with local churches receiving the fruit of work done in the Sunday schools.[38]

Key to the success of the Sunday school movement was the role played by the teachers. In 1917 they were lauded as a 'great missionary agency for the universal spread of the gospel of Christ'. The majority of the workforce for teaching in the Sunday schools was provided by women, bringing the new sense of female collective and public activity. Here they gained opportunities for social organization and leadership, which were significant in enhancing their role in society. A number went on to serve in overseas mission.[39] Teaching was often combined

---

[35] Rice, *Sunday-School Movement*, 3, 59–66, 80–81.

[36] Ibid. 84, 430.

[37] *Northwestern Christian Advocate* 4 (27 August 1856), 138, quoted in J. F. Findlay, *Dwight L. Moody: American Evangelist 1837–99* (Chicago, Ill.: University of Chicago Press, 1969), 73.

[38] Rice, *Sunday-School Movement*, 263.

[39] The significant role played by women in antebellum reform movements is discussed in B. L. Epstein, *The Politics of Domesticity: Women, Evangelism and Temperance in Nineteenth-Century America* (Middletown, Conn.: Wesleyan University Press, 1981); L. Ginzberg, *Women and the Work of Benevolence, Morality, Politics and Class in the Nineteenth-Century United States* (New Haven, Conn.: Yale University Press, 1990).

with pastoral visitation – in 1897 it was reckoned that the teachers of the SSU were visiting 95,000 families per year, reaching up to 500,000 people.[40]

By 1917 the SSU was employing more than 200 agents to promote the gospel and Sunday schools. John McCullagh (1811–88), a Scottish émigré, had as a small boy in Glasgow attended a Sunday school started by Thomas Chalmers, and learned the vital value of Sunday school work. As a result of forty-seven years as an SSU missioner, he was credited with having started 1,000 schools (90 in 1850 alone), which 66,200 children had attended. A number of these schools went on to become churches. The SSU missioner Stephen Paxson (1808–81) was converted after his little daughter took him to a Sunday school meeting. He was believed to have travelled more than 100,000 miles on horseback establishing schools, often in great adversity. He declared, 'A Sunday-school born in a snowstorm will never be scared of a white frost,' and was credited with starting 1,314 Sunday schools.[41]

Most Sunday schools were started in a small room or kitchen. In rural areas often the School house or a storehouse was used, and sometimes a tent. Although such premises were not ideal, they enabled Sunday schools to be seen as part of the community, rather than belonging to the separate province of a particular church. Gradually, distinctive buildings for Sunday schools were built. By the start of the twentieth century the SSU still considered itself the handmaiden of the churches. Although some Sunday schools did become churches, the SSU built none of its own:

> It lays the foundation for multitudes of churches . . . of every evangelical faith. It brings the gospel to all alike . . . it leaves them to unite in or with any local church of whatever evangelical creed they may prefer.[42]

Between 1890 and 1900, 69,988 professed conversions were reported, and as a result of its work 1,359 churches were founded. As these churches then developed their own Sunday schools, more than 100,000 schools were transferred from the SSU to different denominations.[43]

Sunday schools in the USA appear to have been more effective as agents for recruitment to churches than those in the UK, especially in newly settled rural areas where there was no previous religious provision. In 1900 it was claimed that 17.4 per cent of the population of the USA was in membership of a Sunday

---

[40] Rice, *Sunday-School Movement*, 3, 264.
[41] Ibid. 269–273, 421.
[42] Ibid. 288–289.
[43] Ibid. 3–5, 281–289.

school, including 21.9 per cent in Pennsylvania. In 1917 there were 215,000 Sunday schools across the USA, with more than 25 million members, with more than 20 million of them in evangelical Sunday schools that used the Bible as the chief textbook of instruction. However, this left more than 40 million people in the USA who were neither members of a church or of a Sunday school.[44]

One of those whose pathway into ministry lay through Sunday school teaching was D. L. Moody (1837–99).[45] Aged 22, bursting with evangelistic and physical energy but feeling denied opportunities in his local church, he started his own non-denominational mission Sunday school in 1859. The location he chose was the Sands, one of the poorest areas of Chicago's north side, noted as a red-light district filled with saloons, gambling dens and shanty houses. Local children, many living on the streets, were quickly drawn to this larger-than-life character, his pockets filled with 'missionary sugar' (sweets). The school flourished. Moody recruited both children and teachers, and established a library of books, tracts and religious periodicals. His addresses to the children were short, pithy and practical, and he reported thirty-four conversions in the first year. His care extended beyond the children, for some of whom he bought clothes, to their impoverished families for whom he bought food. Despite his unorthodox methods, his force of personality, deep sincerity, unpretentiousness and care for individuals won affection and respect.[46]

His Sunday school was started while Moody was working highly successfully as a shoe salesman. But within a year he had given up his employment and regular income to focus on Young Men's Christian Association (YMCA) work and the mission school. This decision was encouraged after an appeal to Moody, from another Sunday school teacher, who had to leave Chicago because he was dying of tuberculosis, to come and help him lead the girls in his class to Christ before he left.[47] Such evangelistic opportunities were too strong to resist. By 1862 the school had 450 children attending and Moody was also holding meetings for their parents. Three evenings a week classes were held to teach reading and to help immigrant families learn English. The original premises were soon outgrown, and in 1864 a large brick building, with an auditorium holding 1,500, and numerous classrooms, was completed. By 1865, 750 children attended regularly, and it was the second largest mission Sunday school in Chicago. There were a large number of converts, often from poor, illiterate and unruly

---

[44] Ibid. 418–420.

[45] On Moody see W. R. Moody, *The Life of Dwight L. Moody* (London: Morgan & Scott, 1900); J. F. Findlay, *Dwight L. Moody: American Evangelist, 1837–1899* (Chicago, Ill.: University of Chicago Press, 1969); L. Dorsett, *A Passion for Souls: The Life of D. L. Moody* (Chicago, Ill.: Moody Press, 1997).

[46] Findlay, *Moody*, 72–82.

[47] Moody, *Moody*, 64–66.

backgrounds, who did not find an easy or ready welcome in Chicago's churches, leading to the founding of the Illinois Street Church in December 1864. This independent church ran, as well as the Sunday school, evening tea meetings, prayer meetings and a range of social-concern projects. Moody's Sunday afternoon Bible class attracted adults and children, and he illustrated his talks on a large blackboard.[48]

Although church and state were separated, the Sunday school movement helped instil distinctive Christian cultural values within North American life. The absence of an Established Church in America proved no hindrance to voluntary bodies such as the American Bible Society and the SSU in promoting the Christianization of society. They did this through the reading of the Bible and Christian literature, endeavours towards moral improvement, Sabbath observance and education.

Sunday schools were a key component of home-mission strategy on both sides of the Atlantic, and in turn inevitably became part of overseas mission strategy as well. In 1890 there were 135,565 children being taught in Sunday schools in India.[49]

Sunday schools also made significant contributions to wider thinking about education. They helped ensure that in Britain religious instruction was an important, though much debated, aspect of public educational provision. Sunday schools also furthered the idea that education should be available for all, and that it should be free. They offered a Christian leaven to the lives of children who had the potential to be dehumanized by industrialization and its impact on those who had to work. Although the significance of Sunday schools declined in the late twentieth century, their legacy remained. In 1957 a Gallup survey of adults in the UK found that 73 per cent of them had at some point attended a Sunday school.[50]

Character study: Henrietta Mears (1890–1963) – USA

A very significant figure in the development of Sunday schools in the twentieth century was Henrietta Mears.[51] At 7 years of age she announced she was ready to become a Christian and joined the First Baptist Church of Minneapolis. Aged 12 she taught her first Sunday school lessons. Despite suffering from poor

---

[48] Findlay, *Moody*, 106–111.

[49] G. Smith, *The Conversion of India from Pantaenus to the Present Time AD 193–1893* (London: John Murray, 1893), 205–206.

[50] Quoted in D. Bebbington, *Evangelicalism in Modern Britain* (London: Unwin Hyman, 1989), 124.

[51] E. M. Baldwin and D. V. Benson, *Henrietta Mears and How She Did It* (Glendale, Calif.: GL Regal, 1966), 31.

eyesight all her life, and repeated warnings over the risk to her sight from intensive study, Henrietta Mears trained as a chemistry teacher.[52] She taught in various high schools, eventually heading the chemistry department at one of them. She also continued to teach in the Sunday school, and emphasized the importance of applying educational principles and standards to Sunday school programmes. Within two years, the class she had inherited, which comprised just one child, had grown to 530 pupils.[53]

In 1927, as she considered a call to overseas missionary service, Mears undertook a sabbatical during which she visited First Presbyterian Church, Hollywood, California. The minister, Stuart MacClennan, had led the growth of a small country church into a large and prominent congregation, known for biblical teaching, evangelism and supporting many young people into cross-cultural mission. Here she was offered the post of Director of Christian Education, which she accepted in 1928. Her initial focus was on training and mobilizing the teachers, and implementing a graded, age-appropriate curriculum from infants to adults. She was convinced of the potential for Sunday school to reach others with the Bible. Within two-and-a-half years of her arrival, Sunday school attendance had grown from around 450 to more than 4,200 per week, and eventually it reached 6,500 – at the time the largest Presbyterian Sunday school in the USA. It involved a mainly volunteer staff of more than 500, and proved extremely influential on other churches and church leaders. Mears taught the college-age programme herself, encouraging many into theological education.[54]

The key components of effective Sunday schools were, to Mears, a Christ-centred and Bible-based message, and teachers possessed of genuine Christian experience.[55] Their closeness to Christ was essential – the shorter their 'perpendicular' distance from God, the greater the 'horizontal' reach would be.[56] She steadfastly refused to tone down foundational teaching on the atoning work of Christ, the plenary inspiration of Scripture or the spiritual danger those who were without Christ were in.[57]

Mears was certain that the value of the 'business' conducted by her teachers over plain wooden tables in Sunday school far exceeded that conducted by

---

[52] B. H. Powers, *The Henrietta Mears Story* (Westwood, N.J.: F. H. Revell, 1957), 114.

[53] A. C. Migliazzo, '"She Must Be a Proper Exception:" Females, Fuller Seminary, and the Limits of Gender Equity Among Southern California Evangelicals, 1947–52', *Fides et Historia* 45.5 (summer–autumn 2013), 9.

[54] R. J. Leyda, 'Henrietta C. Mears: Evangelical Entrepreneur', *Christian Education Journal: Research on Educational Ministry* 1.1 (November 2003), 57.

[55] Powers, *Henrietta Mears*, 32–33.

[56] Ibid. 57.

[57] Ibid. 55.

businessmen over their glass-topped desks.[58] Organization was key: prayer and planning were not antithetical.[59] She was also convinced of the need for integration between what happened in the Sunday school and the regular pulpit ministry, creating a strong teaching unity throughout the church. By the middle of the twentieth century many Sunday schools looked drab and rundown, and Mears pressed for them to renovate their facilities, making them bright, attractive and welcoming.[60]

Her professional skills and understanding of educational theory were applied to the Sunday school. She wanted to put the 'school' back into Sunday school. Teaching had to be vibrant and clear to be effective.[61] She called her approach 'a new and scientific way of mastering teaching the Greatest Book in the World'.[62] There was a focus on child-centred learning, applying the understanding of the Bible rather than just memorizing texts.[63] Teaching materials were to be age-appropriate, with continuity between levels, from children to young adults to young marrieds.[64] Horrified at hearing of children being bored at Sunday school, Mears came to believe that the Bible was the most widely, but most poorly, taught book in the world. Her philosophy became, 'Give them something to come for, and they will come miles to get it.'[65] She wrote much teaching material herself, and others requested access to the high-quality materials she was producing.[66] This led to the foundation of the Gospel Light Press, which by 1940 was one of the leading independent publishers of Sunday school literature, with 13 depositories and a further 53 bookshops serving more than 2,000 churches.[67]

Although she did not undertake the overseas missionary service she had contemplated, Henrietta Mears adopted a missiological approach to Sunday school work, at a time when confidence in it was waning: 'Don't plan on going to Japan to be a missionary if you cannot start being a missionary where you are.'[68] She set out a missional plan for Sunday schools: start with those nearest you – 'How many unchurched youth are there in your community?'; focus on the Bible – 'other things may be good, but this is the best'; win people

[58] Ibid. 32.
[59] Ibid. 129.
[60] Ibid. 133.
[61] Leyda, 'Henrietta C. Mears', 59.
[62] Quoted in A. C. Migliazzo, 'The Education of Henrietta Mears: A Fundamentalist in Transition', *Baptist History and Heritage*, June 2011, 71.
[63] Baldwin and Benson, *Mears*, 35; Rice, *Sunday-School Movement*, 432.
[64] Baldwin and Benson, *Mears*, 82; Powers, *Henrietta Mears*, 129.
[65] Baldwin and Benson, *Mears*, 60, 62.
[66] Ibid. 68.
[67] Powers, *Henrietta Mears*, 151.
[68] Ibid. 137.

to Christ – 'eighty-five percent of the boys and girls attending the Sunday Schools of America do so without ever taking Christ as their Savior'; enlist for service – 'find a place for every student to work'; look over your building – 'Is it conducive?'; study your programme – is it 'merely an assortment of ideas, or do you have a comprehensive, long-range plan?'.[69]

Most who knew Henrietta Mears referred to her simply as 'Teacher', but she never felt called to be a preacher. She also never married. This was a 'final door, where it was just the Lord and myself'. She reflected, 'He has given me thousands of children; the Lord has supplied everything in my life and I've never felt lonely.'[70]

Hundreds of men and women went through her Sunday school programme and into full-time Christian service, ranging from pastoral work to theological education. Students she taught founded at least fifty ministries and organizations.[71] Her book *What the Bible Is All About* sold more than three million copies. Jim Rayburn, founder of Young Life, said of her, 'She was my teacher long before she ever heard of me. When I began my work among young people in 1933, I read everything she wrote and listened to everyone who could tell me about her.'[72] The *Four Spiritual Laws* developed by Bill Bright for Campus Crusade for Christ, so influential for late twentieth-century evangelicalism, were significantly shaped by Mears' work. He acknowledged her as one of the greatest influences on his life. 'She directly discipled hundreds of young men and women whom God led into full-time Christian ministry. Today, no doubt, thousands of additional disciples whom they influenced are, in turn, introducing millions of other people to Christ.'[73] Billy Graham said:

> I doubt if any other woman outside of my wife and mother has had such a marked influence. Her gracious spirit, her devotional life, her steadfastness for the simple gospel, and her knowledge of the Bible have been a continual inspiration and amazement to me.[74]

Her concern was that Christian education should not just be for children from Christian families. It was a primary outreach tool, and involved visiting the homes of children who attended to show their families personal pastoral

---

[69] Baldwin and Benson, *Mears*, 84–86.
[70] Powers, *Henrietta Mears*, 116.
[71] Leyda, 'Henrietta C. Mears', 60.
[72] E. O. Roe (ed.), *Dream Big: The Henrietta Mears Story* (Ventura, Calif.: Regal Books, 1990), 5–6.
[73] Ibid. 6.
[74] Powers, *Henrietta Mears*, 7.

care.[75] The gospel message was not just to be conveyed in words, but in how people lived. 'Spiritual ideas cannot stalk alone through the world and be of any value. They must be clothed with men and institutions who will serve as hearts and brains, hands and feet to carry them out.' This meant keeping faith and works 'in their proper place'. Works were the fruit of faith – 'True religion produces a pure life, "unspotted from the world", and a useful life, "visit the fatherless and widows."'[76] Through this holistic approach she said, 'You teach a little by what you say. You teach most by what you are.'[77]

Henrietta Mears became a revered figure among theological conservatives of the 1940s and 1950s, and the most famous religious educator in the USA.[78] Her influence was felt in church curricula, teacher training, leadership development and missions education.[79] In her Sunday school work she was able to combine a strong commitment to conservative evangelical Christianity with cautious engagement with modern North American culture. This helped to set a pattern for evangelicals in the decades following the Second World War.[80]

---

[75] Leyda, 'Henrietta C. Mears', 60.

[76] H. C. Mears, *A Look at the New Testament: An Abridged Survey of Matthew–Revelation* (Glendale, Calif.: GL Regal, 1966), 11–12, 215.

[77] Roe, *Dream Big*, 18.

[78] M. L. Bendroth, *Fundamentalism and Gender, 1875–the Present* (New Haven, Conn.: Yale University Press, 1993), 86–87.

[79] Leyda, 'Henrietta C. Mears', 64.

[80] Migliazzo, 'Fundamentalist', 65–76.

8

Care for street children

The streets of towns and cities in nineteenth-century Europe and North America were awash with children, as they still are in many cities in the Global South. By 1826, 24 per cent of England's population was aged between 5 and 14 years, and many had no experience of normal family life.[1] Street children included, as well as orphans, those abandoned by their parents or who had fled from abusive homes or families rendered dysfunctional by problems such as alcohol abuse. Others were sent on to the streets by their parents to earn money. In 1876 Thomas Barnardo estimated 30,000 children under the age of 16 were living on London's streets. Variously called 'Street Arabs', 'ragamuffins' or 'street urchins', they were usually barefoot. Some were naked or semi-naked; others were dressed in rags. They were often found sitting in the gutters of the streets, or scavenging in markets and refuse heaps for scraps of food.[2]

At night they would be found sleeping under the arches of bridges, in doorways or in stables. It was said they were more numerous than the dogs that roamed the streets in packs, and were often treated worse. Many of them did not know what names they had been given at birth, so just went by nicknames. They tried to earn pennies by sweeping crossings, selling flowers or matches, or running errands, but many were forced to beg or steal to survive. They did not attend schools and were unwelcome at many Sunday schools because they were unruly, dirty, smelly and swarming with vermin.[3] Lord Shaftesbury memorably described the street children he met in London as 'bold, pert and dirty as London sparrows, but pale, feeble and sadly inferior to them in plumpness of outline . . . spanning the gutters with their legs and dabbling with earnestness in the latest accumulation of nastiness'.[4]

---

[1] J. Humphries, 'Care and Cruelty in the Workhouse: Children's Experiences of Residential Poor Relief in Eighteenth- and Nineteenth-Century England', in N. Goose and K. Honeyman (eds.), *Childhood and Child Labour in Industrial England: Diversity and Agency, 1750–1914* (Farnham: Ashgate, 2013), 115.

[2] K. Heasman, *Evangelicals in Action* (London: Geoffrey Bles, 1963), 69.

[3] 'The Ragged Schools', *Daily News*, 21 February 1846, quoted in L. Mair, *Religion and Relationships in Ragged Schools: An Intimate History of Educating the Poor, 1844–1870* (London: Routledge, 2019), 51.

[4] S. L. E. Barnardo, *Memoirs of the Late Dr Barnardo* (London: Hodder & Stoughton, 1907), 65.

In his novel *Oliver Twist* (1838) Charles Dickens depicts the gangs of feral children who roamed the streets, typified by the 'Artful Dodger', easily lured into crime by unscrupulous adults. Attitudes to street children varied. Many were deeply motivated by genuine compassion and care, seeing them as victims of events beyond their control, and were deeply concerned for their moral welfare. Some bleakly viewed them as hopeless cases; to others they were a danger to the welfare of society.[5] The presence of street children could hardly be missed, but most gave little thought to where they lived or what could be done to help them.

In 1810 Thomas Cranfield made an early attempt in Camberwell to educate such children, who had been rejected by Sunday schools. Then in 1820 John Pounds, a cobbler from Portsmouth, began teaching a group of ragged children. He was aware that they had to be fed and adequately clothed in order to be capable of benefitting from education. They also needed training to prepare them for future employment, if they were not to be doomed to a life on the streets.[6] A painting of Pounds teaching a group of ragged children proved inspirational to Thomas Guthrie, the case study in this chapter. By the 1840s, running schools for street children had become an important aspect of the London City Mission's work. In 1840 it reported running five schools exclusively for children 'raggedly clothed', in places such as Bethnal Green, Lambeth and Shoreditch, which 570 children were attending.[7]

The interest of Lord Shaftesbury was awakened in 1843 after seeing an advert in *The Times* appealing for funds for a ragged school run by the London City Mission. He visited it and was impressed with what he saw. In 1844 he became President of the recently formed Ragged School Union (RSU), and over the next forty years became synonymous with its work. His name added prestige and popular appeal, and the work grew rapidly.[8] Within the wider religious and philanthropic work Shaftesbury was devoted to, ragged schools played an important part, such that he declared, 'If the Ragged School system were to fail . . . I should die of a broken heart.'[9]

The RSU in London was an evangelical organization designed to provide support for existing schools and assist the formation of others. Its growth was rapid, from an initial 16 schools to 560 schools in 1860. This included 199 Sunday schools, 146 day schools and 215 evening schools, with a total attendance

---

[5] H. Hendrick, *Child Welfare: England 1872–1989* (London: Routledge, 1994).

[6] Heasman, *Evangelicals*, 71.

[7] Ibid. 71–72.

[8] E. Hodder, *The Life and Work of the Seventh Earl of Shaftesbury*, vol. 2 (London: Cassell, 1887), 146.

[9] Georgina Battiscombe, *Shaftesbury: A Biography of the Seventh Earl 1801–1885* (London: Constable, 1974), 196.

of 49,290 scholars. They were taught by 2,690 voluntary and 400 paid teachers. By 1870 the total number of scholars had increased by a further 26 per cent.[10] Many other ragged schools operated independently of the London-based union, and were found in most other towns and cities – in 1861 there were 64 in Liverpool and 17 in Manchester, each of which developed its own ragged-school unions. To Shaftesbury they were the only hope to 'reclaim a wild and lawless race, unaccustomed from their earliest years to the slightest moral influence or even restraint'. He believed the proper response to 'juvenile vagrancy' was not 'coercion and chastisement', but wide-ranging care and education. Only this would raise them from 'the depths of degradation' and give them a chance to 'run the course set before them . . . as citizens of the British empire, and heirs of glorious immortality'.[11]

Ragged schools had a number of distinctive features. Most day schools required a fee (albeit small sometimes) to be paid for attendance, but the education provided by the ragged schools was free: without this it was impossible for the children to be there. They focused on neglected children who were receiving no other form of education. Their care was holistic – alongside education, in which Christian teaching played a key part, food and clothing were often offered. They also operated in small unpretentious premises, in the immediate vicinity of where the children roamed, such as stables, cowsheds, storerooms, cellars, lofts or under railway arches.[12]

Ragged schools would be found in the poorest, most overcrowded and unhealthiest parts of the cities where there was little or no sanitation. Here streets and courtyards were filled with stinking animal, vegetable and human waste and excrement. In such an unwholesome environment, with small rooms closely packed with unwashed children in filthy clothes, the atmosphere was fetid. Teachers were known to faint, overwhelmed by the smell. Infectious diseases spread quickly among both children and teachers – from measles to scarlet fever and typhus, and deaths among both groups were not uncommon. Street children were easily recognizable, with their stunted growth, emaciated bodies, sunken eyes and sallow complexions. Some had stomachs swollen through malnutrition. Many had sores on their legs that were often infected; others were severely disabled by rickets. Poor eyesight was common, and large numbers of children had additional learning-support needs. Such children were regularly involved in accidents on London's busy streets, where they were

---

[10] Mair, *Ragged Schools*, 43.
[11] Lord Shaftesbury, *Quarterly Review* 79 (n.d.), 127–141, quoted in G. B. A. M. Finlayson, *The Seventh Earl of Shaftesbury 1801–1885* (London: Eyre Methuen, 1981), 251–253.
[12] Heasman, *Evangelicals*, 69–73.

unsupervised.[13] As the schools increased in size, they began to rent better premises, and some school owners purchased them. A number provided children with overnight shelter. A concern for the future employment of the children led to the development of industrial schools to offer training. Some ragged schools also started churches, offering worship in a style and location suitable for the children and their parents.

A strong feature of the ragged schools was their interdenominational basis, with evangelicals from different traditions working willingly together. The London Ragged School Union (RSU) was committed 'to act on the broad principles of Christianity, without reference to sect or party'. This was something that Shaftesbury, an Anglican, came to appreciate. He confided in his diary in November 1845, 'it is high time to be thinking where we agree, not where we differ'. The urgency of the need required this: 'tens of thousands of untaught heathens in the heart of a Christian metropolis cry aloud to God'.[14] For working with Christians of other denominations he received criticism, but was undaunted. He believed he was acting 'in the spirit of the Bible and the spirit of the Church of England'. If it was judged that doing this was 'at variance with the doctrines and requirements of the Church', then he would 'prefer to renounce communion with the Church to abandoning those wretched infants of oppression, infidelity and crime'.[15]

Schools were identified by streets or areas, not by association with a church as had eventually happened with Sunday schools. Religious teaching was to be solely based on the Bible, with all catechisms excluded. Sunday school teachers were described as 'members of a great evangelical alliance, not merely recognising each other as brethren on the platform . . . but working together in the schoolroom'.[16] Some denominations developed their own ragged schools apart from the RSU, such as those among the Unitarians led by Mary Carpenter.

The efforts of Shaftesbury in support of this work were prodigious, chairing not only the annual meeting, but also numerous local meetings of the RSU. He spent much time, usually accompanied by a London City missioner and a doctor, in visiting the poorest and most deprived parts of London. His biographer summed up his commitment to the street children:

---

[13] Mair, *Ragged Schools*, 54–55, 81, 85–86, 91–92, 94–95.

[14] Hodder, *Shaftesbury*, 151.

[15] Shaftesbury, diary, 11 December 1845, in Hodder, *Shaftesbury*, vol. 2, 151.

[16] 'Our Principles: A Review', *Ragged School Union Magazine* (January 1869), 2, quoted in Mair, *Ragged Schools*, 45.

he visited them in their wretched homes, he saw them in their daily work, he sat beside them in their schools, he let them come to his home to tell him their troubles; he pleaded for them in religious and political assemblies; he carried their cause into the House of Commons and the House of Lords; he interested the whole country in their welfare.[17]

Shaftesbury also became a significant donor to the work – paying for the running of a class teaching tailoring, shoemaking and needlework at the ragged school at Broadwall. He helped found the Lambeth Ragged School, which by 1846 was helping 370 children.[18] He was convinced that the ragged schools should always be in the poorest areas; and when some schools had opportunities to move to more desirable areas, he opposed this: 'you must keep them . . . in the mire and gutter, so long as the mire and gutter exist'. Otherwise they would not be located where most needed.[19] He was fully aware of the social context of the poorest areas. When one government commission in 1861 recommended that the solution to the educational needs of ragged street children was simply to supply them with decent clothes so they could attend regular schools, Shaftesbury, who knew the hand-to-mouth existence of their parents, begged to differ: 'in the twinkling of an eye, every particle of clothing would have gone into the pawnbrokers' – turned into cash for rent, food and often alcohol. He argued that ragged schools existed only because of deprivation and poverty. Only when those were dealt with would there be no more need for the schools.[20]

The primary purpose of ragged schools was educational. They met at first on Sunday nights, but soon their work spread into weekday evenings. There was a strong emphasis on teaching children to read, especially so they could read the Bible. However, there was not the anxiety about teaching writing or other subjects that there had been in the Sunday schools. Facilities were generally sparse, with children often sitting on the floor, with few books or writing implements, which attracted criticism. With children who lacked structure or rules in their lives, the atmosphere could be riotous. Attendance tended to be irregular, which hampered educational development. That any progress was made at all was an achievement.

It soon became apparent to teachers in ragged schools that a purely educational approach was insufficient. Many children were too hungry to learn.

---

[17] Hodder, *Shaftesbury*, vol. 2, 153.

[18] G. B. A. M. Finlayson, *The Seventh Earl of Shaftesbury 1801–1885* (London: Eyre Methuen, 1981), 253, 264.

[19] Hodder, *Shaftesbury*, vol. 2, 140.

[20] Shaftesbury, quoted in Finlayson, *Shaftesbury*, 418.

Sheriff Watson, who had started a ragged school in Aberdeen in 1841, began providing the children with food, and sought to keep them in attendance through much of the day, rather than just a few hours in the evening or on Sunday. This pattern was followed by Thomas Guthrie in Edinburgh.[21] Ragged schools in England were slower to provide meals, not doing this until the 1860s. In 1867 the Destitute Children's Dinner Society was formed, offering free meals to children at the ragged schools, inspired by the example of Watson and Guthrie. Lord Shaftesbury and Lord Kinnaird were officers of the society. Within a year thirty-seven dining rooms had been opened. Those located in ragged schools and Christian missions were in 1888 serving up to 18,000 dinners a week. After the education acts of the 1870s, the society worked to support the provision of school meals in the local-authority schools that were started, paving the way for the institution of the school dinner.[22]

As Thomas Barnardo found in his mission work in East London, at the end of the school day many ragged-school children had no home to return to, so loitered around the school door. Some teachers began to put up hammocks or informal beds for them in the schools so they could stay overnight, and before long night refuges and dormitories were being established.[23] Another strong emphasis was 'industrial' training for the children, giving them specific skills for future employment and preventing them from falling back into begging, delinquency and crime when they left the school. Training was offered in skills such as shoe-blacking, tailoring, shoemaking, mending clothes, chopping wood, carpentry and leatherwork for boys, and sewing, knitting and embroidery for girls. More than fifty of the ragged schools in London offered such training, although the level of skill-attainment was not high.[24]

The shoe-blacking brigades were probably the most successful employment training ventures. Boys were sent out in teams to work at strategic locations under careful supervision. At the end of the day the earnings were split three ways – a third to the boys, a third put in savings for them and a third used to cover costs. The boys were fed, and given lessons in the evening. By 1878 the RSU was operating nine shoe-blacking brigades. Although the skill level required was low, the boys were able to find order and develop self-discipline where there had been none, and so were prepared for future employability.[25]

---

21 Heasman, *Evangelicals*, 74. See case study in chapter 8 below.
22 Ibid. 75–76.
23 Ibid. 76–77.
24 Ibid. 87.
25 Ibid. 78–79.

Another solution to the problem of street children was helping them to emigrate to Australia and Canada, as with orphan children, which has been much criticized. There were, however, some success stories. Shaftesbury received letters from children who had been helped to migrate to Canada, where they had found work. One girl had found a good home, and wrote about the 'many comforts' she now enjoyed that would never have been possible had she remained on the streets of London.[26]

The holistic care offered to ragged-school children also extended to their parents where they could be found. It was recognized that much of the work done in schools could be quickly undone by way of the home life the children experienced. Therefore, local churches were started by ragged schools, in an attempt to reach the whole family. By 1852 there were thirty-five ragged churches, with an attendance of 2,500. The London City Mission played an important role in this before the Ragged Church and Chapel Union was started in 1853 to help raise funds for the rental of premises and provide adult classes. Some of the churches attracted up to 1,000 people, many from the lowest sections of society – beggars, down-and-outs and an assortment of people involved in crime. Notably, unlike other churches, where male attendance was only around 35 per cent, up to three-quarters of those who attended the ragged churches were men. Significant attention was given to working with both parents and children, to offer support, advice and teaching.[27]

One example of the progressive development of a ragged school was the Field Lane School, which started in a deprived part of London in 1841. It began in a small back room in a dingy courtyard. Its only equipment was a Bible, a prayer book, two stools, two benches, a box that served as a table and some old candlesticks. The first night five teenage girls attended, and they spent the evening giggling. When five teenage boys appeared, chaos ensued. The pioneers struggled to make any progress, and activities were switched to Sundays and help was sought from a local church. Before long fifty boys and girls were attending, and weekday evening classes were resumed. In 1847 a free day school was started, running each morning from 9 am to 12 noon, and then from 2 pm to 4 pm, which attracted seventy street children. Over time a boys' overnight refuge was started, then a ragged church and evening adult school, and refuges for homeless men and women followed. In the 1870s there was also a day nursery to care for infants while women went to work, an industrial training school for boys and a training home to prepare girls to go into domestic

---

[26] Finlayson, *Shaftesbury*, 545.
[27] Heasman, *Evangelicals*, 79.

service. The Field Lane School was by the 1880s a major institution, with large Sunday and evening schools,[28] although the day-school element of Field Lane's work was handed over to the Metropolitan School Board in 1873. This was to the disappointment of Shaftesbury when he heard that little teaching from the Bible was thereafter permitted.[29] The range of activities found at Field Lane were typical of other ragged schools that ran a whole series of associated activities, such as mothers' meetings, ragged churches, nurseries, penny banks, lending libraries, bands, hostels and soup kitchens.[30]

Those involved in running ragged schools came from a variety of social backgrounds, but most were middle-class evangelicals with a concern for the poor and outcast. In 1858 the RSU reported 2,118 voluntary teachers, with a further 332 receiving payment. One of the challenges was recruiting and retaining such a large number of volunteers. A significant number of teachers were, however, from the working class, and one of the achievements of the movement was enabling people from such different parts of society to work together. In 1859 at least 43 per cent of ragged-school teachers in London were women. Some joined their husbands in the work, others worked along with their mothers and sisters, but many were single women without family connections choosing to give up their time to rescue and educate the children of the streets.[31]

One example of the volunteers who devoted their spare time to ragged schools was Martin Ware (1818–95). Although he studied classics and theology at Cambridge University, and his brother was eventually consecrated Bishop of Barrow-in-Furness in 1899, Martin chose a career in law. A man of deep evangelical devotion, he gave his spare time to mission work with a ragged school in Compton Place, Camden, London, of which he left a detailed account. Ware served as superintendent of the Sunday evening boys' class from 1848 until around 1854. Through the rest of the week he undertook visits to the families of the children he taught, attended committee meetings, prayer gatherings and meetings held for teachers in other ragged schools in the Camden area. Ware also found time to support a range of evangelical organizations, including the Bible Society and China Inland Mission. He played a key role in the establishment of the Ragged School Shoe-Black Society (RSSBS), in which he was involved until his death. This society gave work to ragged-school children who had been recommended by their teachers. They were given a

---

[28] Ibid. 79–80.
[29] Finlayson, *Shaftesbury*, 545.
[30] Mair, *Ragged Schools*, 44.
[31] Ibid. 56–63.

uniform and a box of equipment for blacking shoes, and then sent to clean boots at various busy locations for a small fee. The society grew out of a meeting of teachers at the Field Lane Ragged School, and by 1878 it had nine different brigades, each with its own coloured uniform.[32] Ware's deepest desire was to see the children make a profession of religious faith as a result of their teaching. The letters he received from former ragged-school pupils indicate that a number of children did make a Christian commitment, and wrote testifying of their own faith, their Bible reading and church attendance. Some took up some form of Christian work.[33]

The development of infant nurseries, or crèches, in association with ragged schools, became a notable feature from the 1870s onwards. These already existed in factory towns, where many women worked in large mills, but in inner-urban areas the crèches enabled women to go out to work. By 1872 there were fourteen in London, such as that started by Marie Hilton, a Quaker, in Stepney Causeway, which opened in 1871. Children were cared for from 8 am to 8 pm. They were washed on arrival, and their clothes cleaned. Children were given three meals a day, with the infants placed in clean cots and the older ones taught to play with toys. So they could go out to work, mothers paid tuppence a day for this care for their children.[34]

Ragged schools also offered their children an annual treat, such as a day out in the countryside or seaside. This was supported by ministries such as the Children's Fresh Air Mission (1882), which funded short holidays for children from the slums.

In England the passing of the 1870 Education Act, introducing state-funded provision of education alongside the already-existing church schools, signalled a major change for many of the ragged schools. Within four years thirty-nine ragged schools with nearly 9,000 pupils had been taken over by the local-education boards that had been established.[35] The ragged schools had played a vital role through the period when the state had been unwilling to offer free universal education, but that need was now diminishing. For a period, some children did not fit into the new school system, and the work of some ragged schools continued into the 1880s. Other ragged schools became juvenile missions, aiming their work at teenage children and running meetings for them on Sundays and clubs on weekday evenings. The provision of Bible classes, mothers' meetings, savings clubs and free or cheap meals to the poor continued.

---

[32] Ware's work is described in ibid. 19–24.
[33] Mair, *Ragged Schools*, 197–200.
[34] Heasman, *Evangelicals*, 81.
[35] Mair, *Ragged Schools*, 44.

The Barefoot Mission was started to provide children with boots and shoes so they could attend school. The Ragged School Union became the Shaftesbury Society and focused its activities on the care and welfare of children.[36] One significant part of its work was with children with disabilities, ensuring they received medical care and the support they needed. The Shaftesbury Society developed centres to which disabled children, who were largely excluded from mainstream schools, could go each day and receive education and occupational therapy.

Despite the huge amount of work they undertook, the work of the ragged schools is often ignored in histories of education.[37] Yet between the movement starting and 1870 it was believed that in London alone 300,000 children had passed through the ragged schools.[38] The ragged schools' achievement is much debated. In such assessments it needs to be recognized that they were dealing with the dispossessed and marginalized of society, who had lived without structure or order in their lives. Most lacked a settled home life and had little, or no, parental support. Educationally, progress was certainly limited – some children got basic reading and writing skills. The social researcher Henry Mayhew (1812–87) presented statistics indicating that just as ragged schools had increased in number, so had juvenile delinquency, and suggested that a small amount of education made the children even cleverer criminals! Others pointedly disagreed. In 1848 the London City Mission highlighted police reports from the King's Cross district in London of a significant drop in juvenile delinquency since a local ragged school had started. Similar claims were made by Thomas Wright, a prison reformer in Manchester, who attributed a drop in the number of juveniles in prison to the care of the ragged schools for the fatherless and destitute children, who were the chief source of the criminal fraternity.[39]

Lord Shaftesbury concurred, arguing that without the work of institutions such as the ragged schools there would be a need for twice the number of troops and three times the number of police.[40] Towards the end of the nineteenth century one Recorder of London reckoned that juvenile crime in the city had been reduced by 75 per cent 'mainly by the ragged schools', and it was reported that a politician put those rescued from a life of crime by the work of the ragged

---

[36] Heasman, *Evangelicals*, 84.

[37] Thomas Laqueur makes no mention of ragged-school work, even though many grew out of Sunday schools: T. W. Laqueur, *Religion and Respectability: Sunday Schools and Working Class Culture, 1780–1850* (New Haven, Conn.: Yale University Press, 1976).

[38] Mair, *Ragged Schools*, 65.

[39] Heasman, *Evangelicals*, 86–87.

[40] Finlayson, *Shaftesbury*, 593.

schools as 300,000.[41] One historian has asserted that the ragged schools were the 'most successful of the agencies established by the Evangelicals in their efforts to convert the urban poor'.[42]

Character study:
Thomas Guthrie (1803–73) – Scotland

On the south side of Edinburgh's famous Princes Street stands a statue of a tall man in clerical robes. In his left hand is a Bible, and his right arm shelters a small street child. The statue's inscription summarizes the achievements of Thomas Guthrie: 'an eloquent preacher of the gospel, founder of the original ragged industrial schools, a friend of the poor and the oppressed'.

Guthrie studied theology, and then science and medicine, at Edinburgh University, and later in Paris. It was a training well suited for the realities of urban ministry. After an initial parish charge in Arbirlot, near Brechin, he was called to Old Greyfriars Church in Edinburgh. When that parish was divided in two because of its size, he chose St John's Church, the poorer of the two new parishes created. Then, in 1843, with the Disruption in the Church of Scotland, he joined the Free Church, becoming the minister of St John's Free Church, located in the centre of the city adjacent to the area of greatest poverty and disease.[43] Throughout his ministry Guthrie chose to live in the heart of the city, and his home was within three minutes' walk of its most deprived area.[44]

In 1867 William Anderson observed of Edinburgh that it was 'impossible to realise the terrible state of many of the houses and the abject condition of their inhabitants unless they are visited'.[45] Inspired by Thomas Chalmers' aphorism 'a house going minister, a church-going people', Guthrie visited every house in his parish. One tall, rickety structure crammed 150 people into its multiple storeys, from cellar to garret.[46] He later recalled how on these visits he never saw 'a Bible, or indeed any book at all', adding:

> I often stood in rooms . . . where father, mother, and half a dozen children had neither bed nor bedding, unless a heap of straw and dirty rags

[41] Quoted in B. Blackburn, *Noble Lord: The Seventh Earl of Shaftesbury* (London: Home & Van Thal, 1949), 165.

[42] I. Bradley, *The Call to Seriousness: The Evangelical Impact on the Victorians* (London: Jonathan Cape, 1976), 46.

[43] W. H. O. Smeaton, *Thomas Guthrie* (Edinburgh, 1900), 20–36.

[44] Guthrie, *Memoir* (London: Isbister, 1874), 309–310.

[45] W. Anderson, *The Poor of Edinburgh and Their Homes* (Edinburgh: Menzies, 1867), 2.

[46] A. L. Drummond, 'Thomas Guthrie', in R. S. Wright (ed.), *Fathers of the Kirk* (London: Oxford University Press, 1960), 171.

huddled in a corner could be called so. I have heard the wail of children crying for bread, and their mother had none to give them . . . I have known a father turn his step-daughter to the street at night – bidding the sobbing girl who bloomed into womanhood, earn her bread there as others were doing. I have bent over the foul pallet of a dying lad to hear him whisper how his father and mother – who were sitting half-drunk by the fireside had pulled the blankets off his body to sell them for drink.[47]

For this work the brilliant preacher Guthrie was derided for wasting his time on 'paupers and pickpockets'.[48] Guthrie quickly became aware of large numbers of children on Edinburgh's streets, abandoned by their parents or woefully neglected by them. In 1847 he believed there were 'at least a thousand, and some said thousands'.[49] Their circumstances, he argued, were a direct cause of many being led into crime.[50] The governor of Edinburgh Prison reported in 1845 that 740 children under the age of 14 (of whom 245 were under 10) had been committed to his prison in the three previous years.[51] Guthrie visited the slums day and night. In one police station he found homeless children who came in each night to find shelter in the cells, before being sent out each morning: 'this wreck of society, like the *wrack* of the sea-shore, came drifting in again at evening-tide'. He recalled an 8-year-old boy, without mother, father or friends sleeping on the stone floor of the cells, a brick serving as his pillow. Guthrie was appalled at the neglect of 'a society, more criminal than he, and punished for his fate, not his fault'.[52]

Compassion and moral outrage at the cruelty and neglect by adults drove his determination to help the street children. He recalled coming across a little child about 7 years of age, who wore pathetically thin clothes, soaked to the skin in the blast of the storm, standing in a flooded gutter. The poor boy was singing a song and holding out his emaciated hand, which was trembling with the cold, to beg for money. Guthrie did what he could to help him, but recalled:

my indignation burned against the monster of a father or mother who would send out an infant on such a day . . . to get money (as I ascertained

---

[47] T. Guthrie, *Out of Harness*, ch. 1 <http://www.newble.co.uk/guthrie/harness1.html>, accessed 20 April 2020.

[48] Smeaton, *Guthrie*, 40.

[49] T. Guthrie, *A Plea for Ragged Schools: Or, Prevention Better Than Cure* (Edinburgh: Elder, 1847), 9, 16.

[50] T. Guthrie, *Memorial on the Claim of Ragged Industrial Schools to Government Support* (Edinburgh: Jack, 1852), 4.

[51] Guthrie, *Memoir*, 439–440.

[52] Guthrie, *Plea*, 14–15; emphasis original.

was the fact) and spend it in vice instead of spending it on that poor infant.[53]

In 1847 Guthrie published his first *Plea for Ragged Schools*, and a second followed in 1849. They circulated widely and extracts were published in newspapers. With the donations that flowed in, a building near Guthrie's church was rented, where children were each day offered education and a chance to learn the 'truths of the gospel'. Guthrie made 'The Bible, the whole Bible, and nothing but the Bible; the Bible without note or comment – without the authoritative interpretation of priest or presbyter – as the foundation of all its religious teaching.'[54] Children also learned reading, writing and arithmetic, and were offered training in basic job skills.[55] Guthrie recorded the background of some of the street children:

Found homeless, and provided with lodgings 72;
children with their father dead 140;
deserted by parents 43;
Fatherless, with drunken mothers 77;
Motherless, with drunken fathers 66;
Who have been in the Police Office 75;
Who have been in Prison 20.[56]

The school day started with a shower before breakfast, with Guthrie believing that 'improvement in cleanliness' was the 'first step towards moral revolution'.[57] Lessons were provided in the morning, before dinner at noon, and religious education and training in future employment skills in the afternoon, and a meal at the end of the day. Food was made available even on Sundays.[58]

The project won the support of evangelicals across denominations, a major achievement in a time of often bitter religious division. Within a year Guthrie was running three ragged industrial schools in Edinburgh, one for boys, one for girls and one mixed school, and 265 children were being supported.[59] By

---

[53] Guthrie, *Memoir*, 488.

[54] Ibid. 455.

[55] Ibid. 442–447.

[56] T. Guthrie, 'The Edinburgh Original Ragged School', in *Out of Harness* (New York: Strahan, 1867), ch. 1.

[57] T. Guthrie, *Eight Months' Experience of the Edinburgh Original Ragged or Industrial Schools* (Edinburgh: John Elder, 1848), 17.

[58] Heasman, *Evangelicals*, 75, 84–85; O. Chadwick, *The Victorian Church*, vol. 2 (London: A&C Black, 1970), 307.

[59] Guthrie, *Memoir*, 456.

1851 the schools could report that 216 children had completed their education and training, and were earning their living through employment. There was also evidence the schools were reducing juvenile crime. Between 1847, the year the ragged schools were started, and 1851, the percentage of Edinburgh's prison population under 14 years of age fell from 5 per cent to 1 per cent; that is, from 315 children to 56.[60] The Governor of the Edinburgh Prison believed Guthrie's ragged industrial schools had 'been the principal instruments in effecting so desirable a change'. Begging was also reduced.[61] Guthrie's evidence before an 1852 committee of the House of Commons helped the passing of two Acts of Parliament giving magistrates powers to send juvenile offenders under 16 years of age to a reformatory school rather than prison.[62]

Through the ragged schools a significant number of street children had their prospects in life dramatically changed. In 1867 Guthrie asserted that employment had been found for 500 former pupils.[63] Of 60 boys who had recently completed their schooling, 1 was in prison and 3 were in reformatories. But of the remaining 56, 2 were in the army, 2 in the navy and 48 were apprentices. Guthrie was astonished and delighted when attending the Edinburgh University graduation ceremony to recognize that one of those graduating 'had been one of my Ragged School boys'.[64] His vision was holistic and wholesome, attributing success not only to prayer but also to the 'allied powers of patience, and porridge'.[65] What delighted Guthrie most was news of the children showing 'a decided change, not of outward conduct only, but of heart'. He recorded numerous examples of children converted through the ragged-school work. Guthrie also regularly received letters from former pupils including personal testimony of their continuing Christian life and witness.[66]

However, children still flooded on to city streets. After the 1872 Scottish Education Act, the state began to take on the responsibility for the education of all children, something Guthrie welcomed. He believed that no child should be 'allowed to grow up without a good useful education', and it was the responsibility of society to supply that need.[67]

As one of Scotland's pre-eminent preachers, Guthrie attracted one of Edinburgh's largest congregations, and addressed crowds of thousands in

---

[60] Ibid. 459–460.

[61] Ibid. 461.

[62] Ibid. 462–472.

[63] Guthrie, *Out of Harness*, 19.

[64] Guthrie, *Memoir*, 491–493.

[65] T. Guthrie, quoted in J. L. Newton, 'Thomas Guthrie, Preacher and Philanthropist', University of Edinburgh PhD thesis, 1951, 83; Guthrie, *Memoir*, 171.

[66] Guthrie, *Memoir*, 492.

[67] Ibid. 482.

promoting various Free Church causes. He served on the committees of at least five other charities in Edinburgh that offered relief to those who were sick or homeless.[68] Yet it was his firm view that

> I never engaged in a cause . . . that I believe on my death-bed I will look back on with more pleasure or gratitude to God, than that He led me to work for Ragged Schools. I have the satisfaction . . . that God has made me an instrument in His hand of saving many a poor creature from a life of misery and crime.[69]

---

[68] Smeaton, *Guthrie*, 154.
[69] Guthrie, *Memoir*, 496.

9

Care for orphans

From the late eighteenth through to the early twentieth century huge population movements in Europe and the USA brought millions of people hungry for
work into urban areas. They were predominantly young adults, and among
them was a high birth rate. Grim environmental and working conditions reaped
a heavy toll, with a high death rate resulting in large numbers of children
orphaned of one or more parent. The state provision was the workhouse, where
Dickens described the lot of the orphan as a 'humble, half-starved drudge – to
be cuffed and buffeted through the world – despised by all, and pitied by none'.[1]
The desperate and urgent need of orphans suddenly thrown into abject
destitution by the death of their parents made the care and support of orphan
children a deeply embedded part of evangelical social action.

When August Francke was appointed as a lecturer at the University of
Halle, Germany, in 1691, and a pastor in the neighbouring village of Glaucha,
he began a programme of reformation centred on personal commitment to
Christ, devotional reading of Scripture and pious living. Deeply concerned by
the large number of outcast children in his parish, especially the orphans, he
longed to help them. Not paid by the university and poorly paid as a minister,
he had no means to help the orphans apart from trusting in God. An
unexpectedly high collection at the Easter service in 1695 led him to start a
charity school. He then took on the support of a family of four infant children
whose parents had died, and then two more.

Francke later wrote, 'He who is the Father to the fatherless and is able to do
for us far more than we can ask or think, came to my assistance in a matter that
my reason could never have anticipated.' After two very large donations he was
able to start building an orphanage, which was opened in 1701. In his account
of the building and running of the orphanage Francke stressed God's provision

---

[1] C. Dickens, *Oliver Twist* (1838) (London: Thomas Nelson, n.d.), 4.

for their needs at each step, even in the most challenging circumstances. On no occasion had the children ever to go without a meal. By the time of Francke's death in 1727 his schools were providing education for 2,300 children, there were 134 in the orphanage and 240 deprived children were receiving free daily meals. Francke unleashed a wave of generosity – a local apothecary supplied medicines free of charge, and even the local chimney sweep swept the chimneys for free. Francke attributed all to the hand of God: 'He has led me in a way I knew not of . . . He has done for me more than I could have even imagined.'[2] Francke's example was to have a powerful effect on George Müller, as the character study in this chapter shows.

The Congregationalist minister Andrew Reed (1787–1862) epitomized the connection between evangelicalism and social action, and between spiritual and social transformation. In 1811 he began a ministry in Stepney, in London's East End, that spanned more than fifty years. Amid the growing poverty and social problems, he found mothers and children who had turned to crime, including prostitution, to feed their families. Orphan children were particularly at risk.[3] Reed understood his calling in Christian ministry as following the example of Christ, who preached the good news and went about doing good. Within a year Reed took two small orphans into his own home and cared for them with the help of his sister.[4] There were other orphanages in London at the time, such as the famous Foundling Hospital, which catered especially for abandoned illegitimate children, but there were generally few places for orphaned children until the 1860s.[5] Despite his own lack of personal resources, being the son of a struggling watchmaker, in 1814 with the help of friends he started a small orphanage in a rented house. The first two girls admitted were those Reed and his sister had personally supported for nearly three years.[6] They took a deep practical and caring interest in the running of the home, visiting it regularly. When there was an allegation that a child had been disciplined incorrectly, the matter was investigated promptly. When another child complained of being hungry the order was given that children be given 'as much as they could eat' at all meal times. Reed created a family atmosphere. They arranged for each child to have a box under his or her bed in which

---

[2] *Memoirs of Hermann August Francke* (Philadelphia, Pa.: American Sunday School Union, 1831), 109–140; quotations from 111, 136–137.

[3] A. Reed and C. Reed, *Memoirs of the Life and Philanthropic Labours of Andrew Reed* (London: Strahan, 1863), 89. See also I. J. Shaw, *The Greatest Is Charity: The Life of Andrew Reed, Preacher and Philanthropist* (Darlington: Evangelical Press, 2005).

[4] Reed and Reed, *Memoirs*, 86–87.

[5] K. Heasman, *Evangelicals in Action* (London: Geoffrey Bles, 1963), 89.

[6] Reed and Reed, *Memoirs*, 92–93.

to keep personal possessions.[7] In 1815 the orphanage took the name 'The London Orphan Asylum'.[8]

Reed was bold in seeking patrons for his work. In 1815 he secured the support of the Duke of Kent, father of the future Queen Victoria. Other royal patrons followed, including King George IV in 1823, King William IV in 1833 and then Queen Victoria in 1837 and Prince Albert in 1843.[9] By 1818 he needed to raise £3,000 per year to feed, clothe and house the children, a huge sum for the times. Through the project he sought to glorify God, as he wrote in his journal, 'May He who is the judge of the widow and the fatherless prosper our cause and purify our motives.'[10]

In 1820 some 150 children were being cared for, and in the following year the construction began of a purpose-built orphanage at Clapton, in East London. It was to be a true 'home' for the orphan, 'a friend to guide his steps, relieve his wants and wipe away his tears'.[11] Reed acknowledged, 'I am indebted to God for the thought, energy, opportunity, and disposition . . . If the London Orphan Asylum exists, its maker and builder is God, to whom may all the glory be given.'[12] Education was given a high priority and was essential if the children were to obtain future employment. When they left in their mid teens they moved into apprenticeships in various trades, and then increasingly into situations in the offices of City firms or as clerks. This contrasted with other orphanages that at the time sent children as young as 6 to work as apprentices in factories in the Midlands and north of England.[13] Most of the children who passed through George Müller's orphanage in Bristol became domestic servants.[14]

The children who came to the London Orphan Asylum were in desperate need. Eliza Evans was one of five destitute children whose father had died and their mother was terminally ill. John Aveling's mother had perished in a fire, and six months later his heartbroken father died, leaving three children. Jane and Amelia Evans were two of six children whose father had collapsed and died of a heart attack while their mother was in labour with her sixth child.[15]

---

[7] Shaw, *Reed*, 70.

[8] Reed and Reed, *Memoirs*, 93.

[9] Ibid. 95, 99.

[10] Ibid. 96.

[11] Shaw, *Reed*, 103.

[12] Reed and Reed, *Memoirs*, 114.

[13] R. K. McClure, *Coram's Children: The London Foundling Hospital in the Eighteenth Century* (London: Yale University Press, 1981), 150–153.

[14] G. Müller, *A Narrative of the Lord's Dealings with George Müller* (London: J. Nisbet, 1855), 164.

[15] Shaw, *Reed*, 104.

The London Orphan Asylum accepted children aged between 7 and 14, and Reed quickly became aware of a need to do something for younger children. Therefore, in 1827 a project for children under the age of 7 was started, and in 1828 the Duke of Gloucester, the brother of King George IV, agreed to become a patron of the charity. Within a year the Infant Orphan Asylum was catering for twenty-eight children. Reed frequently called at the home, discussing arrangements for the education of the children, their diet and clothing. He bought toys for the nursery, and pictures for the walls. He could not bear to hear little children crying, and insisted that staff should always seek out the cause: Were they unwell, or unhappy? Contact with surviving relatives was strongly encouraged. His practice was underpinned by the theological conviction that in the orphanage were children made in the image of God. They were therefore 'the noblest of the Creator's works' and deserved the best: 'Let this training be worthy of such a being.'[16]

By 1837 the Infant Orphan Asylum had 103 children under its care, with a further 80 seeking admission. The backgrounds of the children were often tragic. Jemima Usher's father, a tallow chandler, had died leaving a wife and three children before Jemima's mother perished in a catastrophic fire. After the death of 9-month-old Ellen Griffiths' father, a seaman, her mother had been killed when run over by a cart while carrying the little infant in her arms. Miraculously, Ellen had escaped.[17]

In 1841 the foundation stone for a permanent home for the Infant Orphan Asylum was laid by Prince Albert at Snaresbrook, on the edge of Wanstead Forest.[18] Sadly, in 1843 Reed had to resign from the charity when Anglicans on the board began to insist that it was an Anglican institution (despite its founder being a Nonconformist), and that only the catechism of the Church of England could be used for the religious education of the little children.[19] For similar reasons he stepped down from the London Orphan Asylum in 1844. Yet the orphanages retained a firm place in his heart. More than ten years later he noted, 'The London Orphan Asylum reports 410 in the house, and 2,228 as having been provided for. Thank God!'[20]

Reed was resolved not to 'carry uncharitableness into the work of charity'.[21] Within a year he had started a new orphanage project, the Asylum for Fatherless Children, designed to avoid denominational rivalries. By the end of July 1844

---

16 Ibid. 124–127.
17 Ibid. 131–132.
18 Reed and Reed, *Memoirs*, 133.
19 Ibid. 135–137.
20 Ibid. 240.
21 Ibid. 234.

six children were in its care. The orphanage initially met in rented properties before, in 1853, a site was bought near Purley, Surrey, with the hope the children would be brought up amid fresh air and rural scenery. The building was opened in 1858 as Reed approached his seventy-first birthday. Although a non-denominational charity, Reed was held in such esteem that Queen Victoria became a strong supporter of the charity, as did her son, the Prince of Wales.[22]

Numbers being cared for rose steadily. In February 1852 there were 89 children, and in 1868 144 boys and 105 girls in the care of the institution.[23] As with the London Orphan Asylum, the educational focus was strong – pitched at grammar school standard, much higher than the basic level offered in most orphanages. Children who left went on to work in the offices of lawyers, bankers and architects, or entered retail trades and worked for drapers, chemists or warehousemen. Girls found employment as teachers or governesses, or worked in shops or as dressmakers, telegraph clerks or nursery maids.[24]

Supporters of the charity believed Reed succeeded in producing a 'Happy Home', where Christian faith and character were cultivated. Reed's model and motivation remained that of Jesus Christ, who 'pitied, loved, and sheltered such little ones when He was Himself on earth'.[25] His greatest desire, that the children would come to a personal faith in Jesus Christ, was fulfilled in many cases, and large numbers went on to become Sunday school teachers. One girl, who died of heart disease soon after leaving the orphanage did so expressing a 'firm though simple trust in the Saviour she learned to love'.[26] By the time of his death in 1862 the Asylum for Fatherless Children had provided care for nearly 500 children, and the Infant Orphan Asylum had cared for more than 1,900 children. Through his orphanage charities more than £750,000 had been raised.[27]

In 1867 C. H. Spurgeon, pastor of the Metropolitan Tabernacle, then the largest congregation in Britain, received a gift of £20,000 from a widow, Mrs Anne Hillyard, to start an orphanage run on 'simple Gospel principles'.[28] A site in Stockwell was chosen. It was established for children bereaved of their father, or both parents, and who were from 'Evangelical churches dissenting from the Church of England'. Spurgeon's desire was that 'all that we believe and hold dear shall be taught to the children of our poorer adherents'. One biographer called the orphanage 'the greatest sermon Mr Spurgeon ever preached'.[29]

---

[22] Shaw, *Reed*, 253–259.

[23] *Asylum for Fatherless Children Annual Report 1868* (London, 1868), xxviii.

[24] Shaw, *Reed*, 265.

[25] Reed and Reed, *Memoirs*, 248.

[26] Shaw, *Reed*, 265–266.

[27] Ibid. 377.

[28] Heasman, *Evangelicals*, 91.

[29] W. Y. Fullerton, *C. H. Spurgeon, A Biography* (London: Williams & Norgate, 1920), 246.

The orphanage depended heavily on giving from Baptist churches, and Spurgeon confessed he lacked Müller's 'courageous silence' and made frequent appeals for his orphanage. The initial sum required was more than £100,000, and in the early 1870s Spurgeon reckoned it cost at least £10 a day to feed the 220 orphans then in his care. Grand bazaars were held to raise funds, and some of the orphanage houses were paid for by individual donors, including the workmen employed in their construction.[30] By 1879 the orphanage was caring for more than 500 children. Spurgeon often visited it, greeted excitedly by the children. He would write personally to them, expressing his hope 'I want to see you all happy here and hereafter.'[31]

The Brixton Orphanage was started by Mrs Montague, who had undertaken extensive social-work visitation in the area in connection with the Metropolitan Tabernacle. In the course of her work she came across many destitute girls, and began by building a home for their care in her garden. This eventually merged into the Stockwell Orphanage. A close associate of Spurgeon was Archibald Brown, pastor of the East London Tabernacle, who also started an orphanage for the 100 destitute children the church was supporting.[32]

In 1869 Thomas Bowman Stephenson, the minister of Waterloo Road Wesleyan Chapel, established what became the National Children's Home in Lambeth. Through his ministry in the area he became aware of the large number of homeless children found in Southwark, who often associated with homeless adults. A workman's cottage was rented and the first boys were accepted for support. Eventually a home was started in Bethnal Green, and branch homes established to accommodate children with different needs. An early appeal for the charity became a famous rhyme:

> Poor little scaramouch, homeless and sad,
> Ragged little scaramouch, dirty and bad,
> Father gone to prison, mother in her grave,
> Vice and crimes learnt betimes; who is there to save?
> 'In the street all day, Sir'; yes, but where at night?
> Where he goes no one knows; somewhere out of sight.[33]

---

[30] G. Holden Pike, *The Life and Work of Charles Haddon Spurgeon*, vol. 4 (London: Cassell, 1894), repr. (London: Banner of Truth, 1991), 219, 221; vol. 5, 41.

[31] C. H. Spurgeon, *Autobiography of C. H. Spurgeon*, vol. 3 (London: Passmore & Alabaster, 1900), 173.

[32] Heasman, *Evangelicals*, 92.

[33] W. Bradfield, *The Life of Thomas Bowman Stephenson* (London: C. H. Kelly, 1913), 95.

The Waifs and Strays Society had similar beginnings after Edward and Robert de Montjoie, teachers in a Lambeth Sunday school, found that two boys were missing from their class. On enquiry they found their father had died and their mother had sent them to beg bread from men at the local gasworks. With their friends the two brothers rented a house in East Dulwich and started to support these and other children. Their policy was to create a series of small branch homes scattered across the country to meet local needs. This work eventually became the Church of England Children's Society.[34]

A number of orphanages developed from ragged schools. The National Refuges for Homeless and Destitute Children, later called the Shaftesbury Homes, were started in a hayloft over a cowshed in the notorious 'rookery' of St Giles in Central London. Eventually a former gin palace was bought and converted into dormitories for around 100 children. The children were also educated and given basic training for work. The Manchester and Salford Refuges, started by Leonard Shaw, similarly developed out of a ragged school. They started in small, dingy premises off Deansgate, with a cellar used as a living room and children sleeping in hammocks upstairs. Eventually a children's garden village was established.

The homes begun by William Quarrier in Glasgow developed out of a ragged school he ran in Jamaica Street. Quarrier owned a boot and shoe shop in the centre of the city and regularly encountered destitute children. In 1876 his City Orphan Home was built, but needs soon outstripped the space available and Quarrier resolved to build a garden village for the orphans at Bridge of Weir in Renfrewshire. Here a series of cottage homes were constructed, where children could live in 'families'.[35] Some orphanages made provision for children needing special care. Quarrier developed homes specifically for children with tuberculosis and epilepsy.

Evangelicals not only took the lead in establishing homes, but also in developing the methods of childcare for orphans. Over time the great barrack-like orphanages – where hundreds of children lived by strict rules, wore a distinctive uniform and were fed in a frugal manner – gave way to smaller units where children received more care and attention. The inspiration for the family system appears to have been the work of Johann Wichern of the Lutheran Inner Mission, which in the 1840s emphasized brotherly love, charity and education.[36]

---

[34] Heasman, *Evangelicals*, 91.

[35] See W. Quarrier, *A Narrative of Facts Relative to Work Done for Christ* (Glasgow: George Gallie & Son, 1872, 1900); J. Climie, *William Quarrier, the Orphan's Friend* (Glasgow: Pickering & Inglis, 1902); J. Ross, *The Power I Pledge, Being a Centenary Study of the Life of William Quarrier and the Work He Pioneered* (Glasgow: Quarrier's Homes, 1971).

[36] On Kaiserswerth and its pioneering nursing training see chapter 14 below.

In 1833 Wichern, who had been running a Sunday school in a poor area of Hamburg, opened the Rauhe Haus (Rough House). This was a cottage that had been donated, and into which Wichern, his wife Amanda and his mother moved, along with twelve destitute boys. Over time further children were admitted, and they too were grouped into families of ten to twelve living in separate cottages, with a house father and mother. Other buildings were added to the site over time, including a gymnasium, schoolhouse, infirmary and workshops, where skills such as carpentry and shoemaking were learned. Central to the site was the prayer house.[37]

Wichern's methods became widely known, and were gradually adopted by others, including Stephenson's National Children's Home. The family system, either in the form of cottage homes grouped together, or scattered in different parts of a town, became common. At the Farningham and Swanley Homes for Boys, established in 1867, every cottage was looked after by a Christian couple. Each family took meals together, shared playtimes together, started and ended the day with family prayers and went to church together. Spurgeon in the Stockwell Orphanage adopted the same pattern.

One of the most famous pioneers of new approaches to orphan care was Thomas Barnardo. Born in Dublin in 1845, he was converted as a teenager in 1862, threw himself into evangelistic work and joined a local Brethren assembly. In 1866 he moved to London and began medical studies at the London Hospital, and was active in urban mission.[38] In 1868 he founded the East End Juvenile Mission in Limehouse, and ran prayer meetings, Bible studies and evening classes. He also started a small church.[39] The young lads he found on the streets were a particular focus of his attention. One bitterly cold night young Jim Jarvis came into the ragged school, without shoes, dressed only in a few rags, asking if he could stay the night. Barnardo told him he should go home to his mother and father, but he replied, 'Got no home . . . Got no mother . . . Got no father . . . Don't live nowhere.' Barnardo asked Jim to show him where he was sleeping, and he was taken to a gutter on a shed roof where eleven other boys were asleep. The discovery, Barnardo recalled, 'determined my subsequent career. Often . . . I have seen before me the upturned piteous faces of these eleven outcast boys, realized their awful misery and destitution, heard their mute appeal for assistance.' Barnardo resolved to devote the rest of his 'future life, by God's help, to their rescue and training'.[40] He was appalled that nobody appeared to care

37 Heasman, *Evangelicals*, 97–98. See also <http://www.childrenshomes.org.uk/RauheHaus>, accessed 14 April 2020.
38 S. L. E. Barnardo, *Memoirs of the Late Dr Barnardo* (London: Hodder & Stoughton, 1907), 28–32.
39 Ibid. 51–53, 58.
40 Ibid. 78–79.

for either their bodies or souls, and resolved that evangelistic work be combined with care for their physical welfare. In 1870 he started a home for homeless boys on Stepney Causeway, providing support for thirty-three teenagers.[41]

Barnardo was a strong advocate of temperance, and in 1872 bought the prominent Edinburgh Castle pub in Limehouse, east London, behind which was a notorious music hall. This he turned into the British Working Men's Coffee Palace, an alternative social gathering place for men. It became the centre of the social work he had started among the needy.[42]

One night Barnardo met with an 11-year-old boy, John Somers, who had lived on the streets for four years, sleeping among the barrels and packing cases near Covent Garden or Billingsgate markets. He was with a group of other boys, and they pleaded with Barnardo for shelter for the night. Space in the home was limited, so he picked the five who looked most in need, promising to return in a week's time. Sadly, John's body was found several days later by a porter at the market. The inquest determined he had died of malnutrition and hypothermia.[43] It was another turning point, leading Barnardo to adopt his 'No Destitute Child Refused Admission' policy. It was far-sighted, but placed huge strain on his work.

After Barnardo was gifted Mossford Lodge, Barkingside, Essex, he used it to provide a home for girls.[44] He raised money to build thirty cottages in the grounds, modelled on the system pioneered by Wichern in Germany.[45] By 1883 the Village Home for Girls, in Ilford, had a school, laundry, church and a population of more than 1,000 children. In 1905, the year of Barnardo's death, 1,500 girls lived in the village.[46] Barnardo also promoted boarding-out (fostering) schemes, which were started in 1887, with more than 2,000 children fostered by 1893. To help the orphans gain future employment, he started a woodchopping brigade and training for other forms of employment.[47]

However, controversy followed Barnardo. He never finished his studies at the London Hospital, but used the title 'Doctor', which attracted significant criticism when it became known. He eventually spent several months in Edinburgh formally completing his medical studies. His practice of taking sole

---

[41] Ibid. 84–86.
[42] Heasman, *Evangelicals*, 92.
[43] Barnardo, *Memoirs*, 353–354.
[44] Ibid. 117–124.
[45] Heasman, *Evangelicals*, 99.
[46] Barnardo, *Memoirs*, 124–141.
[47] G. Wagner, 'Barnardo, Thomas John (1845–1905), Philanthropist and Founder of Dr Barnardo's Homes', in *Dictionary of National Biography* (Oxford: Oxford University Press, 2004), online edition <https://www.oxforddnb.com>, accessed 12 December 2020. See also G. Wagner, *Barnardo* (London: Weidenfeld & Nicolson, 1979).

control of the funds of his organization led to rumours about his financial probity, and costly court cases followed as he sought to clear his name, in which he was partially successful.[48] There were also legal challenges from three mothers whose children Barnardo rescued from neglect, and whom they then demanded back. A particular issue for which Barnardo has faced criticism was his policy of promoting the emigration to the colonies of some of the children he rescued. He believed it gave children a fresh start away from the scenes of their earlier degradation. It also helped relieve the pressure on his children's homes, occasioned by the no-child-turned-away policy.[49]

The pioneer of child migration was Annie Macpherson (1833–1904), a Scottish evangelical Quaker, who developed a scheme for resettling children from her Home of Industry in London. Here the children received training and preparation in skills such as carpentry and farm work to give them employment opportunities in the colonies. She accompanied the first boys she sent to Canada in 1870, and they were set up in apprenticeships with local families and businesses. Subsequent parties of children were taken by other members of the Macpherson family. The scheme proved popular, and children were regularly referred for emigration by Poor Law Guardians, clergy and sometimes the police. Macpherson started similar projects in Edinburgh and Liverpool, and was very influential on Barnardo's policy. However, as the schemes grew, in the 1880s criticism followed over the lack of proper knowledge of the children being sent, and of the conditions in which they were living in Canada.[50]

When Barnardo adopted the policy, it was popular with supporters and the government. Between 1882 and 1939 Barnardo's organization sent more than 30,000 children to Canada, but by 1900 the care the children received there was being questioned. Some were badly treated. Many were lonely, far from home, and had little prospect of ever seeing such family as they had left. This well-intentioned but misguided policy continued until 1967.[51]

Relentless in his drive for expansion, Barnardo opened seven regional centres, each with an open-door policy. By 1905 his homes were caring for some 34,000 children. During his lifetime it is thought he rescued some 60,000 children. Yet his desperation to help as many children as he could, and extend the work, took a heavy toll on his health.[52] Barnardo also withdrew from the Brethren, many of whom had been his staunchest supporters, and became an

---

[48] Wagner, 'Barnardo'.
[49] Ibid.
[50] Heasman, *Evangelicals*, 102–105.
[51] See <https://www.barnardos.org.uk/who-we-are/our-history>, accessed 22 September 2020.
[52] Wagner, 'Barnardo'.

Anglican. The debts had mounted to nearly £250,000 by the time of his death in 1905, before he was 60 years old.[53]

The evangelical commitment to social action in the care of orphans was a powerful example of holistic mission. The growing sensitivity to the welfare needs of children and the recognition that it was the responsibility of the community to care for the weakest and most vulnerable, rather than ostracizing and condemning them to the degradation of the workhouse, owe much to the pioneering efforts of evangelicals. The work established by these evangelicals lasted well into the twentieth century.

Character study: George Müller (1805–98) – England

The question is sometimes asked whether God would give someone £1 million if he or she prayed for it? According to the records of George Müller, through prayer more than £1.5 million was donated for the care of orphans, a vast sum for the time. As a divinity student, Müller had stayed in lodgings at Halle, and every day witnessed the continuing care and education provided in the orphanage founded by Francke. Müller, a Prussian émigré, who by 1835 was leading a modest-sized congregation in Bristol, was inspired by a biography of Francke to attempt something similar. The following year he commenced an orphanage project, drawing on Francke's principle of 'reliance on God alone' to supply its needs. Müller had seen such radical faith devotion among other early members of the Brethren movement, including his brother-in-law, Anthony Norris Groves (1795–1853), an Exeter dentist who served as a missionary in Baghdad and then India. Groves has been called the 'Father of faith missions'.[54] Müller was convinced that an orphanage run on 'faith' principles would be a powerful testament to the trustworthiness of God, who would be glorified as people witnessed his provision, never forsaking 'those who rely on Him'.

Müller's personal resources were extremely limited, having struggled to pay his tax bill the year he launched the orphanage. Nonetheless, he was moved with compassion for orphan children who often came to his door begging for food or money. He longed to provide for both their physical and spiritual welfare.[55] The needs were very great. In 1851, 42 per cent of Bristol's population

---

[53] Ibid.

[54] R. B. Dann, *Father of Faith Missions: The Life and Times of Anthony Norris Groves* (Carlisle: Authentic Media, 2004).

[55] G. Müller, *A Narrative of Some of the Lord's Dealings with George Müller* (London: J. Nisbet, 1855), 138–152.

was under 15 years of age, and through the prevalence of disease and poor living conditions many were bereaved of their parents.[56] Müller focused on destitute children who had lost both mother and father.[57]

The first Orphan House was opened in 1836, with accommodation for thirty children. They were cared for by a matron and a governess. Initially, girls aged between 7 and 12 were admitted, but by the end of the year a home for infants aged 4 and above was also started. In 1837 a home for orphaned boys was also established.[58] Müller's orphanage provision was constrained by his limited resources. Children were offered a 'plain education' and limited training in basic work skills. It was hoped the boys could get into a trade; and if not, they might join the girls in domestic service. Some of the ablest girls obtained work as governesses.[59] Compared to the plight they were in when rescued, this was considered a significant achievement.

Müller was quite open with the children when there were financial and practical needs. By this means he sought to encourage their faith by giving a lived-out example of what it was to trust God, although for some it might have occasioned worry over where the next meal was coming from. Müller also broke away from the system in some other orphanages of donor's votes being needed to get admission. He retained personal control of operational matters, or placed it in the hands of those he appointed. Some who ran homes adopted Müller's faith principles, but others, such as Barnardo, believed that the amount of need was so great that more businesslike methods of fundraising had to be adopted.

As numbers increased, the initial location in Wilson Street, Bristol, where a series of buildings were rented, became less suitable, and neighbours complained about the noise made by the children. In 1846 a plot of land on Ashley Down, just outside Bristol, was purchased. The following year building work started, initially to accommodate 330 orphans. In 1851 Müller decided to expand the accommodation to 1,000 children,[60] and by 1870 five large buildings had been completed, which became the full extent of the premises. The buildings were impressive in size, but they and their furnishings were deliberately plain and utilitarian. Müller was committed to frugality in everything, so that the maximum funds might be available for spiritual work and relief of the poor elsewhere. He also believed that because the future prospects of the children

---

[56] M. Gorsky, *Patterns of Philanthropy: Charity and Society in Nineteenth-Century Bristol* (Woodbridge: Boydell & Brewer, 1999), 22.

[57] Müller, *Narrative*, 153.

[58] Ibid. 172–209.

[59] Ibid. 153, 183.

[60] A. T. Pierson, *George Müller of Bristol* (London: Pickering & Inglis, 1899), 127–129, 205–206.

were inevitably limited, they were likely to live in plain homes, and had to learn how to live on little. He felt that providing anything beyond this loving, clean, but basic, level might lead to discontentment in future life. Training for life was key, and around the buildings were gardens in which the children learned to grow vegetables. Each day was carefully ordered. From 6 am onwards the children were fully occupied through the day, but there were times for play in between school lessons, meals and training activities. Food was simple, but ample and nutritious. The average stay of children in the orphanage was ten years, but some remained as long as seventeen years.[61]

Müller adopted a number of key principles. One was to let the charity never go into debt, based on his interpretation of Romans 13:8, 'Owe no man any thing' (AV).[62] He personally acknowledged every gift, no matter how small, each of which was ascribed a number. This was all that was published in reports, along with the amount given, but no name attached. He saw every gift as a donation from God himself.[63]

There is a misconception that in fundraising Müller did nothing more than pray and the money came. Müller was in fact a very skilled promoter of the orphanage projects. He wrote letters about the needs of the orphanage, spoke to key people, mentioned the project in the pulpit and published accounts of the work. He raised awareness of the needs there were, although did not mention the sums required. Müller believed charity should be done in secret. Donations appear to have come from rich and poor alike. By not publishing a subscriber list, the anonymity provided enabled denominational prejudices to be avoided, which might have limited the charity's appeal. One key supporter was Conrad Finzel, a Bristol sugar manufacturer, who interpreted a fire at his factory as God's judgment on his lack of concern for the needs of others, and resolved to devote one third of his income to charitable projects. Müller saw great fruit from his efforts. Donations to the orphanages rose from £1,664 in 1837–8 to £20,198 in 1869–70. Even during the periods of trade depression, such as the 'hungry forties' and again in the 1860s, income to the charity continued on an upward trajectory.[64] The donations were many and varied. Among those reported in 1864 were a legacy of £800, a half sovereign that had been kept as a widow's memento of a husband who had died in the Crimean War, and a barrel of currants and five boxes of raisins for Christmas puddings![65]

---

[61] Ibid. 213–215, 280.
[62] Müller, *Narrative*, 175.
[63] Ibid. 182.
[64] Gorsky, *Philanthropy*, 158–203.
[65] G. F. Bergin (compiler), *Autobiography of George Müller* (London: Pickering & Inglis, 1929), 401.

The overriding hope was that the children would come to 'the knowledge of Jesus Christ'. Therefore, Müller ensured that staff were 'true believers' as well as being fully qualified for their work.[66] By the time of its founder's death, the Ashley Down Orphanage was able to provide a home to 2,050 orphaned boys and girls, and employed 112 staff.[67] It was not the only example of Müller's charitable work. He raised vast sums for the support of missionaries, channelled through his Scripture Knowledge Institution for Home and Abroad, including for recruits of the newly founded China Inland Mission. Its founder, James Hudson Taylor, adopted Müller's faith principles. In addition to funds for the orphanage, Müller raised a further £1.4 million for missionary causes, including helping to support more than 123,000 children in schools. He remained resolute in being unwilling to ask for money from the unconverted.[68]

Müller presented his orphanage as a testimony to God's faithfulness. He was revered as a model and guide. C. H. Spurgeon declared, 'I never heard a man who spoke more to my soul than dear Mr. George Müller.'[69]

---

[66] Müller, *Narrative*, 152–153.

[67] Bergin, *Autobiography*, 716.

[68] A. Austin, *China's Millions: The China Inland Mission and the Qing Society, 1832–1905* (Grand Rapids, Mich.: Eerdmans, 2007), 96.

[69] C. H. Spurgeon, *Metropolitan Tabernacle Pulpit Sermons*, vol. 29 (London: Passmore & Alabaster, 1883), 389.

10

Care for children at risk

Through running ragged schools, and regularly undertaking pastoral and evangelistic visitation in the poorest and most deprived areas, parts of which were considered no-go areas for the police and other authorities, evangelical Christians were afforded unique and often shocking insights into the underworld of society. They regularly came into contact with children who had been seriously abused – sometimes by their parents or carers, sometimes by strangers – and large numbers of others who were vulnerable and at risk. They were dismayed to find that intervention was extremely difficult, for children had few rights and were considered the property of their parents. Indeed, the legal protection of animals came before that of children. In Britain the Royal Society for the Prevention of Cruelty to Animals (RSPCA) had been founded in 1822, with strong support from evangelicals such as William Wilberforce. Based on this example, a similar organization was started in North America in 1866. However, a strong connection existed between those committed to the protection of animals and to the protection of the 'human animal', especially children. In these developments evangelicals played a central role.

Etta Wheeler (1834–1921) served as a Methodist urban missionary in one of the poorest parts of New York, an area later known as Hell's Kitchen. In 1873 she heard reports of a little girl called Mary Ellen who was rarely seen but whose screams were often heard. When Wheeler visited Mary Ellen's home, she noticed the girl was barefoot and poorly dressed. On her arms were bruises and wheals from a whip lying on the table. When Wheeler spoke to various agencies, including the police, begging that someone should intervene, all reported to her that it was almost impossible to remove a child from a guardian. In 1874 she appealed to Henry Bergh, the founder of the American Society for the Prevention of Cruelty to Animals (ASPCA). This was an appeal to someone outside her evangelical tradition, for Bergh was a Unitarian, but they shared a common humanitarian compassion. Bergh was well known to other evangelicals, and in 1873 had addressed the Evangelical Alliance to encourage support for the ASPCA. With the help of Bergh's associates, Wheeler carefully collected witness statements and accounts to prove that serious abuse was taking place.

Bergh, wealthy and well connected, had the wherewithal to present these to a Supreme Court judge who ordered that the girl be removed from the home and her mother be apprehended. The incident inspired Bergh to found the New York Society for the Prevention of Cruelty to Children in December 1874. Its remit was to rescue children from neglect, abandonment or cruelty, to ensure the conviction and punishment of perpetrators of abuse, and to ensure children who were victims or were at risk of cruelty were removed to places of safety.[1]

News of the American Society was read with great interest in Britain, and in 1881, at a meeting in Liverpool of the RSPCA, the formation of a society to protect children at risk was proposed. The following year the Liverpool Society for the Prevention of Cruelty to Children was formed, and a national society soon followed. The National Society for the Prevention of Cruelty to Children (NSPCC) was led by evangelicals, with Benjamin Waugh, a Congregationalist minister, as secretary and Thomas Barnardo serving on the committee.[2]

The NSPCC sought both to protect children from incidents of cruelty and to change the law so that children were given some legal protection. A series of parliamentary acts in 1889, 1894 and 1904 secured increased legal protections, making it an offence to ill-treat, neglect or abandon a child, or leave him or her in a situation of danger that might cause suffering or injury. The NSPCC employed inspectors, who called on homes when there was a report of possible cruelty or neglect to investigate the report, prevent further abuse happening and, if necessary, take the case to court.[3]

The work of evangelicals in the rescue of children at risk from abuse was not confined to Europe and North America alone, as the character study at the end of this chapter of the work of Amy Carmichael in India shows. One Indian evangelical to play a significant role was Sarasvati Mary (Pandita) Ramabai (1858–1922), a social reformer and educator. She was a high-caste Indian who converted to Christianity, and was such an able linguist that she translated the Bible into Marathi from the original Hebrew and Greek.[4] Pandita had been widowed after just three years of marriage, but went on to study medicine in Britain and North America, before returning to India to start schools and undertake rescue work for girls and women from all castes who were at risk. In 1898 near Pune she founded Mukti Sadan (House of Salvation), a vast settlement for poor widows and orphans, including homes for the elderly and sick, and a

---

[1] Etta Wheeler, *The Story of Mary Ellen: The Beginnings of a Worldwide Child-Saving Crusade* (Albany, N.Y.: American Humane Society, 1913). See also L. B. Costin, 'Unravelling the Mary Ellen Legend: Origins of the "Cruelty" Movement', *Social Service Review* 65.2 (June 1991), 203–223.

[2] K. Heasman, *Evangelicals in Action* (London: Geoffrey Bles, 1963), 83–84.

[3] Ibid. 84.

[4] R. E. Frykenberg, *Christianity in India* (Oxford: Oxford University Press, 2008), 410.

rescue home for prostitutes. By 1907 it was sheltering some 2,000 women and children. Pandita worked to end the practice of child marriage and sought to rescue child widows.[5]

One major issue in the West was the lack of protection for young girls from potential abuse, which left them open to exploitation and trafficking for prostitution. In 1880 in most European countries the age of consent was only between 12 and 14 years of age (and just 10 in Russia). In the USA in 1880 in most states it was between 10 and 12 years of age, but in Delaware it was just 7. As a result of campaigning, the age was progressively raised, so that by 1920 it was between 16 and 18 years of age in different states, but remained at 14 in Georgia until 1995.[6] In England and Wales the age of consent was raised in 1875, but it was only from 12 to 13 years of age, and voices called for urgent change.

Josephine Butler (1828–1906) is best known for her role in the rescue of prostitutes and protection of the rights of women (see chapter 18), but through her work in England she found evidence in the 1860s to 1880s of under-age girls being procured and sold into prostitution. Evidence from a government agent presented in Parliament in 1881 indicated it was possible to obtain trafficked girls 'with impunity in the streets of London'. From this developed a campaign to end what was termed 'White Slavery', although the term 'trafficking of women' would be used today, and a recognition that children and women of all ethnic and cultural backgrounds, as well as vulnerable men, were at risk. The campaigners were greeted by a wall of silence and disinterest, including from the press and churches. It was argued that such matters should never be spoken about publicly. Josephine Butler declared, 'They don't *want* to know it,' and church leaders preferred to focus on exclusively spiritual concerns.[7]

The young and enthusiastic 'Chief of Staff' of the Salvation Army Bramwell Booth joined the cause. As the son of William and Catherine Booth, the founders of the Salvation Army, his ministry took him into some of the most deprived and depraved parts of cities. He learned how women were tricked into prostitution, often as children. He declared it a 'curse over every nation', and consecrated his life to ending 'these abominations'.[8] Bramwell Booth's

---

[5] R. Sarasvati and S. Manohar Adhav, *Pandita Ramabai* (Madras: Christian Literature Society for the Christian Institute for the Study of Religion and Society, 1979), 49.

[6] M. Killias, 'The Emergence of a New Taboo: The Desexualization of Youth in Western Societies Since 1800', *European Journal on Criminal Policy and Research* 8.4 (2000), 459–477. See also M. Odem, *Delinquent Daughters: Policing and Protecting Adolescent Female Sexuality in the United States, 1885–1920* (Chapel Hill, N.C.: University of North Carolina Press, 1995).

[7] A. S. G. Butler, *Portrait of Josephine Butler* (London: Faber and Faber, 1953), 210–211; emphasis original.

[8] H. Begbie, *Life of William Booth*, vol. 2 (London: Macmillan, 1926), 37.

determination was to attack the problem at its root by stopping people being drawn into it. His parents were sympathetic but concerned about risking the reputation of the Salvation Army.

Instead, Bramwell Booth's greatest encouragement came from his wife, Florence. The daughter of a Welsh physician, enjoying a refined, delicate and somewhat sheltered middle-class upbringing, she might be considered the last person to take up such a campaign. But as her husband shared his deep concerns, she undertook her own enquiries. What she discovered was even more shocking than her husband believed. Florence found that children of 13 and 14 were being 'entrapped by a vicious network of carefully devised agencies and in their innocence condemned to a life of shame'. This was associated with a trade between Britain and Europe attended by 'the most atrocious fraud and villany', bringing 'anguish and degradation'. Bramwell Booth remembered Florence crying herself to sleep over her discoveries of the plight of trafficked children.[9]

Not long afterwards a teenage girl was found waiting outside the door of a Salvation Army office in London. She had gone to London in response to an advert for a job as a maid, but when she was given fine clothes she realized she had been tricked into prostitution. When she screamed in protest, she was locked into a room, from which she escaped during the night, climbing down a drainpipe. She fled to the Salvation Army as the only organization she believed could keep her safe. Other girls gave similar accounts of entrapment, virtual imprisonment and being forced into sexual slavery. As Bramwell Booth probed this ghastly underworld, he declared:

> I was like one living in a dream of hell. The cries of outraged children and the smothered sobs of those imprisoned in living tombs were continually in my ears. I could not sleep, I could not take my food. At times I could not pray.[10]

He placed a courageous female Salvation Army worker in a brothel to pose as a prostitute to report on events, giving her money to pay the brothel keeper. Somehow she stayed for ten days while rejecting the advances of various customers. The services of a private investigator were also engaged to make detailed enquiries. The level of sexual exploitation and trafficking discovered far exceeded what they had imagined. Children were in deep physical and

---

[9] B. Booth, *Echoes and Memories* (New York: G. H. Doran, 1925), 118.
[10] Ibid. 118–120.

moral peril, and were being 'bought and sold as irrevocably as in a slave market'.[11]

While these investigations continued, the British Parliament continued to stall the passage of the Criminal Law Amendment Bill, one provision of which was to raise the age of consent. Vested interests blocked progress on this measure in 1882, 1883, 1884 and 1885.[12] The wall of public silence and indifference was broken by W. T. Stead (1849–1912), the brash and headstrong editor of the *Pall Mall Gazette*, who was not averse to sensationalist journalism as a means to driving up the circulation of his paper. Stead admired the Salvation Army's values, having attended their meetings when working as a journalist in Darlington. In 1885 Stead was approached by Bramwell Booth, Josephine Butler and Benjamin Scott, Lord Chamberlain of the City of London. Scott was a Nonconformist, a strong advocate of temperance and devoted to charitable work in the London slums, including supporting ragged schools. He feared the police were turning a blind eye to the issue of child prostitution and sex trafficking, and urged Stead to mobilize public opinion in support of laws against trafficking and to raise the age of consent.[13] Stead felt the opposition from vested interests rendered the task almost hopeless; but when Butler and Booth shared their findings, he was shocked. Further encouragement came from the Congregationalist minister Benjamin Waugh (co-founder of the London Society for the Prevention of Cruelty to Children), who stressed the reality and urgency of the situation. As the campaign unfolded, Frederick Temple, Bishop of London, and Cardinal Manning, Catholic Archbishop of Westminster, lent their support.[14]

Stead spent six weeks undertaking detailed investigations, assisted by workers from the London City Mission and officers of the Salvation Army. He immersed himself in the nether world of the prostitute, the procuress and the brothel keeper, returning each night from his 'descent into hell' to seek prayer support from Booth and wise counsel from Butler.[15] He shuddered at the entrapment techniques used by the procurers of girls. One man he interviewed described his visits into the country to court girls 'under all kinds of disguises', including that of a parson, leading them to believe he would make an offer of marriage. He would take a girl to London to see the sights, go to the theatre and

---

[11] Ibid. 123.

[12] Ibid. 118–120.

[13] Sidney Lee (ed.), 'Scott, Benjamin', in *Dictionary of National Biography*, vol. 51 (London: Smith, Elder, 1897), 14–15.

[14] S. J. Brown, *W. T. Stead: Nonconformist and Newspaper Prophet* (Oxford: Oxford University Press, 2019), 60–61.

[15] Ibid. 63.

have a meal, and when she missed the last train home would offer her a place to stay in his home. Thereby tricked she was handed over to the customer, who sexually abused her, leaving the girl too ashamed to return home. Most ended up on the streets.[16]

Stead was most disturbed by the abuse of young girls brought into brothels, who were drugged and then raped by male abusers, their desperate screams going unheeded. It led him to fear that much of the professed Christianity and civilization of London was a veneer, with real evil underneath. He began to entertain his own doubts. Josephine Butler observed, 'At times he was tempted to give up all faith in God, in justice, in the atoning sacrifice, and the love of Christ.'[17] At other times he seemed close to losing his reason. She met him as he returned one night, crying bitterly, 'Oh, Mrs. Butler, let me weep, let me weep, or my heart will break.' He recounted young girls he had met who had played children's games with him, completely unaware that within hours they would be sold for sex in the fashionable West End brothels, and he was powerless to prevent it.[18]

Much compelling evidence was collected, but Stead felt he needed one conclusive piece. This was proof that it was possible to buy a young girl, with a view to her being trafficked out of the country. Through Josephine Butler, Stead had met Rebecca Jarrett, a former prostitute and recovering alcoholic, who had been rescued by the Salvation Army. Moved by the kindness she found there and deeply repenting of her previous life, she was converted in 1884.[19] She had been employed by Josephine Butler to run a home in Winchester for rescued prostitutes. Stead persuaded Jarrett that helping him expose the evil of children being drawn into prostitution would be a form of atonement for her past. She began to visit her old haunts, and eventually learned of a 13-year-old girl whose mother was an alcoholic with an abusive partner and desperate for money. An agreement was made for the child to be sold, and given over to Jarrett. Elements of the plot were crude and distasteful. Stead wanted proof that the child was a virgin, and Jarrett took her to a midwife she knew for the examination. Then she was taken to a room in Soho and, as with other trafficked children, was drugged, but instead of being abused was taken to France, but only after another medical examination to prove that no sexual assault had taken place. The girl was soon in France, being cared for by members of the Salvation Army.[20]

---

[16] W. T. Stead, 'The Maiden Tribute of Modern Babylon', *Pall Mall Gazette*, London, 6 July 1885.

[17] J. Butler, *Rebecca Jarrett* (London: Morgan & Scott, 1885), 18.

[18] H. Begbie, *Life of William Booth*, vol. 2 (London: Macmillan, 1926), 42.

[19] P. J. Walker, 'The Conversion of Rebecca Jarrett', *History Workshop Journal* 58 (autumn 2004), 248.

[20] Brown, *Stead*, 63–64.

This was the 'proof' Stead needed, and he proceeded to publish the findings of his investigations over several days under the heading *The Maiden Tribute of Modern Babylon*. He declared it an exposé of 'The sale and purchase and violation of children, the procuration of virgins, the entrapping and ruin of women, the international slave trade in girls, atrocities, brutalities, and unnatural crimes.' Crimes were being committed each night against girls 'too young in fact to understand the nature of the crime of which they are the unwilling victims', and this was happening with near impunity.[21] Stead implied leading figures in society, including MPs, were involved in the trafficking and abuse of children, and that members of the police were complicit.[22]

The reaction to the series of articles was sensational. The circulation of the *Pall Mall Gazette* soared from 15,000 to 100,000. The articles were widely republished, with estimates of up to 1.5 million copies finally sold. Some welcomed the revelations, others dismissed them as fictitious and others denounced Stead for spreading 'filth' into decent homes. Letters of support came from evangelicals, including C. H. Spurgeon and the Methodist preacher and journalist Hugh Price Hughes.[23] Although entering the final months of his life, Lord Shaftesbury pressed for the delayed parliamentary age-of-consent legislation to be passed. He addressed the issue in a speech before the Society for the Prevention of Cruelty to Children and met the Home Secretary and Prime Minister to demand action.[24] A huge petition bearing some 400,000 signatures was organized by the Salvation Army in just seventeen days, and was presented to Parliament.[25]

In this fevered atmosphere the Criminal Law Amendment Bill was re-introduced to Parliament in July 1885, including provision to raise the age of consent to 16.[26] Booth and Stead, when consulted by the Home Secretary, had insisted on the age of 16 rather than the age of 15 previously suggested.[27] On such a tide of moral outrage the bill quickly passed through Parliament. Police were given powers to search brothels if they suspected child prostitution was taking place, the solicitation of girls under 16 was outlawed and provision was given to remove children from parents living by immorality.[28] This was not

---

[21] Stead, 'Maiden Tribute'.

[22] Brown, *Stead*, 64.

[23] R. Whyte, *Life of W. T. Stead*, vol. 1 (London: Jonathan Cape, 1925), 173–175.

[24] G. Battiscombe, *Shaftesbury: A Biography of the Seventh Earl* (London: Constable, 1974), 331.

[25] Begbie, *Booth*, vol. 2, 41.

[26] Brown, *Stead*, 67.

[27] Booth, *Echoes*, 124.

[28] Brown, *Stead*, 67–68.

without resistance from opponents, who argued that prostitution was inevitable and prevented widespread sexual immorality by young men.[29]

All seemed to be prospering for the campaign but then, in one of those curious twists Victorian morality seemed capable of, Stead and his co-conspirators, including Rebecca Jarrett and Bramwell Booth, were arrested for committing the very crime they sought to expose – the abduction of a young girl. The evidence of a shamed government being behind this was evident in the prosecution being led by the Attorney General himself. William Booth declared the trial 'the work of the Arch-enemy of Souls and the earthly enemies of the Army, to destroy our work and fair name'.[30]

In the storm that followed the articles Elizabeth Armstrong had reported her daughter missing to the Marylebone police station. Although Eliza's name was changed in Stead's account, there was enough detail for her to identify her own daughter. She then gave her story to a rival newspaper, who pressed for action against Stead. Eliza was found and returned to her mother.[31] The trial proved to be a sensation. In court Eliza's mother insisted she was given money so that her daughter could be a servant with a respectable family.[32] It became her word against that of Rebecca Jarrett, whose own criminal past was mercilessly exposed. The judge acknowledged Stead's good intentions, but he was found guilty and sentenced to three months in prison with hard labour, although he was quickly moved to comfortable prison quarters. Bramwell Booth was exonerated, but Rebecca Jarrett and Louise Mourez, who had assisted her, received sentences of up to six months hard labour. Louise Mourez died in prison. The rest of the press delighted in the downfall and humiliation of Stead, and declared that his other revelations were also fabricated. *The Times* denounced him for manipulating evidence and hiding his own vile lusts behind 'the mask of holy purpose'. *The Observer* asserted, 'journalism, after all, is not a mission, and editors are neither missionaries nor evangelists'.[33] Sales in the *Pall Mall Gazette* plummeted, and advertisers pulled out. Stead remained as editor only until 1888.

There was certainly an aspect of the religious crusade about the *Maiden Tribute* campaign, but Stead's personal spiritual life was extremely complex. A pioneer of investigative journalism, he used the press for moral crusading, but in this case cut corners. He reported a conversion experience in 1861 when at

[29] J. R. Walkowitz, *City of Dreadful Delight* (Chicago, Ill.: University of Chicago Press, 1992), 103–104.
[30] Begbie, *Booth*, vol. 2, 42.
[31] Booth, *Echoes*, 127.
[32] Walkowitz, *City*, 107; Brown, *Stead*, 69.
[33] Quoted in Walkowitz, *City*, 123–125.

the Congregationalist Silcoates School, with the sudden realization that he had been saved from his sins by Christ's sacrifice on the cross. His spirituality was shaped by the 1859–62 religious revival. He attended Salvation Army meetings in Darlington when he was working on the *Northern Echo*, and resolved 'what I had to do was to do good'.[34] After the trial, Wimbledon Congregational Church, of which he was a member, stood by him and Stead made an emotive address 'as a penitent sinner' to the congregation, admitting the mistakes he had made.[35] Spurgeon wrote a letter of support, encouraging him despite the mistakes made, 'when your self-sacrificing spirit is thought of, it is with glowing admiration. You cast yourself into the abyss to rescue & preserve innocent children, & you are held in honour among the honourable.'[36] Josephine Butler and other Christian feminists arranged a mass rally and huge petition calling for his release, viewing him as a hero in defence of the rights of women and a martyr in their cause. Cardinal Manning also stood by him and gave him great support.[37]

Yet William Booth remained cool towards Stead. George Railton's biography of Booth asserted that Booth never trusted Stead's judgment.[38] Similarly, Begbie presents the general's belief that Stead 'shilly-shallied with the great decision of Christian life'.[39] Through the stressful trial and imprisonment Stead's religious views certainly changed, becoming more non-orthodox and even extreme. He believed that if Christ returned to late nineteenth-century London, he would not acknowledge the Christianity he found professed there. Stead believed he was called to start a Church of the Future, to be made up of other Christs, like himself, willing to lay down their lives for others.[40] The journalist was to act as the preacher, or Old Testament prophet, and the reader was the congregation. The portals of the church were to be widened, to include all who could 'minister to the service of humanity', whether they be agnostics or atheists.[41] By the later 1880s Stead had developed an interest in spiritualism and telepathy, and after another mental breakdown in the 1890s became convinced he had paranormal powers. Yet he was enthusiastic about the Welsh revival of 1904–5, in which he participated and wrote a popular account of it.[42] He retained his local

---

[34] Brown, *Stead*, 73.

[35] Whyte, *Life of W. T. Stead*, vol. 1, 211–213.

[36] C. H. Spurgeon to W. T. Stead, 24 December 1885, quoted in Brown, *Stead*, 70.

[37] Brown, *Stead*, 70–71.

[38] G. S. Railton, *Authoritative Life of William Booth* (London: G. H. Doran, 1912), 40–43.

[39] Begbie, *Booth*, vol. 2, 40.

[40] R. Blathwayt (ed.), *Interview of Mr W. T. Stead on the Church of the Future* (London, 1891), 14–15, quoted in Brown, *Stead*, 73–74.

[41] Brown, *Stead*, 74.

[42] Ibid. 75–77, 135–139, 151–153.

Congregational church membership, but his views became increasingly theologically liberal and eclectic, with belief in the essential unity of all religions. His death came in April 1912 in the icy waters of the North Atlantic as he sailed for America, a victim of the first and final passage of the *Titanic*.[43]

Although humiliated in her trial, Rebecca Jarrett maintained her new-found faith and adherence to the Salvation Army in the face of enormous challenges.[44] Despite Stead's discrediting, the 1885 Act remained on the statute book, and demands for the Act's enforcement grew. This prompted the formation in 1885 of the National Vigilance Association for the Protection of Girls. A huge demonstration in favour of 'social purity' was held in Hyde Park, attended by between 100,000 and 250,000 mothers (and some fathers) with their daughters, working-class women, shop girls and milliners, demanding protection from the depredations of upper-class men.[45]

The secretary of the National Vigilance Association, W. A. Coote, was a deeply committed evangelical. One of its remits was to halt the trafficking of women. It sought to meet girls at ports and railway stations whom they had suspicion were being trafficked, or at risk of this happening, and intervene to befriend and help them. Through their persistent endeavours a conference of governments was held in 1899, and a series of international acts against the trafficking of women were passed in 1904 and 1910. In the 1920s the League of Nations took up the issue, covenanting to supervise the application of these agreements against the traffic (a term that replaced 'white slavery') of women and girls.[46]

The issue of human trafficking was difficult to raise and provoked huge controversy. Yet evangelicals, often derided for their prudish 'Victorian values', were at the forefront in the campaign for action in the same way they also involved themselves in responses to the issue of prostitution (see chapter 18). The courage of evangelicals in challenging vested interests, and the sacrifices made in the campaign, eventually inspired international governmental responses and commitments to reduce the trade. Responses were developed and people were rescued, but the issue of human trafficking did not disappear. In 2004 the United States Department of State estimated 600,000 to 800,000 men, women and children were trafficked across

---

43 Ibid. 168–170, 199, 201–202.

44 Her story is told in Walker, 'Conversion of Rebecca Jarrett'.

45 Walkowitz, *City*, 82; Brown, *Stead*, 67–68.

46 Heasman, *Evangelicals*, 164–166. On the wider implications for the campaigns against the trafficking of women see L. Lammasniemi, 'Anti-White Slavery Legislation and Its Legacies in England', in *Anti-Trafficking Review* <https://www.antitraffickingreview.org/index.php/atrjournal/article/view/264/253>, accessed 25 April 2020.

international borders.[47] Of these 80 per cent were trafficked for the purpose of sexual exploitation and 20 per cent were children.[48] The Salvation Army, which placed its reputation on the line in exposing the issue in the 1880s, continued throughout the twentieth century to play a key role in providing victim support.

Character study: Amy Carmichael (1867–1951) – India

Amy Carmichael was brought up in a loving Presbyterian family in Northern Ireland. She remembered, 'I don't think there could have been a happier child than I was.'[49] This blissful childhood abruptly ended with the sudden death of her father, leaving the family in serious financial difficulties. The tragedy gave her a heart for those in serious need. She began mission work in inner-city Belfast, and then in Manchester, where her mother became the superintendent of a home for rescued women. A sense of call to overseas mission deepened after she attended the Keswick Convention, and in 1892 Carmichael became the first missionary chosen to be sent and supported by the Keswick Convention.[50] After brief periods working in Japan and Sri Lanka, in 1895 she arrived in India to work for the Church of England Zenana Missionary Society.[51] Her ministry was especially to women in the zenana, the inner part of a house in India where the women were secluded from men and the rest of society apart from their immediate family.

The centre of Carmichael's work was the village of Dohnavur, in the south of India. In 1898 she formed the 'Starry Cluster', a band of female Indian workers who worked with her in itinerant evangelism in the surrounding villages.[52] One aspect of Indian life that deeply troubled Amy Carmichael was devadasis, a practice dating back several centuries, in which young girls were dedicated to service in the Hindu temples.[53] She and the 'Starry Cluster' began to visit Hindu

---

[47] U. S. Department of State, *Trafficking in Persons Report* (Washington, D.C.: U. S. Department of State, 2004).

[48] UN Office on Drugs and Crime report, 2009 <https://www.unodc.org/documents/Global_Report_on_TIP.pdf>, accessed 25 April 2020.

[49] E. Elliot, A *Chance to Die: The Life and Legacy of Amy Carmichael* (Grand Rapids, Mich.: F. H. Revel, 2005), 26.

[50] F. Houghton, *Amy Carmichael of Dohnavur* (London: Hodder & Stoughton, 1953), 51.

[51] Ibid. 84.

[52] Ibid. 98.

[53] Davesh Soneji, *Unfinished Gestures: Devadasis, Memory, and Modernity in South India* (Chicago, Ill.: University of Chicago Press, 2011), 3. I am grateful for information about devadasis and other aspects of Amy Carmichael's work from the research of one of my doctoral students, Okky Chandra Karmawan. See O. C. Karmawan, 'The Impact of the Keswick and Cambridge Holiness Movement on British Protestant Missions in Asia (1881–1906), with Special Reference to the Church Missionary Society and the China Inland Mission', PhD thesis, University of Edinburgh 2020, 64–65, 131–134.

temples in disguise to undertake investigative work into the causes and nature of this practice. She always remembered gratefully that her childhood prayer that God might give her blue eyes instead of brown was not answered, for otherwise she would have been instantly recognizable as non-Indian.

The reasons behind devadasis were complex. Sometimes parents offered children to the temple god in fulfilment of a vow, or because the parents could not afford to keep them. Some baby girls were abandoned by parents as unwanted and subsequently adopted by temple women.[54] Others were the children of women who worked in the temple. The little girls were ceremonially married to the deity, and given duties in cleaning the temple, carrying lights, singing and dancing before the deity and devotees. They became virtual prisoners in the temples. By Carmichael's time devadasis had degenerated into a form of prostitution, which involved the sexual abuse of these young girls.[55]

A few missionaries, such as those in the North American Madura Mission,[56] had sought to help girls trapped in this system but there was no rescue work near Dohnavur. Some missionaries even denied the existence of devadasis, and others argued that only evangelism was needed, and then as a consequence of changed lives the practice would end.[57] Most in the local population were indifferent to the practice. Because the issue involved sexual abuse of children, Carmichael chose to highlight something deeply offensive to middle-class sensibilities, and something that would not have been spoken about publicly in Victorian Britain.

Then, one night in 1901 one of these little temple girls escaped and was brought to Amy Carmichael. Amy gave the 7-year-old Preena the motherly love the girl was longing for and immediately adopted her, becoming her *amma* (mother). When the temple authorities found where Preena was, they demanded her return, but Carmichael steadfastly refused – the girl was covered by the marks of previous abuse, including where she had been burned with hot irons for trying to escape from the temple earlier. Amy learned from Preena of the exploitation and physical and sexual abuse of children in the temple by worshippers and was outraged: 'We are skirting the abyss, an abyss which is deep and foul beyond description, and yet it is glorified . . . by the sanctions of religion.'[58]

---

[54] Houghton, *Amy Carmichael*, 116; Elliot, *Chance*, 179.

[55] Swami Harshananda, *All About Hindu Temples*, 2nd edn (Mysore: Sri Ramakrishna Ashrama, 1981), 36; Soneji, *Gestures*, 3.

[56] N. Arles, 'Pandita Ramabai and Amy Carmichael: A Study of Their Contribution Towards Transforming the Position of Indian Women', MTh thesis, University of Edinburgh, 1985, 139.

[57] A. Carmichael, *Lotus Buds* (London: SPCK, 1909), 333–339.

[58] A. Carmichael, *Things as They Are* (London: Morgan & Scott, 1903), 88.

So the work for which Amy Carmichael is most famous began – rescuing and sheltering little girls from exploitation and abuse, and rescuing other young orphans or abandoned girls. This became her primary role, to which 'every missionary call had to be subordinated'. Some argued she had put social concern before evangelism, but she believed she was following the pattern of Christ in rescuing and caring for lost lambs, and that her work provided many evangelistic opportunities with the children.[59] By 1904 seventeen children were being cared for at Dohnavur.

One critique of evangelical social concern is that issues are often tackled separately from wider contextual causes and implications. On this issue Carmichael combined both practical and spiritual approaches. She declared, 'pray not less for the Reform movement . . . and the Education movement . . . but far more for the breath of God'.[60] Her book *Things as They Are* raised awareness of devadasis, and she supplied evidence to the Governor of Madras. She addressed educated Indians on 'the evils of the society' faced by the temple girls,[61] and called for Christians to demand the practice be legally prohibited. Believing that in God's law she followed a higher law, she was willing to defy the secular law when some parents demanded their temple children back from Dohnavur. Carmichael was also quite prepared to expose the bribery, corruption and brutality among the police.[62] She criticized the indifference and temerity of British officials, who feared Hindu protests if action was taken. Carmichael also encouraged missionaries teaching Indian children and students to alert these officials to the practice so they might also fight the system from within, and urged Indian reformers to bring about legal changes.[63] However, it was not until 1947 that the Madras government made devadasis illegal, but Carmichael's work and influence were important in that success.[64] In 1919 she was awarded the Kaisar-i-Hind Medal for her service to the people of India, and until her death continued her work of rescuing children at risk.

This work with at-risk children brought huge challenges. They were easily prey to infectious diseases and finance was often short. Carmichael recorded many stories of money and cheques arriving just as resources ran out, often posted weeks earlier by friends who had no idea of the urgent need the work was facing. When she rescued and refused to return 5-year-old Kohila to her

---

[59] A. Carmichael, *Gold Cord* (London: SPCK, 1932), 39–41.

[60] Carmichael, *Things*, 70.

[61] Arles, 'Pandita', 230.

[62] Ibid. 141, 159.

[63] Ibid. 142, 144.

[64] G. A. Oddie, *Social Protest in India: British Protestant Missionaries and Social Reform* (New Delhi: Manohar, 1978), 26.

abusive guardians, she was charged and faced a seven-year prison term before the case was dismissed in 1914.

As others joined Carmichael in this difficult work, she warned them:

> No word of attraction can I write . . . I ask for steel, that quality that is at the back of all that is going on, patience which cannot be tired out, and love that loves in very deed, unto death.[65]

She was supported by a band of faithful Indian women who devoted themselves to the work, surrendering caste to follow her into a life of simplicity and poverty. She adopted Indian dress, spoke Tamil and set an example by being willing to do menial tasks herself. The compound was walled to keep the children safe from further harmful influences, but some felt it left them unprepared for the realities of Indian life when they grew up.

Gradually the work at Dohnavur developed. There was a residential school for girls, and after 1918 boys were also accepted. A house of prayer, nurseries and a hospital were built. By the 1930s a medical superintendent and three doctors were working in the hospital.

The last years of Amy Carmichael's life were spent in pain and immobility after a severe fall, but her ministry of writing continued. She died in 1951, just over a month after her eighty-third birthday. During her lifetime more than 1,000 children had been rescued and given a home. The work of the Dohnavur Fellowship continued under the leadership of Indians, some of whom had themselves been cared for by Amy Carmichael.

---

[65] A. Carmichael, *Toward Jerusalem* (London: SPCK, 1936), 85.

11

Care for people with mental illness and children with learning disabilities

There was little understanding of the causes of mental illness in the late eighteenth and early nineteenth century, and treatments were unregulated and sometimes barbaric. In the eighteenth and early nineteenth centuries a number of hospitals had been built for those suffering from mental illness, but few distinctions were made between those with mental illness and those with learning disabilities. Often people with serious mental illness and those with learning disabilities ended up in the workhouses or prison, or were left to roam the streets without any care or support. This chapter will first explore evangelical responses to the needs of those with mental illness, and then action to support the needs of those with learning disabilities.

For those declared 'insane' and confined to asylums, the main concern was that the general public be protected from them, so they were often restrained with chains and manacles. In the eighteenth century Londoners could pay two pennies to visit, mock or laugh at the people with mental illness detained in Bethlehem Hospital, or Bedlam as it was known. In other asylums the inmates were often whipped or subjected to semi-strangulation in an attempt to control them. 'Shock' treatment, intended to jolt patients back into sanity, included the 'bath of surprise' into which the unsuspecting patient was plunged when walking over a concealed trapdoor through which he or she fell into the waters beneath. Others were chained in deep wells, and water let in until it reached the necks of the terrified patient, or they were spun in a revolving chair at frightening speeds. Others spent their days confined in iron cages, as if they were wild animals.[1]

In Britain a parliamentary Act of 1774 had allowed the compulsory detention of those deemed 'furiously mad and dangerous'. In 1816, after cases of notorious abuses were reported, a further act was passed allowing asylums to be inspected. Much of the care of those suffering from what was called 'lunacy' was in the

---

[1] E. Hodder, *The Life and Work of the Seventh Earl of Shaftesbury* (London: Cassell, 1887), 50.

hands of private 'madhouses', many being private institutions run for profit by unscrupulous proprietors where standards of care were generally low. A great deal of power was placed in the hands of doctors and apothecaries called upon to diagnose cases where mental illness existed and sign certificates of insanity where necessary. People committed to an asylum could lose their liberty, their reputation and even their property. A number of these cases became celebrated trials. There were very real fears of unscrupulous doctors being persuaded, or even paid, by family members to commit people who were not in fact mentally ill to lunatic asylums. Some doctors were also proprietors of asylums and stood to gain from the admission of patients.

Evangelicals pioneering some of the most advanced and humane treatments of those with mental illness challenged techniques such as bleeding and purging, and intimidation to control patients, such as the use of leg irons and straitjackets. A key figure in these advances was the Quaker merchant William Tuke (1732–1822), who started a care facility known as the Retreat near York in 1792. Tuke, an evangelical, was a strong supporter of the Bible Society and of William Wilberforce in his campaign against the slave trade. Tuke's attention was alerted to the needs of those suffering from mental illness when asked to visit a Quakeress who had been committed to the York Asylum. He was concerned at the conditions in which she was detained, especially when some of her friends who had travelled a long distance for a visit were refused permission to see her. Concern turned to alarm when she suddenly died in unexplained circumstances. Tuke was determined to make further enquiries, and when visiting another asylum was distressed to observe the methods of coercion employed, and appalled to find a young woman lying completely naked on some dirty straw while chained to a wall. He resolved that those admitted to his Retreat would receive humane and compassionate treatment. His plan met with significant opposition, some denying there was a problem, and others believing that the provisions of the York Asylum were sufficient.[2]

The Retreat started by Tuke was small, but the methods of treatment employed were far-sighted and helped patients to take some ownership of their own treatment. Coercion, chains and hobbles were rejected in favour of kindness and fairness.[3] The work included a strong spiritual dimension, with special focus on prayer. The name 'Retreat' summed up Tuke's intention that it be a place of refuge, 'a quiet haven in which the shattered bark might find the means

---

[2] D. H. Tuke, 'William Tuke, the Founder of the York Retreat', *Journal of Psychological Medicine and Mental Pathology* 8 (1855), 507–512; K. Heasman, *Evangelicals in Action* (London: Geoffrey Bles, 1963), 209–210.

[3] S. Tuke, *Description of the Retreat* (York: Alexander, 1813), 163.

of reparation, or of safety'. Many of the patients admitted would now be diagnosed as suffering from psychotic episodes or schizophrenia. Tuke provided beautiful gardens and pet animals for the patients, and allowed them some employment opportunities as a diversion from a cycle of depressive thoughts, creating a restorative environment. Despite being a widower for the last twenty-eight years of his life, and suffering from blindness in his eighties, Tuke faithfully continued close involvement in the work until two years before his death. His preference was to prove the rightness of his views by letting the practical example of his work speak for itself. It became a model for other asylums and proved to be highly influential on other pioneers, including Dr John Conolly and Lord Shaftesbury.[4]

Conolly, who became closely associated with the evangelical Congregationalist minister Andrew Reed, as seen in the character study in this chapter, in 1830 wrote his *Inquiry Concerning Insanity*.[5] When Conolly was appointed the superintendent of the Hanwell Asylum in Middlesex, he turned one of the country's largest, and considered ungovernable, institutions into a model asylum, particularly in the use of non-restraint methods in the treatment of the mentally ill. With his emphasis on therapy rather than physical coercion he has been called by some 'the patron saint of English psychiatry'.[6]

In 1828 Parliament in Britain appointed commissioners to control admission to mental hospitals and to inspect them and the treatment they were providing. A key figure in enforcing this legislation was the evangelical Lord Shaftesbury. Recently elected to Parliament, he believed it a path marked out for him by Providence as the 'best means of doing good'. He was especially satisfied that his first speech in Parliament was on a measure 'for the advancement of human happiness'.[7] Within a year he was serving on a House of Commons Select Committee to investigate the treatment of those suffering from 'lunacy'. He showed an 'unusual sympathy' for those with mental illness, not then considered a popular cause.[8]

In 1829, still aged only 27, Shaftesbury was appointed Chair of Her Majesty's Metropolitan Commissioners of Lunacy. It was the first of many social-concern causes he took up, and he was assiduous in his visitation of asylums and concern to improve the treatment of those with mental-health issues. He witnessed patients chained up in dark, foul cells, and left with only bread and water to eat.

---

4 Tuke, 'William Tuke'; Heasman, *Evangelicals*, 209–210.

5 J. Conolly, *An Inquiry Concerning the Indications of Insanity* (London: John Taylor, 1830), 4–5, 17.

6 A. Scull, *The Most Solitary of Afflictions: Madness and Society in Britain 1700–1900* (New Haven, Conn.: Yale University Press, 1993), 290, 377.

7 Shaftesbury, diary, 17 December 1827, quoted in Hodder, *Shaftesbury*, 53.

8 G. B. A. M. Finlayson, *The Seventh Earl of Shaftesbury* (London: Eyre Methuen, 1981), 36.

He vowed he would never cease to appeal for the needs of those who suffered in this way, until their condition was improved. Although it was arduous work, he believed that 'every sigh prevented, and every pang subdued' made the effort worthwhile.[9] As a commissioner he was called on to adjudicate whether to detain or discharge a patient. The responsibility lay heavily upon him: 'In the first case you hazard the commission of cruelty to the prisoner; in the second to his friends and the public.' Such matters sometimes took several days to decide, work done without receipt of any payment, but he was relieved such decisions were taken jointly with the other commissioners.[10]

Shaftesbury was part of a Commission in Lunacy, which reported in 1844 on the national situation in the care of those with mental illness. The report contained shocking and distressing revelations about continued cruel neglect and brutal treatment, but Shaftesbury hoped it would lead to 'the alleviation of moral and physical suffering'.[11] It recommended that the powers of inspection of the commissioners be extended to include asylums located outside London. In the report, most of which he wrote, Shaftesbury praised the efforts of those who like Tuke had 'laboured to make the rational and humane treatment to be the rule and principles of the government of lunacy'.[12] Shaftesbury sought to restore to those with mental illness the rights of personhood.

In 1845 he saw through Parliament bills replacing the Metropolitan Lunacy Commission with a national Lunacy Commission. This required counties or boroughs to build asylums if they had not already done so, thus undermining the unscrupulous private 'madhouses' still operating for profit. Shaftesbury was driven by the desire to come to the 'aid and protection' of people who were 'the most helpless, if not the most afflicted, portion of the human race', who demanded 'our highest sympathies'.[13] His selfless devotion to the cause won the praise of others in Parliament. One fellow MP's admiration was reported in *The Times*:

> It is gratifying to see a man of his high rank, not descending, but stooping from his exalted position, in order to deal with such subjects – not permitting himself to be allured by pleasure or ambition, but impelled by the generous motive of doing good, and by the virtuous celebrity by which his labours will be rewarded.[14]

---

[9] Shaftesbury, diary, 13 November 1828, quoted in Finlayson, *Shaftesbury*, 37.
[10] Hodder, *Shaftesbury*, 124.
[11] Ibid. 308.
[12] Ibid. 309.
[13] Ibid.
[14] Speech of Mr Shiel, reported in *The Times*, 24 July 1844.

Such recognition did not mean the task was easy; indeed, it regularly robbed Shaftesbury of rest, as he recorded in his diary: 'I dream every night, and pass, in my visions, through every clause, and confuse the whole in one great mass. It is very trying – perpetual objections, perpetual correspondence, perpetual doubt.'[15]

One sad feature of these debates was the vehement opposition the bills received in the House of Lords, especially from Shaftesbury's father, the Sixth Earl of Shaftesbury, who seemed to make a point of opposing the humanitarian activities of his son. In August 1845 Shaftesbury was appointed chair of the newly formed national Lunacy Commission. The role involved a huge amount of work in reading reports, conducting meetings and inspecting asylums. He held this position until a year before his death.[16] The work he put in would for many people be considered a full-time job, but Shaftesbury maintained it while active in Parliament and a huge range of other causes. Shaftesbury was motivated by tremendous sympathy for those with mental illness and a recognition of how quickly its onset could be: 'a fall, a fever, a reverse of fortune, a domestic calamity – will do the awful work, and then . . . the most exalted intellects, the noblest-affections, are transformed'.[17] In his view, based on his observations, 70 per cent of cases of mental illness were influenced in some way by alcohol abuse by the person or by his or her parents.[18]

Shaftesbury took a key role in improving standards in asylums and in establishing proper criteria upon which patients were to be admitted. In 1845, reflecting on the extraordinary success of seeing through parliamentary bills in this difficult area, he wrote in his diary:

> Such a thing almost before unknown, that a man, without a party, unsupported by anything private or public, but God and His Truth, should have overcome Mammon and Moloch, and have carried, in one Session . . . such measures . . . Non Nobis, Domine.[19]

A similar role to that of Shaftesbury was played in Scotland by the evangelical Lord Kinnaird, the MP for Perth, who helped secure in Scotland an Act of Parliament in 1857 creating a board of commissioners for lunacy with similar powers to those in England.

---

15 Hodder, *Shaftesbury*, 332.
16 Finlayson, *Shaftesbury*, 231.
17 Hodder, *Shaftesbury*, 332.
18 Ibid. 672.
19 Shaftesbury, diary, 30 July 1845, quoted in Hodder, *Shaftesbury*, 333 ['Not to us, O Lord . . .'].

In 1859 Shaftesbury reported that the system of mechanical restraint of people with mental illness had almost been eliminated in the thirty years since he started as a commissioner. He recalled visiting asylums in the early years of his involvement, declaring he had 'never beheld anything so horrible and miserable' as seeing inmates in one asylum who had been chained to the wall and were shouting and roaring in distress; most of the women were naked. Now most asylums were 'clean, orderly and quiet'. He continued to call for more medical research into the causes of, and treatments for, mental illness, and an increase in the standards of nurses and attendants caring for those with mental illness. Shaftesbury also insisted on the right of the commissioners to visit all patients with mental illness, even the wealthy in private asylums, to ensure their treatment was appropriate. He lamented in 1859 that many who were poor and suffering from serious mental illness were still detained in the workhouse, along with the homeless and unemployed, rather than in specialist hospitals. His preference remained that the state or local authorities should be providers of most of the care for the mentally ill, for as soon as private providers became involved there was a possibility of the profit motive influencing judgments about the care and treatment of patients, with significant money to be made from detaining people in asylums for prolonged periods.[20]

In 1877, as Shaftesbury reflected on fifty years of dedicated work on behalf of those with mental illness, he observed, 'through the wonderful mercy and power of God, the state now as compared with the state then, would baffle, if description were attempted, any voice and any pen that were ever employed in spoken or written eloquence'.[21] Yet difficulties remained for those eventually discharged from the asylums. Many found it impossible to live independent lives and ended up in the workhouse or returned to the asylum. In 1879 Lord Shaftesbury was one of the founders of the Mental After-Care Association, set up to help address this issue. The Association found families who would offer a temporary home to former inpatients from the asylum while they found work and were rehabilitated into society. But considerable prejudice remained against those who had suffered from mental illness, and there was great reluctance to offer them employment.[22]

As late as 1884, within a year of his death, Shaftesbury was still campaigning in the cause of the proper care of those with mental-health issues. He again appealed for early intervention in terms of treatment, despite the stigma brought by attaching the label of 'lunacy' to someone, which held many family members

---

[20] Finlayson, *Shaftesbury*, 413–415.
[21] Hodder, *Shaftesbury*, 700.
[22] Heasman, *Evangelicals*, 211.

and doctors back from prompt action. It remained his fervent hope that through the combination of compassionate care and advances in science it would be possible 'by God's blessing, to arrive at some alleviation, if not a full remedy, for the most mysterious affliction that has been permitted to fall on the human race'.[23]

The plight of those with learning disabilities was especially tragic. They were often chained up along with prisoners or the insane, or held in the common pound or village lock-up. Others were chased from one community to another, hounded by crowds of jeering, taunting children, and even adults. This was the case for both adults and children with learning-support needs. Notable work was especially done at the small home for children with severe learning disabilities established in 1839 by Dr Guggenbühl at Abendberg, above Interlaken in Switzerland. A number of people visited the chalet where the asylum was located and were impressed with his enlightened approach, but his claims to be able to cure mental disability by his treatments were proved to be false.[24]

One person influenced by Guggenbühl's approach was Charlotte White, daughter of a major general who had served in India and then retired to Bath. In April 1846 she started a home for children with additional learning-support needs in the town.[25] Established in a small property, it employed a matron to care for the children and was unique in that it was run by women: the chair of the founding committee was the Marchioness of Thomond and the rest of the committee were all female. Indeed, for the first twenty-five years of the charity the offices of secretary and treasurer were held by women. The only men involved were the visiting physician, the collector and the official visiting clergy, who included the evangelicals the Revds Fountain Elwyn[26] and J. H. Way.[27] They were closely associated with the project and led morning and evening prayers with the children. The home was initially small and low-key, caring for just three girls, although boys were also later admitted. The children were to be under the age of 10 when admitted, and were generally between 7 and 15 years

[23] Finlayson, *Shaftesbury*, 590–592.

[24] K. Day and J. Jancar, 'Mental Handicap and the Royal Medico-Psychological Association: A Historical Association, 1841–1991', in G. E. Berrios and H. Freeman, *150 Years of British Psychiatry, 1841–1991* (London: Gaskell, 1991), 268–270; *Memoirs*, 386–387.

[25] This was called the Bath Institution for Idiot Children and those of Weak Intellect. 'Idiot' was at the time one of the medical terms used to describe a certain form of learning disability. Along with other similar terms such as 'imbecile' and 'cretin', also used by doctors, over time 'idiot' became a term of abuse and is no longer appropriate.

[26] Elwyn's name is as a supporter of the evangelical Church Missionary Society (CMS), in D. Corrie, *Sermon Preached Before the Church Missionary Society, and Report of the Committee Including a List of Subscribers and Benefactors* (London, 1816), 235.

[27] Way was a member of the Bath council of the Evangelical Alliance (*Proceedings of Council of EA*, 1 February 1875).

of age. Its focus was on rescuing those in great need and providing compassionate care, including the provision of education with a Christian basis.

The annual reports highlight the terrible plight of some of the rescued children. Some had been found fastened by ropes. One young girl had been discovered shut up in a room completely alone 'in total mental darkness' with nothing to interest or occupy her for days on end. The report observed, 'Few sound minds could hold out against such a trial or mode of life.'[28] The charity made a specific appeal to the 'cordial sympathy and support of a Christian public', and in 1851 moved to a much larger house, close to a park, for the health and benefit of the children.[29] The institution functioned as a boarding school, with children taught, 'as their capacities permitted', reading, writing, arithmetic and geography, but 'Religious knowledge and moral culture are directly or indirectly kept in view in every pursuit.'[30]

Eight years after the charity began, the founder Charlotte White wrote, 'the general conduct of the pupils is extremely good. Some of them evince much love of religion, and a clear comprehension of its simpler truths.'[31] One blind orphaned girl was admitted in the early years, after being cared for by a very poor relative. She suffered frequently from fits and spoke only incoherently when she arrived, but through care and teaching came to demonstrate a 'clear understanding of the leading truths of Christianity, as fully evinced by her conduct and conversation'. When her health declined, and she had to be removed to hospital for specialist nursing care, she was distressed to leave the teachers for whom she had such affection, and expressed her hope that 'she should meet her teacher in Heaven, naming at the same time the only true ground of acceptance with God'.[32]

Efforts were made to give children training with future life and work skills. In 1853 it was reported how children who when admitted could not feed or dress themselves had by the time they left made considerable progress. The school never became large, accommodating no more than thirty-five children in the first few decades, and children came from as far away as Essex and Glasgow. Teachers were instructed to use the most 'gentleness and forbearance' with the children, no corporeal punishment was allowed and the children were never to be left alone.[33] One boy described as 'extremely helpless in every way'

---

[28] *Report of the Committee of the Institution for Idiot Children and Those of Weak Intellect* (Bath: Hollway, 1850), 18.

[29] P. K. Carpenter, 'The Bath Idiot and Imbecile Institution', *History of Psychiatry* 11 (2000), 168.

[30] *Report*, 19.

[31] Carpenter, 'Bath Institution', 161–162.

[32] *Report*, 22.

[33] Ibid. 20.

had learned reading, writing and arithmetic by the time he left. Of the thirty-seven who had progressed through the school for a number of years, twenty-three were considered to have 'benefitted' appreciably from its work by the time they left.[34]

As will be seen in the following case study the London Congregationalist minister Andrew Reed was a pioneer in England. His researches in the 1840s indicated that at least 30,000 people were suffering from serious learning disabilities in England and Wales, although there was no formal attempt to distinguish between learning disabilities and mental illness. He found that many with serious learning disabilities were indiscriminately mixed in lunatic asylums with those who were mentally ill, or were living in a state of destitution. Some were cared for by relatives who had very low incomes. One doctor in Edinburgh observed that those with learning disabilities in wider society became 'the sport of fortune or of their own imperfect instincts and ill-regulated passions, the prey of the designing, the butt of the idle or the cruel'.[35]

The two homes Reed established – one in Essex and one in Surrey, where children with additional learning-support needs could be both cared for and educated, and offered some form of training for future employment – became models for others. However, even in 1886 they were still the only places outside London that provided such care and education. Concern that those with learning disabilities who had received some education but who could easily be led into crime or immorality when they became adults and left the homes was recognized by the Young Women's Christian Association (YWCA). This grew out of the work of the evangelical Lady Mary Jane Kinnaird (wife of Lord Kinnaird, who worked with Shaftesbury on mental-health issues) and provided accommodation for nurses and others who moved from the country to London to find work. At Addlestone Mrs Meredith started Village Homes for young female adults who had additional learning needs. In 1895 the National Association for the Care of the Feebleminded was started, in which Isabella Head played an important role. She was an evangelical and one of the leaders of the YWCA. This Association pressed for a Royal Commission into adults with learning-support needs, which led to the Mental Deficiency Act of 1913 that established a proper system of care for them.[36]

In the care of people with mental illness or severe learning difficulties it is clear that evangelicals were both pioneers in methods of humane and

---

[34] Carpenter, 'Bath Institution', 172.

[35] W. A. F. Browne, *What Asylums Were, Are, and Ought to Be: Being the Substance of Five Lectures Delivered Before the Managers of the Montrose Royal Lunatic Asylum* (Edinburgh: A&C Black, 1837).

[36] Heasman, *Evangelicals*, 208–213.

compassionate care and ensured that such care extended to the treatment of all with these needs. At the heart of this was the conviction that all people who suffered from learning disability or mental illness were made in the image of God and had inherent dignity and a right to proper treatment. This conviction and its message of love and compassion was to play a central part in sharing the Christian gospel with those in need.

Character study: Andrew Reed (1787–1862) – England

By the time he reached his late fifties Andrew Reed had already started three orphanages (see chapter 9). He was the minister of Wycliffe Chapel in Stepney, East London, with a congregation he had seen grow from around 60 to more than 2,000. He was involved in various other societies and organizations, but resolved to start a charity for the care of children with severe learning difficulties.[37]

On his many preaching visits around the country Reed was distressed to see children with learning disabilities locked up in gaols as if criminals, or chased by crowds of jeering, taunting children, and even adults. Reed was determined to do something for those whom society classed as less than human but who, he was convinced, bore 'the Divine image'. Reed's conviction of the fundamental human dignity of those with learning-support needs was a crucial motivation for him.[38] Before launching any scheme, Reed always undertook thorough research and planning. He read all the literature available from Britain and overseas, travelled to Europe to meet leading experts and formed a close friendship with Dr John Conolly, England's foremost expert on mental illness and learning disability.[39]

Then Anne Plumbe, a member of Reed's church, came to him seeking advice as to where her son Andrew, who had severe learning difficulties, could find long-term care. Reed saw this as God's prompting him to action.[40] He proposed a scheme to 'take care of, and, by skilful and earnest application of the best means, to prepare, as far as possible, for the duties and enjoyments of life' those with learning disabilities.[41] Drawing on all his previous experience of founding

---

[37] On Reed's life and achievements see I. J. Shaw, *The Greatest Is Charity: The Life of Andrew Reed, Preacher and Philanthropist* (Darlington: Evangelical Press, 2005).

[38] A. Reed and C. Reed, *Memoirs of the Life and Philanthropic Labours of Andrew Reed* (London: Strahan, 1863), 384.

[39] Day and Jancar, 'Mental Handicap', 268–270; Reed and Reed, *Memoirs*, 386–387.

[40] D. Wright, *Mental Disability in Victorian England: The Earlswood Asylum, 1847–1901* (Oxford: Oxford University Press, 2001), 20–32.

[41] Reed and Reed, *Memoirs*, 383–389.

charities, he embarked on an exhausting round of visiting and letter-writing, urging the assistance of individuals from all ranks – noblemen, clergymen, bankers, merchants and ordinary lay members of churches.[42]

Reed had come to the view, radical for the time, that children with learning disabilities could be helped, by education and appropriate physical exercise, to overcome at least some of their needs. This made him one of Britain's pioneer thinkers in the field.[43] Reed declared, 'We plead for those who cannot plead for themselves,' and expressed his higher spiritual hope that not only would the children be educated for life, but also that they might have the opportunity to learn of Jesus Christ, 'and look before our present imperfect modes of being to perfected life in a glorious and everlasting future'.[44] It was particularly this hope for the spiritual well-being of the children that inspired him.[45]

Admission to the home was to be open to any in need – most supported were aged between 8 and 14. Premises were secured in Highgate, a headmaster was appointed and staff, including a gym teacher and singing teacher, were employed. When the home opened in 1848, seventeen children were admitted. The stables were converted into a gymnasium, to encourage physical exercise by the children, together with a washing room, workshop, playroom and infirmary.[46]

Working with children with severe learning difficulties who had never lived in a structured or community environment proved challenging for those with no previous experience. Many despaired at any prospect of success in what they had taken on.[47] However, others were far more visionary. One early supporter was Prince Albert, who visited the asylum in 1849 and donated 250 guineas. The following year Queen Victoria granted her patronage to the charity.[48]

Reed was determined that the charity's work would be more educational than medical, and that the children were not just patients requiring treatment.[49] The children and staff were referred to as the 'family'. Careful attention was given to diet, ensuring it was nutritious and easily digestible, and in quality and variety far above that enjoyed by most working families. Any staff guilty of

---

[42] Ibid. 390.

[43] Andrew Reed's leading role is acknowledged in histories of the care of those with mental handicap; e.g. G. E. Berrios and H. Freeman (eds.), *150 Years of British Psychiatry* (London: Gaskell, 1991).

[44] Reed and Reed, *Memoirs*, 391; Annual Reports of Asylum for Idiots, 1849 Report, in Royal Earlswood Hospital Archives, Surrey History Centre, Woking, 392/1/4/1.

[45] Minutes of Board Meetings of Asylum for Idiots, bk 1, 1847–52, in Royal Earlswood Hospital Archives, Surrey History Centre, Woking, 392/2/1/1, Report of Public Meeting 27 October 1847.

[46] Minutes, bk 1, 1847–52, 1847–8.

[47] Reed and Reed, *Memoirs*, 392–393.

[48] Minutes, 22 March 1849, 26 February, 6 March 1850.

[49] Ibid. 16 June 1848.

harshness or 'violence of temper' were instantly dismissed.[50] The daily regime mixed education and physical exercise. Two hours each day were given to free play and one hour to occupational training, such as gardening, carpentry and mat or basket weaving. Wednesday and Saturday afternoons were visiting times for friends and families. High standards for the clothing and cleanliness of the pupils were established, with both showers and aromatic baths available.

An important dimension of the care provided was religious instruction. This was delivered at a level appropriate to the capacity of the children and focused on simple Scripture texts, the Lord's Prayer, the Ten Commandments and the Creed.[51] With such holistic care the children began to respond positively.[52] Any signs of progress were carefully noted. One small boy who was unable to walk was admitted, and could only slide about the floor on his stomach. Through the patient work of the staff in regularly exercising the boy's muscles Reed was delighted to see him first stand, then walk and then run. He gained the power of speech and began to make educational progress.[53] Children began to speak, read, write and do simple arithmetic. At the end of 1849 Reed also discerned signs of increased spiritual awareness in the children, and more participation in simple services of worship.[54] The following year he could report, 'Windows are now safe; boundaries are observed without walls; and doors are safe without locks. The desire now is, not to get away, but to stay. They are essentially, not only an improving, but a *happy family*.'[55] John Conolly expressed his delight that the asylum had created a 'happy family not by coercion but by desire'.[56]

In 1849 the charity took over a home in Colchester for children with learning disabilities that had been founded by the railway baron and prominent Baptist Sir Samuel Morton Peto, and this was then run in a similar fashion.[57] In 1855 the patients from Highgate were moved to a purpose-built home at Earlswood, in Surrey. With its own farm, cricket ground and gymnasium, it was an impressive facility.[58] In the midst of the fundraising for this prestigious building Reed suffered a severe stroke. His cry to God was, 'Thou didst not need me; but perhaps thou wilt condescend to use me. I will endeavour to be more diligent in my work, more faithful in my trust, and more cheerful beneath the burdens

---

[50] Ibid. 3 November 1848, 9 June 1848.
[51] Ibid. 29 September 1848.
[52] Reed and Reed, *Memoirs*, 394.
[53] Ibid. 396–397.
[54] Ibid. 397–398.
[55] Ibid. 400; emphasis original.
[56] Day and Jancar, 'Mental Handicap', 287.
[57] Minutes, 1 August, 21 November, 12 December 1849.
[58] Ibid. 18 December 1850.

and trials of my service!' After rest and recuperation he pressed on, albeit slowly: 'better to walk than to creep, but better to creep than to stand still'.[59]

After early teething problems with the new building, in 1861 the Medical Officers who visited declared their 'most unqualified admiration', observing that the building was 'clean, well warmed, and thoroughly ventilated', with an air of 'neatness and cheerfulness'; the children were 'happy and healthy'.[60] Delighted with the progress her child was making at Earlswood, one mother wrote to Reed, describing how happy her little daughter was: 'She laughs when the sun shines.'[61]

The letters of thanks written by parents or guardians on the discharge of their children are filled with expressions of appreciation for the work of the institution. Many refer to the improvement in their children, far beyond what they imagined possible. Others sadly saw little progress, but all expressed thanks for the care of the charity. The happiness and contentedness of the children were frequently stressed, as was the kindness of the staff. William and Ann Morgan reported that their son James had been made 'more happy under your fostering care than any parents could, even under prosperous circumstances in life'.[62]

Reed hoped that the homes in Earlswood and Colchester would be the first of a chain of asylums that would spring up across the nation, from London to Edinburgh and Dublin. His hopes were not in vain.[63] Earlswood became a world leader in its field. One key decision was to appoint John Langdon Down as the resident medical superintendent in 1858. He undertook outstanding work in the treatment and classification of patients with learning disability: Down syndrome is named after him.[64]

What thrilled Reed above all were indications of a growing spiritual awareness in the children. He once came across a little boy sitting contentedly by a fireside. When he asked him what made him so content, the lad spontaneously replied, 'My Saviour.' Reed persisted, 'What did He do for you?', and the boy expressed his simple, but real, faith: 'Died for me, for my sins, that I may go to heaven.' Reed saw this as his ultimate motivation in the work, that through this work of compassionate care they could learn of God and come to love him. He

---

[59] Shaw, *Greatest Is Charity*, 309.
[60] Lunacy Commissioners Reports, 1858, 1859, 1860, in Visitors Books, Royal Earlswood Hospital, Surrey History Centre, 392/10/1/1; and Medical Officers Reports, Surrey History Centre, 392/10/3/1, 25 September 1861.
[61] Reed and Reed, *Memoirs*, 423.
[62] Letters of thanks to the Board of the Asylum for Idiots, 1849–87, Royal Earlswood Archives, Surrey History Centre, Woking, 392/2/8/2, letters dated 1849–62.
[63] By 1866 this hope was being fulfilled, with hospitals at Exeter, Lancaster and near Birmingham.
[64] Wright, *Mental Disability*, 155–176.

recalled how someone had asked him if children with learning disabilities had souls, and he responded:

> I have always had their *souls* in view . . . Yes, and I remember that little fellow at Highgate who said, 'I love God.' – Nothing that loves Him shall perish. No, they shall not die. I shall meet them soon in heaven.[65]

---

[65] Reed and Reed, *Memoirs*, 423–424; emphasis original.

12

Campaigning against slave trading and slave ownership

As a result of the slave trade some eighteen million black Africans were forcibly transported to the Americas and Asia between 1500 and 1900. A further ten million people had also been enslaved by their fellow Africans by 1850.[1] The trade was driven by greed, conducted with indescribable cruelty and infused with appalling racism against the black women, men and children who were enslaved. It involved ruthless exploitation by African tribal chiefs and traders often of their own indigenous peoples, but some of the worst treatment took place in European ships and colonies, or through the work of traders from the Middle East. Called the 'rape of Africa', it left parts of the continent ruined and divided.

The horrors of the 'Middle Passage' across the Atlantic attracted the greatest outrage from abolitionists. Around one in ten slaves died on this journey. The rewards from slave trading and slave produce could be very large: between 1750 and 1780, 70 per cent of British government income came from taxes on goods from its colonies.

Some challenges to slavery drew on Enlightenment humanitarian sentiment, including concepts of individual liberty and the right to personal happiness. The French Revolution's Declaration of the Rights of Man and of the Citizen in 1789 asserted all are born free and liberty was a 'natural' right of humankind, and in 1794 slavery in France was abolished. When the United States Declaration of Independence of 1776 asserted that 'all men are created equal', that also appeared to herald the end of slavery. Yet opinion among the founding fathers and the states was divided (George Washington owned slaves), and the issue

---

[1] P. Manning, *Slavery and African Life: Occidental, Oriental and African Slave Trades* (Cambridge: Cambridge University Press, 1990), 171; H. S. Klein, *The Atlantic Slave Trade* (Cambridge: Cambridge University Press, 1999), 129.

was left constitutionally unresolved.[2] While 'Life, liberty and pursuit of happiness' was proclaimed, it was denied to millions on the basis of skin colour. Rhode Island was the first state to outlaw slavery in 1775, followed by six others by 1804. Although the slave trade between North America and the wider world ended in 1808, the number of slaves continued to grow from one million in 1800 to four million in 1860.

The pathway to the abolition of slavery was very different in Britain from that in North America. Slave ownership was abolished in Britain as early as 1772. In 1783 Quakers began to campaign against slave trading, and drew evangelicals into the 'great cause'. John Wesley had seen slavery first-hand in North America and deeply opposed it, declaring liberty 'the right of every human creature, as soon as he breathes the vital air'. He was appalled at the inhuman brutality of the slave traders:

> When you saw the flowing eyes . . . or the bleeding sides and tortured limbs of your fellow-creatures, was you a stone or a brute . . . when you threw their poor mangled remains into the sea, had you no relenting?[3]

He warned them of the future judgment 'wherein the just God will reward every man according to his works'.[4]

In 1785 the evangelical Thomas Clarkson wrote *On the Slavery and Commerce of the Human Species*, and in the following years spent most of his fortune on the campaign. While not the sole reason for success in the abolition campaign, the impact of evangelicalism is unmistakeable. This was true among both the abolitionists and the slaves themselves, such as Olaudah Equiano, whose account of his enslavement, release and evangelical conversion became a powerful anti-slavery document.[5]

At the heart of the campaign against British slave trading was the 'Clapham Sect', a group of evangelical thinkers, writers and MPs who gathered around William Wilberforce (the subject of the following character study). Many of them lived in Clapham, then just outside London, and attended Holy Trinity Church, where John Venn was the minister. They included the wealthy merchant Henry Thornton, who provided significant funding. Others, such as Zachary Macaulay and James Stephen, had been colonial administrators and had

---

[2] I. J. Shaw, *Churches, Revolutions and Empires: 1789–1914* (Fearn: Christian Focus, 2012), 140.

[3] John Wesley, *Thoughts upon Slavery* (1774), in Wesley, *Works*, vol. 11, 3rd edn (London: Wesleyan Conference Office, 1872), repr. (Peabody, Mass.: Hendrickson Publishers, 1984), 79.

[4] Ibid.

[5] O. Equiano, *The Interesting Narrative of the Life of Olaudah Equiano, or Gustavus Vassa, the African* (London, 1789).

witnessed first-hand the horrors of slavery in Africa and the West Indies. Hannah More (see chapter 6) was associated with the group.

The Clapham Sect worked together with other evangelical Nonconformists and Methodists, as well as the Quakers and Unitarians, in a popular mass movement that used widespread propaganda techniques. They undertook detailed research into the slave trade, ensuring they had up-to-date evidence as to current practice. They wrote letters, made lecture tours, raised funds, distributed tracts, published graphic images of the cruel practices of slavery and promoted the boycott of the products of slave labour, especially sugar.

The Clapham Sect succeeded in making it a badge of evangelicalism to oppose slavery, something that was not achieved in North America. Yet, because evangelicals remained a religious and political minority they needed to work with those who did not share their faith perspective, such as the Whig leader Charles Fox. They were generally inclined to be politically and socially con-servative; therefore, such tactics were radical, and have been termed 'holy worldliness': seeking, through alliance with the forces of the world, to achieve a greater Christian good.[6] This approach was followed by evangelicals in other moral and religious campaigns.

The first bill seeking to abolish the slave trade was introduced in 1791, and resistance was fierce, especially from merchanting and planter interests. Success came only after twenty years of persistent campaigning, as successive bills were year by year defeated. Finally, in 1807 an act to abolish slave trading in British ships was passed, and the British navy began patrolling the coast of West Africa to intercept the ships of other nations still transporting slaves. Spain and Portugal continued slave trading into the middle of the century. For all the efforts of the abolitionists some three or four million Africans were still shipped across the Atlantic after 1807 as other countries continued the trade.

The Clapham Sect were also determined to provide an alternative model to slave trading within Africa. This led to the development of the Sierra Leone colony in West Africa, where liberated slaves could settle in freedom, be offered education and employment opportunities, and engage in peaceful trading. Sierra Leone was to be the morning star of Africa, a practical demonstration of evangelical social compassion. Located on poor agricultural land, opposed by slave traders, requiring a costly defence force and large subsidies from the Clapham Sect, it faced almost insuperable odds. The founders of Sierra Leone hoped it would be a base for promoting not only farming, industry and

---

6 H. Willmer, 'Holy Worldliness in Nineteenth-Century England', in D. Baker (ed.), *Sanctity and Secularity: The Church and the World* (Oxford: Blackwell, 1973), 200.

education in West Africa, but also Christianity.[7] By 1820 its population included more than 10,000 free slaves from many tribes across West Africa, most of whom had been rescued from slave ships. Those who accepted Christianity developed a passion to share the gospel in their homelands, becoming a highly capable missionary force. They were able to withstand the West African climate and diseases in ways Europeans never could, and already understood the local culture and language. Over a sixty-year period in the nineteenth century, from a population of around 50,000, Sierra Leone produced more than 100 clergy for the Church Missionary Society (CMS), and many more catechists, teachers and mission workers.[8]

Once slave trading was ended in Britain, the campaigners turned to the institution of slavery itself as a 'sin', which it was the religious and moral duty of evangelical Christians to oppose. This required evangelicals to challenge public authorities that supported the repressive slave system and so hindered the spread of the gospel.

In 1823 what became known as the Anti-Slavery Society was formed, with the aim of securing the liberty of the 650,000 slaves in the British colonies in the West Indies. Wilberforce helped launch the movement, but because of growing age and infirmity the lead was taken by Thomas Fowell Buxton (1786–1845), an evangelical Anglican, who was closely connected to Quaker abolitionists by virtue of a Quaker mother and Elizabeth Fry, his sister-in-law.[9] Buxton served as an MP from 1818 until 1837, and declared his views independent of any party: 'I vote as I like.'[10] In 1823 Buxton declared to the House of Commons, that 'the state of Slavery is repugnant to the principles of the British Constitution and the Christian Religion; and . . . it ought to be gradually abolished'.[11] Resistance came not only from slave owners but also a number of Anglican clergymen in the West Indies who were closely associated with the plantation owners.

In the campaign the role of evangelical missionaries in the West Indies proved important. The schools they ran gave them close contact with the slaves, and they saw first-hand the cruelties and injustices suffered. The missionaries supplied vital information to the campaigners and connected the freedom to

---

[7] On Sierra Leone see A. F. Walls, 'A Christian Experiment: The Early Sierra Leone Colony', in G. J. Cuming (ed.), *The Mission of the Church and the Propagation of the Faith*, Studies in Church History 6 (Cambridge: Cambridge University Press, 1970), 107–130.

[8] A. Walls, *The Missionary Movement in Christian History: Studies in the Transmission of Faith* (Edinburgh: T&T Clark, 1996), 86–87, 102–109.

[9] On Elizabeth Fry see chapter 19 below.

[10] On Buxton see T. F. Buxton, *The African Slave Trade and Its Remedy* (London: John Murray, 1838); C. Buxton (ed.), *Memoirs of Sir Thomas Fowell Buxton* (London: J. Murray, 1848).

[11] *Parliamentary Debates (1786–1838)*, vol. 9 (London, House of Commons, 1823), 275, 286.

preach the gospel with the emancipation of the slaves. In 1830 a speaker at the Wesleyan Missionary Society declared, 'We cannot care for the salvation' of the African slave, without 'caring for his emancipation from bondage'.[12] By promoting education and religious instruction, including running Sunday schools, missionaries propagated Christian teaching on spiritual freedom and equality. Slaves appointed as deacons and class leaders became capable spokespersons and were able to organize others. They also brought cases of abuse against slaves to the attention of the authorities.

After a slave rebellion in Demerara in 1823, which was brutally suppressed, John Smith of the London Missionary Society was accused of being an instigator. Smith had ignored instructions not to teach slaves to read and appointed a number of them as deacons in his church. His decision to read the book of Exodus to the slaves was considered by the authorities as an act fomenting rebellion. He was tried and sentenced to death, but died in prison before the sentence was carried out. Smith became a martyr for the anti-slavery cause. The backlash by the authorities against the work of the missionaries was severe. Attempts were made to deny missionaries licences to operate,[13] and some colonial authorities viewed any attendance at a missionary church as subversive.[14] William Knibb, a Baptist missionary in Jamaica from 1824 to 1845, became convinced that all Christians should be abolitionists, and argued it was a crime to be silent in the face of injustice and inhumanity.[15]

In 1830 the policy of the Anti-Slavery Society changed from seeking gradual change to demanding immediate emancipation.[16] The voting habits of MPs on the issue were publicized and many congregations in Britain signed anti-slavery petitions, which was seen as an overtly political act. Women played a key role in the cause, establishing ladies' anti-slavery associations after 1825.[17] But not all evangelical leaders were comfortable with such mass agitation.

As the prospect of emancipation grew in 1831, rebellion broke out among slaves in Jamaica. In this the slave Sam Sharpe (1801–32) played a vital role, drawing on skills gained as a lay leader in his local Baptist church. Sharpe argued that the Bible taught the natural equality of all men, that slaves were entitled to freedom and that white people had no right to hold black people in

---

[12] Richard Watson, quoted by R. Anstey, 'Religion and Slave Emancipation', in D. Eltis and J. Walvin (eds.), *The Abolition of the Atlantic Slave Trade* (Madison, Wis.: University of Wisconsin Press, 1981), 47.

[13] M. Turner, *Slaves and Missionaries: The Disintegration of Jamaican Slave Society, 1787–1834* (Urbana, Ill.: University of Illinois Press, 1982), 107.

[14] S. Jakobsson, *Am I Not a Man and a Brother? British Missions and the Abolition of the Slave Trade and Slavery in West Africa and the West Indies 1786–1838* (Uppsala: Gleerup, 1972), 436.

[15] Letter, 6 July 1831, quoted in J. H. Hinton, *Memoir of William Knibb* (London, 1847), 114.

[16] Anstey, 'Slave Emancipation', 51.

[17] See C. Midgley, *Women Against Slavery: The British Campaigns, 1780–1870* (London: Routledge, 1992).

slavery. Of ninety-nine slaves later tried for their role in the rebellion, it is thought that twenty-five were connected with the Baptists. Sharpe believed that the work of proclaiming freedom was God's work, and would enjoy his favour and assistance. The rebellion started with passive resistance through a refusal to work. Then open rebellion broke out, involving between 20,000 and 50,000 slaves. In the aftermath of the failed rebellion 312 slaves, including Sharpe, were executed.[18]

Evangelical Nonconformist missionaries were again accused of being complicit in the rising. In the choice between loyalty to the state establishment and the white planters, and support for the slaves who appealed to the missionaries as their allies, they sided with the slaves, demanding the freedom to preach and teach them. As a result, fourteen Baptist chapels and six Methodist chapels were demolished and others were closed. The reports the missionaries sent back to Britain helped sway public opinion in favour of immediate emancipation. In the 1832 election tactical voting was encouraged to support abolitionist candidates. As a result, 134 candidates pledged to the abolition of slavery were returned, spanning the political spectrum from Conservative to Radical.[19] The bill to abolish slavery passed through the House of Commons in 1834, and 'emancipation' was proclaimed, together with religious freedom, allowing missionaries to continue their work. Significant compensation was paid to planters for the loss of their 'property', the slaves. The proposal was to end slavery gradually over six years, but the slavery system in British colonies soon collapsed and was gone by 1838.

On Emancipation Day the freed slaves flocked to the missionaries' churches in acknowledgement of the role the missionaries had played. Missionaries had taught slaves to read and write, that they were made in the image of God, that they had rights, including that of self-expression and to be taught Christian truth.

It had taken more than sixty years of campaigning to abolish slave trading and emancipate the slaves in British colonies. Success came through a complex series of religious, economic, social, humanitarian and political influences; but in these, evangelical religion was crucial. It provided the spiritual and moral drive to sustain the 'great cause'. Yet the scars remained, and the ugly legacy of poverty and racial discrimination suffered by black people in Africa and the Americas in the following centuries owes much to the legacy of slavery.

---

[18] Turner, *Slaves and Missionaries*, 148–173.

[19] I. J. Shaw, *High Calvinists in Action: Calvinism and the City c.1810–60* (Oxford: Oxford University Press, 2002), 107–108.

The success of Wilberforce and the Clapham Sect in making anti-slavery sentiment a hallmark of evangelicalism was never achieved in North America, despite the significant size of the evangelical community and the large abolition movement. Slavery was deeply embedded in the economy of the southern states. More than 90 per cent of cotton was grown by slaves, and power was held by a planter elite, who fiercely defended their interests. Slaves were deeply oppressed, with few legal rights or protections: they were unable to marry freely, own property or travel without a pass. Women in particular were subject to physical and sexual abuse. Christianity, often in an evangelical form, was widely practised among African Americans, including slaves, and from this they drew patience and courage, but it was also used by the planters to preserve unity and order.

Among the early evangelical voices opposing slavery was Samuel Hopkins (1721–1803) of Newport, Rhode Island. Another was the revivalist Charles Finney (1792–1875), who argued that repentance, resulting in moral change, would undermine slavery: 'Let Christians of all denominations . . . clear their communions, and wash their hands of this thing . . . and there would not be a shackled slave, nor a bristling, cruel, slave-driver in this land.'[20]

One of the founders of the American Anti-Slavery Society, formed in 1833, was William Lloyd Garrison, from a strongly evangelical Baptist background. He asserted a biblical basis for opposing slavery:

> In the name of God, Who has made us of one blood and in Whose image we are created; in the name of the Messiah, Who came to bind up the broken hearted, to proclaim liberty to the captives . . . I demand the immediate emancipation of those who are pining.[21]

However, he became frustrated by the gradualist approach advocated by the Baptist, Presbyterian and Methodist clergy he approached for support. Over time he began to question their theological views publicly, and after 1840 moved in an increasingly liberal and then radical theological direction, rejecting the authority of the Bible and the atoning work of Christ. He eventually became fascinated with spiritualism.[22]

---

[20] C. Finney, *Lectures on Revivals of Religion*, ed. W. G. McLoughlin (Cambridge, Mass.: Harvard University Press, 1960), 107–108, 112, 302.

[21] Quoted in J. Rutter Williamson, *The Healing of the Nations* (Chicago: Missionary Campaign Library, 1899), preface.

[22] W. L. van Deburg, 'William Lloyd Garrison and the "Pro-Slavery Priesthood": The Changing Beliefs of an Evangelical Reformer, 1830–1840', *Journal of the American Academy of Religion* 43.2 (June 1975), 229–237.

Garrison's demand for immediate emancipation split the anti-slavery movement. The evangelical businessmen Arthur and Lewis Tappan promoted the education of Africans and a more gradual abolitionist approach through their *Journal of Commerce*. The South's small abolitionist movement included the Congregationalist John Fee, of Kentucky.[23] African American churches also proved to be a vital link in the Underground Railroad, which assisted escaping slaves on their journey to slave-free states and Canada, as did white anti-slavery Protestant evangelicals influenced by the Second Great Awakening in states such as Kentucky.[24]

Tragically, the rift that plunged North America into civil war was prefigured by divisions between North and South within denominations, many of them evangelical, over slavery. The Baptist mission agency split over the appointment of slave-holding missionaries: out of this division came the Southern Baptist Convention. Methodists similarly divided over slavery. When Christianity was exerting its strongest ever influence over the nation, it signally failed to provide clear moral leadership on the slavery issue, and even fostered division.

Mirroring other theological traditions, this failure of evangelicals in America to find a common approach to slavery reflected weaknesses in their approach to biblical interpretation.[25] In Britain evangelicals uniformly interpreted the Bible in favour of the abolitionist position, but in America slavery was deeply embedded culturally. Here some evangelicals found it difficult to interpret Scripture without doing so through the lenses of their slave-owning culture. They argued that because the Bible mentioned slavery, the practice was acceptable, even though no other body of Protestants in the English-speaking world shared that conclusion. J. H. Thornwell, the leading Presbyterian theologian of the South, argued that 'the relation betwixt the slave and his master is not inconsistent with the word of God', and that the church should not interfere in such political matters.[26] This produced a shocked reaction from the Scottish United Presbyterian Church, which declared Thornwell's thinking 'the foulest

---

[23] Fee's campaign is discussed in V. B. Howard, *The Evangelical War Against Slavery and Caste* (Selinsgrove: Susquehanna University Press, 1996).

[24] See A. Turley, 'Spirited Away: Black Evangelicals and the Gospel of Freedom, 1790–1890', PhD thesis, University of Kentucky, 2009.

[25] The clearest treatment of this is found in Mark Noll, 'The Bible and Slavery', in R. Miller, H. Stout and C. Wilson (eds.), *Religion and the American Civil War* (New York: Oxford University Press, 1998), 43–73. See also M. Snay, *Gospel of Disunion: Religion and Separatism in the Antebellum South* (Cambridge: Cambridge University Press, 1993).

[26] J. H. Thornwell, 'Our National Sins', in *Fast Day Sermons: Or the Pulpit on the State of the Country* (New York: Rudd & Carleton, 1861), 44.

and most revolting that has ever been enunciated since our blessed Redeemer hung upon the cross of shame'.[27]

Evangelical abolitionists in the North argued that American slavery bore no resemblance to that in the Old Testament, and that Scripture provided the principles by which slavery was to be ended. They highlighted the inconsistency of biblical interpretation in the South: if slavery was justified because it was mentioned in the Old Testament, then so too was polygamy or the dietary and purity laws. Charles Hodge, the leading Presbyterian theologian in the North, pertinently observed that biblical interpretation in the South was 'more or less subject to the controlling influence of public opinion, and of the life of the community to which they belong'.[28] Hodge's views developed over time, but in 1871 he outlined his long-standing conviction that 'slaveholding is in itself a crime, is anti-scriptural and subversive of the Word of God'. He believed emancipation should come through the influence of the gospel,[29] and had reservations over going to war against Christian slave owners.

Many evangelical African Americans saw redemption as the central theme of Scripture, and the liberation from slavery in Exodus as providing hope for their own freedom. They held firmly to the truth of biblical texts such as Acts 17:26: 'From one man he [God] made all the nations'.

Evangelical abolitionists took different approaches to resolving the issue. Through literary means Harriet Beecher Stowe's (1811–96) novel *Uncle Tom's Cabin* provided a powerful evangelical challenge to slavery. In it the Christlike character Tom, a slave, suffers and lays down his life to protect others, and refuses the opportunity of escape. Others sought direct action, including evangelicals from the slave community. Nat Turner (1800–31), a respected African American Baptist preacher from Virginia, led an unsuccessful slave uprising in 1831.[30] The white Congregationalist abolitionist John Brown (1800–59) believed he was called by God to lead a 'holy war' against those seeking to extend slavery, and that America's guilt for the sin of slavery would not be purged without the shedding of blood. After his failed

---

[27] 'The Civil War in America, and Our Present Difficulty', *United Presbyterian Magazine*, new series 6 (January 1862), 2, quoted in M. Noll, *America's God: From Jonathan Edwards to Abraham Lincoln* (New York: Oxford University Press, 2002), 401.

[28] C. Hodge, 'The General Assembly', *Princeton Review* 37 (July 1865), 506, quoted in Noll, *America's God*, 403.

[29] C. Hodge, 'Slavery', in *Biblical Repertory and Princeton Review: The Index Volume from 1825–1868* (Philadelphia: Peter Walker, 1871), 15; 'Slavery', in C. Hodge, *Essays and Reviews* (New York: R. Carter, 1857), 573–611; Noll, 'Bible and Slavery', 60.

[30] Turner's revolt is explored in H. Tragle (ed.), *Southampton Slave Revolt of 1831* (Amherst, Mass.: University of Massachusetts Press, 1971).

uprising in October 1859 on behalf of God's 'despised poor', Brown was executed.[31]

In 1858 Abraham Lincoln declared, 'this country cannot endure permanently half slave and half free'.[32] His election as president in 1860 led slave-holding states to secede from the Union, precipitating a civil war that cost 600,000 lives. Both sides believed they were fighting in Christian armies and that God was on their side, but, as Lincoln observed, 'God cannot be *for* and *against* the same thing at the same time.'[33] Religious revivals were reported among troops of both the North and the South, Bible studies were well attended and religious tracts and books widely read. Soldiers went into battle singing psalms and hymns. General Thomas 'Stonewall' Jackson, a Southern general, was widely known as a Sunday school superintendent concerned for the spiritual state of his soldiers.[34]

The understanding among evangelicals that somehow the appalling suffering was redemptive was pervasive. As Harriet Beecher Stowe explained, 'Ours sons must die, their sons must die. We give ours freely; they die to redeem the very brothers that slay them; they give their blood in expiation of this great sin.'[35] Strangely, for all the blood spilled and devastation reeked, America emerged from the Civil War an even more Christian nation.

Lincoln's emancipation proclamation took effect on 1 January 1863, declaring slaves 'henceforth forever free'. Although he was not an evangelical, and joined no church, Lincoln placed a strong emphasis on Providence and his speeches were redolent with biblical images.[36] Hodge declared victory against the slave-holding states to be 'one of the most momentous events in the history of the world. That it was the design of God to bring about this event cannot be doubted.'[37] In the South victory was attributed to infidel and rationalistic voices. Robert Dabney, a Presbyterian theologian who served as Jackson's chief of staff, was still in 1867 opposing the ordination of African Americans and racial intermarriage, although he based his view on the 'righteous, rational *instinct* of pious minds', rather than specific Bible verses.[38]

---

[31] *Herald*, New York, 3 November 1859, quoted in D. A. Copeland, *The Antebellum Era* (Westport, Conn.: Greenwood, 2003), 399.

[32] S. Thernstrom, *A History of the American People* (San Diego, Calif.: Harcourt Brace Jovanovich, 1989), 363–364.

[33] W. J. Wolf, *The Religion of Abraham Lincoln* (New York: Doubleday, 1963), 147–148; emphases original.

[34] D. W. Stowell, 'Stonewall Jackson and the Providence of God', in Miller et al., *Religion*, 187–207.

[35] H. Beecher Stowe, quoted in L. P. Masur (ed.), *The Real War Will Never Get in the Books: Selections from Writers During the Civil War* (New York: Oxford University Press, 1993), 245.

[36] Noll, *America's God*, 426, 436. On Lincoln's religion see A. C. Guelzo, *Abraham Lincoln: Redeemer President* (Grand Rapids, Mich.: Eerdmans, 1999).

[37] C. Hodge, 'President Lincoln', *Biblical Repertory and Princeton Review* 37 (July 1865), 439–440, quoted in Noll, *America's God*, 433–434.

[38] R. L. Dabney, 'Ecclesiastical Equality of Negroes', in *Discussions: Evangelical and Theological* (1890), vol. 2 (London: Banner of Truth, 1967), p. 207; emphasis original.

The freedoms granted to African Americans allowed them to choose where to worship. Most rejected the white-dominated Southern churches that had been complicit in perpetuating slavery, and formed autonomous black churches, which were largely evangelical in their theology.[39]

Despite evangelical action being central in the victory against slave trading and slavery in Britain and its colonies, and such views being shared by evangelicals in the Northern states of America, there was no such consensus in the South. The result was the deeply distressing spectacle of evangelicals, along with those from other theological traditions, killing each other in the Civil War. The slaves, in whose cause they fought, also included many evangelicals. The deep penetration of the pro-slavery culture in the South prevented evangelicalism from being the radical countercultural movement that had created far-sighted social action elsewhere. There were certainly compassionate evangelical slave owners who treated slaves well, but the overall system remained oppressive and cruel in the South. Anti-slavery was in many ways one of evangelicalism's greatest achievements in social action, but events in America cast a shadow over this positive narrative.

Character study:
William Wilberforce (1759–1833) – England

The person synonymous with the British campaign against the slave trade was William Wilberforce, an MP from the age of 21. As a close friend of the young William Pitt, who became prime minister at the age of just 24, Wilberforce appeared destined for high political office. After his evangelical conversion in 1785, he considered becoming an Anglican clergyman, but John Newton (1725–1807), the leading evangelical preacher in London, persuaded him to remain in Parliament. As his evangelicalism became widely known he was approached by abolitionist campaigners who urged him to become a parliamentary advocate in the cause. It was a challenge he accepted after much prayer and heart-searching and with the encouragement of Newton, who was a converted former slave trader. Newton provided first-hand testimony about the slave trade, 'a commerce so iniquitous, so cruel, so oppressive, so destructive'.[40]

---

[39] C. E. Lincoln and L. H. Mamiya, *The Black Church in the African American Experience* (Durham: Duke University Press, 1990), 25–63.

[40] J. Newton, *Thoughts upon the African Slave Trade* (London, 1788); repr. in P. J. Kitson (ed.), *Slavery, Abolition and Emancipation: Writings in the British Romantic Period*, vol. 2: *The Abolition Debate* (London: Pickering & Chatto, 1999), 117.

John Wesley also urged Wilberforce to help abolish the slave trade, 'that execrable villainy, which is the scandal of religion'. He warned him of the challenges ahead: 'Unless God has raised you up for this very thing, you will be worn out by the opposition of men and devils. But if God be for you, who can be against you?'[41] Wilberforce also worked closely with Thomas Clarkson, and was ably assisted by the Clapham Sect. They were convinced they should use their wealth and influence, especially in Parliament, to promote social reform. Surrendering ambition for high office, Wilberforce effectively became a parliamentary cross-bencher, operating independently.

Wilberforce declared, 'God has set before me two great objects, the suppression of the slave trade and the reformation of manners.'[42] Although evangelicals remained a religious and political minority, Wilberforce strongly identified evangelicalism with opposition to slavery. Important to his success was his political acumen: he recognized the need to form alliances and work steadily and persistently over decades. He also understood the need to mobilize popular support through speeches, letter-writing and popular petitions.

To Wilberforce, the Bible provided the principles upon which slavery was to be abolished. Texts such as Exodus 21:16 and 1 Timothy 1:9–10 were appealed to. The evangelical theological emphasis on redemption stressed deliverance from the slavery of sin, making freeing slaves from the bondage of slavery appear a physical representation of the inward spiritual experience of evangelicals. This theological dynamic of liberation,[43] when coupled with Enlightenment concepts of individual liberty, the right to personal happiness, and growing humanitarian sentiment provided a broad basis on which campaigners appealed. Those impelled to promote social transformation as a fruit of their spiritual transformation were thus able to win sympathy and support from those without the same religious motivation.

Wilberforce drew on Old and New Testament principles:

Inasmuch therefore, as we are repeatedly and expressly told that Christ has done away all distinctions of nations, and made all mankind one great family, all our fellow creatures are now our brethren; and therefore the very principles and spirit of the Jewish law itself would forbid our keeping the Africans, any more than our own fellow subjects, in a state of

---

[41] J. Wesley, letter to William Wilberforce, 24 February 1791, *Letters of John Wesley*, vol. 8, ed. J. Telford (London; Epworth, 1921), 265.

[42] By 'manners' he meant morality.

[43] R. Anstey, *The Atlantic Slave Trade and British Abolition 1760–1810* (Atlantic Highlands, N.J.: Humanities Press, 1975), 406.

slavery ... Fraud, and rapine, and cruelty, are contrary to that religion, which commands us to love our neighbour as ourselves, and to do to others as we would have them do to us.[44]

This theological understanding drew Wilberforce and other evangelicals into the abolitionist cause with a zeal and perseverance not matched by others. It gave an opportunity to enact the ethics of the gospel. Coupled with this was a sense of guilt at being associated with a nation and its colonies that profited from putting humans in bondage. This profiting, it was feared, was placing the nation under the judgment of God – the loss of the American colonies was viewed as evidence of judgment.[45] Abolition was a means by which God's grace could be restored to the nation.[46]

Wilberforce faced a phalanx of political and economic opposition, including plantation owners in the West Indies and British merchants and traders involved in the Atlantic trade. The French Revolution and the resultant social collapse brought resistance to any change that might destabilize the status quo. Wilberforce also battled constant ill health, suffering from what appears to have been ulcerative colitis, leaving him debilitated and in pain each day.

In 1787 Wilberforce introduced into Parliament resolutions condemning the slave trade, declaring, 'So much misery condensed in so little room is more than the human imagination had ever before conceived.' Its wickedness appeared 'so enormous, so dreadful, so irremediable'.[47] The first bill to abolish the slave trade was defeated in 1791,[48] but was reintroduced the next year, calling this time for 'gradual' abolition. This passed in the House of Commons, but was stalled by the House of Lords. A succession of eleven parliamentary bills were rejected. In 1804 a bill did eventually pass through the House of Commons, but was then delayed by Pitt's death. Finally, in 1807, the measure for the Abolition of the Slave Trade in British ships was passed by both Houses and received its royal assent. Only sixteen MPs opposed it. After eighteen years of campaigning, dedication and determination Wilberforce attributed the victory to the hand of God.

---

[44] W. Wilberforce, *A Letter on the Abolition of the Slave Trade: Addressed to the Freeholders and Other Inhabitants of Yorkshire* (London: Cadell & Davies, 1807).

[45] Anstey, *Atlantic Slave Trade*, 406.

[46] This is outlined in Granville Sharp's *The Law of Retribution: Or a Serious Warning to Great Britain and Her Colonies* (London: W. Richardson, 1776).

[47] G. C. B. Davies, 'Simeon in the Setting of the Evangelical Revival', in A. Pollard and M. Hennell (eds.), *Charles Simeon (1759–1836)* (London: SPCK, 1959), 16.

[48] W. Hague, *William Wilberforce: The Life of the Great Anti-Slave Trade Campaigner* (London: HarperPress, 2007), 178–183.

The social concern of Wilberforce extended far beyond slavery. In 1787 he persuaded King George III to issue a 'Royal Proclamation against Vice and Immorality'. Efforts to enforce the proclamation were undertaken by the Proclamation Society, which in 1802 became the Society for the Suppression of Vice. His book *A Practical View of the Prevailing Religious System* (1797) set out his evangelical convictions, challenging the nominal Christianity of many of the middle and upper classes in Britain, and reminding the rich of their duty to the poor. Although his political instincts were conservative and he opposed the development of the early trade unions, Wilberforce also worked for prison and factory reform, and protecting children used to sweep chimneys. He sought to reduce excessive penalties imposed for some minor crimes. Wilberforce was a founder of the Society for Bettering the Conditions and Increasing the Comforts of the Poor, helping those suffering most through harsh working and living conditions. The society promoted the welfare and education of children working in factories, and the provision of soup kitchens for the unemployed. Wilberforce was a strong supporter of Joseph Lancaster's British and Foreign School Society, and inspired and, as mentioned in chapter 6, supported Hannah More in her educational efforts in Somerset. In 1824 he was also a founder of the Royal Society for the Prevention of Cruelty to Animals.[49]

Wilberforce combined moral earnestness with practical philanthropy. During his lifetime he was a member of sixty-nine charities, generously giving away from the fortune he had inherited from his father thousands of pounds each year to needy causes and individuals. His whole life was underpinned by intense evangelical devotion – he often spent three hours a day in prayer.[50]

Although Wilberforce formally launched the campaign for the abolition of slave ownership, its leadership was undertaken largely by Buxton. When Wilberforce heard the news three days before his death that the slave emancipation bill had passed, he declared, 'Thank God that I should have lived to witness a day in which England is willing to give twenty millions sterling for the abolition of slavery.'[51] Through the bill nearly 800,000 slaves were freed.

The achievement over fifty years of Wilberforce and his friends in the Clapham Sect was aptly summed up by Charles Smyth: 'the Evangelicals, although a minority, converted the Church of England to foreign missions,

---

[49] M. Hennell, *Sons of the Prophets: Evangelical Leaders of the Victorian Church* (London: SPCK, 1979), 4–6. On Lancaster and More see chapter 6.

[50] Davies, 'Simeon', 15.

[51] R. I. and S. Wilberforce, *Life of William Wilberforce*, vol. 5 (London: John Murray, 1838), 370.

effected the Abolition of the Slave Trade and Slavery, and initiated Factory Legislation and humanitarian reform, healing the worst sores of the Industrial Revolution'.[52]

---

[52] C. Smyth, 'The Evangelical Movement in Perspective', *Cambridge Historical Journal* 7.3 (1951), 160.

13

Racial equality and the protection of minority ethnic groups

The previous chapter demonstrated how closely the practice of slavery was connected with racist attitudes, which it perpetuated. It was black Africans who were enslaved and transported by both European and Arab traders. African Americans and native American peoples failed to reap much benefit from the 1776 American Declaration of Independence, which stated that 'all men are created equal, that they are endowed by their Creator with certain unalienable rights, and that among these are Life, Liberty and the pursuit of Happiness'. Indeed, the legacy of discrimination and marginalization of black and ethnic racial minority groupings lasted into the twenty-first century.

Under the 1787 United States Constitution, in terms of reckoning a state's total population, slaves were counted only as three-fifths of a person. Although there were evangelicals who addressed such racially discriminatory thinking, sadly this constitutional discrimination was replicated within some of their churches, and even affected both free African Americans as well as slaves. The African Methodist Episcopal Church was formed out of a shocking incident in Philadelphia in 1787 that involved Richard Allen (1760–1831), a slave converted through the itinerant preaching of Methodists. By 1800 one in three American Methodists was black and, despite his status as a slave, Allen began to preach. After hearing Allen preaching, Freeborn Garrettson, his master, renounced slaveholding and allowed Allen and his family to purchase their freedom. Allen preached both to black and white congregations, and settled in Philadelphia, where he mainly ministered to the growing numbers of black members of St George's Methodist Episcopal Church. Despite its location in the North, the African Americans were met with growing hostility from white members of the congregation, who required them to sit in separate parts of the church.

One Sunday in November 1787 the number of African Americans joining the service at St George's was so large that some of them sat in an area of the church set aside for the white congregants. During a time of prayer they were pulled from their knees and removed to another part of the church. Outraged at this and other incidents, Allen and other African Americans withdrew to form separate churches. Initially, they attempted to remain within the Methodist Episcopal Church, but with African American self-government. This arrangement was not successful and a separate denomination, the African Methodist Episcopal Church, was formed in 1816. It began with just five churches, but by 1906 had 500,000 members.[1] The church was African in name and membership, combining the early nineteenth-century evangelical theology of the Methodist denomination with a distinctive social concern. It helped African Americans to find strength, unity and religious self-expression in the face of racial discrimination, and celebrate their African American identity. The African Methodist Episcopal Church was a product of the failure of white Christians to escape the racial prejudices of their culture. It was also an example of how, as Eugene Genovese put it, 'The slaves shaped the Christianity they had embraced; they conquered the religion of those who had conquered them.'[2]

The racial inequalities of the pre-Civil War American South were reflected in its churches. Most slaves attended the same churches as their masters, heard the same sermons, sang the same songs, were even baptized in the same water, but did so from segregated parts of the church. Most white preachers were moulded by the social agenda of their white hearers, many of whom were wealthy and influential, and so concentrated their message narrowly on the spiritual needs of their congregations. However, the way they emphasized biblical teachings on obedience and submission to earthly authorities was a way of enforcing social control, whereas topics related to freedom and liberation were avoided. Even African American preachers felt constrained to preach in ways that did not give offence to white masters, although some were skilled in using language with double meanings, which slaves readily picked up. African American preachers were also to play significant roles as community leaders. However, in the South some churches run by free African Americans separated themselves from slave churches or barred slaves from membership. Aware that their free status depended on the sanction of white Southerners, they disassociated themselves from anything that might destabilize their social position.[3] Despite the discrimination and lack of opportunities they faced, African American church leaders often demonstrated an impressive level of

---

[1] Allen's account of these events is in R. Allen, *The Life Experience and Gospel Labours of the Rt. Rev. Richard Allen*, 2nd edn (Nashville, Tenn.: Abingdon Press, 1960); see also C. V. R. George, *Segregated Sabbaths: Richard Allen and the Emergence of Independent Black Churches, 1760–1840* (New York: Oxford University Press, 1973).

[2] E. D. Genovese, *Roll, Jordan, Roll: The World the Slaves Made* (New York: Random House, 1972), 212.

[3] W. E. Montgomery, *Under Their Own Vine and Fig Tree: The African-American Church in the South, 1865–1900* (Baton Rouge, La.: Louisiana State University Press, 1993), 10–37.

theological knowledge and spiritual understanding. Andrew Reed attended an African American church in Lexington, Virginia, in 1834, heard a fine sermon from a black preacher, heartfelt singing of an Isaac Watts hymn and judged the worship and level of spirituality superior to what he had observed at white services.[4]

The racial discrimination exercised by whites against the black population in North America was repeated in parts of Africa colonized by Europeans. Johannes van der Kemp (1747–1811), a medical doctor from the Netherlands, arrived in Cape Town in 1799 under the auspices of the London Missionary Society (LMS). His ministry was very successful and he attracted a large congregation. He worked closely with the Xhosa evangelist Ntsikana (c.1780–1821), who proved remarkably effective among his own people. When van der Kemp refused to view the local African people as inferior and denounced the behaviour of the Boer settlers towards them, he became a controversial figure. He caused shock to the European settler community by marrying an African woman.

A key figure in further asserting the equal rights of Africans alongside European settlers was the London Missionary Society's John Philip (1775–1851), who arrived in the Cape Colony (later to become South Africa) in 1819. Here he became superintendent of the LMS's work. Philip, from Kirkcaldy, Scotland, had a strongly formed biblical anthropology enabling him to view everyone, including non-Western peoples, as made in the image of God. He followed other evangelical missionaries in believing that through the fall people of every racial background were equally lost, but were also equally able to respond to the gospel and be saved through Christ's atoning work on the cross.[5] Philip's humble family background affirmed his commitment to equality of opportunity. The son of a handloom weaver, he had risen from working as a weaver to become manager of a spinning mill. He then trained for the Congregational ministry, before working very successfully as a minister in Aberdeen for fifteen years. He was therefore a leader of experience and seniority when he arrived in Cape Town.

The European population in the Cape were largely Dutch, but the government officials were British. Philip arrived at a time of significant conflict between the Dutch settlers and the African population, the latter of whom found their land being lost and their rights significantly reduced through the encroachment

---

[4] A. Reed and J. Matheson, *A Narrative of a Visit to the American Churches*, vol. 1 (London: Jackson & Walford, 1835), 216–222.

[5] B. Stanley, 'Christian Missions and the Enlightenment', in B. Stanley (ed.), *Christian Missions and the Enlightenment* (Grand Rapids, Mich.: Eerdmans, 2001), 8–11.

of European settlement. Black Africans fell into a vulnerable and dependent state, needing a letter from a white employer stating their business in order to travel in the colony, without which they could be arrested for vagrancy.[6] The seeds of what became the apartheid system, with its separation between whites and other racial groups, were already being sown.

Philip argued that Christianity should be the agent for moral and social change across the Cape. This included mission to the African population, but also required Europeans to live out their professed Christian values. Philip combined evangelicalism's high estimation of the spiritual potential of each individual with an Enlightenment emphasis on human rights and freedoms. His approach was framed by biblical egalitarian perspectives and, as a Congregationalist, he was committed to the governance of the local church by members of the congregation rather by an imposed external authority. Indeed, he asserted that the black African population displayed a higher level of moral virtue than the supposedly civilized Europeans. In the Khoi villages he observed, 'you will find as rational ideas, as large a quantum of intelligence, as much religion and morality' as any in Britain. He concluded, 'the natural capacity of the African is nothing inferior to the European'.[7]

The evidence Philip sent to the British government about how the African population was consigned to a state of abject economic dependency proved significant. Although Africans were being trained by missionaries in key skills such as carpentry, bricklaying or stonemasonry, they found themselves, and even their children, subjected by European settlers to bonded or forced labour, which was little better than slavery. This forced labour destroyed the businesses they were trying to start.[8] Coming at a time when the campaign to abolish slavery in British colonies was in full swing, Philip's evidence from South Africa was crucial. Philip asserted that ending slavery also required proper protections for Africans in Africa. As a result of Philip's appeals, Thomas Fowell Buxton successfully introduced a motion into the House of Commons that the African population of South Africa should receive the same 'freedom and protection as other free people in the colony'. This brought an end to the compulsory labour and vagrancy laws that so penalized the African population.

---

[6] On this see R. Elphick and R. Davenport, *Christianity in South Africa* (Oxford: Oxford University Press, 1997).

[7] A. Ross, *John Philip (1775–1851), Missions, Race and Politics in South Africa* (Aberdeen: Aberdeen University Press, 1986), 95–96.

[8] Ibid. 98–100.

Buxton encouraged Philip to write an account of the situation in South Africa, which became *Researches in South Africa*,[9] a significant piece of missiological and sociological writing. Much of it was a negative portrayal of white colonists and officials, and included a challenge to reform. For the revelations of the shocking treatment of the African population by white settlers he was sued for libel and had to pay significant damages. Nonetheless, throughout the controversy Philip maintained his assertion that the testimony of a black person was valid, even when it was in conflict with that of a white person.[10] His revelations helped secure the adoption of a non-racial constitution in the Cape Colony. They also demonstrated the continuing pernicious effect of slavery within Africa.

These efforts to develop a non-racial basis for the Cape Colony provoked a negative reaction, and were a factor behind the Great Trek, or Voortrek, of Boer settlers who rejected British rule and relocated to settle across the Orange River in what became the Orange Free State and the Transvaal. This choice by the Boers to live outside the range of British jurisdiction left the African tribes in those areas without the protections that had been secured in the Cape Colony. Philip unsuccessfully urged the British to extend their rule to these regions, believing that with that protection, and the religious and educational efforts of missionaries, the situation of the Africans in these areas would be transformed. He presented a model of colonial rule being exercised with a sense of humanitarian responsibility to the African peoples, demanding that colonial authorities should restrict the excesses of white settlers who wished to rule without any accountability to London.

Philip saw his work as 'civilization' – promoting the education and civil rights of the African population as preparatory work for the gospel. He was convinced that one was a prerequisite for the other: 'Civilisation is to the Christian religion what the body is to the soul; and the body must be prepared and cared for, if the spirit is to be retained upon earth.' Extending education and human rights was disseminating some of the 'blessings which the Christian religion scatters in her progress'.[11] Philip promoted the view that developing legitimate trade and commerce among the African population was essential to overcoming the evil commerce in human flesh that slavery represented, and that this development should be one dimension of missions policy. This helped shape the Christianity, commerce and civilization approach of Buxton and David Livingstone to ending slavery within Africa.[12]

---

[9] J. Philip, *Researches in South Africa* (London: James Duncan, 1828).

[10] Ross, *Philip*, 105–111.

[11] J. Philip, 'Report to the American Board of Commissioners for Foreign Missions', in ibid. 217.

[12] A. Porter, *Religion Versus Empire? British Protestant Missionaries and Overseas Expansion, 1700–1914* (Manchester: Manchester University Press, 2004), 94–97.

Despite Philip's achievements, the 1840s proved to be a disappointment. For all the treaties and agreements, the situation in the Cape Colony deteriorated. Africans continued to be poorly treated by European settlers, including those from Britain. Growing racist attitudes, unstable frontiers and drought and war in 1846 left the African population even more marginalized. After Philip's death in 1851, other missionaries argued for an exclusive focus on individual conversion, with little role for the preparatory work he had urged in creating a secure social context in which Africans could freely embrace the gospel. His thinking was radical for the time, and the type of civil rights he won for a period for Africans in the Cape was achieved only in the twentieth century for African Americans in the USA. Nonetheless, for all the setbacks, in 1853 the Cape Colony was granted the right to have an elected legislature open to people of all racial backgrounds, which lasted until 1910.

Within Europe other groups faced significant racial prejudice. The Jewish population of Eastern Europe, especially Russia, faced terrible persecution. In Europe evangelicals played a prominent role in promoting civil and religious liberty for the Jews. Although Oliver Cromwell had allowed Jews to settle in England, they lacked full civil rights until the nineteenth century. The Strict Baptist pastor of the Surrey Tabernacle, London, James Wells, strongly advocated religious liberty for all, declaring in 1860 that it was 'the right of every man to come before God in what form or manner his conscience may dictate'.[13] He argued that it was the duty of civil government to ensure religious liberty and protect the rights of 'all sects and parties', providing that they did not 'commit anything disorderly' or 'interfere with the rights and liberties of others'.[14] He looked forward to a day when no one filled a civil office or appointment in the government based purely on his religious background. This included members of the Jewish faith, and Wells backed Jewish emancipation in 1870, asserting that 'the Jew has just as much right in the British Parliament as any other man, as a citizen considered; and it is no more a Christian Parliament than the seats on which they sit are Christian'.[15]

Although Lord Shaftesbury opposed the attempt to admit Baron Rothschild to Parliament as an MP in 1846 because it meant changing the Christian basis of the parliamentary oath, he said he did so on religious grounds, rather than

---

[13] J. Wells, 'A Word of Instruction for Duty-Faith People', *Surrey Tabernacle Pulpit*, vol. 2, no. 61 (London: G. J. Stevenson, 1860), 10.

[14] J. Wells, *Address Delivered at Surrey Tabernacle, the Day of the Funeral of the Late Prince Consort* (London: G. J. Stevenson, 1861), 11.

[15] I. J. Shaw, *High Calvinists in Action: Calvinism and the City c.1810–60* (Oxford: Oxford University Press, 2002), 273; J. Wells, 'Mount of Olives', in *Surrey Tabernacle Pulpit*, vol. 12, no. 621 (London: G. J. Stevenson, 1870), 471.

of race. Shaftesbury declared the Jews 'the most talented of all races' and 'the descendants of the most remarkable race that has ever appeared on the face of the earth and . . . the forefathers of those who were yet to play the noblest part in the history of mankind'.[16] Shaftesbury was deeply involved in the establishment of an Anglican bishopric in Jerusalem, a shared appointment with the German Lutheran Church. This was an expression of his passionate concern for evangelization of the Jews, the conversion of whom he saw as a sign of the last days and a prelude to the second coming of Christ. When asked for advice on a new Bishop of Jerusalem in 1879, he declared the incumbent should be 'a man of earnestness and sound judgement, with a true and deep zeal for the welfare and honour of the Jewish people'.[17] In 1882, in the midst of the pogroms in Russia against the Jews, Shaftesbury became president of a society established to help Jewish refugees fleeing the persecution.[18]

The deep and pervasive inequalities and racial discrimination faced by black Americans continued after the Civil War. Despite their freedom they lived the marginalized life of second-class citizens with limited economic opportunity, and suffered significant local hostility. In places they had restricted access to the law, were subject to stringent black penal codes and were denied equal access to education, hospitals, theatres and churches – even in death they were treated as inferiors in cemeteries. After the end of the post-Civil War Reconstruction Era in 1877, former slave states used different strategies to disenfranchise African Americans, and then made use of this to defeat federal legislation against racial violence and abuses.

Racist thinking was not only fuelled by slavery but also by evolutionary theory, which proposed separate points of human origination, rather than a single set of parents, Adam and Eve. This encouraged racist theories of different racial groups being at different levels of human development, with the white Aryan race considered the best developed. Social Darwinists spoke of 'the survival of the fittest' to describe how powerful societies overran less well-developed ones. Such theories underlay the rise of Nazism in Germany, with its appalling Holocaust, the attempt to exterminate the Jewish racial group as well as Roma people (gypsies), the disabled and others deemed undesirable. Sadly, racist attitudes, which demeaned non-white peoples, were evident in some Christian thinking. Such views have been discerned among evangelical holiness missionaries in Africa, resulting in degrading attitudes to black evangelical

---

[16] Shaftesbury, papers, December 1847, quoted in G. B. A. M. Finlayson, *The Seventh Earl of Shaftesbury 1801–1885* (London: Eyre Methuen, 1981), 265.

[17] Letter to Lord Beaconsfield, 16 May 1879, quoted in Finlayson, *Shaftesbury*, 583.

[18] Ibid. 583.

leaders.[19] Even the impeccably conservative evangelical China Inland Mission's flagship Chefoo School in China came to exclude Chinese children. The CIM was also deeply opposed to European missionaries marrying Chinese Christian leaders, fearful it would offend the sensibilities of middle-class supporters back home.[20]

Although D. L. Moody practised racial integration in his schools in Northfield, Massachusetts, he found more difficulty in insisting on this in his evangelistic preaching crusades in the South. His practice was shaped by events in Augusta, Georgia, in 1876, where his open-air meetings began on an unsegregated basis. When African Americans were found sitting on many of the front seats, the organizers put up railings to divide them from the white attendees. Moody opposed this, observing that white people would be astonished one day to see these African Americans 'marching into the kingdom of heaven while they themselves were shut out'. This aroused protest from local politicians, and local white Christians assured Moody that his gospel preaching would be viewed with 'contempt and abhorrence' if he persisted with unsegregated meetings. Fearful of losing his audience, Moody backed down and preached to segregated audiences or to separate services for African Americans and whites, conforming to the social pressures of the time. This, however, deeply offended African American evangelicals. When he preached in Louisville, Kentucky, in 1888, to segregated audiences he offered a special campaign exclusively for the city's black population. This they refused, one African American minister asserting, 'I recognize no color line in the church of God.' Moody did hold private sentiments in favour of racial justice; but when those appeared likely to reduce the numbers of those who would hear the gospel and offend prominent white supporters and advisors, he pulled back. He saw the evangelistic task, in the light of the imminent return of Christ, as overriding all other considerations.[21]

A thoroughgoing response to racial inequality had to wait until the civil-rights movement of the 1950s and 1960s. In their response to this, white Christian leaders often replicated the equivocal stance of D. L. Moody, rather than the clearly articulated biblical anthropology of John Philip and James Wells. Most of the white supporters of Martin Luther King tended to come from theologically liberal churches rather than the evangelical tradition.

---

[19] A. Porter, 'Cambridge, Keswick, and Late-Nineteenth-Century Attitudes to Africa', in *Journal of Imperial and Commonwealth History* 5.1 (1976), 5–34.

[20] R. A. Semple, *Missionary Women: Gender, Professionalism, and the Victorian Idea of Christian Mission* (Woodbridge: Boydell Press, 2003), 155, 168–169.

[21] J. F. Findlay, *Dwight L. Moody: American Evangelist, 1837–1899* (Chicago, Ill.: University of Chicago Press, 1969), 278–281.

Many evangelicals remained content to defend the status quo, which meant white dominance, and some opposed the civil-rights movement. Calls for social justice were adjudged 'political', and therefore in conflict with gospel ministry. Interracial marriage was in general opposed, and many white evangelicals opted to live in areas physically separate from African Americans, and so failed to see the inequalities the latter suffered daily.[22]

Southern Baptists who spoke openly of the need for social action to secure racial justice were rare.[23] Similarly, Presbyterians in the South generally opposed the civil-rights movement. W. A. Gamble, stated clerk of Central Mississippi Presbytery, ardently supported the segregation laws between the races and opposed mixed-race marriages. L. Nelson Bell, associate editor of the *Presbyterian Journal* and founder of *Christianity Today*, and Billy Graham's father-in-law, took a more moderate view, opposing segregation as a hindrance to the preaching of the gospel to all. However, he believed Christian love would bring about integration naturally, rather than its needing to be legally imposed. Compared to the early 1950s, by the late 1960s segregation was much more widely opposed, including by some of the future founders of the Presbyterian Church in America in 1973. They argued that the product of true gospel preaching should be a racially inclusive church.[24]

A leading role in promoting this view was played by Billy Graham, who in 1952–3 decided that he could no longer preach the gospel to segregated meetings, because this was a betrayal of the gospel itself. He asserted, 'Jesus Christ belongs neither to the coloured nor the white races. He belongs to all races.' He was disturbed how the attitude of the church to racial equality was lagging far behind that of sport and politics.[25] Graham faced significant opposition from extremists for these views, and believed that 'Christ alone can give the love in the hearts of the two races that ultimately will ease all tensions and solve all problems in this matter.'[26] Social change would follow when the gospel was preached and believed: changed men and women would create a changed society.

Although many evangelicals showed personal kindness to African Americans, such evangelicals remained content with a society that left whites in control.

[22] M. J. Hall, in J. Taylor (ed.), 'A Conversation with Four Historians on the Response of White Evangelicals to the Civil Rights Movement' <https://www.thegospelcoalition.org/blogs/evangelical-history/a-conversation-with-four-historians-on-the-response-of-white-evangelicals-to-the-civil-rights-movement>, accessed 11 April 2020.

[23] See D. Swartz, 'Glimmers of Hope: Progressive Evangelical Leaders and Racism, 1965–2000', in J. R. Hawkins and P. L. Sinitiere, *Christians and the Colour Line: Race and Religion After Divided by Faith* (New York: Oxford University Press, 2013).

[24] S. M. Lucas, in 'Conversation with Four Historians', in Hall, n. 22 above.

[25] J. Pollock, *Billy Graham* (London: Hodder & Stoughton, 1966), 134–137.

[26] W. Graham, letter to Ralph McGill, 31 October 1953, quoted in Pollock, *Graham*, 137.

Some opposed efforts to desegregate schools and sought to justify this from the Bible. The rejection of church involvement in politics led to the condemnation of civil-rights activists, such as Martin Luther King, who were church leaders. Funds were withheld from church agencies that advocated equality, and pastors who supported the civil-rights struggle could face removal from office. Black worshippers still found themselves turned away from services; and when segregated schools became unlawful, many white evangelicals put their children into private schools sponsored by the churches of which these evangelicals were members. Most white evangelicals opposed violence being used to support segregation, but that did not mean they supported desegregation. They were convinced their task was solely the spiritual regeneration of the individual, and that personal spiritual change was the only answer to social problems. This led to a failure to address the issues that rendered African Americans second-class citizens, condemned by the colour of their skin to live in areas of poor housing, inferior education and limited job prospects.[27]

Although the National Association of Evangelicals in 1964 and 1965 faced demands from white Christian leaders not to support the civil-rights movement, the NAE had already decided it was not the place of the church to be involved in such matters. The sacred and secular were to be kept firmly apart in this area. Some persisted in maintaining that segregation between the races was 'God's plan'.[28] Tragically, this meant separation from their fellow evangelicals in the African American community who were living in segregated neighbourhoods.

One of the clearest statements of changing evangelical approaches to the issue of racial equality, and a return to the values of Philip, came with the publication of John Stott's *Issues Facing Christians Today* in 1984. When Stott wrote this, apartheid still prevailed in South Africa, anti-Semitism lingered in Europe, and the USA and other Western societies remained very unequal racially. Stott argued that Acts 17:22–31 conclusively proved the unity of the human race. All derived their life and breath from God the Creator, who from one man made every nation of men. Therefore, 'every human being is our brother or sister' and 'we are equal in his sight in worth and dignity, and therefore have an equal right to respect and justice'. Alongside this he called for 'a respectful diversity of *cultures*', so that, while 'our racial, national, social and sexual distinctions remain, they no longer divide us', having been transcended by the unity of the

---

[27] See C. R. Dupont, *Mississippi Praying: Southern White Evangelicals and the Civil Rights Movement, 1945–1975* (New York: New York University Press, 2013).

[28] J. R. Hawkins in 'Conversation with Four Historians'; see also J. R. Hawkins and P. L. Sinitiere (eds.), *Christians and the Color Line* (New York: Oxford University Press, 2014).

family of God (Gal. 3:28). The implications of this teaching for racial justice were enormous:

> Because of the unity of mankind we demand equal rights and equal respect for racial minorities. Because of the diversity of ethnic groups we renounce cultural imperialism ... Because of the glory of the church, we must seek to rid ourselves of any lingering racism and strive to make it a model of harmony between races.[29]

As with the issue of slavery, and for similar reasons, the record of evangelicals in their response to racial inequality is a mixed one. Certainly, evangelicalism produced leaders who radically challenged their culture and its prejudices, and were often far ahead of their time, but there remained those who read Scripture through their culture and failed to challenge injustice or practise integration. Sadly, some churches remained more racially segregated than the society surrounding them. This tragically meant segregation of white evangelicals from the large numbers of black evangelicals in their neighbouring churches and communities.

Character study: Jeremiah Evarts (1781–1831) – USA

It was not only African Americans who suffered discrimination and oppression on the basis of their racial backgrounds in North America. The drive west by settlers was into territory already possessed by 125,000 Native Americans, and First Nations peoples in Canada. Courted as allies by the American rebels in the War of Independence, by the early nineteenth century their close proximity was increasingly feared. This was despite the efforts of evangelical leaders such as the US Congressman Elias Boudinot (1740–1821), one of the founders of the American Bible Society, to promote the rights of Native Americans.[30]

Jeremiah Evarts also campaigned resolutely for the rights of Native Americans, and strongly opposed their removal from their ancestral lands. He was deeply influenced by the Second Great Awakening.[31] Between 1805 and 1820 Evarts worked as editor of *The Panoplist*, a religious monthly magazine, where he published essays about education, social and moral reform, including

---

[29] J. Stott, *Issues Facing Christians Today* (Basingstoke: Marshall, Morgan & Scott, 1984), 205, 206, 207–208 (emphasis original), 209.

[30] I. J. Shaw, *Churches, Revolutions and Empires: 1789–1914* (Fearn: Christian Focus, 2012), 339.

[31] J. A. Andrew III, *From Revivals to Removal: Jeremiah Evarts, the Cherokee Nation, and the Search for the Soul of America* (Athens, Ga.: University of Georgia Press, 1992), 30–31.

Sabbath observance and temperance, the training of ministers, and for-eign missions. He also wrote twenty-four essays on the rights of Native Americans. Evarts challenged leaders in early nineteenth-century America to demonstrate self-denial, and place civic responsibility before profit.[32] Central to Evarts' theology was the love of God. This love, demonstrated to them through Christ, was experienced by the believer and should be returned to God. Charity was the outflow of a changed heart and a genuine faith: 'No worship is acceptable to God unless it proceeds from a heart filled with benevolence to man.'[33]

Evarts served as treasurer of the American Board of Commissioners for Foreign Missions (ABCFM) from 1812 to 1820 and then as secretary from 1821 until his death in 1831. His vision for missions encompassed not only overseas fields but also those unreached with the gospel in North America, especially the Indigenous population of America. His strategy focused on education, training for settled agricultural life and employment, and religious education.[34] The approach was similar to the missions policy later advocated for Africa – Christianization, civilization (education) and commerce, or at least settled farming. The first schools were started in 1816 and 1817, and by 1826 there were a series of mission stations among the Cherokees in Arkansas, Tennessee, Alabama and Georgia, and the Choctaws in Mississippi. They faced consider-able opposition from settlers, land speculators and even local officials, who desired these people's lands for their own purposes.[35]

Evarts' policy could be criticized for perpetuating Thomas Jefferson's assimilation policy, rather than preserving the culture of the Indigenous peoples of the Americas. Furthermore, while supporting the rights of Native Americans to remain on their ancestral lands, an unfortunate by-product of assimilation was that it undermined their claims to possess their own dis-tinctive national identity, on the basis of which treaties had been signed and from which they could claim rights for protection. However, Evarts argued that the work of the missionaries protected their rights more effectively than any armed force, ensuring their survival and alleviating the fears of white settlers, because the Native Americans were increasingly becoming Christian peoples.

This mission work, and commitment that Native Americans should remain on their lands, became a significant barrier to the growing removals policy from

---

[32] E. C. Tracy, *Memoir of the Life of Jeremiah Evarts, Esq.* (Boston: Crocker & Brewster, 1845), 65–69.
[33] Andrew, *From Revivals to Removal*, 51.
[34] Ibid. 86.
[35] Ibid. 86–87, 89.

1817 onwards. Federal government funding was obtained for the educational work, and under missionary influence the Native Americans became less willing to sign new treaties and cede further land.[36] White settlers and some state officials, such as those in Georgia, turned their hostility on the missionaries.

Evarts found that mission to the Native Americans was slow and expensive compared to overseas missions, where progress among the 'heathen' was often quicker and more dramatic, and seen as less political. Also, through the 1820s Native Americans gradually became more resistant to the civilization aspects of the plan. Evarts found it an increasing struggle to raise money for the missions and was also battling his own failing health, with the onset of tuberculosis.[37] His fear remained that the Indigenous peoples of the Americas would simply 'melt away, destroyed by vices copied from unprincipled whites, having sold their birthright for a *mess of pottage*, and being left in the land of their fathers, without property, without a home, and without a friend'.[38]

'Indian' removal became a popular electoral cause. Andrew Jackson asserted, 'I have long viewed treaties with the Indians an absurdity not to be reconciled with the principles of our government,'[39] arguing that Native Americans were subjects like any others, not sovereign rulers with whom treaties needed to be made. Their lands should be surveyed as any other land was, and then put on the market for sale.[40] Some missionaries supported removal. In 1823 Isaac McCoy, a Baptist missionary to the Native Americans, argued that the Christianization and civilization policy was working too slowly, and it would be safer for the Native Americans to be removed west of the Mississippi, where they would be free from white encroachment on their lands. Here missionaries could continue their work without hindrance from the white community. To Evarts this amounted to removing them to wild and uncivilized lands in order to civilize them, which was unlikely to be successful.[41]

After Jackson was elected president in 1828, Evarts found himself locked in confrontation with him. He was convinced Jackson was using political power to promote unchecked individualism and discard religious and moral values and responsibilities.[42] When Jackson introduced the Indian Removal Bill of

---

[36] Ibid. 94–97.

[37] Ibid. 130–131.

[38] Evarts, letter to ABCFM Board, May 1822, quoted in Tracy, *Memoir*, 179; emphasis original.

[39] Letter from Andrew Jackson to James Monroe, 1817, in E. H. Spicer, *A Short History of the Indians of the United States* (New York: D. Van Nostrand, 1969), 228–229.

[40] Andrew, *From Revivals to Removal*, 93.

[41] Ibid. 122–123.

[42] Ibid. 155, 183.

1830, Evarts threw himself into the campaign against it, mobilizing congressmen and senators who opposed removal, in the hope that enough Jacksonians would oppose the measure. He also sought to turn the tide of public opinion through letter and pamphlet writing and publication of articles.[43] Evarts came agonizingly close to succeeding. In May 1830 the measure passed through the House of Representatives with a majority of just four. Evarts was dismayed that some who opposed removal had set aside the dictates of conscience and morality in favour of party loyalty, and they had voted for the bill just to support the administration.[44] His sentiments were echoed by the *Christian Advocate*, which declared, 'If it shall be such as we fear, the iniquity of this single transaction will overshadow, as with one broad cloud of deepest darkness, the whole lustre of our national glory.'[45]

Jackson immediately removed government funding for the mission stations among the Native Americans.[46] The forced expulsion of tens of thousands of Native Americans to barren reservations in the west, along what was known as the 'Trail of Tears', followed. In theory the removals were voluntary, backed by provisions and cash incentives, but those who refused to relocate were rounded up by the army.[47] Evarts urged the Cherokees to take their case to the US Supreme Court. It initially refused to hear the case, but when the state of Georgia prohibited whites from living on Native American territory without a licence, Evarts encouraged the white missionaries to defy this. After a number were arrested, one of them, Samuel Worcester, fought a test case, as a result of which the Supreme Court ruled in 1832 that the Cherokee nation was sovereign, and that Georgia did not have the right to enforce state laws in Cherokee territory.[48] Jackson chose to ignore the ruling and enforced the expulsion of some 15,000 Cherokees. It was thought that some 4,000 died on the journey to their new territory in Oklahoma.[49]

Evarts died in May 1831, aged just 50, having burned himself out in the cause of the Native Americans. In many ways the Christian campaign against the removal of the Indigenous peoples of the Americas died with him. Despite never being an ordained minister, he had greatly furthered the cause of mission at home and overseas among the North American churches, and fought

---

[43] Ibid. 220–221.

[44] Tracy, *Memoir*, 378–379.

[45] *Christian Advocate*, 8 May 1830, 263, in Andrew, *From Revivals to Removal*, 231.

[46] Ibid. 232–233.

[47] Ibid. 234–235.

[48] Ibid. 260–261.

[49] On this see W. L. Anderson (ed.), *Cherokee Removal: Before and After* (Athens, Ga.: University of Georgia Press, 1991).

resolutely for the rights of the minority Native American population.[50] Evarts'
hope that the Second Great Awakening would spread evangelical humanitarian
sentiment through the political sphere, creating a new Christian and benevolent
consensus, was not fulfilled. Many continued to keep their inward spiritual life
separate from the secular realm, including the political. Evarts remained sure
that in God's time change would come: his abiding prayer resolutions included
that 'the rights of the Indians may be vindicated, and the honour of the country
preserved'.[51]

---

[50] Tracy, *Memoir*, 428.
[51] Ibid. 429.

14

Medical mission

The example of the preaching and healing ministry of Christ provided a strong motivation for Christians to include medical work as an aspect of missionary service. The 'double cure' of body and soul, powerfully demonstrated in the healing of the paralysed man (Luke 5:17–26), became the ideal of medical mission from the nineteenth century onwards.

As Protestant missionaries travelled from Europe in the eighteenth century, even those who had not been medically trained were regularly consulted for medical advice and assistance. The first Hindu convert reported by the Baptist Missionary Society in India came through the work of Dr John Thomas, William Carey's fellow worker, who was a surgeon. While resetting the dislocated shoulder of Krishna Pal, Thomas shared the gospel with him, which led to the conversion of the Hindu carpenter.[1]

Thomas never appears to have styled himself a medical missionary, and there is some uncertainty over the formal beginnings of the Protestant medical missionary movement. Thomas Colledge (1796–1879), a surgeon with the East India Company and then for the British Crown, seems to have made the first significant attempt to connect medical work with mission formally in the 1820s. He undertook part-time missionary work alongside his surgical work as the occasion presented itself. He also began to treat local Chinese people, and in 1827 started a mission hospital in Macao.[2] Colledge focused on ophthalmic work and crowds of Chinese people flocked there for treatment. The hospital

---

[1] C. B. Lewis, *The Life of John Thomas, Surgeon of the Earl of Oxford and First Baptist Missionary to India* (London: Macmillan, 1873), 363–373.

[2] Reports and testimonies of Colledge's work are given in the *London Saturday Journal*, 1840, 298–299.

demonstrated how Western medicine could be used as a way of introducing Christianity to China.[3]

Colledge also began to promote the cause of medical missions and helped found the Medical Missionary Society in China in 1837.[4] Colledge patterned the work of the missionary doctor on that of Christ, arguing that his last command 'preach the gospel' did not abrogate his earlier one to 'heal the sick'. To Colledge, 'benevolent deeds cannot fail to be a means, which must ultimately lead to the propagation of the truths of *His* gospel'. The medical missionary was to combine medical excellence with profound Christian commitment. Colledge strongly objected to missionaries who possessed an 'imperfect knowledge of the healing art', using their limited medical knowledge to try to gain the confidence of the local people, but ending up harming both the cause of medicine and religion.[5]

The question of the balance between the two dimensions of medical mission was seen in the work of Dr Peter Parker (1804–88), who completed both medical and divinity studies at Yale before being ordained a Presbyterian minister in 1834. In the same year he was commissioned by the American Board of Commissioners for Foreign Missions, becoming the first full-time Protestant medical missionary to China. In 1835 he opened an ophthalmic hospital in Canton, which treated more than 2,000 patients in its first year of operation. Parker trained Chinese students in medical skills and preached to the patients.[6] Parker believed 'no medium of contact, and of bringing people under the sound of the Gospel, and within the influence of other means of grace, can compare with the facilities afforded by medical missionary operations.'[7]

Despite his success, Parker's ministry was questioned by his mission board. The instructions he received after his commissioning in 1834 by the ABCFM told him to use 'medical and surgical knowledge' in 'relieving bodily afflictions', but 'only as they can be made handmaids to the gospel. The character of a

---

[3] 'Colledge, Thomas Richardson', in *Dictionary of National Biography* (London: Smith, Elder, 1885).

[4] T. R. Colledge, *Suggestions for the Formation of a Medical Missionary Society Offered to the Consideration of All Christian Nations* (Canton, 1836); see also T. R. Colledge, *A Letter on the Subject of Medical Missionaries* (Macau, China, 1836).

[5] T. R. Colledge, *The Medical Missionary Society in China* (Canton, 1838), 4–5, 7. See also L. Fu, 'The Protestant Medical Missions to China: Dr Thomas Richardson Colledge (1796–1879) and the Founding of the Macao Ophthalmic Hospital', *Journal of Medical Biography* 21.2 (2013), 118–123; emphasis original.

[6] F. Heule, 'Thomas Richardson Colledge and Peter Parker: Two Early Nineteenth-Century Missionary Ophthalmologists in China: A Case of (Inter) Cultural Anthropology', *Anthropology: Open Access*, AOAP-113. DOI: 10.29011/AOAP-113/1000013. See also G. B. Stevens and W. F. Marwick, *The Life, Letters and Journals of the Rev. and Hon. Peter Parker, M.D.; Missionary, Physician, and Diplomatist: The Father of Medical Missions and Founder of the Ophthalmic Hospital in Canton* (Boston: Congregational Sunday School and Publishing Society, 1896); L. Fu, 'Healing Bodies or Saving Souls? Reverend Dr Peter Parker (1804–1888) as Medical Missionary', *Journal of Medical Biography* 24.2 (2016), 266–275.

[7] Parker, quoted in J. Lowe, *Medical Missions; Their Place and Power* (London: T. Fisher Unwin, 1886), 59.

physician . . . you will never suffer to supersede or interfere with your character as a teacher of religion.' Despite regular services being held in the hospital, and the best efforts of Parker and other North American missionaries in Canton, it was 1847 before they reported their first convert. Frustrated at his lack of progress, in that same year his role was terminated by the American Board, although he continued working in China.[8]

In 1840 probably the most famous missionary doctor, David Livingstone, was appointed by the London Missionary Society (LMS) to work as a medical missionary to Africa. He understood the spread of the gospel as involving preaching, education and medical care, and throughout his missionary journeys in Africa Livingstone maintained his knowledge by having medical journals mailed out to him. He also studied the influence of climate and diet on certain illnesses, and conducted medical experiments, including developing a malaria treatment comprising quinine and purgatives, which proved successful. Livingstone was respectful of the insights to be gained from African traditional healers at a time when missionaries generally condemned them.[9] As with Parker, the direct fruit of Livingstone's missionary work in terms of conversions was limited, but he opened doors for others to follow with the gospel.

Despite Parker's struggles with his mission board, a lecture he gave in Edinburgh proved very significant. A number who heard it were evangelical leaders in the city, several of whom were professors in the faculty of medicine. They formed in 1841 what became the Edinburgh Medical Missionary Society (EMMS) to train doctors to serve as medical missionaries, and to persuade missionary societies to recruit them. The society argued that those trained should be of the highest academic quality, and have experience of practising in Scotland the sort of medical work they would subsequently undertake abroad.[10]

The first doctor trained by the EMMS went to India in 1857, and the second, Dr Wong, returned to his home country of China supported by the LMS. Other graduates founded the Christian Hospital in Nazareth (1866), a medical missionary dispensary in Damascus (1885) and the EMMS's work was further extended to Malawi.[11]

By the middle of the nineteenth century medical work was being promoted as essential to mission. William Burns Thomson argued in *Medical Missions*

---

[8] G. H. Anderson, 'Peter Parker and the Introduction of Western Mission in China', *Mission Studies* 23.2 (2006), 203–238; G. H. Anderson, 'The Legacy of Peter Parker', *International Bulletin of Missionary Research* 37.3 (July 2013), 152–156.

[9] A. Ross, 'The Scottish Missionary Doctor', in D. A. Dow (ed.), *The Influence of Scottish Medicine* (Carnforth: Parthenon Publishing, 1988), 95.

[10] Ibid. 91–92.

[11] Ibid.

(1854) that, based on the life of Jesus, 'the best method of *introducing* the Gospel to the notice of those who know it not, or who are opposed to it, is to join to proclamation the healing of the sick'. As Thomson argued, Jesus 'did not preach alone, nor heal alone, but he preached and healed'. Medical mission was a demonstration of the gospel in all its fulness, combining 'the promise of the life that now is and of that which is to come'.[12]

The need to provide a specific locus for this practical part of the EMMS training led to the establishment in 1858 of the Medical Mission Dispensary and Training Institute, in an old whisky shop in the Cowgate, an overcrowded and disease-ridden slum barely a stone's throw from the university. Here students worked alongside the resident doctors, undertaking visitation in the area and leading prayer meetings and Bible study groups.[13] The mission dispensary was open each day, with a doctor and nurse in attendance. In the waiting room before the surgery opened, someone would read the Bible to the patients – for some it was the first time they had ever heard its message – and there followed a short gospel message and prayer. Then each patient was seen individually by the trained doctor in attendance, often with a number of trainee students being present. The medical consultation and medicines dispensed were free; those too ill to get to the surgery were visited at home. Soon some 7,000 people per year were making use of this service.[14]

Burns Thomson, who led the Edinburgh medical missionary dispensary, promoted the foundation of similar missions in cities such as Liverpool (1866), Glasgow (1868), Manchester (1870) and Birmingham (1875). In 1870 he moved to work at the Mildmay Institution, set up by the evangelical vicar William Pennefather. Mildmay became a model for medical mission overseas. The Mildmay Mission Hospital, opened in Bethnal Green in 1877, had wards for men, women and children, together with a maternity wing. When it was rebuilt in 1892, there were beds for 400 people, a convalescent home and a care home for the elderly. There were also dispensaries and surgeries in surrounding areas.[15]

John Lowe, Secretary of the EMMS, offered a detailed exposition of the double cure in his 1886 work *Medical Missions; Their Place and Power*. He declared that medical mission was about the whole person:

---

[12] William Burns Thomson, *Medical Missions: A Prize Essay* (Edinburgh: Johnstone & Hunter, 1854), 10–11, 14; emphasis original.

[13] Ross, 'Missionary Doctor', 91–92.

[14] W. Burns Thomson, *Reminiscences of Medical Missionary Work* (London: Hodder & Stoughton, 1895), 42–43.

[15] K. Heasman, *Evangelicals in Action* (London: Geoffrey Bles, 1963), 226–228.

the welfare of my brother, the welfare of his body, the welfare of his soul – his welfare for time, his welfare for eternity. To hold forth the word of life, along with a practical manifestation of the spirit of the gospel, is therefore the true meaning of 'preaching the gospel'.[16]

Those without the assistance of a medical missionary were bound to 'die the double death' for want of help.[17] Lowe recognized that the fruit of medical work was temporal, and that ultimately the gospel remained 'the Divinely appointed, and only means, for the world's regeneration; it, and it alone, under the influence of the Spirit, can turn men from darkness to light'. Medical mission supported this, being a way to 'gain a readier access to the homes and hearts of those whom we desire to reach with the Gospel message'.[18]

The EMMS model of gospel witness was holistic, combining preaching and the reading and study of the Scriptures with healing the sick and those who had suffered accident or injury, and assisting the marginalized and oppressed, including the poor and disabled. There was a recognition that physical illness and deprivation often needed to be dealt with before people were able to give a hearing to the gospel. Lowe recalled visiting an aged woman, living in abject poverty and lying in tattered garments who appeared to be nearing death. He asked her whether she had any hope for the life to come, but her reply was that she could only think of how she was 'cold and hungry'. Lowe concluded that 'to succeed in the highest aim of Christian love, our ministry must contemplate man in the whole extent of his being'.[19]

A significant element of medical mission was nursing work. In 1822 the evangelical Lutheran pastor Theodore Fliedner and his wife moved to Kaiserswerth in Germany, and in the early 1830s began training deaconesses, especially in the care of the sick. A hospital was opened at Kaiserswerth in 1836, and Fliedner's lecture notes became the standard nursing textbook. The high standards they set and their devotion to the needs of patients contrasted with the poor standards of care and cleanliness found in most hospitals. Kaiserswerth proved to be an inspiration to others in training nurses to the highest possible standards.[20] These included the evangelical Quaker Elizabeth Fry, who visited in 1840, and started an Institute of Nursing in Whitechapel in 1841.

---

[16] Lowe, *Medical Missions*, 10–11.
[17] Ibid. 85.
[18] Ibid. 87.
[19] Ibid. 5, 29–30.
[20] Heasman, *Evangelicals*, 234.

Another person profoundly influenced by Kaiserswerth was Florence Nightingale, who visited in 1849 and worked with the deaconesses there for three months on her second visit in 1851. Although she had an evangelical upbringing, as an adult she expressed no formal Christian commitment and focused on nursing as professional rather than religious work. However, Agnes Jones, who trained under Florence Nightingale and was a strong evangelical believer, also visited Kaiserswerth. She was appointed Nursing Superintendent of the Liverpool Poor Law Infirmary in 1865, which had some 1,200 patients but fewer than 600 beds and was beset by filth, drunkenness and foul language. With twelve nurses and eighteen probationers, Agnes Jones transformed the hospital within a year. She died in 1868 of typhus fever caught in the course of her work, but Liverpool became a model for other hospitals across the country.[21]

Women undertook much of the visitation done by churches and chapels. In 1857 Ellen Ranyard developed a project to pay working-class women as evangelistic agents in the slums of London. By 1867 the London Bible and Domestic Female Mission (or Ranyard Mission) was employing 234 Bible women. On their visits they were often called upon to give advice about childcare and medical matters. As a result, the Bible Nursing scheme was formed. Training included three months on a hospital ward, and three months in domestic visitation. The Bible Nurses ventured into the darkest, foulest smelling and unsafest parts of towns and cities, dressed in a dark gown and flannel apron, carrying a basin containing nursing utensils, a Bible, some tracts and Florence Nightingale's *Nursing Notes*. By 1894 it was reckoned that 82 Bible Nurses had made 215,000 visits to 10,000 patients. By 1901 the period of hospital training was extended to two years.[22] Out of this ministry grew district, or community, nursing work later taken over by the state.

The recruitment of 'slum sisters' who worked and lived among the poor was an important part of the Salvation Army's strategy. As one sister commented, 'if you do nothing, you had better say nothing; people will not listen to words only'.[23] Charles Booth considered these nursing schemes the most directly influential and successful form of Christian social concern work in nineteenth-century London.[24] The approach was carried over into overseas mission by many women.[25]

[21] J. Jones, *Memorials of Agnes Elizabeth Jones by Her Sister* (London: Strahan, 1871).

[22] Heasman, *Evangelicals*, 36–37, 236–238.

[23] W. Booth, *In Darkest England and the Way Out* (London: Salvation Army, 1890), 167, 169.

[24] C. Booth, *The Life and Labour of the People of London*, 3rd series, *Religious Influences*, vol. 7 (London: Macmillan, 1902), 203.

[25] F. K. Prochaska, 'Body and Soul: Bible Nurses and the Poor in Victorian London', *Historical Research* 60.143 (1987), 338, 340, 341–346.

Although started early in the nineteenth century by Colledge and Parker, overseas medical missionary work received a considerable boost from such ministry in the poorest parts of Britain and North America. In 1878 the Medical Missionary Society was founded, with a training centre for students.[26] It emphasized that the proclamation of the gospel was to be accompanied by the highest standards of medical practice, founded on a scientific basis.[27] Lowe argued that medical mission was a 'powerful auxiliary to the spread of the Gospel', and that 'Medical work in China has been one of the most fruitful departments of missionary labour.'[28] This was certainly the experience in Korea, where the work of Horace Allen (1858–1932), medical officer to the American legation, opened the way to Protestant mission in that once-closed country after he was appointed physician to the royal court.[29] Similarly, William Elmslie (1832–72) of the Church Missionary Society in Kashmir, opened doors in a previously hostile field.[30] Hard-to-reach parts of the Middle East – Palestine, Syria and Turkey – saw increased openings through medical missionary work because, as Lowe commented, 'Men naturally care more for their bodies than their souls.' Medical missionaries gained many more opportunities for contact with local people of other faith communities than 'ordinary' missionaries were allowed. In these overseas medical missions, the pattern of reading and preaching from the Bible before patients were seen was continued, sometimes leading to conversations about matters of faith, or requests for Bibles. At Tientsin, in China, Dr MacKenzie, of the LMS, and Dr Howard, a female physician from the American Methodist mission, helped to cure the wife of the Governor General of the province, who subsequently allowed them to establish a large dispensary in a former temple, covered their expenses and gave them freedom to preach in his province. In time a hospital was also established.[31]

Despite the reservations of the American Board in the 1840s, medical mission gradually became embedded in the work of other mainline missions. The mission station in Almora, northern India, was started by the LMS in 1850, initially with a school, and then in 1860 the missioners took on a hospital for lepers.[32] By 1901 the hospital was performing 560 operations and treating 8,000

---

[26] Heasman, *Evangelicals*, 228–229.

[27] Ibid.

[28] Lowe, *Medical Missions*, 57–59.

[29] I. J. Shaw, *Churches, Revolutions and Empires: 1789–1914* (Fearn: Christian Focus, 2012), 424.

[30] Lowe, *Medical Missions*, 64.

[31] Ibid. 59–62, 72; See also D. L. Robert, *American Women in Mission: A Social History of Their Thought and Practice* (Macon, Ga.: Mercer University Press, 1997), 165.

[32] R. A. Semple, *Missionary Women: Gender, Professionalism, and the Victorian Idea of Christian Mission* (Woodbridge: Boydell Press, 2003), 74.

outpatients a year.[33] Services were held as outpatients waited. It offered a holistic model – facilities were extended to include a chapel and a co-operative savings bank, and relatives and friends were allowed to stay with patients. The approach was to knit 'closely the evangelical aim of the missionaries with the needs of the local population'. The medical missionary Robert Ashton wrote in 1920, 'To us Christian workers, philanthropic effort is the fruit, not the root . . . Let us then be all things right and helpful to all men, if by any means we may save some.'[34] This was not without cost. In the early 1890s Miss Reed, an American missionary, was found to have caught leprosy and was invalided home to North America. She later recovered and eventually returned to Almora, where she continued to work with leprosy patients until her death in 1943, aged 88.[35] By 1890 in India there were 97 foreign and 168 native Christian medical missionaries, with 166 hospitals and dispensaries.[36]

James Hudson Taylor (1832–1905), founder of the China Inland Mission, was also medically trained. Although the CIM emphasized the priority of evangelism, in the late nineteenth century it took a growing interest in medical mission.[37] By 1909 the CIM had 10 hospitals, and 68 dispensaries. Although this was significant, it was dwarfed by the medical mission work of other Protestant missions. In 1905 there were 310 medical doctors working in China as medical missionaries (94 being women), running 166 hospitals and 241 dispensaries.[38] However, the fact that the CIM as a 'faith mission' came also to accept medical mission, despite being shaped by premillennial teaching in which urgent evangelism was given the primacy, is notable.

Across much of Africa and Asia into the twentieth century medical mission remained a key component of missionary activity. In 1929 Mary Scharlieb declared 'Medical mission work indeed constitutes the most attractive exposition of the work and aims of the Good Physician', and that joy found in the mission hospitals was the 'nearest approximation to the spiritual gladness of the early Christian Church'.[39] Medical mission was reaching people who would otherwise never have had the opportunity to hear the gospel.

---

[33] Ibid. 86–87.
[34] Kachwa Mission Records, 1920, quoted in ibid. 88.
[35] Ibid. 101–102.
[36] G. Smith, *The Conversion of India from Pantaenus to the Present Time AD 193–1893* (London: John Murray, 1893), 205.
[37] A. Austin, *China's Millions: The China Inland Mission and the Qing Society, 1832–1905* (Grand Rapids, Mich.: Eerdmans, 2007), 205.
[38] J. H. Broomhall, *Hudson Taylor and China's Open Century*, bk 7: *It Is Not Death to Die* (London: Hodder & Stoughton, 1989), 529–531.
[39] M. Scharlieb, preface to M. Balfour and R. Young, *The Work of Medical Women in India* (London: Oxford University Press, 1929), 10–11.

One important dimension of medical mission was the increased opportunities it provided for women not only to serve in missionary capacities but also to gain formal medical training – both as nurses and professionally trained doctors, although full medical training was prohibitively expensive for many.[40] In 1873 Lucinda Coombs, graduate of the Woman's Medical College in Philadelphia, was appointed as the first female medical missionary to China. The first women's hospital in China was opened in 1875, and Chinese women also began studying medicine and nursing, trained by the female missionary doctors.[41]

One area of missionary concern was for women in Asian communities living in the zenana, or purdah. As we saw in chapter 10, this meant they were excluded from male company apart from their husband and children. Specialist missions developed to meet their needs, often with a medical component, such as the Zenana Bible and Medical Mission, started by the evangelical Lady Kinnaird.[42] This issue also motivated the development of specialist medical training for women, and the professionalization of such treatment.[43] In 1885 Sophia Jex-Blake, one of Britain's first female doctors, argued that even those who opposed female physicians practising in Britain could not deny the urgency of the need for them in the East, where 'native customs make it practically impossible that women should be attended by medical men'.[44] Women living in the zenana became a powerful argument for the need to train female doctors for such work.

The London School of Medicine for Women (LSMW), which started in 1874, attracted a number of evangelical women who took the radical stance of seeking medical training. One was Fanny Butler, a member of the Church of England Zenana Missionary Society. Strongly committed to evangelism, she expressed reservations about 'lady doctoring', feeling it unwomanly. Yet, because of the zenana, she believed that the only way to evangelize women in India was through offering medical care. The message of missionaries was impossible to resist 'when it was expressed in acts of mercy'. Fanny Butler became the first British woman to practise as a doctor in India, for which she set sail in 1880, and where she died in 1889.[45] With a strong woman-to-woman care ethic, many

---

[40] Semple, *Missionary Women*, 2, 10, 22, 231.

[41] Robert, *American Women*, 165.

[42] Jeffrey Cox, *The British Missionary Enterprise Since 1700* (London: Routledge, 2008), 189, 190.

[43] See Mary Carpenter, *Six Months in India*, 2 vols. (London: Longman's, Green, 1868).

[44] Sophia Jex-Blake, *Medical Women: A Thesis and Its History* (London: Hamilton & Adams, 1886), 23, 154.

[45] E. M. Tonge, *Fanny Jane Butler: Pioneer Medical Missionary* (London: Church of England Zenana Missionary Society, 1930), 10, 50; A. Burton, 'Contesting the Zenana: The Mission to Make "Lady Doctors for India," 1874–1885', *Journal of British Studies* 35.3 (July 1996), 368–397.

doctors specialized in gynaecology. The LSMW was determined to send out the best-trained doctors, believing that if people were to be helped in the name of Christianity, nothing less than the highest standards were required.[46] In 1881 Dr Elizabeth Garrett Anderson, then a lecturer at the LSMW, wrote to *The Times* declaring, 'It will not recommend Christianity to Hindoo ladies to send them missionaries in the disguise of indifferent doctors.'[47] Criticisms of the poor medical skills shown by some missionaries forced missions to employ more professionally qualified doctors.[48] Schools for training female Indian doctors were also started, such as the 'North India School for Medicine for Christian Women', attached to the mission at Ludhiana founded by Edith Brown in the 1890s. The expanding role of women serving as nurses and doctors on the mission field was part of the increasing 'feminization' of missions.[49]

Other women focused on antenatal and obstetric work. One of the first to do so was Annie McCall who, after graduation from the London School of Medicine, trained in midwifery and obstetrics in Berne, Switzerland. In 1885 she was invited to superintend a medical mission started in Battersea. Two years later she opened a clinic providing antenatal and post-natal care, and in 1889 started the Clapham Maternity Hospital, offering the highest standards of medical care. As a temperance advocate, McCall allowed women patients neither to smoke nor drink in the hospital. Her concern was for women throughout pregnancy and in the first months after childbirth and so she visited women in their homes, offering instruction in basic childcare. A School of Midwifery was started and Annie McCall helped to set national standards. A hospital in South London was later named after her.[50]

The range of organizations established in the nineteenth century by evangelical Christians for the sick and disabled was immense. Heasman notes that it was not just the funds raised or the time invested that was significant, but the spirit and ethos with which these organizations operated – bringing 'a more human understanding and desire to help those they befriended'. As a result, 'homes' replaced 'asylums', and there was an emphasis on 'personal care' that has become normative today.[51]

---

[46] Burton, 'Zenana', 380.

[47] Elizabeth Garrett Anderson letter 'Medical Women for India', in *The Times*, 31 October 1881, in Burton, 'Zenana', 384.

[48] Ibid. 389.

[49] J. Hunter, *The Gospel of Gentility: American Women Missionaries in Turn of the Century China* (Newhaven, Conn.: Yale University Press, 1984), 14.

[50] Heasman, *Evangelicals*, 230–231.

[51] Ibid. 244–245.

The legacy of medical mission went far beyond the institutions founded. They established the principle that health care should be available to all in need, and that even the poorest should receive the best possible treatment.[52] Medical missions emphasized care not just for medical conditions but for the whole person. This included their spiritual needs, which could impact their health. They viewed the provision of food, clothing and clean housing as essential to restoring and maintaining health. They also pioneered understandings of health care as a matter for the community, tackling the causes of disease, as well as its symptoms. The emphasis on training indigenous people for medical work was central to the approach in medical mission, and the training of women as doctors and nurses profoundly changed the medical treatment of women in India and China.

In opening doors for other mission work, the medical missionaries were highly successful. Some questioned whether medical mission was focusing on people when they were most vulnerable, as the social observer Charles Booth observed slightly ambivalently: 'Advantage is taken of the softening of the heart in sickness and sorrow to point to the "Great Physician".'[53] Yet, at home or abroad, it was the only medical care available to many people in great need, the alternative being prolonged suffering or death. The large numbers who sought the help of medical missionaries shows how much their work was needed and valued.

Character study: Clara Swain (1834–1910) – India

Clara Swain was born in Elmira, New York State, the youngest and frailest of ten children. Her mother's prayer was that she might 'grow up to be a good and useful woman'. Clara was converted in the family Methodist church just before she was 10 years old, influenced by a powerful sermon on personal commitment. Her Christian life was marked by deep devotion, especially attendance at prayer meetings, and she spent a year studying at a local seminary for women.[54] She worked for three years at the Castile Sanitarium before being accepted at the Woman's Medical College in Philadelphia, from which she graduated in 1869.[55]

That year the Women's Foreign Missionary Society of the Methodist Episcopal Church appealed for a female doctor to work among Indian women

[52] Ross, 'Missionary Doctor', 101.

[53] Booth, *London*, 286.

[54] R. Hoskins, *Clara Swain MD: First Medical Missionary to the Women of the Orient* (Boston, Mass.: Women's Foreign Missionary Society Methodist Episcopal Church, 1912), 2–10.

[55] D. C. Wilson, *The Palace of Healing: The Story of Dr Clara Swain, First Woman Missionary Doctor, and the Hospital She Founded* (New York: McGraw-Hill, 1968), 17.

secluded in the zenana. Missionaries observed seriously ill women being taken by their relatives to the banks of the Ganges, where they were left to pass away before their bodies were pushed into the river, whose sacred waters it was believed would bring the blessing of salvation.[56] An opportunity arose for a female doctor at the Methodist Mission in Bareilly, a north-Indian city in Uttar Pradesh that ran a boys' and girls' orphanage. The vision of the resident missionaries, Mr and Mrs D. W. Thomas, was to recruit a female medical missionary and start a small medical school to train Indian women. The Woman's Medical College recommended Clara Swain on the basis of her competence and dedication to Christian service. It was a huge step, and it took her three months to decide on the rightfulness of abandoning her hoped-for medical career in North America, to work in an under-resourced location and unfamiliar climate. She chose the latter with all its challenges, despite many predicting she would fail.[57]

After an arduous journey, Clara Swain arrived in Bareilly at 5 am in January 1870. She found a crowd of patients already awaiting her, and indomitably treated 14 patients on that first day. Within a year she had treated 1,225 people and made 250 home visits.[58] Her work covered the full spectrum of medical conditions, including ophthalmic and dental work. Sometimes she acted as both anaesthetist and surgeon because of a lack of trained assistants. Some patients presented with highly contagious diseases such as smallpox and cholera.

Her work was an intentional combination of medical activity with opportunities for faith-sharing. Wherever possible she read the Scriptures and explained them to each family visited. Scripture texts were written on the back of prescription cards. She also took opportunities to question the practice of keeping women in seclusion, and encouraged a number of high-caste men to allow their wives to leave the zenana to visit her for medical consultation. She also spoke out against the practice of the infanticide of female babies by families.[59] Swain's dual commitment was clear: 'while we endeavor to heal their bodies, we are trying just as earnestly to minister to their souls'.[60] In both of these she enjoyed considerable success. Children in the orphanage were regularly converted.[61] In 1872 she reported the conversion of a devout Hindu man and his wife, with the

---

[56] Ibid. 3.

[57] J. T. Gracey, *Medical Work of the Women's Foreign Missionary Society, Methodist Episcopal Church* (Boston: Women's Foreign Missionary Society, 2015), 34.

[58] Hoskins, *Swain*, 14–15.

[59] See C. Swain, *A Glimpse of India: A Collection of Extracts from the Letters of Dr. Clara A. Swain* (New York: James Pott, 1909; repr. New York and London: Garland Publishing, 1987), 56.

[60] Ibid. 96–97.

[61] Ibid. 51, 54.

wife's elderly mother also deciding to become a Christian believer, saying, 'If Christianity is good for my daughter and her husband, it is good for me, and where they go, I will go.'[62] Swain boldly declared the ability of Christ to overcome the barriers of caste, and the love of God for the lowest castes as much as the respected Brahman caste.[63] Her holistic approach was characteristic of women in the modern missionary movement.[64]

A key part of Clara Swain's ministry was heavy investment in training. A theological school was started in Bareilly, where Bible women were trained to explain the Christian gospel and provide medical care. She also began training Indian women for medical work, providing them with three hours of instruction each day. After three years of study, and having been examined in their skills by three highly qualified doctors, the first class of thirteen graduated in 1873. They were granted 'certificates for practice in all ordinary diseases'.[65]

A significant need was a hospital as a base for the work. In a remarkable provision, after an appeal from Clara Swain and the Thomases, the Nawab of Rampore gifted the mission 40 acres of land and an old mansion house for a dispensary and hospital. As a devout Muslim he had at one time vowed he would never allow Christian missionaries in his area, but had been deeply impressed with the care and compassion for the needy shown by the missionaries. It is thought to be the first women's hospital in India, with separate wards for Hindus, Muslims and Christians, and attracted patients from as far as Burma. By 1875 she was treating almost 2,000 patients.

Swain had the ability to combine skills as evangelist, doctor and teacher with considerable administrative ability. Through her devoted work in India she gained professional influence, responsibility and autonomy she would never have had in America. Her response to the often bitter criticism of her work was to strive for excellence, especially of training Indian women, and her one-time critics later sought her advice. Swain's method was uncomplicated:

we go among the people in a quiet, unobtrusive way, doing good to their bodies and praying God to bless their souls. When they call us to their houses in sickness, we can speak a word for Him in whom we trust, and recommend them to search after Him.[66]

---

[62] Ibid. 73.

[63] Ibid. 106.

[64] D. L. Robert, *American Women in Mission: A Social History of Their Thought and Practice* (Macon: Mercer University Press, 1997), 162.

[65] Hoskins, *Swain*, 16–17.

[66] Gracey, *Medical Work*, 17.

Six years of relentless work in India, with constant exposure to sickness and infections, took its toll. In 1876 Swain returned to North America to recover her health, before returning to Bareilly in 1880. She continued for a further five years of remorseless work, before her health deteriorated again. This led to a decision to accept the post of medical doctor to the rajah and his rani, of Khetri state, Rajasthan, in north-west India. Swain believed that from this position she could bring a Christian influence to both the ruling family and society more generally. It enabled her to reach devout Hindus with the gospel who were otherwise unreachable by normal missionary methods. She held Bible studies with the rani (who developed a great love for the Bible), the princesses and some of the rajah's staff.[67] A dispensary for women was opened, and at the encouragement of his wife the rajah allowed a school for girls to be started, despite opposition from Hindu traditionalists to women gaining education. Swain also challenged the ruler on key social issues, such as increasing the marriageable age of girls.[68]

At the age of 61 Swain took the difficult decision to retire from India and return to work at the Castile Sanitarium. However, in 1906, when more than 70 years of age, the 'frail little daughter' of the 'frail little mother' returned to India for a further eighteen months to encourage the work she had started.

She died in 1910, leaving a significant and lasting legacy. Her work encouraged Lady Dufferin, wife of the viceroy of India, to begin a fund for the training of women as medical doctors and establishing hospitals for women across India. In 1894 a medical training college for women was started in Ludhiana, and another in Delhi in 1905. Swain's work inspired Indian women to seek high-quality medical training in the West. The first was Anandibai Joshee, who graduated from the Woman's Medical College – where Swain had studied – just seventeen years after Swain had embarked for India. By 1909 the overseas medical missionary workforce included 147 female physicians and 91 trained nurses, supporting 82 dispensaries and 80 hospitals around the world.[69] Training indigenous women for medical work profoundly changed the medical treatment of women in India and China.[70] Swain helped break down patriarchal barriers in both America and India, and opened doors for women to be liberated from the zenana, and play a fuller role in Indian society.

---

[67] Hoskins, *Swain*, 25–26.
[68] Ibid. 21–24.
[69] Robert, *American Women*, 162.
[70] M. Balfour and R. Young, *The Work of Medical Women in India* (New York: Oxford University Press, 1929).

15
Care for people with alcohol addiction

The abuse of alcohol was recognized from the eighteenth century onwards as a major social problem, the source of much crime, immorality and poverty. Alcohol was plentifully available, and after a reduction in the tax on spirits in Britain in 1822 it was cheap. Along the New Cut, off Blackfriars in London, there were no fewer than sixteen public houses.[1] In the early nineteenth century in central Glasgow there was one public house for every thirty people.[2] One German traveller to the city in the 1850s described it as 'the most religious and the most drunken city in Europe', and another spoke of 'Augean pandemonium' in the city at night.[3] In 1850 Glasgow recorded 15,751 cases of drunkenness, or 1 for every 22 people in the population. Much social life centred on the public house – from christenings to weddings and funerals, to job changes and the start and end of apprenticeships. Saturday, as pay day (and wages were often paid in a pub), was when most alcohol was consumed. Holidays saw excessive drinking, as witnessed at Glasgow Fair in 1853: 'Groups of excited men were fighting here and there . . . no small number of human forms lay in the kennel, in a state of swinish beastitude.'[4] Excessive alcohol consumption caused poverty, but was also a product of it – alcohol offered a way to forget need.

John Wesley cautioned his followers against buying and selling alcoholic spirit liquor. He argued that a person filled with alcoholic spirits had no room for the Holy Spirit. In his *Word to a Drunkard* he asserted:

> You are an enemy to every man that sees you in your sin; for your example may move him to do the same . . . Above all, you are an enemy to God . . . Him you are continually affronting.[5]

---

[1] *Report of the Select Committee of the House of Lords on Public Houses*, 1854, 4, in K. Heasman, *Evangelicals in Action* (London: Geoffrey Bles, 1963), 126.

[2] J. E. Handley, *The Irish in Scotland, 1798–1845* (Cork: Cork University Press, 1943), 160.

[3] 'Shadow', *Midnight Scenes and Social Photographs: Being Sketches of Life in the Streets, Wynds and Dens of the City* (Glasgow, 1858), 99, 115.

[4] *Glasgow Herald*, 18 July 1853.

[5] J. Wesley, *Word to a Drunkard*, in *Works of John Wesley*, vol. 11 (London: Wesleyan Methodist Book Room, n.d.), 170.

Wesley had the task of disciplining Methodists for drunkenness and declared, 'What! drunken Christians! cursing and swearing Christians! lying Christians! cheating Christians! If these are Christians at all, they are devil Christians'.[6]

Both the American and the British temperance movements developed out of a strong self-help ethos among working people (at times independent of churches and chapels) and a growing view that avoidance of alcoholic spirits was beneficial to health.[7] A key feature of early temperance societies was the encouragement to sign the 'pledge', a promise not to touch alcohol for a set period.

By 1828 there were more than 400 temperance societies across North America, some of them being statewide bodies, such as those in New Hampshire, Pennsylvania, Virginia and Illinois.[8] They sought to educate people as to the extent of the alcohol problem, and placed pressure on shops not to sell alcohol by boycotting them. The temperance societies had a considerable impact. By 1850 per capita consumption of alcohol in America had plummeted by 80 per cent since the start of the century.[9]

The relationship between evangelicalism and temperance became close. In America it was an area in which evangelicals had a significant impact in the public arena. In 1826 Lyman Beecher founded the American Society for the Promotion of Temperance, convinced that alcohol consumption lay behind poverty, violent crime and family conflict and break-up. The Society's focus was the opposition to 'the daily use of ardent spirits', rather than total abstention.[10] Teetotalism gained ground in the 1830s in the north-east, and then spread to frontier areas. An important figure in this was Charles Finney. While he always made personal conversion the priority, Finney married revivalism with temperance, asserting that turning from alcohol was a sign of spiritual change. Temperance became an important by-product of evangelistic outreach.[11] When the temperance lecturer Theodore Weld was invited by Finney to speak at his revivalist campaign in 1830–31, in Rochester, New York, he dramatically called for an end to the alcohol trade. The next day merchants and shopkeepers who had heard him smashed barrels of alcohol in the street, or emptied them in the

---

6 J. Wesley, *A Plain Account of the People Called Methodists*, in *Works of John Wesley*, vol. 5 (New York: J. Emory & B. Waugh, 1831), 178.

7 W. R. Ward, *Religion and Society in England, 1790–1850* (London: B. T. Batsford, 1972), 289.

8 J. G. West, 'Nineteenth Century America', in D. Eberly (ed.), *Building a Healthy Culture: Strategies for an American Renaissance* (Grand Rapids, Mich.: Eerdmans, 2001), 183.

9 J. Q. Wilson and R. J. Herrnstein, *Crime and Human Nature* (New York: Simon & Schuster, 1985), 433.

10 J. Wolffe, *The Expansion of Evangelicalism* (Nottingham: Inter-Varsity Press, 2007), 170–172, quotation from Beecher on 172.

11 C. Hambricke-Stowe, *Charles G. Finney and the Spirit of American Evangelicalism* (Grand Rapids, Mich.: Eerdmans, 1996), 174.

canal. Church leaders, politicians, newspaper editors, business leaders and ordinary Christians all called for an end to alcohol sales, and for boycotting businesses that continued with that trade. Evangelism brought significant social change.[12] Teetotalism became a part of the gospel message as evidence of forsaking sin and of genuine conversion, and 'emphasizing separation from the world which revivalists thought essential'.[13]

The methods used to promote revivalism were also used to promote teetotalism, including open-air meetings, processions, literature campaigns, advertising and testimony meetings. The decisions called for at evangelistic meetings were mirrored in calls to 'sign the pledge' to abstain from alcohol. Alcohol was seen as a major barrier to the gospel. The spread of the temperance movement among the churches in Britain was slower, something that shocked visitors from North America. William Collins (1789–1853), a member of Thomas Chalmers' congregation during Chalmers' Glasgow ministry, and later famous as a publisher, was an early advocate of the cause and spent the winter of 1829–30 lecturing across Scotland on the evils of strong drink. His printing company published some 500,000 tracts on temperance in 1830 alone. Collins successfully started temperance societies in Liverpool, Manchester, Bristol and London. He passionately believed that alcohol abuse was so deeply embedded that 'to tear up the spirit-drinking practices is like tearing up the whole system of society'.[14]

Strong support for Collins' work came from the Glasgow City Mission, whose visitation of the poorest areas highlighted the problem of alcohol abuse and its harmful effect on families. One city missioner reported in 1832:

In one house, found a man almost in a state of insanity, by ardent spirits. His wife, quite a young woman, was sitting crying and the blood flowing copiously from a wound inflicted by him, on one of her eyes.[15]

William Logan (1813–79), a Glasgow City missioner, became an expert on the connections between alcohol abuse and crime, including prostitution, and was a strong advocate of temperance.[16] Evangelical urban and medical missions recognized the close connection between heavy drinking and poverty, and made temperance an important part of their work, especially in the worst slum

---

[12] Hambricke-Stowe, *Finney*, 110–112.

[13] L. Billington, 'Popular Religion and Social Reform: A Study of Revivalism and Teetotalism, 1830–1850', *Journal of Religious History* 10 (1978–9), 268.

[14] E. King, *Scotland: Sober and Free* (Glasgow: People's Palace Museum, 1980), 6–7; W. Collins, in *Parliamentary Papers*, 1834, vol. 8, 139.

[15] *Glasgow City Mission Fifth Annual Report* (Glasgow, 1831), 13.

[16] King, *Sober and Free*, 8.

areas. The Glasgow United Evangelistic Association ran meetings in a large tent on Glasgow Green from the mid 1870s onwards, attracting many who never attended church. A lasting part of its work included ministry to those rendered homeless by alcohol abuse.[17] The Glasgow City missioner John Paton (1824–1907), who worked in Calton, one of the poorest parts of the city, argued that practising total abstinence was essential to his work, believing drunkenness was inseparable from vice, immorality, criminality and poverty. Efforts to help the poorest were thwarted when clothes donated to poor children were regularly pawned for drink. Some of the strongest opponents to Paton's very successful urban mission work, which saw a thriving church planted in Calton, were owners of public houses.[18]

Temperance was gradually absorbed into the life of Nonconformist chapels in Britain in the 1830s, especially those in the Methodist tradition.[19] Hugh Bourne, founder of the Primitive Methodists, who had been influenced by American revivalist teaching, stressed the importance of opposition to drink. The Primitive Methodist Conference discussed the issue in 1831 and 1841, and a ministerial temperance declaration was issued in 1848.[20] Revivalists argued that whereas temperance was merely a respite and preventative approach, teetotalism was considered a cure.

A number of temperance-related movements spread from North America to the UK. One such, the Independent Order of Rechabites, based on the group mentioned in Jeremiah 35, were formed in Salford in 1835. It operated as a total abstinence Friendly Society, offering sick and funeral pay-outs for relatively low contributions, with sections for women and children. Members wore distinctive regalia, including silk and satin sashes, and carried banners with blue trimmings. The movement spread rapidly, and was particularly strong in Scotland. It brought a sense of group identity, considered important for working men as they stood together against the wider social and cultural pressures towards alcohol consumption among their peers. The Good Templars and the Sons of Temperance were similar organizations.[21]

Teetotalism also impacted those who had no time for revivalism. Sometime between 1832 and 1834 the Manchester Strict Baptist minister William Gadsby became a teetotaller. Although averse to taking pledges in public, it was a private

---

[17] Ibid. 21–22.

[18] I. J. Shaw, 'John Paton and Urban Mission in Nineteenth-Century Scotland', *Records of Scottish Church History Society* 35 (2005), 178–180.

[19] I. Sellers, *Nineteenth-Century Nonconformity* (London: Edward Arnold, 1977), 41.

[20] R. Davies, A. R. George and G. Rupp, *A History of the Methodist Church in Great Britain*, vol. 3 (London: Epworth, 1983), 173.

[21] Heasman, *Evangelicals*, 128; King, *Sober and Free*, 14.

commitment he kept until death. He regularly saw the harmful effects of alcohol not only on the drunken gangs that marauded around Angel Meadow, where his church was located, but also on those church members he had to discipline for intoxication.[22] He condemned magistrates for excusing crimes because they were committed when the offender was drunk.[23] The London Strict Baptist James Wells also became a teetotaller, but publicly took the pledge in order to be strengthened against 'self and against flesh, and against the devil'.[24] In a funeral sermon for one of his deacons, also a teetotaller, he declared that drink 'robs the family, brutalises the feelings, insults the Most High, turns a home that ought to be a paradise into confusion, wretchedness, and woe; leads to every privation and a premature grave'.[25] Some ministers changed their views. Although a moderate drinker early in his ministry, the leading Baptist preacher C. H. Spurgeon adopted total abstinence. He placed gospel proclamation at the centre of rescue work: 'go in for winning the real drunkards, and bring the poor enslaved creatures to the feet of Jesus, who can give them liberty'.[26]

Total abstinence was much less popular among Presbyterians in Scotland. One of those who did adopt it was Thomas Guthrie. His ragged school work, and his pastoral ministry in the Cowgate area, one of the poorest parts of Edinburgh, demonstrated to him the harmful effect of alcohol abuse. He recalled:

> I wandered from house to house, and from room to room, misery, wretchedness and crime; the detestable vice of drunkenness, the cause of all, meeting me at every turn, and marring all my efforts . . . The murder of innocent infants in this city by drunkenness 'out-Herods Herod'.[27]

He studied the problem closely and was appalled that public houses were found in Edinburgh in the greatest numbers in areas of greatest poverty, and where people were least able to resist temptation. Throughout his ministry he found drunkenness 'defeating me in every effort', and resolved that the only way to challenge the evil was to become an abstainer himself, setting an example not

---

[22] P. Ramsbottom, 'A Chiliasm of Despair? The Community Worshipping at St George's Road Baptist Chapel, Manchester', *Baptist Quarterly* 37.5 (January 1998), 234.

[23] W. Gadsby, *A Memoir of the Late Mr. William Gadsby, Compiled from Authentic Sources* (Manchester, 1844), 105.

[24] T. Jones and W. Crowther, *Services in Connection with the Decease and Funeral of the Late Mr James Wells* (London: G. J. Stevenson, 1872), 8.

[25] J. Wells, *The Faithful Man: A Funeral Sermon Preached on December 28, 1851* (London: G. J. Stevenson, 1852), 27.

[26] S. Spurgeon and J. Harrald, *C. H. Spurgeon Autobiography*, vol. 4 (London: Passmore & Alabaster, 1899), 70.

[27] T. Guthrie, *Memorial on the Claim of Ragged Industrial Schools to Government Support* (Edinburgh: Jack, 1852), 378–379.

only to his parishioners but also to civic leaders and other ministers, some of whom he had seen deposed from office for drunkenness. He was a powerful advocate and one of the founders of the Free Church Temperance Society, which attracted up to 300 ministers. Similar societies were founded in the United Presbyterian Church and the Church of Scotland. Guthrie visited local fairs, so often the scenes of dissipation, and preached in the open air against drunkenness. In 1850 he helped found the Scottish Association for the Suppression of Drunkenness and published 'A Plea on Behalf of Drunkards, and Against Drunkenness', which had a circulation of around 450,000. The Scottish Association helped secure the passage of the Forbes Mackenzie Act, limiting the hours public houses could be open on weekdays in Scotland to 8–11 pm.[28] His famous work *The City: Its Sins and Sorrows* contained a series of sermons on the destructive impact of alcohol on urban life.[29] Guthrie was a strong encourager of movements such as the British Workman Public House movement, which offered an attractive alternative for working men through creating a pub atmosphere without alcohol.[30]

Temperance was particularly strong among some Methodist groups. The Cornish tin miner Billy Bray (1794–1868) had experienced bouts of drunkenness before his dramatic conversion after escaping a serious mining accident. He joined the Bible Christians, a Methodist group, and became a well-known preacher, renowned for his dramatic sermons. Bray adopted teetotalism, characteristically declaring, 'If Satan ever catches me, it will be with the ale-pot . . . Satan sets wine-bottles and ale-pots to catch fools, but I will not touch a drop.' To him public houses were 'hell-houses', and it was impossible to help those with alcohol problems by temperance – total avoidance was the only option. He also strongly opposed smoking tobacco because of its addictive properties and effect on health.[31]

The early ministry of the American evangelist D. L. Moody was undertaken in Chicago's poorest areas, where he saw families devastated regularly by alcohol abuse. His own father may have had a serious drink problem, and Moody saw a strong connection between drunkenness and poverty.

In a sermon in 1877 he declared:

It strikes me this curse of intemperance is worse even than our civil war. That cut off a great many men – ten, twenty, thirty, perhaps forty years

---

[28] Ibid. 571, 577, 579–580.

[29] T. Guthrie, *The City: Its Sins and Sorrows* (Edinburgh: A&C Black, 1857).

[30] Guthrie, *Memoir*, 587.

[31] F. W. Bourne, *Billy Bray, The King's Son* (1871), repr. (London: Epworth Press, 1937), 98–100.

earlier than their time; but think of the men that are being ruined body and soul by this terrible curse.[32]

He was convinced that the only lasting cure for addiction to drink was conversion: 'Taking away a man's appetite for strong drink is a supernatural work, and that is what God does.'[33] Moody particularly cared for those most damaged by having an alcoholic man in the family – the wives and children.

Moody encountered the temperance movement when growing up in Northfield and declared, 'I am a total abstainer; have never touched liquor and never intend to do so.'[34] It became a strong theme both in his sermons and in his writings.[35] However, Moody never let temperance become a more dominant theme in his ministry than gospel proclamation. This led to a breach with Frances Willard, who had helped to form the Woman's Christian Temperance Union, becoming its president in 1879. This movement campaigned against alcohol abuse through demonstrations in the streets, holding prayer meetings in saloons and picketing places that sold alcohol. It was even introduced into China in 1886, and broadened its scope to oppose opium and tobacco smoking, and sought to help women free themselves from poverty and illiteracy.[36] Working with Moody, Willard had run special meetings for women and emphasized the salvation of the whole home. However, Moody felt she was emphasizing temperance as much as evangelism, and discontinued the collaboration.[37] To Moody, working for a changed lifestyle without conversion would never succeed. He declared, 'To drinking men, as to everyone else, [I say] believe on the Lord Jesus Christ.'[38] A pledge to abstain was much more likely to succeed if it came after a pledge to Jesus as Lord.

As well as the efforts of individual ministers and Christian workers, a range of groups made tackling alcohol abuse central to their ministry. In 1847 the Band of Hope was started, which ran weekly evangelistic meetings and promoted temperance among children, educating them about the dangers of alcohol abuse and encouraging them to sign the pledge. This led to the formation

---

[32] D. L. Moody, *To All the People* (New York: E. B. Treat, 1877), 136.

[33] Ibid. 198.

[34] Quoted in W. R. Moody, *Life of Moody* (New York: F. H. Revell, 1900), 449.

[35] For Moody's talks on temperance see James B. Dunn (ed.), *Moody's Talks on Temperance: With Anecdotes and Incidents in Connection with the Tabernacle Temperance Work in Boston* (New York: National Temperance Society and Publication House, 1877).

[36] See L. M. N. Stevens, 'The Work of the National Woman's Christian Temperance Movement', *Annals of the American Academy of Political and Social Science* 32 (November 1908), 38–42.

[37] J. F. Findlay Jr, *Dwight L. Moody: American Evangelist* (Chicago, Ill.: University of Chicago Press, 1969), 282; L. Dorsett, *A Passion for Souls: The Life of D. L. Moody* (Chicago, Ill.: Moody Press, 1997), 252–254.

[38] Cited in Findlay, *American Evangelist*, 283.

of the UK Band of Hope Union in 1855, which in 1900 had three million regular members, with 26,000 bands being attached to churches. Their work helped encourage the 1886 legislation that forbade the sale of alcohol to all children under the age of 16.[39] Even in 1932 the Primitive Methodist Church alone was still running nearly a thousand Bands of Hope, with some 50,000 members, and its Abstainers League branches had a membership of around 19,000.[40]

In 1856 the National Temperance League was formed in order to co-ordinate the work of temperance societies, and was closely connected with evangelicals – its supporters included Lord Kinnaird and C. H. Spurgeon. It appealed to city missionaries, Scripture readers, social workers, those in the medical professions and chaplains to teach temperance among those they worked with.[41] This was followed in 1878 by the Blue Ribbon Movement, introduced into Britain from North America. Spurgeon, Meyer and Barnardo were strong supporters. By 1882 more than one million people had taken to wearing the blue ribbon to show they were both Christians and total abstainers.[42]

Some evangelicals went beyond persuading individuals to abstain from alcohol to directly seeking to prohibit its sale. In Hillsboro, Ohio, in 1873 Eliza Jane Thomson, daughter of the governor, led a group of seventy women from the Presbyterian church to protest outside saloons and hotels against the sale of alcohol, praying and singing hymns day after day. They were so successful that all the drinking saloons in the town were closed.[43] Others sought political solutions to the problem. In 1853 the UK Alliance for the Suppression of the Traffic in Intoxicating Liquors was founded in Manchester by the Quaker Nathaniel Card and the Baptist minister Dawson Burns. The UK Alliance was influenced by the passing of the Maine Law in North America, which restricted the sale of alcohol. The UK Alliance argued that, as with slavery, the evil of alcohol should be legislated to extinction. It had some evangelical support, but it was not a solely evangelical society.

In Scotland, where alcohol abuse was particularly prevalent, the Temperance (Scotland) Act became law in 1913, allowing local areas to vote whether or not to prohibit the sale of alcohol, and through a series of polls a number of areas became 'dry'.[44] In 1917 the Wesleyan Conference declared the manufacture and sale of intoxicating liquor as 'opposed to the best interests of the State and the Kingdom of God'. It called for people to 'work and pray for the total

[39] Heasman, *Evangelicals*, 135–137.
[40] Davies et al., *Methodist Church*, vol. 3, 176–177.
[41] Heasman, *Evangelicals*, 128–129.
[42] Ibid. 131–133.
[43] Ibid. 129–130.
[44] King, *Sober and Free*, 20–21, 24.

and permanent prohibition of the common manufacture and sale of alcoholic drinks'. In 1922 the first Prohibitionist MP, Edwin Scrymgeour, was elected to the British Parliament. Methodism was strongly associated with temperance, an emphasis that continued into the twentieth century. Methodists in Parliament played their part in restricting licencing hours, and bringing about the 1923 bill that restricted the sale of alcohol to those over 18 years of age.[45] However, the promotion of temperance through political efforts was a far less prominent feature of evangelical social action in Britain than in America, where a legal prohibition on the production, importation, transportation and sale of alcoholic beverages was achieved from 1920 to 1933.

A significant approach by evangelicals in tackling the alcohol problem was through providing alternatives to the temptations of the public house. The British temperance activist Sarah Robinson (1834–1921) started the Aldershot Mission Institute in 1863. It was an alcohol-free place of recreation for soldiers and for outreach to them. Although initially opposed by the army chaplains, the success of the project led to similar initiatives in other garrison towns, offering not only a place for recreation but also for education for the soldiers. From 1865 to 1873 she visited army camps and distributed Bibles and literature to soldiers and held prayer meetings. She also visited brothels in these towns, seeking to improve the health of the sex workers there. In 1874 she founded the Portsmouth Soldiers' Institute in a former public house, along with night schools and a public laundry, and in 1876 published *Christianity and Teetotalism*. Robinson became known as the 'Soldier's Friend' and raised awareness of the need of the army to improve the welfare of its soldiers. By the 1880s the scope of her work had extended to Alexandria in Egypt.[46]

In 1854 a coffee house was opened in Dundee with the support of the evangelical Lord Kinnaird, a place for working men to meet together in comfortable surroundings and get a cheap meal. Others followed in Edinburgh and Lichfield. Some coffee houses had a reading room or a games room. William Pennefather of Mildmay opened coffee huts for navvies at locations where railways were being constructed. Coffee carts selling hot drinks, breakfast or biscuits were set up by other missions outside factories and dockyards, and markets such as Billingsgate in London. Dining rooms were also established where cheap meals could be bought by working men during the day, rather than by their resorting to the pub at lunchtime. In 1875 the British Workman Public House Company was formed

---

[45] Davies et al., *Methodist Church*, vol. 3, 354–355.

[46] On Sarah Robinson see S. Morgan, 'Robinson, Sarah (1834–1921), Evangelist and Army Temperance Activist', *Oxford Dictionary of National Biography* <https://doi.org/10.1093/ref:odnb/49197>, accessed 2 May 2020.

in Liverpool, opening five houses in six months, and the idea quickly spread to other towns. These houses provided a convivial 'pub atmosphere' without the presence of alcohol. By the 1880s most large towns had several such premises, although without the sale of alcohol few made money and were sustained by donations from supporters. D. L. Moody, a strong encourager of these developments, argued that preventative measures to avoid the temptation of alcohol were vital.[47] The People's Café Company, started in 1874 with Lord Shaftesbury as president, also provided tea and coffee, cheap meals and non-alcoholic drinks.[48] By these efforts evangelicals played a key role in transforming the catering trade and breaking its strong connection with the sale of alcohol.

When Thomas Barnardo bought the Edinburgh Castle pub in the East End of London in 1873, and then the Dublin Castle in 1876, he attempted to make them look and feel as much like a pub as possible, with bright lights and plate glass windows with bright colours. They were run as centres for outreach and social-concern projects, and where working people could gather socially without the presence of alcohol.[49] In Glasgow temperance campaigners ran a teetotal paddle steamer offering pleasure trips down the Clyde as an alternative to the other excursions on offer that were literally 'booze cruises', notorious for their intoxicated passengers.[50] A notable attempt to provide an alternative to the alcohol-dominated places of amusement, such as the music hall, took place at the Old Vic Theatre in London from 1880 to 1912, under the management of the social reformer Emma Cons. It became a temperance amusement hall, where musical concerts and scenes from Shakespeare and opera were performed. John Pearce, leader of one of the coffee-house missions, provided the catering and non-alcoholic drinks, and Samuel Morley, the evangelical industrialist, offered finance.[51]

As well as the provision of alternatives to recreation that involved alcohol, evangelicals were deeply involved in the reclamation of alcoholics. Those who had been rescued from alcohol addiction had a particularly strong ministry to other alcoholics. One such was Mel Trotter, who in 1897 staggered drunk into the Pacific Garden Mission in Chicago. He was converted that night through hearing the testimony of Harry Monroe, another converted alcoholic. Trotter went on to found a series of missions across the USA established to rescue men whose lives were being ruined by alcohol addiction.[52]

---

[47] Heasman, *Evangelicals*, 137–139.
[48] Ibid. 143–144.
[49] Ibid. 140.
[50] King, *Sober and Free*, 12.
[51] See I. Bradley, 'The Old Vic', *History Today* 26.10 (October 1976), 4–9.
[52] See C. F. H. Henry, *The Pacific Garden Mission* (Grand Rapids, Mich.: Zondervan, 1942).

Many addicts repeatedly found themselves in court. The Habitual Drunkards Act of 1879 in England allowed for the provision of retreats for alcoholics to which those repeatedly arrested for drunkenness could be referred. A number of these were set up by evangelical groups, such as the Salvation Army, the Church Army and the Wesleyans. The National Institute for Inebriates, started by former police-court missionary H. N. Burden, ran five rescue homes. Such ministries deepened the understanding of alcohol addiction as a form of illness that needed treatment followed by therapeutic care.[53]

The success of linking temperance to gospel proclamation was mixed. Many were saved from a life of addiction and poverty, and families were spared the consequences of alcohol abuse, but for others temperance created an additional barrier to overcome in accepting the gospel.[54] Nonetheless, by the 1930s there was clear evidence of declining rates of alcohol abuse and associated crime, especially among young people, compared to the later years of the nineteenth century. A range of factors lay behind this, including limitation of licencing hours, better housing and education. In this evangelicals played a significant role, especially educating as to the dangers of alcohol abuse and providing alternative places of recreation and amusement to the public house.

Character study: William Booth (1829–1912) and Catherine Booth (1829–90) – England

The evangelical ministry most associated with work to rescue those suffering from alcohol addiction was that of the Salvation Army. Its co-founders, William and Catherine Booth, came from the Methodist tradition, where temperance advocacy was strong. From the time of his conversion in 1847 William Booth was a passionate evangelist, but his heart for the poorest residents of Nottingham was not shared by the leaders of the Wesleyan chapel he attended, who bridled at dirty and undisciplined lads from the slums being brought in to sit on their polished pews. He moved to London, explored other Methodist traditions and swapped work as a pawnbroker's assistant for lay preaching. In 1855 William married Catherine Mumford, daughter of a Methodist preacher and temperance worker, who played a strong, often guiding, role in his future ministry. Catherine was a very capable preacher. Their subsequent ministry in Gateshead, in the north-east of England, was a great success, turning a church of 120 people into a congregation of 1,500. But

---

[53] Heasman, *Evangelicals*, 145–146.

[54] B. Harrison, 'Religion and Recreation in Nineteenth-Century England', *Past and Present* 38 (December 1967), 123–124.

William's passion was evangelism, rather than settled pastoral ministry. In 1861 he resigned from the Methodist New Connexion and began life as an itinerant evangelist, promoting holiness revivalism. In 1865 he started holding tent meetings on Mile End Road, in London's East End, aided only by 'God the Holy Ghost and an open Bible'.[55]

The Booths believed that if the poorest were to be reached it was necessary to go to them in the streets, open-air spaces and pubs. They developed techniques to attract a crowd, including the use of brass-band music, which was also effective when there was a need to 'blow down' the opposition. The use of military-style uniforms, dramatic advertising and women preachers all proved effective. The name the 'Salvation Army' was adopted in 1878, its leaders known by military ranks: Booth was General Superintendent, and then simply 'the General'. Women played a key role – in 1878 they made up 41 of the Salvation Army's 91 officers. Its work attracted crowds, but also opposition, including from the 'Skeleton Army', spurred on by owners of public houses to disrupt their meetings, and even the police. Many in established denominations recoiled at what they considered Booth's uncouth debasing of the Christian message. Nonetheless, the work grew rapidly, from 13 preaching stations in 1868 to 1,006 corps, 2,260 officers and attendances of more than 53,500 in 1887.[56]

Booth's mission was to the 'submerged tenth' – the poorest and least reached who numbered, he reckoned, some three million in Britain. His years as a pawnbroker's assistant showed him how precarious life was for them. Particular focus was given to the homeless, discharged prisoners and alcoholics. Salvation Army officers were to be abstainers. Yet the primary focus remained evangelistic – as Catherine Booth declared, 'Oh! how I see the emptiness and vanity of everything compared with the salvation of the soul.'[57] In 1884 the Women's Special Services was started, which worked particularly with homeless women, deserted wives, prostitutes or those addicted to alcohol. In 1886 the first slum post was opened, and two years later a depot was opened in Limehouse, East London, where food and shelter were provided.[58] Whether this represented radical change or natural development of earlier work is debated, but these emphases were encapsulated in the publication by William Booth of *In Darkest England and the Way Out* (1890). This married the need for urgent evangelism with deep social concern, and critiqued other churches too busy with their

---

[55] O. Chadwick, *The Victorian Church*, vol. 2 (London: A&C Black, 1970), 288–299.
[56] K. S. Inglis, *The Churches and the Working Classes* (London: Routledge, 2006), 195.
[57] *Pall Mall Gazette*, 22 November 1883; *War Cry*, 7 July 1881, in Inglis, *Working Classes*, 175–176.
[58] Inglis, *Working Classes*, 198.

internal concerns to heed the cry of the poor at their door. Booth declared the current state of Christian rescue work to be 'lamentably inadequate for any effectual dealing with the despairing miseries of these outcast classes. The rescued are appallingly few'. He sought a way to make 'it easy where it is now difficult, and possible where it is now all but impossible, for men and women to find their way to the Cross of our Lord Jesus Christ'.[59]

Booth proposed a comprehensive scheme beginning with the evangelistic outreach work of the slum crusade, where immediate shelter, lodging and cheap food were offered to those in need, and the opportunity given to move into rescue homes. Here people were provided with permanent support – employment training in skills such as carpentry and brickmaking; and for those who progressed, opportunities were provided to resettle in the country or overseas. Booth reckoned that at least half a million people in Britain were 'completely under the domination' of alcohol. He called alcohol abuse 'a national vice', and spoke of the 'despair' of those involved in rescue work.[60] He believed that those with alcohol addiction were some of the hardest people to reach. Without some 'extraordinary help', Booth observed, 'they must hunger and sin, and sin and hunger'.[61]

The struggle of the alcoholic was graphically depicted: 'The insatiable craving controls him. He cannot get away from it. It compels him to drink, and, unless delivered by an Almighty hand, he will drink himself into a drunkard's grave and a drunkard's hell.' Although for some, excessive use of alcohol was a bad habit, for others, 'it must be accounted a disease'. While the former simply needed to be removed from the place of temptation, for the latter it was necessary to 'bring to bear upon it every agency, hygienic and otherwise, calculated to effect a cure'.[62] External reform, or resolution based on will-power, was rarely likely to succeed:

> you may clothe the drunkard, fill his purse with gold, establish him in a well-furnished home, and in three or six or twelve months he will once more be on the Embankment, haunted by delirium tremens, dirty, squalid, and ragged.[63]

Many factors were recognized as contributing to addiction issues – poverty and poor living environment, but also personal character. Booth was wary of

---

[59] W. Booth, *In Darkest England and the Way Out* (London: Salvation Army, 1890), preface.
[60] Ibid. 186; on p. 178 he gives the number as one million.
[61] Ibid., preface, 178.
[62] Ibid. 181, 186.
[63] Ibid. 86.

utopian schemes of social reconstruction, recognizing that spiritual regeneration was needed alongside practical assistance to bring lasting personal change: 'if the inside remains unchanged you have wasted your labour. You must somehow or other graft upon the man's nature a new nature, which has in it the element of the Divine.' *In Darkest England* contains a number of cases where this happened, such as that of 'Barbara', driven to drink and a suicide attempt by an unhappy marriage and an abusive husband, but then saved through the Salvation Army's open-air meetings and 'delivered from her love of drink and sin'.[64]

In recognizing that the cause of many social problems was not just personal but also the impact of societal factors beyond human control, the Salvation Army helped break down prejudicial attitudes towards the poor. Salvation Army officers understood the gospel was for all, and recognized the worth of each individual, whether poor, criminal or addict, and believed they deserved another chance and, given the right circumstances, most could become valuable and productive members of society.[65] Those addicted to alcohol recognized the Salvation Army rescue centres as a safe port of call when in need. Booth also established a series of rescue homes to which those repeatedly arrested for drunkenness could be referred, rather than repeatedly being sentenced to prison.[66]

How effective the Salvation Army was in reaching the 'submerged tenth' is debated. Most Salvation Army recruits were from the respectable working classes and above rather than the destitute. In some ways the Salvation Army was more effective as a channel of service to the poorest, rather than in bringing large numbers of them to Christ.[67] Yet the work of the Booths could be described as Christianity with its sleeves rolled up. They understood the biblical meaning of love as 'practical helpfulness'.[68] Booth believed that meeting the needs of the poorest, or most helpless, opened the door for opportunities to provide care for the soul. The evangelist was more likely to gain a hearing from someone 'if he comes to know that it was you who pulled him out of the horrible pit and the miry clay in which he was sinking to perdition'.[69]

---

[64] Ibid. 45, 181.

[65] N. Magnuson, *Salvation in the Slums – Evangelical Social Work, 1865–1920* (Metuchen, N.J.: Scarecrow Press, 1977), 176–177.

[66] Booth, *Darkest England*, 187.

[67] C. Parkin, 'The Salvation Army and Social Questions of the Day', in M. Hill (ed.), *Sociological Yearbook of Religion in Britain*, vol. 5 (London: SCM Press, 1972), 117.

[68] Magnuson, *Salvation*, 178.

[69] Booth, *Darkest England*, 45.

By 1890 the Salvation Army's work reached to other parts of Europe, North America, Australia, the West Indies, Africa and India. Opposition turned to admiration and then to imitation: the Church Army was established by the Church of England in 1882.

16

Care for people with drug addiction

Drug addiction is often considered a problem of the 1960s onwards, when the drug culture came to attention through its association with popular music culture and events such as the Woodstock festival. However, the issue has been around far longer than that, and so have attempts by evangelical Christians to rescue those gripped by drug addiction. This chapter will focus on the rescue of opium addicts, and particularly on China in the nineteenth century.

A lucrative trade in opium, grown in India and shipped by British merchants to China, developed from the 1790s to meet the growing demand for the drug. By the 1830s the opium trade was one of the most valuable in the world. Opium was used widely for medical purposes – for pain relief, suppression of the symptoms of lung and throat diseases, the treatment of diarrhoea, dysentery and cholera, and various nervous diseases. Laudanum, an opium-based medicine, was widely used as a painkiller and cough suppressant, and was openly sold by chemists without prescription until the twentieth century, with little awareness of its addictive properties. Laudanum included about 10 per cent opium and most of the opium alkaloids, including morphine and codeine, and was a constituent of many patent medicines. Morphine, a derivative of opium, was refined in medical form in Germany in the 1840s. It was widely used by doctors on the battlefields of Crimea and the American Civil War, relieving the pain of many casualties but also sadly causing wounded soldiers to become dependent on it. Opioid addiction is not a new issue.

In China opium was widely smoked. Addiction became such a serious problem that in 1839 the Chinese emperor attempted to outlaw opium smoking and stop the trade. When opium stocks worth more than £2 million were seized and dumped at sea, the British government intervened and demanded reparations for the destroyed goods. War ensued from 1839 to 1842, and again from 1857 to 1859. When British gunboats blockaded the Yangtze River, cutting off trade, the Chinese were forced to sign the Treaty of Nanjing in 1842. Hong Kong became a British colony and five treaty ports were opened allowing foreign merchants to trade and operate under self-governance.[1] Opium also began to be grown in China itself, and it was highly profitable, yielding a price five times that of wheat.[2]

Out of this catalogue of distasteful events that promoted such a harmful addiction in the name of free trade an unexpected opportunity for mission arose. The Treaty of Nanjing saw strictures against Christianity in China being removed and foreigners being allowed to move freely across inland China. Pioneers such as Karl Gützlaff responded to opportunities to promote the gospel across China. Although Gützlaff's work was much criticized,[3] it influenced James Hudson Taylor.

By 1857 some eight million Chinese were regular opium smokers and many were addicts.[4] As opium smoking developed into a massive social problem in China in the 1870s, the government responded with draconian laws against addicts, opium growers and settlers, but these drove the problem underground.[5] Missionary work in inland China brought missionaries into contact with many people trapped in opium addiction. From the middle of the nineteenth century, Catholic missionaries were running opium refuges, and being free of opium addiction was required before a catechumen could be accepted for baptism.[6] In December 1871 Dr James Galt and his wife, sent out by the Edinburgh Medical Missionary Society, opened a hospital for opium addicts at Hangzhou.[7]

Hudson Taylor's China Inland Mission (CIM), deeply influenced by the holiness movement, had a strong evangelistic priority, but its compassionate response to the terrible famines in China through relief work has already been mentioned in chapter 3. The CIM also rescued and cared for opium addicts. This challenges the assertion that missions such as the CIM, influenced by

---

[1] A. Austin, *China's Millions: The China Inland Mission and the Qing Society, 1832–1905* (Grand Rapids, Mich.: Eerdmans, 2007), 43–50.

[2] G. Taylor, *Pastor Hsi: Confucian Scholar and Christian* (London: CIM, 1900; repr. London: OMF, 1972), 77.

[3] On Gützlaff's work see J. G. Lutz and R. R. Lutz, 'Karl Gützlaff's Approach to Indigenization: The Chinese Union', in D. H. Bays (ed.), *Christianity in China: From the Eighteenth Century to the Present* (Stanford: Stanford University Press, 1996), 269–291.

[4] A. J. Broomhall, *Hudson Taylor and China's Open Century*, bk 2: *Over the Treaty Wall* (London: Hodder & Stoughton, 1982), 380–381.

[5] Austin, *China Inland Mission*, 244.

[6] A. R. Sweeten, 'Catholic Converts in Jiangxi Province: Conflict and Accommodation, 1860–1900', in D. H. Bays (ed.), *Christianity in China from the Eighteenth-Century to the Present* (Stanford: Stanford University Press, 1996), 25–27.

[7] A. J. Broomhall, *Hudson Taylor and China's Open Century*, bk 5: *Refiner's Fire* (London: Hodder & Stoughton, 1985), 314.

holiness, were too 'other-worldly' and lacked transformational attitudes towards the world.[8]

In 1876 the CIM periodical *China's Millions* reported the terrible consequences of opium addiction:

> It is the source of poverty, wretchedness, disease and misery, unparalleled in . . . any other country. It debases the debased to the very lowest depths of degradation . . . See that poor wretch with the emaciated frame; he has parted with his land, his house, his furniture, his children's and his own clothing and bedding, and either sold his wife or hired her out for prostitution, and *all for opium*, to satisfy an insatiable appetite.[9]

It was not long after Hudson Taylor arrived in China in 1854 that he began to witness the devastating effects of opium addiction. As a trained doctor he was called to a number of suicides occasioned by overdoses that eventually stopped the heart beating. After a wave of such deaths in 1859, he opened his first opium asylum in Ningbo for the treatment of addicts. At once he was overrun by people requesting help, and in three months 133 addicts were admitted. It was not a success, and the patients continued to smuggle opium in or regressed to the habit after being discharged.[10] This initial lack of success did not prevent the CIM from making opium refuges a key aspect of their work, often as an initial missionary venture, from which tract distribution and preaching could eventually follow.

There was a debate among missionaries as to whether treating opium addiction was a medical matter or a spiritual issue to be cured simply by prayer and faith. In time, the medical argument won, although treatment was not to be separated from spiritual means. The most difficult problem was how to counteract withdrawal symptoms. Dr John Dudgeon of the London Missionary Society (LMS), a leading figure in developing effective treatments, experimented with the use of morphine to counteract the side effects of withdrawal by giving a gradually diminishing dose. Then, in 1882, Dr Harold Schofield (1851–83), a CIM medical missionary who had set up a hospital and dispensary in Taiyuan, Shanxi, began experimenting with weaning addicts off opium by injecting

---

[8] D. Bebbington, *The Dominance of Evangelicalism: The Age of Spurgeon and Moody* (Leicester: Inter-Varsity Press, 2005), 176. This is also discussed in Okky Karmawan's PhD thesis 'The Impact of the Keswick and Cambridge Holiness Movement on British Protestant Missions in Asia (1881–1906), with Special Reference to the Church Missionary Society and the China Inland Mission', University of Edinburgh, 2020.

[9] *China's Millions*, July–August 1876, 82, in Austin, *China Inland Mission*, 202–203; emphasis original.

[10] Austin, *China Inland Mission*, 76–77.

steadily decreasing amounts of morphine using the newly developed hypodermic needle.[11] Many of those treated successfully were soldiers. Gradually other CIM missionaries adopted the approach, with varying degrees of success. This was combined with prayer and Bible teaching, in the belief that both medical and spiritual means were needed to break addiction and keep a person clean of it. The rule in Protestant congregations was that an opium smoker could not be baptized until after he or she had given up opium smoking.[12]

Opium addicts were considered the hardest group of people to reach in China, especially in areas where opium growing was profitable, and opium smoking was ingrained in the culture. In Shanxi province, where the problem was at its worst, it was estimated that 80 per cent of the urban population, and 60 per cent of the rural population, smoked opium. One missionary lamented, 'If there is a place in the whole world where it is harder to do missionary work than right here in opium-drugged Shansi province . . . I do not want to know of it.'[13] David Hill, who had been so active in famine relief, regularly observed the dire effects of opium addiction and its association with poverty and prostitution. In 1877 he quoted the Chinese saying

If you want to be revenged on your enemy, you need not strike him, you need not go to law with him, you have only to entice him into smoking opium. If you can give him that taste, you will take the surest means in your power of ruining him utterly.[14]

Hill's work led to the conversion of the Chinese scholar Hsi, whose subsequent indefatigable work in running opium refuges is the character study in this chapter. Hill also offered a prize of up to £100 in an essay competition on the topic of the best cure used in opium refuges. Those who approached Hill for help knew that the Christian message he offered alongside his practical care with giving up addiction brought the 'moral fibre' that made the cure more likely to be lasting. In dealing with opium addiction Hill emphasized the need for a 'higher healing'.[15]

Missionaries were often summoned after there had been an opium overdose. If the person was reached in time, they tried emetics, flushing the stomach with potassium permanganate, which made opium non-absorbable, and 'artificial

---

[11] Ibid. 247.
[12] Ibid. 244, 249.
[13] Quoted in ibid. 270.
[14] W. T. A. Barber, *David Hill: Missionary and Saint* (London: Charles H. Kelly, 1898), 162–163.
[15] Ibid. 212, 281.

respiration' to keep a person breathing. Harold Schofield reported forty cases in Taiyuan in 1882 alone. He was able to save four of the six he was called to attend.[16]

Great care was needed with those seeking to break with opium addiction. 'Cold turkey' could prove fatal without expert guidance and care. Opium slowed the bodily system, and internal organs responded by working extremely hard to overcome this. When the drug was withdrawn, mucus would pour from the nose, followed by chronic diarrhoea, raging thirst, shivering and depression. This could last for a week, followed by incessant craving to return to the drug.[17]

Those who gave up addiction and were converted to Christianity did so in the face of great challenges. In a drug-dominated culture there were, sadly, those who professed to be free of addiction, and to have experienced conversion and been baptized and admitted into churches, but later went back to the habit and abandoned their faith profession. A small group of missionaries from Oberlin College, Ohio, reached China in 1881. They laboured in Shanxi for eight years without a convert, struggling with ill health, discouragement and the challenge of learning the language. After they opened an opium refuge at Taigu, Liu Feng Chih, who had been a rich merchant trading in tea, coffee and sugar, approached them in 1889 seeking help. He had lost everything through becoming hopelessly addicted to opium. At the refuge he heard a sermon on the story of the Gadarene demoniac (Luke 8:26–39) and realized how closely it mirrored his situation under the power of addiction. Despite terrible withdrawal symptoms, he stayed at the refuge for forty days, with the missionaries using the diluted morphine solution to ease his pain. After one dreadful night, as dawn approached, Liu found his craving for opium had gone, and he fell into a deep sleep. When he awoke, he felt totally transformed. He stayed at the mission station for several months, learning about Christianity, before, as the man had done in Luke 8, he returned to his own village to spread the news of Jesus, taking copies of the Bible with him. He eventually took up a role as a teacher in the missionary school.[18]

By 1890 the CIM was running opium refuges in at least eight provinces, although some offered only a very basic level of shelter and care. These were often the first points of contact with the local people, and provided further opportunities for tracts and books to be distributed and sold once the ground

---

[16] Austin, *China Inland Mission*, 243.

[17] Ibid. 243.

[18] The story is told in Nat Brandt's account of the mission, *Massacre in Shansi* (Syracuse, N.Y.: Syracuse University Press, 1994), 9–12.

had been prepared by works of compassionate care.[19] The CIM's approach in its refuges was to use gradually reduced doses of morphine over a four-week period, during which time the gospel was regularly shared, together with prayer and Bible reading. Medical and spiritual remedies were offered hand in hand.[20]

The fruit of the work of the opium refuges was astonishing, especially considering the work involved long-standing addicts, and in a Chinese culture that was suspicious of the Christian message because it was delivered by missionaries from countries that had done so much to promote the opium trade. One CIM missionary reported of his congregation in South Shanxi that 28 out of 41 baptized converts were former opium addicts. At Pingyang the number of ex-addicts was reported as at 50 per cent, and in one of the largest churches in Shanxi, at Ta-ning, it was 9 out of 10. The missionary added, 'some of our best men in the church have been opium-smokers'. Although the CIM missionary Stanley Smith recognized that the refuges often attracted 'scamps and vagabonds', he was not daunted: 'God loves them; that is enough.'[21] C. T. Studd reported the case of a man who approached him, saying, 'I am a murderer, an adulterer, I have broken all the laws of God and man again and again. I am also a confirmed opium smoker. He cannot save me.' However, the man was remarkably converted and became a preacher. When he returned to the town where he had done so many wrong things, he was arrested, beaten and imprisoned, but he would not give up preaching.[22] In Shandong a CIM missionary reported, 'If I had gone through the city in order to select THE VILEST AND MOST DISGRACEFUL MAN that could be found, I should certainly have picked out that man. And now he adorns the doctrines of GOD OUR SAVIOUR.'[23]

The medical approach continued to be debated. The Shanghai Missionary Conference of Protestant missionaries held in 1890 feared the black-market trade in morphine, and sought to prevent 'the sale of such anti-opium medicines as contain opium or any of its alkaloids', although their use in 'carefully managed refuges' was not rejected.[24] However, it seems that missionaries, with no alternatives available, continued to use morphine. W. G. Peat of the CIM for a time attempted to cure addicts without the use of morphine, encouraging

---

[19] Austin, *China Inland Mission*, 246–248.

[20] See *China's Millions* (London), February 1887, 28.

[21] Duncan Kay, 'Encouraging Progress in South Shan-si', *China's Millions*, August 1893, 110–111; July–August 1887, 101, quoted in Austin, *China Inland Mission*, 381.

[22] N. Grubb, *C. T. Studd: Cricketer and Pioneer* (London: Lutterworth Press, 1933), 84–85.

[23] Charles H. Judd, 'Turned to God from Idols', *China's Millions* (North America), July 1895, 91, quoted in Austin, *China Inland Mission*, 381; capitals original.

[24] *Records of the General Conference of the Protestant Missionaries of China, Held in Shanghai, May 7–20, 1890*, li.

prayer and urging them simply to 'hold out'. Only two in a hundred managed to withstand the pain of withdrawal, and so he resorted to the use of morphine. Many who came were old, and some seriously ill, broken by addiction and fearing death. Large numbers died soon after conversion because of the long-term health damage caused by their addiction.[25]

The fruit from the marriage between social action and evangelism seen in the rescue work among addicts was remarkable, especially from the CIM's work. Those converted came from many religious backgrounds, and included Buddhist priests, Daoists and members of various secret societies. C. T. Studd reported the conversion at Lucheng of an opium addict who had been a 'sorceress', but who was now 'determined to press on the heavenly way'.[26] Usually the CIM expected two years' probation before baptism, but sometimes baptism took place sooner. Other missions were suspicious of the reports of success, and expected many to fall away quickly. Some did, especially in the face of difficulties, but large numbers did not, and bearing strong witness to family and friends of the incredible change the Christian gospel had brought in their lives, they became effective evangelists.

It was surprising that an organization such as the CIM should invest heavily in rescuing addicts, strongly influenced as it was by holiness and premillennial teaching to focus primarily on direct and urgent personal evangelism in the light of Christ's expected imminent return. There were various reasons it did so. One was that it was seen as a struggle against another power, addiction, which claimed the allegiance of the sufferer, and breaking addiction's chains so someone could embrace Christ was a manifestation of spiritual deliverance. The desperation of the Chinese opium addicts and their families, in the face of hopeless addiction could also not be ignored, and the CIM workers responded with compassion to their cries for help. With the help of Schofield and others they had developed effective forms of treatment, and so had something to offer. There was also a sense, through such work, of making atonement for Britain's involvement in opium trading. Hudson Taylor wrote in *China's Millions* in 1877, 'it is scarcely possible to think of England's responsibility in this matter without feelings of unspeakable humiliation and grief'.[27]

Evangelical missionaries and politicians not only sought to help those caught in addiction, but also spoke out in the political arena, opposing the opium trade itself. The Church Missionary Society (CMS) medical missionary W. Welton,

---

[25] Austin, *China Inland Mission*, 368.

[26] *China's Millions* (North America), June 1895, 82, in Austin, *China Inland Mission*, 382.

[27] J. H. Broomhall, *Hudson Taylor and China's Open Century*, bk 6: *Assault on the Nine* (London: Hodder & Stoughton, 1988), 164–165.

serving at Fuzhou, lamented in 1855 that 'England should have given twenty millions sterling to emancipate her slaves, and yet pocket annually six millions sterling by the opium contraband traffic'.[28] In the British Parliament Lord Shaftesbury condemned the iniquitous opium trade, from which British merchants were profiting hugely. In 1857, on the eve of the second Opium War, he brought a motion to Parliament against the opium trade, partly in an attempt to avert the conflict.[29] Shaftesbury maintained his resolute opposition to the opium trade for more than forty years, and was for many years President of the Anti-Opium League. In 1880 he became president of the newly formed Anglo-Oriental Society for the Suppression of the Opium Trade. He strongly supported a resolution to Parliament that condemned the trade as unchristian and immoral. On religious grounds he believed the trade as 'altogether and unequivocally abominable'.[30]

Missionaries were well aware of the obstacle placed in the way of their work by being associated with the country at the forefront of the opium trade.[31] The General Conference of Missions held in Shanghai in 1877 denounced the opium trade as

deeply injurious not only to China, but also to India, to Great Britain and all countries engaged in it . . . It is a most formidable obstacle to the cause of Christianity and should be speedily suppressed . . . That which is morally wrong cannot be politically right.

The missionaries declared that the British government should have nothing to do with the production and sale of opium, and the Chinese government should not be hindered in its efforts to suppress these. Britain had helped to create a nation of addicts.[32] Similarly, the 1890 Shanghai Missionary Conference expressed its 'unflinching opposition to the opium-traffic'.[33] In addition to his rescue work among addicts, David Hill also spoke out against the trade. It was a moral issue, and the British government could not justify the collection of any revenue from it. He urged prayer that 'the Lord . . . would open the way for some action in the matter'.[34]

---

[28] Quoted in A. J. Broomhall, *Hudson Taylor and China's Open Century*, bk 2: *Over the Treaty Wall* (London: Hodder & Stoughton, 1982), 237.

[29] E. Hodder, *The Life and Work of the Seventh Earl of Shaftesbury*, vol. 3 (London: Cassell, 1887), 38–46.

[30] Ibid. 430–431.

[31] Broomhall, *Treaty Wall*, 314.

[32] Broomhall, *Assault on the Nine*, 165.

[33] *Records*, li.

[34] Barber, *Hill*, 163–164.

In 1876 C. H. Spurgeon denounced how Britain could 'make a monopoly of the growth of opium, and then claim a right to sell it to China, a right enforced by cannon and gun-boats'. It was, he declared, 'practically a right to poison the Chinese', and went on, 'We sent out missionaries to the heathen Chinese, while acting more heathenly than he does.' Spurgeon railed against British politicians, urging them to renounce the policy, despite the loss of revenue that would result from this. He was well aware of the power of the merchanting lobby in opposing this: 'Gold and the gospel seldom do agree.'[35]

Through 1877 and 1878 Hudson Taylor also campaigned against the opium trade with crusading intensity, alongside his vigorous campaign for people to meet the spiritual needs of China. Despite his strong premillennial views, he had no problem with entering the political realm by condemning merchants and politicians over the opium trade. At the 1888 Centenary Missionary Conference in London he declared the trade was 'destroying the Chinese and counteracting the good works of missions'. It was all apiece with the West's exporting its worse vices – opium in China and cheap alcohol in Africa – in exchange for manufactured goods. The CIM's secretary in England, Benjamin Broomhall, was a strong anti-opium campaigner, and the anti-opium movement was promoted in the CIM's publication *China's Millions*.[36]

The Society for the Suppression of the Opium Trade (SSOT) had been started in 1874. Its founders were Edward Pease and his relative Sir Joseph Pease, a Liberal MP and an evangelical Christian. Lord Shaftesbury was the President and Henry Venn, General Secretary of the CMS, was on its committee. The committee included representatives of the LMS, the Wesleyan Methodists, the Baptists and the British and Foreign Bible Society. The SSOT declared, 'The misery and demoralizatioa occasioned by the use of opium are almost beyond belief. Any man who has witnessed its frightful ravages and demoralizing effects in China, must feel deeply on this subject.'[37] It worked as a pressure group lobbying public opinion with a view to political action, and drew together politicians and medical doctors with missionaries and leaders of Nonconformists and evangelicals.[38] Between 1878 and 1895 the SSOT promoted debates in the

---

[35] C. H. Spurgeon, *Sword and Trowel* 11 (1876), 433. On the opium issue and British policy in China see J. Hevia, *The Imperial Security State: British Colonial Knowledge and Empire-Building in Asia* (Cambridge: Cambridge University Press, 2012).

[36] D. Robert, *Occupy Until I Come, A. T. Pierson and the Evangelisation of the World* (Grand Rapids, Mich.: Eerdmans, 2003), 168–169.

[37] A. J. Broomhall, *Hudson Taylor and China's Open Century*, bk 4: *Survivors' Pact* (London: Hodder & Stoughton, 1984), 28–29.

[38] On the SSOT see V. Berridge and G. Edwards, *Opium and the People: Opiate Use in Nineteenth-Century England* (London: St Martin's Press, 1981); and for the campaign in China see K. L. Lodwick, *Crusaders Against Opium: Protestant Missionaries in China 1874–1917* (Lexington, Ky.: University Press of Kentucky, 1996).

House of Lords in every year but one. In 1881 Lord Shaftesbury was one of the joint chairs of a meeting demanding the British government work with that of China to suppress the opium traffic and prevent opium being grown in India. In 1882–3 the society held 180 public meetings and presented a petition of 75,000 signatures to the House of Commons. Broomhall published *The Truth About Opium Smoking*, describing the terrible social consequences of addiction.[39] He also launched the journal *National Righteousness* to arouse Christians and their churches from their apathy on the matter, campaigning for the removal of the evil of opium traffic. Much of the information on which the campaign depended came from missionaries who had seen the blight of addiction on the mission field. *China's Millions* also reported the efforts of Chinese leaders to oppose the trade, and their hostile sentiments towards Britain for promoting it. They showed that selling 'foreign mud' (opium) could not be separated from the 'foreign religion' (Christianity) of those who perpetuated it. Broomhall was told on his deathbed in 1911 that the British government had promised the 'extinction of the opium trade with China within two years'. Echoing the words of Wilberforce, who heard on his deathbed of the abolition of slave-owning, Broomhall declared, 'Thank God I have lived to see the day.'[40] By 1915 the opium trade was over. The legacy in broken lives and broken homes was huge, but evangelical missionaries and leaders back home had played a role in ending it.

Some sought to turn this in favour of further promotion of mission, arguing that the West owed China the opportunity to embrace Christianity to offset the evil caused by the opium trade encouraged by the West. Fears also grew of the retribution that might be exacted against foreigners and their converts to Christianity by the Chinese for inflicting the curse of opium on the people, fears sadly fulfilled in the tragedy of the Boxer Rebellion of 1899–1901.

The problems of addiction never went away, but gained more widespread popular attention with the growth of the drug culture of the 1950s and 1960s. Evangelicals again took a role in developing social-action projects to rescue people from addiction. The American evangelist David Wilkerson (1931–2011) undertook rescue work in New York among those involved with drugs and crime, reaching out especially to gangs, and saw remarkable converts, including the one-time gang leader Nicky Cruz. Wilkerson was the founder in 1958 of the addiction recovery programme Teen Challenge, which spread internationally.[41]

---

[39] B. Broomhall, *The Truth About Opium Smoking* (London: Hodder & Stoughton, 1882).

[40] Austin, *China Inland Mission*, 199–203.

[41] The story of Wilkerson's work is told in D. Wilkerson and J. and E. Sherrill, *The Cross and the Switchblade* (New York: Random House, 1962).

Although the government of Mao Zedong in China repressed opium production and dealing in the 1950s, and forced some ten million addicts into compulsory treatment, the problem shifted into neighbouring parts of South East Asia. In 1966 Jackie Pullinger (1944–), a trained musician, travelled from England to begin work as a primary school teacher in the Kowloon Walled City, Hong Kong, which had become a major opium producing centre and was run by Chinese Triad gangs. Despite considerable risk to herself, she befriended some of the gang members and began sharing the gospel with them. Central to her message was that Jesus could give them purpose for living without the need for drugs. She went on to establish a youth centre that helped the drug addicts inside the walled city. In 1981 she started the St Stephen's Society, providing rehabilitation for recovering drug addicts, prostitutes and gang members. By December 2007 it housed 200 people. Her method of helping addicts recover from addiction focused on the power of creating a family environment, prayer and personal support. The story of the early years of her Hong Kong ministry, and its charismatic ministry emphasis, is chronicled in the book *Chasing the Dragon* (1980).[42]

Character study: Hsi Liao-chih (1836–96) – China

As the Methodist missionary David Hill sought a way to reach Confucian thinkers with the gospel, in 1879 he devised an essay competition for Chinese scholars on the theme of the 'Heavenly Way'. The essays were to be based on Christian scriptures, tracts and pamphlets.[43] The winner of the substantial prize was Hsi Liao-chih, a capable Confucian scholar whose academic prospects had been ruined by opium addiction. Hsi was suspicious of Christianity as a foreign religion, and of the British for trading in the 'black mud' – opium. When Hsi met Hill, he quickly realized he was 'in the presence of a true, good man', highly regarded because of his relief work in the famine of the 1870s. Hsi began reading the Bible regularly with Hill. When he came to the gospel accounts of the sufferings and death of Christ, he wept 'with tears that flowed and would not cease', and gave himself 'unreservedly' to God.[44]

Hsi had fallen into addiction after developing a persistent cough in his thirties. This proved resistant to all treatments, and he began smoking opium to alleviate it. Ten years of addiction left him fearful and haunted by hideous faces tempting him to commit suicide. After his conversion Hsi knew he needed

---

[42] J. Pullinger, *Chasing the Dragon* (London: Hodder & Stoughton, 1980).

[43] Barber, *Hill*, 217; Taylor, *Hsi*, 34–40.

[44] Taylor, *Hsi*, 43, 46–48.

to break the opium habit and turned to Hill. They tried various remedies to ease the withdrawal symptoms, with little effect. For seven days he could not eat or sleep, and was overcome with terrible shivering and aches. Hsi saw the struggle as spiritual warfare, with the devil refusing to surrender his soul and seeking to destroy him. In his agony he cried out, 'Devil what can you do against me? My life is in the hand of God. And truly I am willing to break off the opium and die, but not willing to continue in sin and live!' As he threw himself on God's mercy, seeking the comfort and strength of the Holy Spirit, his soul was flooded with peace. He learned a key lesson for future ministry: 'I knew that to break off opium without real faith in Jesus would indeed be impossible.' Medicine and personal resolve would help, but could not be relied on in themselves for an ultimate break with addiction.[45]

After this struggle Hsi took the name 'Hsi Shengmo', meaning 'the Overcomer of Demons'.[46] He was deeply aware of the immensity of God's grace to him:

> I know my sins are great; I ought to go to hell. I know, too, that Jesus is able to forgive my sins, able to save me from sin, able to save me from hell, and to give me to live in heaven forever.[47]

In 1880, aged 44, Hsi was baptized and quickly began to tell others the gospel that had transformed him. He began a church in his own village near Pingyang and persuaded its residents to give up praying to their idols for their harvests for a year, and pray instead to the 'One True God'. When a year of good harvests followed, the village was won for Christ.[48]

Hsi travelled widely to preach, dressed in a white robe with a red ribbon across his chest on which was written, 'Jesus Christ came into the world to save sinners'. He saw a response on a scale the missionaries never witnessed.[49] Having a strong sense of the reality of spiritual warfare, he ascribed the success of his ministry to the power of prayer, seeing many remarkable answers.[50] One such was the conversion of his wife, who became a key figure in the ministry.[51]

Hsi's family ran a business making and selling traditional Chinese medicines. Helping opium addicts became a central part of his ministry, and he developed

---

[45] Ibid. 50–53.
[46] Ibid. 55, 58.
[47] 'Testimony of Mr Hsi', quoted in Austin, *China Inland Mission*, 176.
[48] Taylor, *Hsi*, 73–74.
[49] Austin, *China Inland Mission*, 258–260.
[50] Taylor, *Hsi*, 54, 71–72.
[51] Ibid. 68–70.

medicines to alleviate the agonizing withdrawal symptoms.[52] He established a chain of refuges for addicts that by the early 1890s extended from Zhili in the east to North Henan, Xian, Shaanxi and Gansu.[53] Hsi trained former addicts to be keepers of the refuges. They were to be converted, compassionate and caring, and preachers of the gospel. Their training included working in the shop where his anti-opium pills were prepared to his special recipe. Hsi stipulated that each day there be 'united prayer that by the help of the Holy Spirit the medicine may be properly prepared, may be able to rescue people from opium smoking, and lead them to believe in the Gospel'.[54] Hsi inspected the refuges carefully to ensure they were run well, and only ever had to close one, which was found to be 'filthy, and in the most hopeless disorder', and had run up huge debts.[55]

Hsi made a charge for the anti-opium pills, which caused some criticism, but it was part of his policy of ensuring the refuges did not become dependent on outside missionary funds. Their success far exceeded that of the missionary-run refuges, and Hsi's medical skills, knowledge of Chinese culture and business ability were key to this.[56] The cost of sustaining the whole scheme was huge – thought to be up to $5,000 a year at the time.[57]

Most refuges paved the way for a local church to be started, as seen in the spread of the work into Xian. Here European missionaries had been unable to get permission to rent property, but Hsi befriended a local mandarin who was a Muslim and shared with him the plan to help opium addicts. The mandarin confessed he too was an addict and assisted with finding premises. Through its successful work a mission station was established.[58]

Hsi recruited very able helpers. At Huaiqing, attempts to preach the gospel had been met with rioting, so Hsi sent Ch'eng, one of his workers, to open an opium refuge as a preparatory step. Although Ch'eng's work was initially rejected because he too had 'Eaten the foreign devils' doctrine', through persistent faith things changed. A key incident came after a visitor to the town was attacked and robbed of his money and clothes. Like the good Samaritan, Ch'eng rescued, fed and clothed the man, and when he had recovered gave him money to complete his journey. The people of the town were deeply moved at Ch'eng's actions, and permission for a refuge to be opened followed. As Hsi's

---

[52] Austin, *China Inland Mission*, 266–267.
[53] Taylor, *Hsi*, 214.
[54] Pastor Hsi, 'Rules for the Middle Eden', in Austin, *China Inland Mission*, 380.
[55] Taylor, *Hsi*, 227–230.
[56] Ibid. 221–224.
[57] Ibid. 225.
[58] Ibid. 218–221.

biographer commented, 'Christlike deeds, prompted by His own Spirit, open closed hearts to Christ.'[59]

In Hsi's refuges there was Bible reading, hymn singing and prayer each morning and evening. The day was marked by orderliness, structure and discipline, which counteracted the erosion of personal care and responsibility that came with addiction.[60] Hudson Taylor was deeply impressed with Hsi's leadership abilities and spirituality. Hsi joined forces in working with the CIM in Shanxi, and surrounding areas that had hardly been touched by the gospel. The famous CIM recruits the 'Cambridge Seven', who abandoned wealth and influence for missionary work, all chose to work under him for a period when they arrived in China. Hsi retained a strongly 'independent' spirit, and was not always easy to work with,[61] but Dixon Hoste, Hudson Taylor's eventual successor as CIM director, worked and prayed alongside him for ten years. Hoste observed, 'We mutually help one another, without any distinction of native or foreigner, because the Lord has made us one.'[62] In 1886 Hsi encouraged the CIM to recruit single women to work under his wife's direction in opening opium refuges. By 1887 eleven women were pioneering stations supervised by Mrs Hsi.[63]

The overall achievement of Hsi's combination of evangelism and social action was enormous. It is thought that he started some forty-five refuges, and claimed to have treated more than 300,000 addicts, although most of this was done by those trained by him, and the overall figure may need to be treated with some caution.[64] The many churches associated with Hsi were outward-looking, evangelistic and growing.[65] After his death in 1896 his wife continued working with female addicts in Huozhou, and built up a congregation of around 60 women.[66] During the Boxer Rebellion Chinese converts of Hsi and his wife bore the brunt of the attacks on Christians in Shanxi for embracing the 'foreign' religion of Christianity, but their courage in the persecution saw a large number of converts after the rebellion ended.[67]

---

[59] Ibid. 221–223.

[60] Ibid. 258–261.

[61] Ibid. xiii; Austin, *China Inland Mission*, 173; For a popular treatment of the Cambridge Seven see J. Pollock, *The Cambridge Seven* (Basingstoke: Marshall Morgan & Scott, 1985).

[62] J. H. Broomhall, *Hudson Taylor and China's Open Century*, bk 7: *It Is Not Death to Die* (London: Hodder & Stoughton, 1989), 245.

[63] Austin, *China Inland Mission*, 387–389.

[64] Ibid. 14.

[65] Ibid. 381.

[66] Ibid. 375, 394.

[67] Taylor, *Hsi*, 373.

17

Care for the elderly and those with incurable illness

The plight of the elderly before the advent of state pensions and social security was especially pitiable. In nineteenth-century Britain most of those unable to look after themselves, or who did not have relatives to care for them, ended up in the workhouse, where there was basic, but not very humane, provision. Elderly married couples were generally kept apart in separate wards. Possibly 30 per cent of all those who were elderly at the end of the nineteenth century sought assistance in this way. Those with incurable health conditions were in an even worse situation. It was estimated in 1860 that of 80,000 people who died from the main types of incurable illness, 50,000 of them were destitute.[1] With support from Lord Shaftesbury efforts were made from 1860 onwards to create separate wards within workhouses for the elderly and incurable, and to allow visits from friends and relatives.[2]

From the late medieval period onwards charitable bequests had been made to provide pensions, or almshouses, for a number of elderly people. By 1795 some 740 of these existed in England. However, the huge growth of population in the nineteenth century, and the increasing number of elderly people, made the care of the elderly a much greater challenge. Also, the dislocation of family units occasioned by the industrial and urban revolution often left aged parents living far from their children, who had moved to obtain work. These numbers overwhelmed the small number of places available in almshouses.

One of the earliest bodies in Britain to provide a number of homes where the elderly could be cared for was the Aged Pilgrims' Friend Society (APFS). This was started in August 1807 as a pan-evangelical venture by a number of laymen attending London churches, including Whitefield's Tabernacle, Moor-fields; Tottenham Court Road Tabernacle; Gower Street Chapel; and St Mary Woolnoth Church – where John Newton was minister until his death later that

---

[1] K. Heasman, *Evangelicals in Action* (London: Geoffrey Bles, 1963), 239.
[2] Ibid. 241.

year. Its 'Truths of Revelation', the faith statement it adopted, contained core
evangelical doctrinal affirmations. Over time its supporters came mainly from
churches in the Calvinistic tradition.[3] It was established to assist the 'aged,
infirm, Christian poor', who, after a life of poorly paid labour, found themselves in old age 'shut up in garrets and cellars, lingering the remainder of their
days in distress and wretchedness'. Some had been found on the verge of
starvation, their only bedding some straw on the floor, and no bedclothes apart
from the rags on their backs. The APFS argued that it was the duty of the household of faith to provide for those in such need, to which they 'are bound by the
positive command of Christ and the nature of their calling to support them'.[4]

The APFS quickly grew from its small-scale beginnings with expenditure
of just £67 in 1810 to outgoings of £676 in 1830. It was run by a committee of
twenty-four men, selected from churches of different denominations. William
Wilberforce was its vice president from 1824 to 1833, and a generous subscriber.
Earl Roden was president between 1862 and 1870.[5]

The APFS was established to support the 'Lord's poor'. Those seeking help
were to provide evidence of conversion, but there was no denominational
requirement placed on applicants – the society claimed it knew nothing of
'party spirit; it shuts the door on contention'.[6] However, those assisted were to
offer evidence of a continuing commitment to Scripture principles. In 1825 one
woman was removed from the roll of pensioners for being 'in the constant habit
of using very bad language highly inconsistent with a Christian character'.[7] At
first the society just provided financial support to the elderly, enabling people
to continue to live in their homes. In 1852 the society granted 340 people
assistance. Thirty-nine received 10 guineas per annum, 198 received 5 guineas
and 103 received smaller sums. Annual expenditure was by then £1,936, and a
total of more than £41,500 had been expended since the formation of the
society.[8]

Awareness that some of the APFS pensioners were still living in poor
conditions led to a resolution in 1825 to construct a home for 40 residents. It
took until 1837 to raise the funds and complete construction in Camberwell,
at a cost of £6,000. By 1852 it had 44 residents. They came from a variety of

---

[3] J. Hazelton, *Inasmuch: A History of the Aged Pilgrims' Friend Society, 1807–1922* (London: APFS, 1922),
9–15.

[4] Ibid. 14.

[5] Ibid. 36–38, 62.

[6] Ibid. 47.

[7] APFS Minute Book, 1825–32, Minute of 20 December 1825, APFS Archives.

[8] I. J. Shaw, *High Calvinists in Action: Calvinism and the City c.1810–60* (Oxford: Oxford University
Press, 2002), 228.

denominational backgrounds – Anglican, Baptist, Methodist, Congregational and Independent. The home became closely associated with Grove Chapel, Camberwell, the minister of which, Joseph Irons (1785–1852), was a trustee. Irons believed that the work of the society was both practical and spiritual, 'ministering a cup of cold water in the name of the disciples, and because they belong to Christ'.[9] Irons did not attribute poverty to moral or personal failings. Support for the poor from their fellow Christians was divinely commanded.

Other Calvinistic churches in South London supported the APFS. The Surrey Tabernacle began an association with it as early as 1836, and in 1852 the church established an auxiliary for the society. Between 1852 and 1863 a total of £2,170 was raised for the society.[10] The Surrey Tabernacle championed the APFS as one of the best societies for helping the poor 'at a time when necessity presses the hardest'. By 1868 thirty persons from the Surrey Tabernacle were dependent on the APFS for support.[11] The minister of the church, James Wells, also regularly preached to raise funds for the APFS, including on one remarkable occasion in March 1858 when he delivered a gospel sermon to a congregation of more than 10,000 persons at the Surrey Gardens Music Hall.[12] Wells saw active social compassion as part of the law of liberty and love that constrained Christians to every good work and act, and was proof of the work of God's grace within the believer. Working in one of the poorest parts of London meant he was familiar with conditions of extreme poverty in the area surrounding his chapel, and was moved to social action in response.

A number of evangelical churches established their own almshouses. The Surrey Chapel started Vaughan's Almshouses in 1866 at Ashford in Middlesex, and two homes for 'gentlewomen in reduced circumstances' were also supported. Residential care for the elderly was provided by societies such as the Homes for the Aged Poor (1869) and the South London Homes for the Aged Poor (1885). Some missions in London also provided small accommodation units for the elderly, including the Mildmay Institution, which had a home for destitute elderly men and women.[13] An important principle behind many of these homes was that of allowing the elderly a measure of independence until they could no longer look after themselves, and then providing them with full

---

[9] J. Irons, 'True Riches, a Sermon Preached at Sion Chapel, Whitechapel, 24 September 1847', in *Miscellaneous Sermons*, vol. 3 (London: The Pulpit Office, n.d.), 72.

[10] *Earthen Vessel* 23 (October 1867), 317.

[11] Ibid. 8 (March 1852), 76; 8 (April 1852), 89; J. Wells, 'True Patience', *Surrey Tabernacle Pulpit*, vol. 11, no. 504 (1869), 214.

[12] J. Wells, *The Right Faith: A Sermon Preached in the Royal Surrey Gardens Music Hall, Sunday Evening, 21 March 1858, on Behalf of the Aged Pilgrims' Friend Society* (London: Partridge, 1858).

[13] Heasman, *Evangelicals*, 242–243.

residential care. This approach prefigured late twentieth-century approaches to the care of the elderly, with an avoidance of institutional care until absolutely necessary.

Evangelicals brought a compassionate approach to the care of the elderly that contrasted to that of the Poor Law, which viewed people in a negative light for becoming dependent and often offered the bare minimum of care. Asylums were called homes. Supplementary missions sent letters and flowers to the elderly, bringing a focus on the individual person rather than just meeting the need that person presented.[14]

As well as the establishment of societies and institutions for the elderly, individuals in the evangelical tradition from their own resources also took on the care of a number of elderly people. The Calvinist preacher William Huntington, who began life in great poverty, later in life had significantly more income and supported a number of pensioners out of his own pocket. Such a lifestyle, Huntington believed, was pleasing to God, who would honour it: '"Dwell in the land and do good, and verily thou shalt be fed". This was a bank note I put in the hand of my faith, when I got poor, I pleaded before God, and He answered it.'[15]

Some evangelical societies were established to provide small pensions to those who did not have sufficient income in old age, such as Miss Sheppard's Annuitants' Home in Bayswater, started in 1855, and Miss Smallwood's Society for the Assistance of Ladies in Reduced Circumstances (1886). Late in the nineteenth century evangelicals offered their support for the introduction of state pensions, recognizing that the scale of need for the support of the elderly was far beyond the capacity of voluntary charitable provision. Such pensions would also allow elderly people to maintain their independence for longer. The pensions cause was strongly supported by the Methodist churches, the Congregational Union, trade unions and co-operative societies, in which many evangelical working people played a key role. The campaign, uniting various groups, was a protracted one. In 1909 old-age pensions of 5 shillings per week were introduced in Britain, made payable to all who were over 70, and whose income was below a certain threshold.[16]

The fate of those suffering from incurable illness was particularly difficult. Hospitals refused to allow people who could not be cured to remain as patients, and they often ended up in workhouse wards. The hospital system of London

---

[14] Ibid. 244–245.

[15] W. Huntington, *The Bank of Faith, or God, the Guardian of the Poor* (London 1786), repr. (London: C. J. Thynne, 1913), 58–61, 169.

[16] Heasman, *Evangelicals*, 243–244.

in the mid nineteenth century was a complicated mixture of voluntary hospitals, funded by charitable donations and subscriptions, and workhouse hospitals for the very poor. High-quality health care and medicine were available for the wealthy only. Hospitals such as the Westminster, the Middlesex and the London were intended to assist those unable to afford to pay for medical help, but were not aimed at those who were already destitute, who were sent to the Poor Law infirmaries. However, through an accident or sudden onset of serious or incurable illness people could quickly become destitute.[17]

The work of the major hospitals was aimed at acute and curable cases, but those with long-term, degenerative, incurable or terminal illness were simply discharged and left to fend for themselves. Often they were too incapacitated to look after themselves, and many were destitute and friendless. Their last years were frequently spent in pain and misery, as the bleakness of a lonely death slowly closed in upon them. Those in the grim, prison-like Poor Law infirmaries had little medical care and were often surrounded by alcoholics, dropouts and the mentally ill. Cases were reported in the Poor Law infirmaries of elderly patients found lying on filthy bed sheets with undressed, festering sores: in 1865 *The Lancet* declared that 'the workhouse system is a disgrace to our civilization'.[18] In the mid nineteenth century, of those who had been in the workhouse for more than five years, 42 per cent were there because of old age.[19]

Many staff in the Poor Law workhouse infirmaries were paupers themselves. Ill-educated and with no training for nursing work, some were ignorant, incompetent or abusive. Others were found drunk on duty, indifferent to the needs of patients, ignoring their desperate cries for help or were themselves suffering from illness. Poor standards of hygiene and nursing care, with sick patients scattered indiscriminately around the general Poor Law wards, led to shocking conditions. In the early 1860s, before Agnes Jones reformed it, Florence Nightingale declared the Liverpool workhouse infirmary to be 'worse than Scutari'.[20] To be discharged from hospital as incurable and to know that future years of declining health would probably be spent in a destitute state was an awful prospect for many.

This was a situation the London Congregationalist minister Andrew Reed, who had already started three orphanages and a home for children with learning disabilities, in 1850 resolved to tackle. Reed was determined to

---

[17] G. Rivett, *The Development of the London Hospital System 1823–1982* (London: King Edward's Hospital Fund for London, 1986), 24–29.

[18] *Lancet* 1 (1865), 410, quoted in Rivett, *Hospital System*, 68.

[19] M. A. Crowther, *The Workhouse System 1834–1929* (London: Routledge, 1981), 224–226, 239.

[20] Ibid. 160–166. Scutari was the military hospital in the Crimean War that Florence Nightingale famously reformed.

establish a hospital where 'every comfort may be enjoyed to mitigate affliction, and where the best medical skill and care may be had, with the hope of making disease something less than incurable'.[21] The project grew out of Reed's steady determination to do something that would improve the conditions of needy individuals, convinced that each person was made in the image of God. Although Reed was at the time already engaged in building projects for the Earlswood Hospital and the Asylum for Fatherless Children, and had himself suffered a stroke in 1851, he was aware, 'I must begin to move in double quick time; for the noiseless foot of death is behind me, and before me there are some faint streaks of morning light.'[22]

Reed researched the issue and found that St Thomas' Hospital, Guy's and St Bartholomew's discharged between 5 and 10 per cent of patients as incurable as the result of an accident, chronic illness, congenital disease or degenerative conditions: the total discharged for these reasons was around 1,500 per year across London's twelve hospitals.[23] Unaware of Reed's researches, a merchant from the city of London offered him £500 to start a home for people diagnosed as incurable. Then Charles Dickens devoted an article in the magazine *Household Words* to the lack of a medical charity for the incurable, who

> of all others, must require succour, and who must die, and do die in thousands, neglected and unaided … Hopeless pain, allied to hopeless poverty, is a condition of existence not to be thought of without a shudder. It is a slow journey through the Valley of the Shadow of Death, from which we save even the greatest criminals.[24]

Reed began fundraising in earnest, and by November 1853 £2,000 had been pledged towards the scheme and he felt the way was becoming clearer. His project was a home for 'the permanent care and comfort of those who, by disease, accident, or deformity, are hopelessly disqualified for the duties of life'.[25] Reed saw the charity as the final offering of his life: 'The hospital is an offering to the Lord, and I may not offer that which costs me nothing.'[26]

---

[21] L. French, *The Hospital and Home for Incurables, Putney* (London: Royal Hospital and Home for Incurables, 1936), 19–20.

[22] A. Reed and C. Reed, *Memoirs of the Life and Philanthropic Labours of Andrew Reed* (London: Strahan, 1863), 427.

[23] Reed and Reed, *Memoirs*, 429. Similar figures are found in J. Woodward, *To Do the Sick No Harm: A Study of the British Voluntary Hospital System to 1875* (London: Routledge & Kegan Paul, 1974), esp. 159–165.

[24] C. Dickens, *Household Words*, 1850, cited in Reed and Reed, *Memoirs*, 430.

[25] Ibid. 431.

[26] Ibid. 432.

It was not just to be a hospital, but a home. It was to be a place of care and tranquillity, and above all where the comforts of the Christian faith were to be ministered, bringing consolation and hope in the face of diseases 'otherwise beyond remedy and all but intolerable'. He called on the fellow feeling of the Christian public:

> Our condition is essentially one; let our sympathies be one. Have we health? Let us relieve the sick. Have we wealth? Let us help the poor. Are we strong? Let us uphold the weak. Are we happy? Let us feel for the miserable. Let us bear each other's burdens, and so fulfil the law of Christ, – the law of kindness and of love.[27]

The project was non-denominational, 'carried out with Christian kindness and liberality, apart from all party distinctions whatever, whether political or religious, and in the spirit of that love which cometh down from heaven and is the bond of perfectness'. Reed's motto for the charity was 'All the good for the good of all'.[28]

Supporters included Samuel Gurney from the Quaker banking family, Alderman David Wire, former Lord Mayor of London, Thomas Calloway of the Royal College of Surgeons and John Conolly, who had proved such a pivotal figure in the Earlswood Hospital for children with additional learning-support needs.[29]

There was a flexibility to Reed's scheme. Where patients were capable of being cared for at home by their families or friends, they could be treated as 'extra-patients', or outpatients, receiving a monthly allowance and medical visitation and attendance. This allowed patients to find support, 'without destroying the most natural sources of comfort'. Although their illnesses were incurable, patients were not to be considered 'hopeless' cases – they were to be treated by the 'best medical science *hopefully*', rather than being abandoned to an inevitable and lingering death.[30]

Patients in the London hospitals were required to provide sureties, or a deposit, that should they die in hospital their body would be removed – a precaution unlikely to inspire confidence in the treatment they were about to

---

[27] Appeal No. 1, in Royal Hospital for Incurables Minute Book 1, 1854, 9–15, at Royal Hospital for Neuro-disability, Putney, London.

[28] Report of Preliminary Meeting, 13 July 1854, ibid. 1–3, 435.

[29] Report of the Public Meeting Held 31 July 1854 at the Mansion House, Royal Hospital Minute Book 1, 27–32.

[30] Constitution and Bye-Laws of The Royal Hospital; and Report of First Annual Meeting, 26 November 1855, Royal Hospital Minute Book 1, 19–27; emphasis original.

receive![31] The lack of available beds for urgent cases led to tragedies, such as that which befell the 18-year-old girl found dying on the steps of St Andrew's Church, Holborn, because she had been unable to gain the necessary subscriber's letter to secure admission to a hospital. As a result, William Marsden, the doctor who discovered her, was inspired to found the Royal Free Hospital in 1828, where no subscriber's or governor's letter was required for admission. The Metropolitan Free Hospital followed in 1837, but these were pioneer ventures.[32] The Hospital for Incurables was to follow suit in having a free ward.

In November 1854 a property in Carshalton was rented, and after suitable alterations the first patients were admitted the following year, with all forty beds quickly filled. Rooms were made homely by bringing in treasured items from the patients' homes – a favourite old clock, picture or item of furniture. After the rented home was filled, cases of need continued to be brought before the charity.[33] Chronic neurological disease was the most common condition suffered by those who applied for admission in the early years, usually due to an injury to the spine or disability from birth. Other cases included those disabled by chronic rheumatism, cancer and severe epilepsy.[34]

In May 1857, at the annual dinner of the Hospital for Incurables, Charles Dickens described his visit to the home in Carshalton: 'in all the inmates of this house whom I saw, – there was not only a hopefulness of manner, but a serenity of face, a cheerfulness and social habit, that perfectly amazed me'. All were saved the ignominy of appealing to the Poor Law.[35] By the end of July 1857 alternative and much larger premises at Putney House, in Richmond Road, Putney, had been rented, where the charity was to remain until 1865.[36] Influential figures lent their support – the Bishop of London and Lord Shaftesbury, and in 1855 vice presidents included the Duke of Devonshire, the Duke of Bedford, two Marquises, four Earls and three Viscounts, including Lord Palmerston, who became prime minister. The involvement of such figures who had wealth and influence was highly necessary, for large-scale charitable hospitals were notoriously expensive to run. In the late eighteenth and early nineteenth centuries the major London hospitals were repeatedly short of

---

[31] Woodward, *No Harm*, 36–49.

[32] A. E. Clark-Kennedy, *The London: A Study in the Voluntary Hospital System*, vol. 1: *The First Hundred Years 1740–1840* (London: Pitman Medical, 1962), 222–226.

[33] Reed and Reed, *Memoirs*, 440–442.

[34] First Case Book, Royal Hospital, at Royal Hospital for Neuro-disability, Putney, London, cited in G. C. Cook, *Victorian Incurables: A History of the Royal Hospital for Neuro-disability, Putney* (Spennymoor: Memoir Club, 2004), 59–62.

[35] Reed and Reed, *Memoirs*, 443–446.

[36] Board Meetings, 23 May, 11 June and 23 July 1857, Royal Hospital Minute Book 2, 307, 318, 323–324.

funds, and on occasion had to close wards or restrict the medicines being used.[37]

By 1860 there were 84 patients in the Hospital for Incurables at Putney, and 62 outpatients were also being supported with an allowance of £20 per year towards their maintenance, care and medical needs.[38] It was believed the general health of the patients had improved considerably, and this owed much to the high standards of medical and personal care and the sense of security that came from patients knowing they were to be supported for life. Leading doctors regularly visited them, and after 1857 the hospital had its own medical officer. On occasion the charity could report even that patients admitted as incurable had in fact, with such high standards of care, recovered and been discharged as cured. For others, distressing symptoms were alleviated and comfort and support offered as life drew to a close. One woman nearing death handed a note to the matron for Andrew Reed. She wrote of the home in heaven to which she was going, and added:

> I should have had no home but for this, and no friend to watch by my dying couch and comfort me. May God bless those who instituted and keep up this home! Will you tell them what a pleasant place this has been, and how grateful I am for all the kindness I have received?[39]

Reed regularly visited the patients and spent time listening to their comments and concerns. Those resident in the hospital were always referred to as 'the family', reflecting an atmosphere of welcome, acceptance and commitment achieved by the staff and directors. Although they were a much-afflicted family, it was repeatedly observed that they were a 'happy family'.

Everything possible was done to spare terminally ill patients the lonely deaths they might otherwise have been consigned to. With a policy that long predated the enlightened work of the modern hospice movement, staff members normally sat with patients as they neared death, to minister a caring presence and comfort in their last moments of life.[40] In the design of the building the needs of disabled people were paramount, with ramps, lifts and hoists freely used. Reed focused on the needs of four types of patient: the bedridden, the less disabled who needed some nursing assistance, those who could live

---

[37] Rivett, *London Hospital System*, 32–33.
[38] Annual Report, 10 October and 14 November 1861, in Royal Hospital Minute Book 4, 19 and 42.
[39] Reed and Reed, *Memoirs*, 450.
[40] F. Nightingale, *Suggestions on the Subject of Providing, Training, and Organising Nurses for the Sick Poor in Workhouse Infirmaries* (London, 1867), 1, quoted in Woodward, *No Harm*, 32.

semi-independently with regular support and those who could live with a degree of privacy without the need for constant attendance.[41] Eventually, after Reed's death, a permanent site was secured on West Hill, Putney Heath, in a parkland setting surrounded by other large houses. By 1862 the Hospital for Incurables was firmly established, and some 150 patients were comfortably housed in the Putney House, receiving the highest standards of care.[42] The charity Reed had established was at the leading edge in providing care for some of the most vulnerable and needy individuals in society. It was a cause that had little glamour and outward popularity attached to it, as evidenced by the difficulties in obtaining royal patronage for it. It drew on the best of medical expertise, but demonstrated the highest aspects of Christian compassion. As one visitor reported:

> it would be impossible for any stranger to visit the Hospital and not be struck by the cheerfulness and contentment that prevail among the family, arising from the knowledge that they are permanently released from worldly cares and anxieties, and from all unnecessary and hurtful exertion.[43]

The inspiration for the project was the example of Jesus Christ, who turned away none of the suffering and infirm who came to him. Reed's sincere hope was that that would one day be true of the Hospital for Incurables, and nobody in need would ever be turned away. It was a hope that predated the creation of the UK National Health Service by almost a century.[44]

Reed's project was not the only one developed to care for those with incurable and terminal illness. The British Home for Incurables was founded by some of those initially involved in Reed's scheme, including Lord Raynham and around a dozen board members. The model of Reed's scheme was closely followed. It was initially located in rented premises in Clapham, where the first nine patients were admitted in 1863. A purpose-built hospital was opened in Streatham in 1894. By 1898 it had 66 patients, and a further 300 received pensions to assist with their living needs.[45] The West London Mission, led by Hugh Price Hughes, also started St Luke's Home for the Dying in 1893. This was run by the Sisters

---

41 Board Meeting, 14 May 1861, Royal Hospital Minute Book 3, 360–361.

42 Board Meetings, 22 October and 12 November 1863, Royal Hospital Minute Book 4, 100, 107, 111–120.

43 Reported at Board Meeting, 27 November 1862, Royal Hospital Minute Book 4, 323–324.

44 The hospital continues its work in Putney, now known as the Royal Hospital for Neuro-disability.

45 French, *Hospital*, 23.

of the People, a group of female workers established by his wife, Katherine, in 1887, especially to minister to the poor and disadvantaged.[46]

Character study: Charles Haddon Spurgeon (1834–92) – England

Spurgeon is renowned as the 'Prince of Preachers', ministering regularly to a weekly congregation of more than 6,000 people at the Metropolitan Tabernacle in London. Also a prolific author, he started a training college for pastors and a host of other gospel ministries and played a role in the formation of more than 187 Baptist churches during his lifetime.[47]

An important part of his message was the duty of Christians to demonstrate their faith in lives of both evangelistic witness and compassionate care for others. Believers were to 'act out deeds of mercy, persevere in labour, and continue in service before God', showing the fruits of salvation: 'if the poor be fed, it must be by these hands'.[48] When preaching in 1877 on behalf of the Hospitals of London, he explained how 'the gospel' was more than doctrinal statements. Much of Christ's teaching concerned the demonstration of the fruits of the Spirit in everyday life:

> Read the Sermon on the Mount and judge whether certain people would be content to hear the like of it . . . They would condemn it as containing very little gospel and too much about good works . . . [Christ] lays great stress on the love which should shine throughout the Christian character.[49]

He urged Christians to 'Be on the side of temperance and sobriety; be on the side of peace and of justice; be on the side of everything that is according to the mind of God, and according to the law of love.'[50]

He longed for the day when 'the mischievous division between the secular and the religious things be no more heard of, for in all things Christians are to glorify God'.[51] This included the area of politics: Christians should use their

---

[46] See P. S. Bagwell, *Outcast London, A Christian Response: The West London Mission of the Methodist Church, 1887–1987* (London: Epworth Press, 1987), 30–56.

[47] M. Nicholls, *C. H. Spurgeon: The Pastor Evangelist* (Didcot: Baptist Historical Society, 1992), 99.

[48] Spurgeon, 'Where to Find Fruit', 85–87.

[49] C. H. Spurgeon, 'The Good Samaritan', sermon, 17 June 1877, at Metropolitan Tabernacle, in *Expository Encyclopaedia*, vol. 4 (Grand Rapids, Mich.: Baker, 1984), 105–106, 116.

[50] C. H. Spurgeon, 'The Present Crisis', sermon, 13 July 1879, *The Metropolitan Tabernacle Pulpit (MTP)*, vol. 25 (Pasadena, Tex.: Pilgrim Publications, 1972), 391.

[51] C. H. Spurgeon, 'The Candle', sermon, 24 April 1881, *MTP*, vol. 27, 226.

rights as citizens for Christ's glory.[52] Spurgeon's gospel focus reflects a bias to the poor: 'If one class can be more prominent than another, we believe that in the Holy Scripture the poor are most of all appealed to.'[53] He condemned how many were 'oppressed and ground down with awful poverty in many parts of this great city. Shall not God avenge the cry of starving women?'[54] The gospel was particularly suited to their situation: 'it needs a great gospel to meet dire necessities'.[55]

This theological understanding of the connection between faithful witness and social action, and Spurgeon's personal experience of suffering, resulted in active and practical gospel compassion demonstrated in the range of different social-concern agencies run by the Metropolitan Tabernacle, including the orphanage. Compared with the orphanage, the most prominent of those projects, the development of a series of almshouses for the elderly, might be seen as something of a sideline, but Spurgeon was deeply invested in their development.

The almshouses associated with the chapel had been started by one of Spurgeon's predecessors, John Rippon. When Rippon proposed the project to his deacons, they were unenthusiastic, so he raised most of the £800 required himself. In 1803 six houses were constructed for the 'aged poor' of the flock, all allocated for the use of elderly women from the congregation. They were located near the old chapel building in Southwark, but it was an environment that was deteriorating, the atmosphere polluted by local factories and two breweries.[56]

After the Metropolitan Tabernacle was opened at Elephant and Castle in 1861, the former church building was sold and the proceeds used to build new schools and almshouses. A site close to the new church was chosen, and Spurgeon considered it appropriate that almshouses and schools should share the same site, the young and old side by side. The buildings, opened in 1868, doubled the accommodation for the pensioners to twelve homes; but demand was huge, and the deacons had the painful choice of selecting the most eligible pensioners. Eventually the almshouses were extended to provide seventeen individual units for the elderly, and the adjoining school had space to accommodate

[52] C. H. Spurgeon, 'The Peacemaker', sermon, 8 December 1861, MTP, vol. 7, 593.

[53] C. H. Spurgeon, 'Preaching for the Poor', sermon, 25 January 1857, The New Park Street Pulpit, vol. 3 (Pasadena Tex.: Pilgrim Publications, 1975), 63.

[54] C. H. Spurgeon, 'Israel and Britain: A Note of Warning', sermon, 7 June 1885, MTP, vol. 31, 322.

[55] Quoted by R. J. Helmstadter, 'Spurgeon in Outcast London', in P. T. Phillips (ed.), The View from the Pulpit: Victorian Ministers in Society (Toronto: Macmillan, 1978), 161.

[56] C. H. Spurgeon, The Metropolitan Tabernacle: Its History and Work (London: Passmore & Alabaster, 1876), 52–53; G. Holden Pike, The Life and Work of Charles Haddon Spurgeon, vol. 1 (London: Cassell, 1894), 121.

380 children on weekdays. The school rooms were also used for Sunday schools and evangelistic meetings at the weekends.[57]

The residents of the almshouses were women aged over 60 who attended the church and were in serious need. One resident in 1876 was Fanny Gay, then aged 87, who had been a member of the church for 69 years. Spurgeon described her as 'an eminently devout, prudent, godly woman', who had over the years greatly helped young women in need of instruction or comfort. Spurgeon delighted to visit the elderly residents: 'Our aged sisters are worthy of all that we can do for them, and their grateful faces often make our heart glad.'[58]

The almshouse residents were also provided with food and clothing, and a small weekly pension. Spurgeon felt a particular sense of responsibility for this project, and himself paid a number of the bills for the heating and lighting of the almshouses, often before the church deacons were aware there was any sum owing. The vast Metropolitan Tabernacle congregation included large numbers living in poverty, and funds for their support came from the 'communion fund', taken regularly in the church. Spurgeon was reluctant to draw on this to pay the pensions, and his solution was the creation of an endowment to cover the needed sum. When Spurgeon was given a testimonial of £6,233 for his personal use, a huge sum for that time, on the twenty-fifth anniversary of the commencement of his pastoral ministry in London,[59] he chose to give £5,000 of it to the endowment for the pensions and the rest to other projects, declaring 'not a penny comes to me'. What made him most happy was

> making other people happy, and easing the sorrows of others by entering into hearty sympathy with them. Using the sum for my Lord's work . . . and for His poor, is the sweetest way of using it for myself.

Spurgeon likened the offering to the incident in 2 Samuel 23:15–17, 'we feel that we must not drink thereof: it must be poured out before the Lord . . . O Lord accept it!'[60] Spurgeon made further donations to the almshouses of sums presented to him, including £4,500 in 1884 after he had completed thirty years of pastoral ministry in London.[61] Similarly, the £100 spontaneously collected

---

[57] Spurgeon, *History*, 93–94.
[58] Ibid. 94.
[59] S. Spurgeon and G. Holden Pike (eds.), *Autobiography of C. H. Spurgeon*, vol. 2 (Chicago, Ill.: F. H. Revell, 1899), 123–126; Spurgeon, *History*, 94–96.
[60] Spurgeon and Holden Pike, *Autobiography*, vol. 2, 126–128.
[61] Nicholls, *Spurgeon*, 56–57.

on the recovery of Spurgeon's wife, Susannah, from serious illness in 1869.[62] However, when he was left a legacy of £4,500 and then found that there were members of the deceased person's family who were left in need by the testator's wishes, he refused to accept it.[63]

Behind the almshouse project was Spurgeon's extremely positive view of old age as a time of spiritual growth and proof of the 'firmness of God's grace'. His pastoral visits to the aged and infirm showed him how 'the Lord cheered the desolate chamber'.[64] The Christian was to approach the end of life in such a way that 'the grace of God may be admired in us', noting 'the finest thing in Jacob's life was the close of it'.[65] Life's end provided opportunity to 'bring forth fruit in old age', including 'Testimony to the goodness of God, the unchangeableness of his love, and the certainty of his revelation'.[66] His dearest hope was that the elderly residents would have full opportunity to enjoy such a gracious, fruitful close of life.

---

[62] Holden Pike, *Spurgeon*, vol. 3, 149; vol. 4, 223, 233, 313.

[63] Spurgeon, *History*, 140; Spurgeon and Holden Pike, *Autobiography*, vol. 2, 135.

[64] C. H. Spurgeon, 'Sermon LXXVII, a Sermon for the Aged' (Isa. 46:4), in *My Sermon Notes, from Ecclesiastes to Malachi LXV to CXXIX* (London: Passmore & Alabaster, 1885), 237.

[65] C. H. Spurgeon, 'Jacob Worshipping on His Staff', sermon (n.d.), in *Expository Encyclopaedia*, vol. 9, 276.

[66] Spurgeon, *Sermon Notes LXV to CXXIX*, 238.

18

Rescue of prostitutes

Prostitution was a significant social and moral issue well before the eighteenth century, but with rapid urbanization its presence became more concentrated and apparent, and urban poverty was a contributory factor. As Hippolyte Taine reported on his 1872 visit to Shadwell, London, 'Every hundred steps one jostles twenty harlots; some of them ask for a glass of gin; others say "Sir, it is to pay my lodgings." This is not debauchery which flaunts itself, but destitution.'[1] A report from Manchester, England, in 1840, noted 285 brothels in the city, with 629 prostitutes, although other sources put the number of prostitutes at 1,500.[2] The Glasgow City missioner William Logan, who undertook a survey of prostitution, reckoned in 1849 that there were 2,000 prostitutes in Glasgow. He noted how alcohol was a significant factor in prostitution, for both the women and their clients. He also noted that the high level of prostitution in the city reflected the high demand for it, and estimated that a quarter of young men in the city had paid for the services of a prostitute. Domestic service was also an issue. One prison chaplain reckoned that half the women sentenced for prostitution had been one-time domestic servants, who had 'fallen' at the hands of their employers and ended up earning a living on the streets.[3] Overcrowded housing was another factor, fostering widespread immorality, as did life in common lodging houses where prostitutes mingled with young unmarried women.

Christians from a range of theological traditions were involved in the rescue and reform of prostitutes, including High Church Anglicans and Roman

---

[1] H. Taine, *Notes on England* (London: W. Isbister, 1874), 36.
[2] L. Faucher, *Manchester in 1844* (London, 1844), repr. (London: Frank Cass, 1969), 33–51.
[3] W. Logan, *The Great Social Evil: Its Causes, Extent, Results and Remedies* (London: Hodder & Stoughton, 1871), 61, 75, 107–110, based on his *An Exposure of Female Prostitution* (Glasgow, 1843), and *The Moral Statistics of Glasgow* (Glasgow, 1849).

Catholics. However, the effort of evangelicals to rescue and redeem prostitutes was notable, again challenging perceptions of the supposedly narrow and condemnatory evangelical moral vision.[4] Indeed, evangelicals on the whole had a good understanding of the reasons behind prostitution, recognizing it as more than just a sinful and criminal act – sometimes women were forced into it by factors beyond their control. Yet the difficulties of evangelical involvement in rescue work in the nineteenth century were summed up by William Booth's biographer:

> Religious people felt, and many still feel, an aversion almost like nausea at any mention of this subject. The unfortunate is most unfortunate in the universal disgust she inspires. Men of the world invent brutal and disdainful terms for her, religious people avert their faces as they pass her in the street, and shudder even to think of her. A fallen woman seems to carry with her into the pit of perdition all the horror of humanity for the desecration of the most sacred of its ideals.[5]

Booth declared 'no evil more destructive of the best interests of society' than prostitution.[6]

Early attempts to help women involved in prostitution, such as the Magdalen Hospital for Penitent Prostitutes, founded in London in 1758, focused on penitence and strict treatment. It was an offshoot of the Lock Hospital, which treated women suffering from the equally shameful sexually transmitted diseases. The Magdalen Hospital accepted women under 30 who had recently fallen into prostitution and who showed signs of genuine penitence. To signify this, their hair was cropped short and they wore a dismal uniform. Penitents received religious instruction and stayed for two years while they were trained in laundry and domestic work, in preparation for domestic service.[7]

The Society for the Suppression of Vice, founded in 1802 by William Wilberforce, included in its work the suppression of blasphemy, profane swearing and cursing, lewdness and dissolute, immoral or disorderly practices. It made significant efforts to stop the publication of immoral literature, and to close down brothels.[8] But by the middle of the nineteenth century the society had

---

[4] E. Bristow, *Vice and Vigilance: Purity Movements in Britain Since 1700* (Dublin: Gill & Macmillan, 1977), 77–80.

[5] H. Begbie, *Life of William Booth* (London: Macmillan, 1920), vol. 2, 38.

[6] W. Booth, *In Darkest England and the Way Out* (London: Salvation Army, 1890), 188.

[7] K. Heasman, *Evangelicals in Action* (London: Geoffrey Bles, 1963), 149.

[8] See M. J. D. Roberts, 'The Society for the Suppression of Vice and Its Early Critics, 1802–1812', *Historical Journal* 26 (1983), 159–176; M. J. D. Roberts, *Making English Morals: Voluntary Association and Moral Reform in England, 1787–1886* (Cambridge: Cambridge University Press, 2004).

become associated with a negative and condemnatory attitude, and in 1838 Shaftesbury called for different approaches, including more understanding of the causes of prostitution, and legislation to 'protect women . . . from fraudulent practices used to procure their defilement'.[9]

The Manchester and Salford Asylum for Female Penitents was founded in 1821. Key figures in its establishment were the evangelicals John Hollist, minister of St James's Church, William Nunn of St Clement's Church and John Marsden, a Methodist. In addition to the committee of thirty members, there was a ladies' committee, on which Mrs Nunn served, which organized the internal running of the home. The asylum assisted those wishing to leave prostitution, but also sought to preserve public morals by their removal from the streets. In 1836 the president of the charity declared his hope that it would be a place of shelter for fallen women, where

> through the merits of her Savour she may at length be received into a state of salvation, that her penitence might wipe away for ever her sins, through his merits, and restore her to some degree of respectability in society.[10]

The women were offered training to enable them to have gainful employment when they returned to society. A religious service was held each Sunday and one evening a week. Two members of the ladies' committee visited the asylum each day, to befriend the penitents, inspect their work and read to them from the Bible, sermons, tracts and other religious books. Family prayers were held morning and evening, and the women were presented with a Bible on admission. The work struggled for lack of finance in its early years, but after 1828 the support of J. B. Sumner, the evangelical Bishop of Chester, was a significant boost. Between 1822 and 1841, 375 women were admitted to the Asylum for Female Penitents. There was a level of success: of the total, 72 were found employment as domestic servants and 93 were restored to family and friends. Accounts of spiritual interest among the women and personal reading of the Bible regularly feature in the annual reports. The charity's leaders recognized that there were various contributory factors to women falling into prostitution other than simply moral weakness. Of the 38 residents in 1838, 17 were orphans and 16 had only one parent. Twenty-three were under 20 years of age and two were only 14. Many had been driven into prostitution by poverty, and most were

---

[9] Bristow, *Vice and Vigilance*, 56.
[10] Reported in *Manchester Guardian*, 15 September 1836.

in a state of destitution when they applied for help. Around half of them could barely read.[11]

As a result of their outreach work in the poorest parts of cities, evangelicals saw first-hand the nature and extent of prostitution and gained an in-depth knowledge of the problem. In 1850 one Glasgow City missioner reported visiting a series of houses in the city, all of which turned out to be brothels: 'Some of them presented scenes the most disgusting . . . when there are men present, the females are disposed to be rude and uncivil.'[12] Generally, efforts to rescue long-term female prostitutes were notoriously difficult, and only when women were in extreme situations of illness or age did they seek help.

By the middle of the nineteenth century the work of evangelicals shifted from demanding overt penitence, and on to rescue work, through the befriending of prostitutes and showing them compassion and offering them a new start. The change is reflected in the names of the societies founded to promote this. In the 1830s the London Female Mission was started with a rescue home in Islington for women. The 1850s saw other major evangelical societies founded, including the Rescue Society (1853), with Lord Shaftesbury as its president, which concentrated on helping women new to the streets, the London Female Preventative and Reformatory Institute (1857) and the Homes of Hope (1860). These operated with an outreach policy. Rather than waiting for women to apply for help when in desperate need or illness, they sought them out, offered them tracts, pleaded with them to change their ways and invited them to the home.[13] Many rescue homes were small and hidden away from public notice to avoid attracting attention to their work.

In order to provide a bridge between the streets and the rescue homes, in 1860 the Midnight Movement was started in London. Evangelicals, including Baptist Noel, the vicar of St John's, Bedford Row, played a key role in this. Invitations were given out to prostitutes to meet at midnight in a restaurant, where they were given a meal and female volunteer workers sought to befriend them. A short gospel message was given and offers of help were made to any seeking to change their way of life. The volunteer workers left their addresses with the women they had spoken with and invited them to make contact. In 1860 nineteen such meetings were held, attended by a total of 4,000 women. The movement flourished for six years, and spread to other cities, including Glasgow, Manchester, Liverpool and Cardiff. Speakers included the well-known

---

[11] I. J. Shaw, *High Calvinists in Action: Calvinism and the City, c.1810–60* (Oxford: Oxford University Press, 2002), 95–98.

[12] *Glasgow City Mission Annual Report, 1850* (Glasgow, 1850), 13.

[13] K. Heasman, *Evangelicals in Action* (London: Geoffrey Bles, 1963), 151.

evangelicals Newman Hall, of the Surrey Tabernacle, Daniel Wilson, Vicar of Islington, and Catherine Booth. Some were shocked at this open association with women engaged in an immoral trade. Others ridiculed it as an attempt to resolve one of the world's oldest social problems by 'Tea and Toast'. Nonetheless, around one in ten of those who attended sought further help.[14]

Much evangelical rescue work among prostitutes was led by women. In 1858 the Female Mission to the Fallen began to employ women (as opposed to male city missioners) to go out at night to meet with women, offer them tracts and invite them to turn from prostitution. By 1871 there were workers in nine districts in London. They visited not only the streets and brothels, but also hospitals, courts and lodging houses to meet women involved in prostitution and offer them temporary shelter and a way out of their current lifestyle.[15]

Successes among those hardened by a life of prostitution were few, but those that occurred were celebrated. The Salvation Army reported in 1890 a country girl who had 'fallen' at the age of 13, ended up in London and was drawn into prostitution. When she became seriously ill with a sexually transmitted disease, she was abandoned by her previous associates and left homeless. William Booth recalled:

> When we found her she was hard and impenitent, difficult to reach even with the hand of love; but love won, and since that time she has been . . . a consistent soldier of an [Salvation] Army corps, and a champion *War Cry* seller.[16]

Booth considered such successes 'worthy to be placed side by side with the greatest triumphs of Jesus Christ' such as the 'savages' saved through overseas missions.[17]

It was Booth's son, Bramwell, who urged the Salvation Army to include as a key part of its work the rescue of the prostitutes Bramwell regularly came across in his outreach work on London's streets.[18] Although his mother, Catherine Booth, had been part of the Midnight Meeting Movement of the 1860s, and occasionally prostitutes were converted through Salvation Army work, it was the 1880s before its first rescue home was opened by Mrs Cotterill, a Salvation Army officer. She started sheltering rescued prostitutes in her own home in

---

14 Ibid. 152–153.
15 Ibid. 153.
16 Booth, *Darkest England*, 191.
17 Ibid. 133.
18 Begbie, *Booth*, 37.

Whitechapel, before moving the work to a rented property in 1883.[19] In that year the Women's Social Services was started by the Salvation Army, which operated independently from its other branches, specializing in work with fallen, homeless and alcoholic women.[20]

In 1884, aged only 22, Bramwell's wife, Florence, was placed in charge of the Women's Social Services. A scheme to raise £20,000 for the rescue homes was launched. By 1890 William Booth was reporting that the Salvation Army had some 13 rescue homes and accommodation for 307 women, under the care of 132 officers. He believed that 3,000 women had been rescued through this work and restored to 'lives of virtue'.[21] Under Florence Booth's skilled leadership the work grew, and by 1914 there were 117 rescue homes for women around the world.[22] These homes also ran an enquiry bureau to which relatives could send details of girls who had gone missing from home. The Church Army ran a similar rescue work, although on a smaller scale.[23]

The Salvation Army's Women's Special Services (WSS) also supported pregnant single women or unmarried mothers with children. Requests for such help began to be received soon after this rescue work started. By 1890 the Salvation Army had two separate homes for unmarried mothers, together with Ivy House, started that year, as a maternity home for them. The demands for this work were great: in 1904 30 per cent of letters to the WSS included appeals for help from pregnant single girls. In 1909 a maternity hospital, which cared for several hundred unmarried mothers each year, was started in Hackney. Other organizations, such as the Rescue Society, did similar work, but none on the scale of the Salvation Army. The work was considered crucial because most unmarried mothers in late nineteenth-century Britain would be expected to give birth in the workhouse infirmary, where they might mix with people who were, or had been, prostitutes, and could easily be drawn into prostitution.[24]

The success rate was high; indeed, Florence Booth claimed there was 'no class of women for whom we have worked which has yielded such uniformly encouraging results'.[25] About one third of those helped returned to their families, and half went into positions as domestic servants found for them by the Salvation Army. The daily regime in the homes included singing and prayers, and some

---

[19] B. Booth, *Echoes and Memories* (New York: G. H. Doran, 1925), 117.

[20] A. R. Higginbotham, 'Respectable Sinners: Salvation Army Rescue Work with Unmarried Mothers, 1884–1914', *Journal of Social History* 36.3 (2003), 217–218.

[21] Booth, *Darkest England*, 188.

[22] Begbie, *Booth*, 38.

[23] Heasman, *Evangelicals*, 154–155.

[24] Higginbotham, 'Respectable Sinners', 219–220.

[25] R. Sandall, *History of the Salvation Army*, vol. 3 (London: Nelson, 1955), 201.

of the women attended education classes. A number of conversions were reported, but most women left after a few months, having being helped through childbirth, grateful for the care they had received through a traumatic period of shame and often rejection, and with hope for a return to some form of employment or to their families. Some of those supported in the maternity home were as young as 12. Florence Booth believed that for many, faced with such a crisis, the only choices were starvation, sin (prostitution) or the Salvation Army. Others less willing to change gave birth to several illegitimate children, each time turning to the Salvation Army for temporary help, and then returning to the streets. The cases were very different – some were young girls seduced by older men; others were abandoned by lovers who had promised marriage; others were long-standing prostitutes. Those who sought help were not turned away. The view was that the shame associated with having an illegitimate child was suffering enough, and that rather than prolonged punishment and penitence, compassionate care, support for the child and help to return to lawful employment was needed. If such care did not save women spiritually, at least lives of future poverty, or even worse, acts of infanticide or a resort to prostitution, were avoided. As their work became known, more and more women in difficulties recognized the Salvation Army as an organization to which they could turn for help.[26]

Similar projects were started by other evangelicals. The Anchorage Mission was founded in 1882 by Colonel Stuart-Wortley, who had been converted through the work of D. L. Moody. His wife had been a Mildmay deaconess, and the Anchorage Mission provided a home for single mothers. The mission worked closely with The Haven, which was a Mildmay rescue project for girls who had 'fallen' and wanted to start again.[27] The existence of homes that accepted both mother and child prevented illegitimate children being put in the workhouse or being 'farmed out' to women for payment, where standards of care were very low. In 1864 the Refuge for Deserted Mothers was started, again in close contact with the Mildmay Institution. The Refuge made use of carefully chosen and controlled fostering arrangements, while the mother received training for employment.[28]

Similar rescue work was undertaken by the Salvation Army in North America; and by the Young Women's Christian Association (YWCA), which also ran residencies as safe places for young women to live sheltered from the

---

[26] Higginbotham, 'Respectable Sinners', 222–227.
[27] Heasman, *Evangelicals*, 156.
[28] Ibid. 157.

risks of vice in unsavoury neighbourhoods.[29] In 1869 the Cleveland Women's
Christian Association (WCA; after 1893 the YWCA) started the 'Retreat' – a
refuge for women who had 'lost the glory of their womanhood'. This continued
its work until 1936. The Salvation Army also started a rescue home for women
in Cleveland in 1892. This was aimed at prostitutes who were seeking to leave
'a house of sin'. Workers from the WCA and Salvation Army regularly visited
red-light districts to meet prostitutes and persuade them to change their lives.
The majority of those helped seemed, however, to have been young women
seduced or abandoned by lovers and who had illegitimate children. Others were
deceived by the 'sophistry' of married men. The homes worked to bring repentance, conversion and restoration. Each day Bible study, prayer and the Christian
witness and example of the matron and volunteers were provided. Some reports
of conversions are recorded, and on occasions men who had abandoned the
women returned to marry them. Families also referred girls considered 'wild'
and uncontrollable to the homes. Again, alcohol and poverty were recognized
as major factors in women falling into prostitution, and an important part
of the 'rescue' work was rescue from poverty by means of providing training
for future employment. Cooking, sewing, laundry work and childcare were
all taught, with the hope that the rescued women might gain employment,
especially in domestic service.[30]

A particular concern was girls being drawn into prostitution after having
been brought up as children with their mothers in a brothel. It was almost
inevitable that they would end up becoming prostitutes themselves. A report
in London in 1880 claimed that 10,000 children were being raised in brothels.
The Bridge of Hope Mission was opened in 1880 on the Radcliffe Highway in
London as a place where children living in brothels could be offered care.
Eventually a small home in Chingford, Essex, was started to provide a settled
home life for the children, and similar facilities were started by Dr Barnardo.[31]

The lack of effective sanction against those who openly profited from prostitution was also a concern to evangelicals. In 1885 Catherine Booth petitioned
the Queen over the court case of a woman in Chelsea who was charged with
keeping twelve 'immoral houses', and who was involved in the trafficking of
young girls abroad. She arrived from her luxurious home in a fine coach,
pleaded guilty and was fined just £200. The leniency of the sentence was

---

[29] Marian Morton, '"Seduced and Abandoned in An American City": Prostitution and Fallen Women',
Journal of Urban History 11.4 (1985), 444.

[30] Morton, 'Abandoned', 446–448.

[31] Heasman, *Evangelicals*, 159.

attributed to the influence of her wealthy friends, some of whom had frequented her high-class brothels.[32]

Evangelicals were also unwavering in their opposition to the double standards in attitudes surrounding prostitution. In an 1838 pamphlet in support of the Manchester and Salford Asylum for Female Penitents, the Baptist William Gadsby outlined factors that had driven the women into prostitution – teenage girls seduced by their masters, abused by foremen in factories, abandoned by fiancés or even parents. Others were tricked by procurers. Gadsby savagely condemned all such men as 'little better, in the sight of God, than murderers'.[33] Josephine Butler believed that 'A moral sin in a woman was spoken as immensely worse than in a man; there was no comparison to be found between them.' Fallen women were treated with 'murderous cruelty'.[34] The same double standard held true in North America. The Cleveland WCA warned of the snares that beset women moving to cities, especially from men who went about 'like roaring lions seeking whom they might devour'.[35]

During the Midnight Meeting Movement in the 1860s Baptist Noel had held meetings for young men attending music and dancing halls to challenge them to avoid immorality. C. H. Spurgeon condemned how sexual sin in young men was accepted as youthful indiscretion, but with

> a poor woman who has gone astray, 'society' cries, 'Put her out! Drive the wretched creature away from us.' I have known one such turned out of hotel after hotel. They could not bear their righteous selves to come anywhere near to one who had in the least degree broken the laws of society.[36]

The prominent role taken in these campaigns by women is notable, many of whom were evangelicals boldly prepared to challenge oppressive sexual attitudes to women that predominated in a patriarchal society. A notable figure was Ellice Hopkins, a High Churchwoman whose writings combined an evangelical emphasis upon personal conversion with an incarnational Anglo-Catholic theology. She worked closely with evangelical women, including Catherine Booth; Laura Ormiston Chant, a Congregationalist nursing sister at the London

---

[32] Begbie, *Booth*, 41.

[33] W. Gadsby, 'The Lamentation of a New-Born Soul: A Dialogue Between Three Inmates, a Female Visitor, and the Matron, in a Female Penitentiary', *Works of William Gadsby*, vol. 2 (London: John Gadsby, 1851), 112–114.

[34] J. Butler, *Recollections of George Butler* (Bristol: Arrowsmith, 1892), 97–98.

[35] Morton, 'Abandoned', 443.

[36] C. H. Spurgeon, Sermon No. 2300, 'The Whole Gospel in a Single Verse', preached on 28 February 1889, in *Spurgeon's Sermons Vol. 39: 1893* <https://www.ccel.org/ccel/spurgeon/sermons39.xii.html>, accessed 18 April 2020.

hospital who wrote hymns and poems, and lectured on social purity, temperance and women's rights; the Methodist Mary Bunting; and the temperance worker Sarah Robinson. Robinson undertook Bible reading and evangelism among the troops in Aldershot and Portsmouth. As part of her work she visited brothels in the town, taking the gospel to sex workers and their clients and promoting the improvement of their health.[37]

The White Cross Army, formed in 1883, was an international non-denominational movement, modelled on those promoting temperance, in which men pledged to maintain sexual purity before marriage and not to indulge in foul language or indecent behaviour. In its name, 'white' stood for purity, 'cross' for the self-sacrifice of Christ that recruits were to imitate and 'army' for disciplined obedience. It was aimed especially at working-class men in the industrial cities. By 1884 there were 102 affiliated branches in Britain, and other branches were formed in Australia, Canada, Germany, India and the USA.[38] Preventative work among young women was also promoted. These included the establishment of projects to support 'friendless girls', usually from poor homes and who had left school, but who had no settled job and were easily drawn into unsuitable company and sometimes prostitution. These projects provided training programmes, social clubs and lectures on childcare, cooking and homemaking.[39] Similar values were promoted by the Gospel Purity Association (1884), led by J. G. Wookey of the Salvation Army. This evangelical movement was aimed at both men and women, and sought to address openly issues about appropriate relationships between young men and women.[40]

Such movements were influenced by the moral preventative arguments of Ellice Hopkins that removing demand for the services of prostitutes was key to resolving the prostitution problem. Erecting a fence at the top of the cliff was better than just stationing an ambulance at the bottom to rescue the fallen.[41] Hopkins and Sarah Robinson have been dismissed as 'sublimated and suffering evangelical spinsters' driven to rescue work, yet these theologically conservative women were willing to take radical action to challenge double standards and

---

37 S. Morgan, 'Faith, Sex and Purity: The Religio-Feminist Theory of Ellice Hopkins', *Women's History Review* 9.1 (2000), 14, 17.

38 R. M. Barrett, *Ellice Hopkins, a Memoir, London* (Wells: Gardner, 1907), 157; F. K. Prochaska, *Women and Philanthropy in Nineteenth-Century England* (Oxford: Oxford University Press, 1980), 215–216; S. Morgan, 'Knights of God: Ellice Hopkins and the White Cross Army, 1883–95', Studies in Church History 34 (Woodbridge: Boydell & Brewer, 1998), 431–445.

39 Heasman, *Evangelicals*, 160–161.

40 Ibid. 163.

41 O. Lovesey, 'Ellice Hopkins (1836–1904)', *Victorian Review* 37.1 (spring 2011), 25, 22–26.

promote sexual purity.[42] They also celebrated the importance of sexuality within marriage.[43]

Into the early twentieth century rescuing and restoring women remained a dimension of evangelical gospel outreach, and especially in the poorest areas. John Pugh (1846–1907), the founder and first superintendent of the Calvinistic Methodist Forward Movement, set up to promote outreach in the unreached parts of Wales, was shocked by revelations from the notorious Saltmead area of Cardiff. Here it was reported that there were more than 100 houses in the area used for immoral purposes, with many girls encouraged into prostitution by their parents. As a result, 'Sisters' undertaking rescue and preventative work were appointed to work in the area – by 1909, two years after Pugh's death, there were eight of them. Pugh had also encouraged the establishment of a home for single women trapped in prostitution, and a maternity home for single women with babies. The work accelerated as a result of the large number of prostitutes converted during the 1904–5 Welsh revival: the salvation of 15 was reported in April 1905 alone. The lack of a suitable place for them to live without returning to their previous haunts led to the opening in November 1905 of 'Treborth' as a rescue home. By 1907, 63 rescued prostitutes had been given accommodation, training and help with finding employment.[44]

Much of the pioneering work of evangelicals in this area inspired others. There was an important willingness to look not just at the issue of prostitution but at its causes, and offer education, alternative training and social opportunities to stop children and young women from being drawn into this lifestyle. For those caught up in prostitution, practical action involved rescue homes and mother and baby hostels. By the early twentieth century the open practice of prostitution on the streets of towns and cities had significantly declined. Better wages and more employment opportunities for women were a factor, as were improved living conditions, slum clearances and lower levels of alcohol abuse. But, alongside this, the actions of evangelicals played a significant role in changing understanding and attitudes, and supporting those desiring to leave prostitution.

Character study:
Josephine Butler (1828–1906) – England

Recent studies of Josephine Butler have demonstrated how her theological views, family background and devotional practice were strongly

---

[42] Bristow, *Vice and Vigilance*, 95–96.
[43] Lovesey, 'Hopkins', 23.
[44] G. Fielder, *Grace, Grit and Gumption* (Fearn: Christian Focus, 2000), 104–105.

evangelical.[45] That there should be any questions about this reflects the causes she took up, and the radical way in which she expressed her views, which seemed so unlikely for an evangelical. As earlier chapters have shown, the combination of evangelism and social action was demonstrated in ways that shatter conventional stereotypes of evangelicals, and especially evangelical women.

She was born Josephine Grey and her father, an evangelical Anglican, was a passionate advocate of anti-slavery, supporting the work of Clarkson and Wilberforce. From childhood she developed a deep-seated opposition to any system or action that deprived people of lawful freedom and happiness. She recognized that slavery often involved the sexual abuse of slaves. In her teenage years Josephine underwent a crisis followed by a deep spiritual experience of God, and thereafter spent many hours in prayer and Bible study. In 1852 she married George Butler. Although ordained in 1853, he chose a career as a schoolmaster, wishing to be both 'pastor as well as teacher' to the boys he taught at Cheltenham College (1857–65) and as the principal of Liverpool College (1866–82). In retirement he became a canon of Winchester Cathedral. George was inclined to Broad Church views, but through Josephine became more open to evangelicalism, and they read the Bible and prayed together each day. At George's suggestion they rescued their first 'fallen' woman, taking her into their home and employing her as a maid.[46]

Tragically, Eva, the youngest of the Butlers' four children was killed in a fall at their home aged just 5. They were overcome with grief and Josephine felt an overwhelming desire to 'go forth and find some pain keener than my own, to meet some persons more unhappy than myself . . . to say, I understand, I too have suffered'.[47] After they moved to Liverpool in 1866, Josephine began to visit the women in the workhouse. She showed these 'wretched, draggled, ignorant' outcasts compassion, and taught them about Jesus Christ. Over the following years, from the workhouse, gaols and streets of Liverpool she brought back to her home a series of prostitutes and 'ruined' and friendless young women. She nursed them back to health and many came to faith in Christ. Some of their stories are told in her book *The Dark Side of English Life*.[48]

In 1869 she was asked to lead the national campaign to repeal the Contagious Diseases Acts of 1864, 1866 and 1869. To Josephine this was the 'very

---

[45] H. Mathers, 'The Evangelical Spirituality of a Victorian Feminist: Josephine Butler, 1828–1906', *Journal of Ecclesiastical History* 52.2 (April 2001), 282–312.

[46] H. Mathers, 'Butler, Josephine Elizabeth (1828–1906)', in T. Larsen (ed.), *Dictionary of Evangelical Biography* (Leicester: Inter-Varsity Press, 2003), 105–106.

[47] J. R. Walkowitz, *City of Dreadful Delight: Narratives of Sexual Danger in Late-Victorian London* (Chicago, Ill.: University of Chicago Press, 1992), 88.

[48] Ibid.

mission' she had prayed for. These acts had been passed because of the widespread venereal disease found in army and naval towns that was debilitating soldiers and sailors. However, rather than targeting the activities of the men, the acts allowed police to detain any woman they suspected of being a prostitute on the streets, and force her to undergo a medical inspection for venereal disease. Refusal led to imprisonment. To Josephine Butler this was the worst form of discrimination, putting large numbers of quite innocent women at risk of detention and forced medical inspection. The acts, denounced as 'deadly poison', resulted in the 'legalised degradation of women'[49] and reflected and perpetuated the double standard of morality. But the cost of taking on such a cause was great. She was vilified for even mentioning such subjects as prostitution and sexually transmitted disease. In a campaign that was continued for nearly twenty years before the Contagious Diseases Acts were repealed, she spoke out, wrote letters, published pamphlets, drew up petitions, spoke on platforms and lobbied Parliament. George Butler resolutely stood by his wife, despite the negative impact on his reputation. When he read a paper in support of the repeal of the Contagious Diseases Acts campaign at the Church of England Congress in 1872, the response was so hostile he was unable to complete his address.[50]

Josephine Butler, a very capable leader and gifted speaker, succeeded in the campaign by constructing an alliance of women, middle-class Nonconformists and working men who were challenged to defend their wives and daughters against such suspicion and indignities. The campaign exposed male sexual brutality and tyranny, both in the practice of prostitution and in its regulation. She denounced women being subject to the 'slavery of men's lust'.[51] Taking up the cause required considerable courage. Meetings were disrupted by gangs of ruffians shouting threats of violence, including of sexual violence. On one occasion the building they were speaking in was set on fire.[52] At the heart of this campaign was the well-brought-up, refined and beautiful Josephine Butler, who remained firm in her evangelical views.

In 1874 Josephine Butler took up a campaign against the legalization of prostitution in Europe, and the following year became the joint secretary of the British and Continental Federation for the Abolition of Government Regulation of Prostitution. Through this work evidence came to light in 1880 that young girls were being trafficked from England to Belgium. This brought her into the campaign to pass the Criminal Law Amendment Act, which raised the age of

---

[49] Mathers, 'Evangelical Spirituality', 286–287.
[50] Ibid. 282–283, 310–312.
[51] Walkowitz, *City*, 90.
[52] Ibid. 91.

consent from 13 to 16, and her encouragement of W. T. Stead in his journalistic exposure of the trafficking of children (see chapter 10).[53] In this campaign Josephine Butler worked with other evangelicals, including Charles Birrell, President of the Baptist Union.[54]

Her rescue work continued wherever she made her home, and when George Butler became a canon of Winchester Cathedral, Josephine began a rescue home for former prostitutes in the city. In 1884 she also started a maternity home associated with the rescue home.[55] Yet criticism of this work was also bitter. Benjamin Jowett, an Oxford don and proponent of theologically liberal views of the Bible, declared that the prostitutes she rescued were 'a class of sinners whom she had better left to themselves'.[56] Instead of such harsh and unfeeling attitudes from some in the Anglican hierarchy, Josephine Butler was in far closer sympathy with the simplicity of the Salvation Army's work. She praised their outstanding success in rescue work among the lost, based on their 'humanness' and belief in 'the power of the name of Jesus ... and the transforming power of the Holy Ghost'.[57]

In 1886 Butler joined the National Vigilance Association for the Repression of Criminal Vice and Immorality, but her preference was to avoid efforts to repress immorality legally. She felt that the prosecution of prostitutes went against the spirit of Jesus' actions in John 8.[58] In her work of 1882, *The Hour Before Dawn*, she argued that it was the duty of men to live in purity and so allow women also to live in purity.[59]

Butler's biblical convictions were a powerful motivation to her campaigning and practical action. Scripture taught her of the terrible consequences of sin – both for the sinner and those sinned against. She believed that ultimate, lasting, personal and social reformation required an individual spiritual reformation, if it were to be sustained.[60] She spoke against the sexual discrimination faced by women across society and contrasted this to the way Jesus treated women on the basis of equality, which 'ought to have changed the whole life and character of men's treatment of women from that time forward'.[61] The actions of Jesus were the model for her Christian feminism, demonstrated in Jesus' response to the woman who had lived a sinful life and washed his feet with her tears and wiped

53 Mathers, 'Butler, Josephine Elizabeth', 106.
54 Mathers, 'Evangelical Spirituality', 301.
55 Heasman, *Evangelicals*, 156.
56 Quoted in E. M. Bell, *Josephine Butler: Flame of Fire* (London: Constable, 1962), 79.
57 Mathers, 'Evangelical Spirituality', 307–308.
58 Ibid. 309.
59 Heasman, *Evangelicals*, 162.
60 Mathers, 'Evangelical Spirituality', 282–283.
61 J. E. Butler (ed.), *Woman's Work and Woman's Culture* (London: Macmillan, 1869), 'Introduction', lix.

them with her hair (Luke 7:36–50). Through her conversion Butler believed that she had been liberated by Christ and given spiritual equality with converted men. This evangelical basis for understanding equality between men and women has perplexed feminist scholars of Butler. So too has her conviction that sexual fulfilment for men and women should be found only within marriage, with personal purity being exercised outside marriage. Her actions helped to extend the sphere of women in the nineteenth century.[62] Her challenge to the 'white slavery' of girls being trafficked for sex has been likened to that of Wilberforce against the African slave trade, and for her achievements she has been called 'the most distinguished Englishwoman of the nineteenth century'.[63]

---

[62] Mathers, 'Evangelical Spirituality', 303, 310–311.
[63] Millicent Garrett Fawcett, quoted in Mathers, 'Butler, Josephine Elizabeth', 107.

19

Prison reform
and care for prisoners

William Booth of the Salvation Army reported that 153,000 people had been sentenced to imprisonment in Britain in 1889. Of this number, half were habitual criminals, having been sentenced at least ten times. To Booth this represented 'a wreckage whose cost to the community is very imperfectly estimated when we add up the cost of the prisons, even if we add to them the cost of the police'. He highlighted the large numbers of women and children either drawn into a life of crime, or plunged into hardship, by a parent in prison. Some were hereditary criminals; others were driven to crime by 'sheer starvation' or 'absolute despair'. Even if a crime had resulted from the stark choice of 'steal or starve', the taint of criminality was almost impossible to escape. Once marked as having been a prisoner, they were 'hunted from pillar to post', spending the rest of their days oscillating 'between one prison and another'.[1]

The penalties for crimes from the eighteenth century onwards ranged from fines to the death penalty. In 1718 transportation to the colonies became a formal sentencing option. Hangings at Tyburn in London, although becoming less common as a sentencing option, still drew vast crowds.[2] Attention shifted to the treatment of long-term prisoners and the prospect of their being rehabilitated into society. Prisons ranged from the lock-ups and short-sentence gaols found in most towns to long-term institutions.

J. Wesley Bready observed, 'The penal code, together with its legal administration and the prison system ... reveals the thinness of the cultural veneer disguising the deep savagery of much of the eighteenth century.'[3] Prison conditions were often atrocious. In 1753 John Wesley visited the Marshalsea Prison in London, and reported it was 'a nursery of all manner of wickedness.

---

[1] W. Booth, *In Darkest England and the Way Out* (London: Salvation Army, 1890), 57–59.

[2] P. Jenkins, 'From Gallows to Prison? The Execution Rate in Early Modern England', *Criminal Justice History* 7 (1986), 52, 56, 61; J. A. Sharpe, *Judicial Punishment in England* (London: Faber and Faber, 1990), 27–36.

[3] J. Wesley Bready, *England Before and After Wesley* (London: Hodder & Stoughton, 1939), 126–127.

O shame to man, that there should be such a place, such a picture of hell, upon earth!'[4] Almost a century later, in 1836, the newly created prison inspectorate of England and Wales reported conditions in most prisons were still disgraceful, with many prisoners locked up in cells for most of the day. Those sentenced to 'hard labour' generally did pointless work, turning cranks or walking the treadmill, or other backbreaking work such as stone breaking.[5]

From the eighteenth century onwards evangelicals were active in promoting efforts to improve the conditions in which prisoners were held and in visiting prisoners to show humanitarian compassion and share the gospel. In 1745 John Wesley highlighted conditions in Newgate Prison, in London:

> The very place strikes horror into your soul. How dark and dreary! How unhealthy and unclean! How void of all that might minister comfort! . . . I know not, if, to one of a thinking, sensible turn of mind, there could be anything like it on this side of hell.[6]

When he visited the French prisoners of war being held near Bristol in 1759, Wesley found 1,100 of them confined in a small space, 'without anything to lie on but a little dirty straw, or anything to cover them but a few foul, thin rags, either by day or night, so that they died like rotten sheep'. He was so moved that he preached that evening on 'Thou shalt not oppress a stranger' (Exod. 23:9 AV), and took up a collection. The £24 raised was used to procure clothes and socks for the prisoners, and the Corporation of Bristol was also moved by the appeal to send mattresses and blankets.[7]

When they were able to get into positions of influence, evangelicals were able to bring significant changes. One example was reported by Wesley in 1761, after Mr Dagge, an early convert of the Evangelical Revival, was appointed keeper of Bristol's Newgate Prison. Under Dagge's guidance the prison was cleaned, drunkenness and visits from prostitutes were stopped and male and female prisoners separated. For a modest remuneration and free medical treatment, work was provided for the prisoners. A religious service was held every Sunday and a sermon preached every Thursday. Wesley contrasted the transformation of Bristol's Newgate with its namesake in London.[8] Sadly, the reforms did not

---

[4] Wesley, 'Journal', 3 February 1753, in *Works of John Wesley*, vol. 2 (London: Wesleyan Conference Office, 1872; repr. Grand Rapids, Mich.: Zondervan, n.d.), 279.

[5] K. Heasman, *Evangelicals in Action* (London: Geoffrey Bles, 1963), 169–170.

[6] J. Wesley, 'A Farther Appeal to Men of Reason and Religion', 1745, in *Works*, vol. 8, 173.

[7] Wesley, 'Journal', 15 October 1759, in *Works*, vol. 2, 516.

[8] J. Wesley, letter to *London Chronicle*, 2 January 1761, quoted in 'Journal', *Works*, vol. 3, 33–34.

outlive the keeper, and when John Howard visited it in 1775 he declared it 'white without and foul within'.[9]

The leading prison reformer of the eighteenth century, John Howard (1726–90), was a Congregationalist. In 1756, when sailing to Portugal, his ship was captured and he was taken to France as a prisoner of war before being released in a prisoner exchange. This experience of the inside of a prison cell inspired his interest in reform. After the death of his wife in 1765, Howard was inconsolable with grief and, finding it unbearable to stay at home, threw himself into benevolent activity. In 1770 he had a deep religious experience and promised God he would serve him wherever he was needed. When in 1773 he became High Sheriff of Bedfordshire, he saw just such an opportunity, especially as the role included oversight of the county's prisons. These he began to visit regularly, and then prisons in other counties. He was shocked to find dirt, disease and corruption throughout the system, and often drunkenness. Some prisoners who had served their sentences were unable to leave because they could not afford the fees prison keepers charged for their upkeep. Howard resolutely collected statistics as to the space in which prisoners were kept and the amount of food, water and exercise they were given. He travelled across Europe to compare prison conditions in other countries, finding in some places, such as the Netherlands, well-run prisons with healthy prisoners who were given meaningful tasks throughout the day. He published his findings in 1777 in *The State of Prisons in England and Wales*. The revelations it contained were shocking. Of Knaresborough Prison he wrote, 'Only one room about twelve feet square; earth floor; no fireplace; very offensive; a common sewer from the town running through it uncovered.' As the scars on prisoners' faces showed, it was infested with ferocious rats.[10]

Behind Howard's prison-reform work lay his evangelical Christian faith. He was a Calvinist, deeply aware of his sin, but confident of the all-sufficient grace of God. He knew most prisoners had committed terrible acts and deserved their incarceration, but this was no excuse for their mistreatment. Instead, he showed them kindness and spent considerable amounts of money to help them. He died in what is now the Ukraine in 1790 after catching typhus fever on a prison visit.[11] Few could dispute the evidence he presented, and a series of Acts of Parliament followed based on his recommendations, many of which, sadly, were not rigorously implemented.

---

[9] J. Howard, *The State of Prisons in England and Wales* (Warrington: W. Eyres, 1777), 370.

[10] Ibid. 372.

[11] On Howard see J. Aikin, *A View of the Life, Travels, and Philanthropic Labours of the Late John Howard* (Boston: Manning & Loring, 1794).

Thomas Fowell Buxton not only worked to end slavery, but was also strongly committed to prison reform. He argued that the eighteenth-century penal code, by which someone could be hanged for stealing sixpence, was completely contrary to the Christian religion. His 1818 report *An Inquiry, Whether Crime and Misery Are Produced or Prevented by Our Present System of Prison Discipline* highlighted the poor state of prisons.[12] This encouraged the Home Secretary, Robert Peel, to introduce penal reforms in the 1820s.

In the later part of the eighteenth century most prisons began to appoint chaplains,[13] who played a significant welfare role and provided a point of contact with prisoners' families. Although employees of the prison, a number of chaplains highlighted poor conditions, although there was risk in this. When the chaplain of Wandsworth Prison, Dr Morrison, challenged the in-humane regime of its governor, he was dismissed. He then launched a public campaign for reform, which led to the 1895 Gladstone Report and whole-sale changes.[14] The Howard Association, founded in 1866 in memory of John Howard, later the Howard League for Penal Reform, sought to allow volunteers to visit prisoners regularly, stressing the beneficial effects of such visits. By 1892 voluntary visitors were permitted in male prisons, and in half of women's prisons. It was 1924 before all prisons permitted such voluntary visitors.

Penal reform was undertaken in the British colonies by George Arthur (1784–1854). During the Napoleonic Wars he underwent a deep personal conversion, becoming convinced of the 'truth and power' of the gospel. He developed close connections with the Clapham Sect. From 1834 to 1836 he served as Lieutenant Governor of Tasmania, then called Van Dieman's Land, a penal colony to which convicted criminals were transported. Here he introduced a system by which convicts could be rewarded for good behaviour, being able to progress through different stages and finally to full freedom. The process of reform involved both the masters who employed the convicts and religious ministers who worked with them. They strove not just for a 'reformation of expediency', but a 'reformation of principle', cultivating the 'inward (moral and religious) regulator', which promoted personal reformation. Arthur saw significant success in the scheme, but it did not long outlast his recall in 1836 before he was moved to another assignment in Canada. Ironically, those uncomfortable with the scheme claimed its success in

---

[12] T. F. Buxton, *An Inquiry, Whether Crime and Misery Are Produced or Prevented by Our Present System of Prison Discipline* (London: J. & A. Arch, 1818).

[13] Howard, *Prisons*, 28.

[14] Heasman, *Evangelicals*, 170–171.

restoring convicts was undermining the deterrent effect of transportation as a punishment.[15]

Alongside efforts to improve conditions for prisoners, visiting prisons to preach and show pastoral care formed another important part of evangelical social action. During their 'Holy Club' days in Oxford John and Charles Wesley began in 1730 visiting the Castle and Bocardo prisons; George Whitefield similarly visited prisons and 'bridewells'. This attracted some opposition, leading to John Wesley's wry comment 'we are forbidden to go to Newgate for fear of making them wicked'.[16] He argued that he was simply fulfilling the command of Christ to do good, feed the hungry, clothe the needy and visit the sick and prisoners. This was all part of 'a higher purpose, even the saving of souls from death'. Wesley even sought to help a man in prison charged with homosexuality, a crime in those days, which brought more criticism.[17] Whitefield and Wesley also provided support for education classes for the children of the prisoners.[18]

In November 1738 John and Charles Wesley visited the condemned cells at Newgate, just before the prisoners held in them were executed. John declared it 'the most glorious instance I ever saw of faith triumphing over sin and death'. One man who wept openly after hearing and believing the gospel for the first time declared, 'I feel a peace which I could not have believed to be possible. And I know it is the peace of God, which passeth all understanding.'[19] Thirty years later Wesley was still preaching to prisoners on death row. In 1767 he took as his text the words of Christ to the dying thief, 'Today shalt thou be with me in Paradise' (AV). Wesley reported, 'All of them were struck, and melted into tears: Who knows but some of them may "reap in joy?".'[20]

The American evangelist D. L. Moody regularly preached to prisoners. On nine different occasions during the American Civil War he ministered to troops on the front line, and regularly preached to the 17,000 prisoners of war from the Southern forces at Camp Douglas, just south of Chicago. In 1862 congregations of up to 400 gathered to hear him.[21] Moody gained permissions from

---

[15] R. Ely, 'Arthur, Sir George (1784–1854)', in T. Larsen (ed.), *Biographical Dictionary of Evangelicals* (Leicester: Inter-Varsity Press, 2003), 20–22. See also A. G. L. Shaw, *Sir George Arthur, Bart, 1784–1854* (Melbourne: Melbourne University Press, 1980).

[16] W. L. Clay, *The Prison Chaplain: A Memoir of the Rev John Clay B.D.* (Cambridge: Macmillan, 1861), 35.

[17] Questions for the Castle Work, in John Wesley, *Letters*, vol. 1, 339, quoted in H. D. Rack, *Reasonable Enthusiast: John Wesley and the Rise of Methodism* (London: Epworth Press, 1989), 89, 91.

[18] A. Dallimore, *George Whitefield: The Life and Times of the Great Evangelist of the Eighteenth Century Revival*, vol. 1 (Edinburgh: Banner of Truth, 1970), 68.

[19] Wesley, 'Journal', 8 November 1738, in *Works*, vol. 1, 163.

[20] Ibid., vol. 3, 303–304.

[21] W. R. Moody, *Life of Moody* (New York: F. H. Revell, 1900), 82.

county sheriffs in 1895 to donate Christian books to prison libraries. He also sent New Testaments and copies of his sermons to prisoners, and encouraged those who had been converted to read aloud from them to the other inmates.[22] Moody recognized there were complex causes of criminal behaviour:

> Many a young man has committed a crime in a moment of anger, or under the influence of liquor. The records show that nearly half the prisoners are under twenty-five years of age . . . If he can be reached by the gospel message before he sinks lower and lower, there is every hope for his salvation for this life.[23]

To Moody evangelism was central to moral reform – from personal spiritual change would come a transformed lifestyle, and the conversion of convicted criminals would bring significant changes to society.

After prisoners were discharged, Evangelicals also sought to help them. Many had no place to stay, and quickly returned to their old haunts and associates, and were drawn back into crime. Prison gates were often surrounded by gangs of criminals who met newly released prisoners and offered them a place to stay, before drawing them into malevolent networks. Early efforts to provide a Christian befriending and support system for discharged prisoners were started at Great Yarmouth by Sarah Martin, who in the 1830s offered them education classes and training for future work. Similar work was done by Thomas Wright at Manchester Prison in the 1840s.[24] Others started refuges for discharged prisoners, so those without families had a place to stay. The London Reformatory for Adult Criminals was started in Westminster, London, in 1848, for the rehabilitation of long-term prisoners released from Brixton Prison. In 1857 the Royal Society for Discharged Prisoners was set up with the aid of the evangelical Lord Kinnaird. It helped prisoners return to their families and find a job or, for those who had no family, to emigrate.[25]

Susanna Meredith (1823–1901) began visiting Brixton Prison in the 1860s. Her father had been governor of the county prison in Cork. She had married at the age of 19, but was widowed eight years later. She combined her strong evangelical faith with a determination that support for those in need should be well organized and make use of the latest thinking. She rented small premises

---

[22] L. W. Dorsett, *A Passion for Souls: The Life of D. L. Moody* (Chicago, Ill.: Moody Press, 1997), 338, 342–343.

[23] Quoted in Moody, *Life of Moody*, 433.

[24] Heasman, *Evangelicals*, 174.

[25] Ibid. 178.

outside Tothill Fields Prison where women could go for breakfast after discharge, and here she befriended them. This became Mrs Meredith's Prison Mission in 1864. She established the Marble Laundry for the employment of discharged female prisoners, for which they received a shilling a day in wages and free meals. Having proved themselves in this work, most were placed into regular employment. The Prison Mission grew to a considerable size, and reported in 1895 that it had 70 paid workers and 300 volunteer workers (all women), and was helping 3,000 ex-prisoners and their children each year. In 1868 the prison authorities made Susanna Meredith's mission a recognized discharged-prisoners' aid society. Funded by voluntary contributions, a home on Wandsworth Road known as The Mission to Women was started. Prisoners could petition for early release from prison, making part of their case that they would go to Mrs Meredith's Home. Women usually stayed in the refuges for around six months, although they could remain for up to a year, before being reintegrated into society by being placed under close supervision in lodgings. Women rarely reoffended when they were in the refuges.[26]

Further prison-gate missions were established, modelled on the Prison Mission. George Hatton, superintendent of the St Giles Mission, started similar work at Holloway, Wandsworth, Pentonville and Millbank prisons. Prison-gate missions were also opened in Dublin and Belfast, and then in Boston and Toronto. There was inevitably some duplication of effort, and some of the small missions lacked the resources to support properly those whose care they undertook. The Salvation Army began its first Prison Gate Brigade at Wandsworth Prison in 1884, and the Church Army started work outside prisons in 1888.[27]

Behind the Salvation Army's approach was the recognition that many prisoners became institutionalized during their sentences. This left them unable to think for themselves and readily susceptible to their former associates in crime or others who easily took advantage of them. The Salvation Army's prison-gate missioners offered 'an open door of hope', providing food and shelter from the moment of discharge. They also worked with prison authorities in undertaking the supervision and care of prisoners at the end of their sentences. Key to the strategy was finding employment for them, or teaching them a trade if they had none. William Booth reported significant success from the prison-gate work. One example was 'G. A.', aged 72, renowned as 'a drunkard, gambler and swearer', who had spent 23 years of his life in gaol. Booth records he was, 'Met

---

[26] J. Turner and H. Johnston, 'Female Prisoners, Aftercare and Release: Residential Provision and Support in Late Nineteenth-Century England', *British Journal of Community Justice*, 2015 <https://www.mmuperu.co.uk/bjcj/articles/female-prisoners-aftercare-and-release-residential-provision>, accessed 18 April 2020.
[27] Heasman, *Evangelicals*, 179.

on his discharge by the Prison Gate Brigade, admitted into [a Salvation Army] Home, where he remained four months, and became truly saved. He is living a consistent, godly life and is in employment.' Another, 'S. T.', was 'an idler, loafing, thieving, swearing, disreputable young man' who had lived with prostitutes. The Prison Gate Brigade officers found him a place to live and work on his discharge. After he was converted, Booth reports, 'such was his earnestness that he was accepted and has done good service as an Army officer . . . He is, indeed, a marvel of Divine grace.' Another man, 'B. C.', had 'good birth, education, and position', but 'drank himself out of home and friends and into gaol'. Rescued by the Prison Gate officers, he was 'saved, exhibiting by an earnest and truly consistent life the depth of his conversion'. He had a major impact on others, 'being made instrumental while with us in the salvation of many who, like himself, had come to utter destitution and crime through drink'. He was restored to his wife and family, obtained a good job position and was 'the possessor of a happy home, and the love of God shed abroad in it'.[28]

Susanna Meredith was deeply influenced by Elizabeth Fry (see the character study below) in seeing the need for support for other members of the family when a wife or mother was incarcerated. Care for prisoners needed to be set within their wider context.[29] In addition to her work with the Prison Mission she became the Treasurer of the Female Prisoners' Aid Society, which was particularly concerned with the plight of children when their mother was imprisoned. She found cases of girls forced to steal or go into prostitution when left to fend for themselves. In 1870 she started Mrs Meredith's Prison Mission School at Addlestone in Surrey, for the children of long-term female prisoners. The children lived in small cottages, were cared for by a house mother and received education and training, often as domestic servants. When they left school, they were assisted in finding employment. They were eventually renamed Princess Mary's Village Homes.[30]

In order to reach prisoners who were in solitary confinement, so could not receive visitors, Meredith also started the 'Letters to Prisoners' project. On Christmas Day 1881 she and her friends sent handwritten letters to women in the Millbank Prison, each containing a Christian message and greeting. With the permission of governors and chaplains, the project extended to other prisons, and eventually became a global work.

In Leicester the Prison Aid Society was formed by F. B. Meyer after he was approached by a member of the Melbourne Hall congregation whose father

---

28 Booth, *Darkest England*, 176, 178–179.
29 Heasman, *Evangelicals*, 176–177.
30 Ibid. 75–76.

was due to be released from prison the next day. She feared he would be met by his previous associates. Meyer met the man at the prison gate and walked with him to a local coffee house, thereby keeping him away from the public house. Success with this case became the basis of the project, and over his years in Leicester, Meyer and his workers met with more than 6,000 discharged prisoners.[31] The difficulties discharged prisoners had in finding employment encouraged him to develop work-creation schemes.[32]

Juvenile offenders caused particular concern. Members of the Clapham Sect who investigated the problem as early as 1816 found that there were 8,000 boys involved in some form of criminal activity in London. By 1849 prison inspectors classified 13,000 prisoners in England and Wales as 'juveniles'. They often operated in gangs and terrorized parts of the inner cities, living without any form of parental supervision. Some of their parents had simply neglected them or had abandoned them to the streets. Alcohol abuse by parents, which plunged families into poverty, was considered a major reason for children living by crime or depredation. Many children ended up in the prison system after committing minor offences. The feeling grew that they were better off going to some form of 'reformatory' school rather than prison, and in 1854 the Reformatory Schools Act was passed. This led to the formation after 1858 of the Reformatory and Refuge Union (RRU), with Lord Shaftesbury as its president, and other evangelicals, including Arthur Kinnaird and Lord Radstock, on the committee. A close interest in the RRU work was taken by Thomas Barnardo, George Müller and William Quarrier. The RRU focused on children who had already fallen into crime, or were being led into crime by association with others, who were homeless and destitute or who through the poverty and adverse circumstances of their families were likely to commit crimes. It connected local projects working with juveniles and provided magistrates with lists of homes willing to take juvenile offenders. Its officers also went to courts to meet child offenders and advise magistrates on the reformatory options available. In 1933 the Home Office took over the running of these reformatory schools, renaming them 'approved' schools. The RRU became the Children's Aid Society, and focused its work on children in need struggling with difficult home backgrounds.[33]

In 1877 William Wheatley of the St Giles Christian Mission found that young offenders leaving Coldbath Fields Prison had often reoffended within hours of discharge. He started a ministry to befriend and support them, and to

---

[31] A. C. Mann, *F. B. Meyer: Preacher, Teacher, Man of God* (London: G. Allen & Unwin, 1929), 88–89.
[32] See chapter 4.
[33] Heasman, *Evangelicals*, 183–187.

help them find employment and prevent them returning to crime. In 1887 the First Offenders' Act was passed, allowing those convicted of their first crime of larceny or false pretences to be placed on probation. Wheatley was accepted as a person considered suitable to supervise those on probation, and local magistrates began to commit first offenders into his care. He became a trusted figure, able to visit the court and identify those who would respond well to such an opportunity. He supervised them for periods of one or two years, during which they attended evening classes, and organized recreation was provided. The young ex-offenders were found employment and used their wages to contribute to their board and lodgings. Most of those offered this opportunity did not return to crime. Wheatley's methods were later adopted by the borstal and approved hostel system developed for young offenders.[34]

The London Police Court Mission, started in 1876, offered assistance to people arrested for drink-related crimes. Their missioners, known for their strong evangelical beliefs and mostly connected with the Church of England, visited prisoners in cells and waiting rooms to meet them before their case was heard, seeking those who would be open to receiving help after they were discharged. The missioners became familiar faces to the magistrates, who often consulted with them as to the best course of action, and discharged some prisoners into their care. They were also able to connect discharged prisoners with churches in their home areas for further pastoral support. In 1902 the mission reported that it had, 'by the Grace of God, reclaimed many from the depths of sin . . . One man, for instance, who had been charged five hundred times, at various English Police Courts.'[35] After the passing of the 1887 Probation Act, Police Court missioners were sometimes asked to assist those released on probation. A further act in 1907 made such supervision compulsory, and many Police Court missioners were selected to act as probation officers. They continued to play this important role until 1937, when probation services were taken over by the government – for sixty years this vital public-welfare service had largely been run by evangelicals. Much of the later practice of the probation services, which earned the trust of the courts, grew out of what evangelicals had done so successfully. Kathleen Heasman attributes the success of the Police Court missioners to their ability to 'combine a lively Christian faith with a sound scientific and practical approach to the problems of the offender'.[36]

Evangelicals from the eighteenth to the twentieth century played a significant role in working to improve the conditions of prisoners, and in moving the

---

[34] Ibid. 177–178.

[35] *London Police Court Mission Annual Report*, 1902, quoted in Heasman, *Evangelicals*, 181.

[36] Heasman, *Evangelicals*, 183.

emphasis in the treatment of criminals from purely punishment and segregation from society to offering them opportunities for moral reform and rehabilitation, including employment on discharge. These evangelicals also emphasized the need for prisoners to maintain contact with the outside world through the work of prison visitors and letter writers. They recognized the need of the families of prisoners for care and support, not least to stop children following their parents into a life of crime. Their ideas were gradually adopted more widely by prison authorities towards the end of the nineteenth century. However, they were not the only group who contributed to prison reform: Utilitarians, such as Jeremy Bentham, and Unitarians, such as Mary Carpenter, played significant roles in improving conditions and individual care for prisoners.

Character study: Elizabeth Fry (1780–1845) – England

Born into a wealthy Quaker banking family, Elizabeth Gurney underwent a profound conversion experience in 1798 after hearing the American Quaker preacher William Savery, who laid stress on the atonement in his message. She wrote afterwards in her diary, 'I feel there is a God and Immortality; happy, happy thought.'[37] She gave up the socializing, theatre, opera-going and fine clothes her family, despite being Quakers, were accustomed to. Bible reading and personal prayer became central to her life. Her new faith helped her overcome the terrible fears she had of robbers that left her 'ready to jump out at my own shadow'.[38] She developed an active social concern, visiting the poor and sick in the local village, the inmates of the local house of correction, and starting a school for the education of poor children.[39]

In 1800 Elizabeth married Joseph Fry, a wealthy Quaker merchant from Bristol. Between 1801 and 1822 she bore eleven children and constantly battled nervousness, illness and depression. In 1809 she began to speak in Quaker worship meetings and was recorded as a Quaker minister in 1811. After this she spoke extensively, promoting evangelical emphases in Quakerism, including an emphasis on the atoning work of Christ, the authority of Scripture and the need for a personal conversion experience.

In 1813 she visited the female inmates of Newgate Prison in London, the most notorious prison in England. Here 300 women lived in appalling, overcrowded conditions, provided with no bedding, with some sleeping on the floor. One

---

[37] K. Fry and R. E. Creswell, *Memoir of the Life of Elizabeth Fry*, 2nd edn, vol. 1 (London: John Hatchard & Son, 1848), 25, quotation from the diary of Elizabeth Fry, 40.

[38] J. Rose, *Elizabeth Fry: A Biography* (London: Macmillan, 1981), 22–24.

[39] T. D. Hamm, 'Fry, Elizabeth', in Larsen, *Biographical Dictionary of Evangelicals*, 240.

visitor described how 'half-naked, drunken women clawed through the iron railings with wooden spoons tied to sticks to beg the public for pennies for porter . . . Shrieking curses, brawling, spitting and tearing each other's hair.'[40] Many had their children with them, and often the first words they learned, sometimes the only words, were swear words. Such an environment was not only alarming, but also dangerous to respectable middle- and upper-class female visitors. The prison authorities maintained control only by means of physical brutality. Yet, despite her early personal timidity, Elizabeth Fry found that when she could speak calmly and confidently to the prisoners about the Christian gospel, they listened carefully and respectfully.[41] Over the next three years she discussed the situation with others in her family interested in prison reform, before at Christmas 1816 returning to Newgate to begin her famous work.[42]

She faced opposition, but not from the prisoners as might have been expected. Her brother wrote to her in 1817, cautioning whether 'that wisdom which dwells with prudence justifies thy entering at Newgate into that most trying line of service'.[43] The prison authorities considered her plans admirable, but impossible, because of the wildness of the inmates. Elizabeth Fry, despite her tendency to 'be much affected by the opinions of man',[44] through patient persistence obtained permission to start a school for the children of the prisoners. The cell set apart for the classes was crowded, and other women, who also desperately wanted an education, stood outside listening to the lessons. Mary Connor, an educated young prisoner, assisted with the teaching. Through the work of the visitors, Mary 'humbly believed, obtained everlasting pardon and peace, through the merits of her Lord and Saviour'. Fifteen months later she received a pardon and was released.[45]

Elizabeth Fry described the heart-rending daily scenes she witnessed in Newgate, with some prisoners under sentence of death:

on my left hand sat Lawrence, alias Woodman, surrounded by her four children, and only waiting the birth of another, which she hourly expects, to pay the forfeit of her life; as her husband had done for the same crime, a short time before.[46]

---

40 Rose, *Fry*, 79.
41 Ibid. 69–71.
42 Fry and Creswell, *Memoir*, 255.
43 Quoted in Rose, *Fry*, 82.
44 Fry and Creswell, *Memoir*, 258.
45 Ibid. 287.
46 Ibid. 271.

At times she despaired as to whether any good could be done at all in such desperate situations, aware that what she was witnessing was only 'an atom in the abyss of vice, and consequent misery' in London.[47]

Her plan was to introduce the prisoners to 'a knowledge of the Holy Scriptures and to form in them, as much as possible, habits of order, sobriety and industry which may render them docile and peaceable while in prison, and respectable when they leave it'. She started the 'Association for the Improvement of Female Prisoners in Newgate'. Its female members visited the prison daily and a matron was appointed to work with the women.[48] Elizabeth Fry sought wider reforms, including removing male warders from the female part of the prison.

The Governor of Newgate remained sceptical about her proposals. Respecting them as individual human beings, Elizabeth Fry took the vital, and unheard of, step of inviting the prisoners to be partners in the project, which could only succeed with their co-operation. They approved the proposal unanimously. The female prisoners were provided with sewing work, for which they were paid, supervised by other prisoners working as 'monitors'. Mrs Fry's calm presence, her insistence on reading to them from the Bible each day and her deep care for the inmates were key to the success of her work. Within weeks 'Hell on earth' had become a 'well-regulated family'. Some called the transformation 'miraculous'.[49] The prison authorities were persuaded to take on the responsibility for the school and for paying the salary of the matron. Fry had quickly become a widely respected prison reformer, and in 1818 was afforded an unprecedented honour for a woman when she gave evidence to a House of Commons Committee on London Prisons.

In 1818 Elizabeth Fry sought to prevent the hanging of Harriet Skelton, a much-liked prisoner sentenced to death for passing forged bank notes. Her appeals for clemency to the Home Secretary, Lord Sidmouth, who was suspicious of her reforming work as being soft on crime, were unavailing.[50] However, awareness was raised of the number of women condemned to death for such crimes, into which they had often been forced by men. Elizabeth Fry was also concerned for prisoners after their discharge, and in 1822 started an institution to support them, followed in 1824 by a home for girls aged 9–13 convicted of minor offences. In an attempt to stop their falling into more serious crime they were provided with education, life skills and Christian influence. By 1832, 103 girls had been admitted. Of them, only 2 had returned to prison, and 4 had gone

---

[47] Ibid.
[48] Rose, *Fry*, 84.
[49] Ibid. 88–89.
[50] Ibid. 96–98.

back to crime.[51] She similarly worked to improve the conditions on ships transporting prisoners to Australia, and to reform the penal settlements of New South Wales.[52]

All this had a cost. Her frequent absences meant her home life was sometimes neglected. Because of the family's growing financial difficulties, six of her nine surviving children spent time living with other close relatives. It was a profound shock when in 1828 Joseph Fry was declared bankrupt after the bank he had established failed. This was considered a cause of great shame in a Quaker family, and significantly reduced her capacity for further social-concern projects.

By the 1830s the humanitarian approach to prisoner care of John Howard and Elizabeth Fry was being challenged by the 'efficient' approach advocated by Edwin Chadwick. Prison was for punishment and short, sharp periods of imprisonment were preferred, ideally in solitary confinement from other prisoners. She deeply opposed this, concerned over the suicide rate and the impact on the mental health of prisoners held in isolation, and their difficulties on release in adjusting to normal life.[53]

In 1840 Elizabeth Fry started a training school for Protestant Sisters of Charity, based on the example of the Kaiserswerth deaconess training institute in Germany. The sisters were trained in local hospitals and devoted themselves to tending to the needs of the poor and sick in their locality and reading the Scriptures to them. By 1854 there were forty 'Fry Sisters', and some assisted Florence Nightingale in her work at Scutari.

Elizabeth Fry died in 1845, aged 65, nationally and internationally influential as a prison reformer. Her legacy was lasting: between 2002 and 2016 her picture appeared on the British £5 note. She inspired other women, including Florence Nightingale, into more public spheres of social-reform work.[54] Through deep personal piety, a strong evangelistic impulse and compassion for the poorest and most degraded people, she transformed not only the conditions but also the lives of hundreds of prisoners and ex-offenders. From her, one biographer comments, 'flowed a wave of tolerance and compassion which swept through nineteenth-century Europe'.[55]

---

[51] Ibid. 123–124, 150.
[52] Ibid. 115–116.
[53] Ibid. 146–147.
[54] Ibid. 179–181.
[55] Ibid. 204–205.

Conclusion

The previous chapters have demonstrated the great variety of activism among evangelicals from the eighteenth century onwards, motivated both by the evangelistic imperative and deep social concern for those in need. There was a fear that if Christians stood idle, 'people who could have been saved might perish'.[1] Despite concerns there might be a subtle shift from justification by faith to justification by works,[2] to most evangelicals evangelism and social action were two sides of the same coin. Evangelism changed people, and changed people would change society.[3] Social action was not an optional extra but an inevitable part of intentional missional activity. As John Venn put it:

> Faith, to be genuine, must produce good works . . . It is inherent in the very nature of the Gospel, that whosoever really believes it will do what is right in the sight of God . . . Such is the power of faith as a principle of action.[4]

The results were notable. Evangelism and social action extended the reach of the gospel to those outside the pale of respectable society, including addicts, prostitutes, prisoners, trafficked women and homeless people. David Hempton observed that the unique combination within evangelicalism of conversionist zeal and practical action rendered Britain 'more stable, more humane, and more religious than it otherwise would have been'.[5] The same was true internationally.

However, as David Bebbington has noted, 'the Evangelical record in the philanthropic field was not an unqualified asset for evangelism'.[6] Mistakes were made. There was also a growing recognition that state involvement was

---

[1] K. S. Inglis, *Churches and the Working Class in Victorian England* (London: Routledge & Kegan Paul, 1963), 6.

[2] R. W. Dale, *Laws of Christ for Common Life* (London: Hodder & Stoughton, 1884), 34.

[3] I. Sellers, *Nineteenth-Century Nonconformity* (London: Edward Arnold, 1977), 92.

[4] John Venn, 'On Good Works', in *Sermons by the Rev. John Venn, MA, Rector of Clapham*, 3rd edn (London: Ellerton & Henderson, 1818), 62–64.

[5] D. Hempton, 'Evangelicalism and Reform, c.1780–1832', in J. Wolffe (ed.), *Evangelical Faith and Public Zeal: Evangelicals and Society in Britain 1780–1980* (London: SPCK, 1995), 33.

[6] D. Bebbington, *The Dominance of Evangelicalism: The Age of Spurgeon and Moody* (Leicester: Inter-Varsity Press, 2005), 121.

necessary to address the vast problems of modern society, such as mass un-employment, slum housing and poor sanitation. The 'Christendom model', so influential on Thomas Chalmers, was unworkable by the middle of the nineteenth century. William Booth argued that parts of British cities were spiritually darker than Africa. With some justification, part of New York was known as 'Hell's Kitchen'. The work of evangelicals, and their calls for inter-vention, helped push the state into a more paternalist and interventionist guise. It was almost inevitable that local authorities and the state, with greater resources at their disposal, would subsume into their regular pattern of activities a number of agencies initiated by evangelicals. The success of evangelicals led eventually in some ways to their loss of influence.

For all their activism, evangelicals did not 'cure' all social problems, nor bring all the population to a profession of personal faith in Christ. In the 1890s Charles Booth reported the discouragement of one London Mission worker: 'the work was heavy and the results so small that we have been tempted to murmur against God and relax our energy'.[7] Church attendance was falling across Europe by the 1890s, although there was continued growth in attendance in America in the late nineteenth and early twentieth centuries. The effort of sustaining so many agencies became more difficult. Yet the decline of Christian influence might well have been far greater without their endeavours. Even if conversions were fewer than hoped for, a diffusive form of Christian under-standing and morality remained widely accepted until at least the middle of the twentieth century in Britain – and remained strong in the USA for most of that century.

The 'Great Reversal' of several decades of the twentieth century proved a temporary engagement of reverse gear rather than a wholesale shift away from the prevailing pattern among evangelicals. The reversal's legacy, however, remains. Evangelical confessional statements, in contrast to those of the Reformers, still often emphasize what evangelicals believe, rather than how they should live. The Lausanne Covenant sought to redress this, but it was a personal covenant, with less attention given to precise doctrinal formulation. The Cape Town Commitment of 2010 reflects the more integrated and holistic approach of the seventeenth-century confessions.[8]

Mark Greene has warned of 'a great divide, leaving most Christians without a vision for engagement and service in the places they go on a daily basis – the

---

[7] C. Booth, *The Life and Labour of the People of London*, 3rd series, *Religious Influences*, vol. 7 (London, 1902), 96.

[8] *The Cape Town Commitment: A Confession of Faith and a Call to Action*, Didasko Files, Lausanne Movement, 2011.

fields, the factories, the school gates, the shops, the clubs, the offices'. The vision is lacking because 'this is not the vision that grips the global evangelical church'.[9] N. T. Wright has noted a tendency among many Christians towards a 'detached spirituality (a heavenly-mindedness with a questionable earthly use), and an escapist eschatology', leaving limited place for engagement with earthly realities and needs.[10]

Some writers have sought to move the primacy on to ethical and social action. Brian McLaren urged a shift from asking 'whose lineage, rites, doctrines, structures, and terminology are right' to 'whose actions, service, outreach, kindness and effectiveness are good'.[11] Rob Bell, in *Velvet Elvis*, suggests, 'Perhaps a better question than who's right, is who's living rightly.'[12] While a corrective may be needed to parts of evangelicalism where the practical outliving of the gospel is insufficiently emphasized, these views appear to take this too far. If the message is 'Get the action and the experience right, and then correct doctrine will follow,' it reverses the classic Protestant evangelical understanding that works acceptable to God grow as fruit from new life in Christ, and develop along with the correct theological understanding of that. A person's changed spiritual status is reflected in changed belief and practice. As John Stott wrote, 'Social responsibility becomes an aspect not of Christian mission only, but also of Christian conversion. It is impossible to be truly converted to God without being thereby converted to our neighbour.'[13]

The discomfort of some evangelicals in giving verbal expression to the gospel is typified in the oft-used phrase 'Preach the gospel at all times. If necessary use words' – as mentioned in chapter 1a, incorrectly attributed to Francis of Assisi. In the context of social action, proclamation must certainly be appropriate to the context, not crass or manipulative of those in need or the vulnerable. William Booth recognized this:

> What is the use of preaching the Gospel to men whose whole attention is concentrated upon a mad, desperate struggle to keep themselves alive . . . the first thing to do is to get him at least a footing on firm ground . . . you will have all the better opportunity to find a way to his heart if he comes

---

[9] M. Greene, 'Naming the Issue in Our Churches and Institutions', in *Whole-Life Mission for the Whole Church: Overcoming the Sacred–Secular Divide Through Theological Education* (Carlisle: Langham Global Library, 2021), 10.

[10] N. T. Wright, *The Day the Revolution Began* (London: SPCK, 2016), 35.

[11] B. McLaren, *A Generous Orthodoxy* (Grand Rapids, Mich.: Zondervan, 2004), 223; *The Last Word and After That* (San Francisco, Calif.: Jossey-Bass, 2003), 197.

[12] R. Bell, *Velvet Elvis: Repainting the Christian Faith* (Grand Rapids, Mich.: Zondervan, 2005), 21.

[13] J. Stott, *Christian Mission in the Modern World* (Downers Grove, Ill.: InterVarsity Press, 1975), 53.

to know that it was you who pulled him out of the horrible pit and the miry clay in which he was sinking to perdition.[14]

In those situations, lovingly sharing the good news of Jesus Christ is a vital part of the expression of wider compassion for a person's blessing in this world and for all eternity. Because James declares 'faith by itself, if it is not accompanied by action, is dead' (2:17), then surely works without faith are unavailing. And works without words do not seem to be the biblical or historical pattern for bringing people to faith. The historical pattern of the ministry of evangelicals shows their seeking the totality of the well-being of people in their physical and spiritual natures.

The foregoing chapters indicate evangelicalism historically to be a highly integrated expression of Christianity. Evangelicalism touches the cognitive, affective and active dimensions of a person, and is expressed with the head, heart and hands. This has not always resulted in a consistent social theory or political theology. Part of this, Stott argues, is a reaction against the 'social gospel': 'When Rauschenbusch politicized the kingdom of God, it was understandable (if regrettable) that, in reaction to him, evangelicals concentrated on evangelism and personal philanthropy, and steered clear of socio-political action.'[15] However, a number of examples in this book are of evangelical politicians and others exercising 'holy worldliness' in a variety of causes. Evangelical Christianity is a countercultural world view. The dangers of failure in this regard were demonstrated in the nineteenth-century American South, where, as Hodge put it, biblical interpretation was 'more or less subject to the controlling influence of public opinion' – with tragic consequences.[16] Elsewhere, evangelicals have regularly critiqued, challenged and even defied the culture and values of 'the world', sometimes under threat of prison, violence or death for doing so. John Smith of the London Missionary Society in the 1820s paid with his life for doing this.

The watching world needs to see a consistency between action and proclamation among evangelicals. David Wells observed, 'proclamation must arise within a context of *authenticity* . . . to embody that truth in the way that the Church actually lives . . . believing and being, talking and doing, all joined together in a seamless whole'.[17] It is disappointing when evangelicals who speak

---

[14] W. Booth, *In Darkest England and the Way Out* (London: Salvation Army, 1890), 45.

[15] J. Stott, *Issues Facing Christians Today*, rev. edn. (London: Marshall Pickering, 1990), 7.

[16] C. Hodge, 'The General Assembly', *Princeton Review* 37 (July 1865), 506, quoted in M. Noll, *America's God: From Jonathan Edwards to Abraham Lincoln* (New York: Oxford University Press, 2002), 403.

[17] D. F. Wells, *Above All Earthly Pow'rs – Christ in the Post Modern World* (Grand Rapids, Mich.: Eerdmans; Leicester: Inter-Varsity Press, 2006), 315; emphasis original.

out against social evils find themselves marginalized by other conservative churches, as happened in the South over the slavery issue. This has pushed some towards the radical end of the theological spectrum. It is important that evangelicals slip neither into liberalism nor marginalize those who seek to uphold the cause of the oppressed.

Another subtler trend has also been apparent. Mark Noll observed in nineteenth-century America a shift in the understanding of divine characteristics away from 'ontological' to 'operational' categories, from 'final value' to 'instrumental' values, with a consequent shift from theocentric activism to activistic anthropocentrism.[18] To Jonathan Edwards, true virtue was chiefly 'love to God; the Being of beings, infinitely the greatest and best'.[19] While anthropocentric activism is important, the theocentric dimension should not be lost. Indeed, when the theocentric vision is restored through salvation by God's grace, anthropocentric activism flows as the fruit. Compassion so channelled to the glory of God means that social concern becomes truly doxological.

The character studies in this book have repeatedly demonstrated the need for balance to avoid being 'heavenly minded yet morally and socially useless'. As Don Carson put it:

> we must remember to help the poor, seek justice for all, insist on integrity and demonstrate it ourselves . . . At the same time, Christians must avoid identifying the goals of the kingdom of God with political, economic or social goals; or, more accurately, such identification must never be exclusive.[20]

The eternal perspective of following the exalted Jesus in service and self-denial 'enables us to be more useful in our society than we would be otherwise'.[21]

It is noticeable through the centuries how many activities in evangelism and social concern have been prompted by personal awareness of deep needs. Increased prosperity among some Christians and physical separation from scenes of deprivation have accompanied a declining pattern of activity. Evangelical Christians have a duty to be informed of the chronic needs of the world in which they live. With globalization and information revolutions such

---

[18] Noll, *America's God*, 440–442.

[19] J. Edwards, 'The Nature of True Virtue', in P. Ramsey (ed.), *The Works of Jonathan Edwards*, vol. 8: *Ethical Writings* (New Haven, Conn.: Yale University Press, 1989), 550.

[20] D. A. Carson, *Jesus and His Friends: His Farewell Message and Prayer in John 14 to 17* (Leicester: Inter-Varsity Press, 1986), 22.

[21] Ibid.

Christians cannot plead ignorance, and the issues discussed here are not simply matters of the past. Mike Davis in *Planet of Slums* argues that the cities of the future are being constructed not from glass and steel as urban theorists expected, but from 'crude brick, straw, recycled plastic, cement blocks . . . most of the twenty-first-century urban dwellers squat in squalor, surrounded by pollution, excrement, and decay'.[22] That is where vast numbers of Bible-believing Christians live every day, facing hardship and short life expectancy. Here both proclamation and compassionate activity are a necessity in the absence of state-funded welfare programmes – the lives of millions depend on it. As the Micah Declaration puts it, 'If we ignore the world, we betray the word of God which sends us out to serve the world. If we ignore the word of God, we have nothing to bring to the world.'[23]

Evangelicals are called to live with both present and eternal perspectives. Philip Ryken has observed how those who long for the 'new creation' are also those who should

> work for that world now, doing everything they can to set things right . . . We do it by giving our time to fatherless children . . . We do it by saving the unborn, healing the sick, feeding the poor, releasing the oppressed, and serving the elderly, . . . by responding with love and mercy wherever things are ugly, unjust, or inconsistent with the redemptive purposes of God.

Words of gospel truth, and deeds of Christian love, are 'not just making this world a better place . . . we are showing this world what the next world will be'.[24]

As those who place a strong emphasis on the authority, reliability and sufficiency of Scripture, evangelicals should be the most serious about acting upon what the Bible says, which includes the words of Jesus in Matthew 25:35, 'I was hungry and you gave me something to eat'. It means living out the Sermon on the Mount and the parable of the good Samaritan. If they do not, evangelicals are in danger of a functional liberalism, accepting only certain parts of Scripture. Evangelicals need to decide whether or not they stand with the rich history of Wesley, Spurgeon, Carmichael, Hsi Liao-chih and Moody. Maintaining a dichotomy between evangelism and social concern cannot be sustained either

---

[22] M. Davis, *Planet of Slums* (London: Verso, 2006), 19.

[23] 'The Micah Declaration on Integral Mission', in T. Chester (ed.), *Justice, Mercy and Humility: Integral Mission and the Poor* (Carlisle: Paternoster Press, 2002), 19.

[24] P. Ryken, *Kingdom Come* (Nottingham: Inter-Varsity Press, 2013), 127–128.

biblically or historically. Words and works are an inseparable couplet. As Tim Chester asserts:

> as valid as cultural and social involvement is in its own right, it cannot be seen in isolation from the task of reconciling people to God through the gospel ... the doctrine of sin and the offer of salvation mean that to engage in culture and creativity without evangelism is indulgent.[25]

Study of this host of witnesses between the times of John Wesley and John Stott has shown evangelicals steadily espousing this 'holistic' gospel of evangelism walking hand in hand with social action. The history of evangelicalism suggests that concern for both the evangelization of the lost and active compassionate care for people in all kinds of need have been stitched into the regenerated DNA of evangelical believers.

---

[25] T. Chester, *Good News to the Poor: Sharing the Gospel Through Social Involvement* (Leicester: Inter-Varsity Press, 2004), 55.

Index

Note: Pages in **bold** denote Character studies.